# New Approaches to Religion and the Enlightenment

# New Approaches to Religion and the Enlightenment

*Editors*
Brett C. McInelly
Paul E. Kerry

FAIRLEIGH DICKINSON UNIVERSITY PRESS
*Vancouver • Madison • Teaneck • Wroxton*

# New Approaches to Religion and the Enlightenment

Published by Fairleigh Dickinson University Press
Copublished by The Rowman & Littlefield Publishing Group, Inc.
4501 Forbes Boulevard, Suite 200, Lanham, Maryland 20706
www.rowman.com
6 Tinworth Street, London, SE11 5AL, United Kingdom

Fairleigh Dickinson University Press gratefully acknowledges the support received for scholarly publishing from the Friends of FDU Press.
British Library Cataloguing in Publication Information Available
Library of Congress Cataloging-in-Publication Data Is Available
ISBN 9781683931614 (cloth : alk. paper) | ISBN 9781683931621 (electronic)
TM The paper used in this publication meets the minimum requirements of American National Standard for Information Sciences Permanence of Paper for Printed Library Materials, ANSI/NISO Z39.48-1992.

Printed in the United States of America

# Contents

# Preface

Early in the process of assembling this collection, I received word that Bob Tennant, a contributor to the collection, had prematurely passed away. I never had the pleasure of meeting Bob face to face, but I had come to know him through this and other projects. I also knew him through his contributions to eighteenth-century studies, particularly his efforts to map the developing field of eighteenth-century sermon studies. I was deeply saddened when I learned of his passing. Not surprising to those who knew him, Bob was active and industrious right up until the end, and before the cancer took him, he completed several articles, including the one in this collection, an exploration of how the Society for Promoting Christian Knowledge managed its missions in the Isles of Scilly. I dedicate this collection to Bob and those loved ones who survive him. Bob will be missed, though we will continue to feel his lasting influence on religious and eighteenth-century studies through his work here and elsewhere.

Unlike most edited collections, this volume is not oriented toward a relatively narrow topic; rather, it demonstrates a breadth of disciplinary perspectives on and approaches to the study of religion during the age of Enlightenment. The chapters included here take us from the Isles of Scilly to the American colonies, from the Haskalah in Eastern Europe to the Methodist revival in England and the late German Enlightenment and ruminations on religious topics by Goethe and Schiller. Topics range from the argument for religious tolerance made by Jean Marteilhe, a Huguenot galley slave in Catholic France, to artistic renderings of the 1745 Jacobite rebellion, to the clash between Enlightenment thinkers and Puritan theologians in the Massachusetts Bay Colony. Other authors compellingly present the religious influences on the burgeoning field of entomology in the eighteenth century, the ways that Protestant intellectuals retained strong beliefs about the influence of God and evil spirits on human affairs, and the extent to which John Wesley's and George Whitefield's ideas regarding political liberty informed revolutionary ideas in America. Another author examines the ways Samuel Clarke's Newtonian theology informed his views of moral agency, while several contributors show how literary texts inform our understanding of religion and enlightenment by, in one case, mapping the political influences that shaped Milton's and Dryden's interpretations of the Bible and, in another case, detailing the ways M. M. Kheraskov's *Numa Pompilius* contributed to the discourse on civil religion in eighteenth-century Russia. Literary critics likewise offer new readings of Aphra Behn's *The History of the Nun* and Sarah Fielding's *David Simple*.

I express my appreciation to the contributors to this volume, including Paul E. Kerry, who played an instrumental role in bringing it to press, as well as Melvin J. Thorne and Suzy Bills of the BYU Faculty Publishing Service and their student editors for their help with copyediting, design, and layout of this volume.

*Brett C. McInelly*
*Brigham Young University*

# Notes from Many Hands: Pierre Lyonnet's Redesign of Friedrich Christian Lesser's *Insecto-Theology*

*Kevin L. Cope*

The argument from design enjoyed a happy immunity during the prosecutorially skeptical Enlightenment. Confident that nature follows empirically discoverable laws, even reputed atheists and freethinkers—whether the Third Earl of Shaftesbury, Anthony Collins, David Hume, or even Voltaire—routinely marveled at the order, ingenuity, and apparent purposiveness of both the inorganic and the biological kingdoms. Affirming that nature, in its interrelatedness and predictability, pointed to some sort of master author, architect, or inventor was an interdisciplinary and egalitarian pastime. Elite philosopher-scientists such as Isaac Newton, John Flamsteed, Gottfried Wilhelm Leibniz, William Herschel, Bishop Burnet, and Benjamin Franklin concurred with satirists such as Alexander Pope, landscape enthusiasts such as John Dyer and James Thomson, Scottish songsters such as James Beattie, and intercontinental explorers such as Georg Forster, Johann Wolfgang von Goethe, Alexander von Humboldt, and the two Cassinis in crediting the arrangement of nature to the divinity. Along with a commitment to a straightforward, causal model of experience, in which every effect results from a specific influence, an intuitive, everyday notion of the content and scale of nature—an assumption that events, causes, and purposes resemble one another at a scale suitable to the human eye and a correlated assumption that nature can be explained in vernacular language and imagery—ensured that most everyone would see traces of design emerging from the complexities of experience. The search for design further guaranteed its success by hailing the discovery of design as the surest measure of the quality of research.

Enthusiasm for the easy revelation of order—for the effortless unveiling of the divine intentions underlying what Alexander Pope characterized as "A mighty maze! but not without a plan"[1]—easily overshadows less unanimous aspects of Enlightenment design theology. Variations, even contradictions, lurked only a few interpretive steps beyond broad pronouncements about "Nature and Nature's Laws."[2] For one, the idea of design took both temporal and atemporal forms. Scientific illustrators sketched plants, animals, microbes, and asterisms in an attempt to unveil instantaneous, timeless, schematic order; geologists, chemists, ornithologists, and astronomers, by contrast, explicated an evolving plan of nature that slowly emerged across eons. Emblematic, pictorial, and process-oriented accounts of design all described different ranges of experience and illustrated diverging ideas about what design might be. Scale became a nagging concern; the expectation of simple linkages between the design of the gigantic solar system and the design of tiny microscopic life remained emotionally compelling but forensically unsupported. Readers of Voltaire's *Candide* know that natural disasters raised more eyebrows than answers when it came to divine plans. And what of the role and purpose of the design argument? Should it confirm, supplement, or simply complicate revelation and church tradition?

In our time, the grandeur of the subject matter in astronomy, physics, and geology tends to set them at the center of discussions of the argument from design. Closer to the epicenter of this eighteenth-century discussion was the diminutive world of seashells, microbes, bivalves, and, above all, insects. Unlike what twenty-first-century popular science calls "life as we know it," insects presented special challenges for those hoping to discover teleology in every corner of creation. Eighteenth-century taxonomists stationed insects in the animal kingdom, yet their manifest differences from dogs, cats, horses, goats, cattle, squirrels, and people obscured their contribution to universal design. Perhaps insects filled in the countless loops in the chain of being; perhaps they depicted moral lessons, like the busy bee stocking up on winter sustenance; perhaps insects had secret duties such as the infliction of corrective plagues on apostate Egypt. As worldwide exploration continued and the number of offbeat species increased, the puzzling behavior of exotic insects left scientific heads spinning. Research seemed to worsen the problem as physiologists revealed anatomical novelties with no apparent value in proclaiming the greater glory of God.

The long eighteenth century swarmed with a surprising number of entomologists as well as scientific illustrators devoted to entomology. In addition to the usual candidates among the virtuosi—with John Ray and Samuel Hartlib leading those who celebrated the commercial utility of insects and their products—a formidable legion of researchers, drafters, and painters collaborated in the advancement of insect art and science. Included in this international ensemble were accomplished painters and engravers such as Maria Sybilla Merian, Benjamin Wilkes, Jan Goedart, August Johann Rösel Aug von Rosenhof, Jacob L'Admiral, and Mark Catesby; microscope enthusiasts such as Robert Hooke; encyclopedic, taxonomic wits such as René Antoine Ferchault de Réaumur, Johan Christian Fabricius, Steven Blankaart, and Jan Swammerdam; science popularizers such as Gilles Bazin; high-culture scientists such as Robert Boyle; and a plethora of regional writers dedicated to recording the inventory of insect species in their homelands, often with an eye toward compiling books of local "wonders." Possibly owing to the modesty of the equipment required, entomology attracted the leading talents of more nations than did the more expensive projects of stargazers, explorers, and geographers. Eighteenth-century entomological research extended almost literally, as Dr. Johnson has it, from "China to Peru," or at least from Prussia to Ireland to the colonial New World and on to the Philippines.

Among the most unlikely participants in the combined scientific, artistic, and ultimately religious drive to deal with the burgeoning insect kingdom was Friedrich Christian Lesser, a prolific writer of tracts on physical theology as well as on assorted topics in traditional divinity. Lesser's minimally documented life in the small German city of Nordhausen remains the province of regional historians and local hagiographers.[3] Despite the remoteness of his setting and the obscurity of his role as a parish pastor in a small town alongside the Harz Mountains, Lesser's breakthrough work, the *Insecto-Theologia* (1799), was quickly translated into both French and English, drawing a large, erudite readership as well as a supplemental, popular readership wherever the aforementioned languages were spoken. Lesser's *Insecto-Theologia*—in its English translation, *Insecto-Theology, Or, A Demonstration of the Being and Perfections of God, from a Consideration of the Structure and Economy of Insects*—consists of a vast array of scientific observations coupled with anecdotes relating to the strange doings of insects and enhanced with abundant digressions of the marvels that the putative Creator inserted into nature. Combining wonder book with travel account, scientific treatise, and religious rhapsody, the *Insecto-Theology* seems an easy, general-audience read even while bristling with the contrasts, contradictions, and tensions endemic to the eighteenth-century search for natural design. The work as a whole glosses over these tensions by presenting itself as a review of the splendors of divine handiwork—as an unveiling or revelation rather than a component in a debate.[4] Lesser applies his formidable entomological knowledge to the service of two goals: the encyclopedic compilation of insect lore and the praise of the Divinity who engineered the insect empire. At once list and hymn, Lesser's *Insecto-Theology* mixes the selective with the comprehensive in what appears to be the ultimate work on righteous entomology.

Appearances can deceive. It was not long before Lesser's popularity led to critical responses to his works. Befitting the strange mix of scientist and votary that was Lesser, the reaction to Lesser combined laudatory astonishment at the breadth of his accomplishment with critical attention to glossed-over detail. At the head of the queue among those who responded both worshipfully and quizzically to Lesser was Pierre Lyonnet (sometimes spelled "Lyonet"), something of a child prodigy who was descended from a noble French family that had suffered badly during the Reformation, abandoned France, sheltered in Switzerland, and finally deposited the cleverest member of its third to fourth generation in the tolerant Hague. Like many prodigies, Lyonnet burned through several careers, having applied himself to physics, law, medicine, theology, cryptography, art, engraving, printing, and languages before securing a small sinecure as secretary of the cyphers to the Dutch throne. The remainder of his life, as reported by a memorial review in the *Gentleman's Magazine* and then adapted in a superficial rewrite for the *Edinburgh Magazine*,[5] was passed in reading, collecting (of horns, shells, and biological artifacts), and in sporadic attempts at artistry. His quick mastery of drawing and engraving, for example, allowed him first to execute the drawings for Abraham Tremblay's study of the polypus and then to complete the engravings when the commissioned professional artist, Jan Wandelaar, fell behind schedule. Even sculpture was not out of the reach of his spontaneously skillful, if amateur, hand.

Following the 1742 translation of Lesser's *Insecto-Theology* into French, Lyonnet, sensing the possibility of hopping onto a bestseller, produced an elaborate body of annotations to the writings of the bug-brained German divine. It is as the host for Lyonnet's annotations that Lesser's treatise enters the English-speaking world, the entire lot—Lesser's book and Lyonnet's notes together—being jointly and simultaneously translated into English. So ardent is Lyonnet's concern for and identification with Lesser that his annotation apparatus grows to an equal, even slightly greater length than Lesser's original text, becoming a treatise in its own right. Lyonnet's annotations serve multiple purposes: provision of empirical evidence in support of (or sometimes against) Lesser; supply of details missing from Lesser's sometimes grandiose and sometimes offhand observations; clarification of Lesser's obscure passages; extension of Lesser's ideas into comparative studies through juxtapositions of Lesser's original remarks against new data concerning similar species; the proposing of experiments to confirm or deny Lesser's opinions; amplification (and occasionally muting) of Lesser's religious interpretations of insect physiology and behavior; and, most importantly, the simultaneous explicating, disciplining, realigning, and often extending of Lesser's theological extrapolations. It is this rewriting of Lesser's widely distributed and influential yet now largely forgotten work that is the topic of this essay.

## Suspended Analogies: The End of Anatomical WYSIWYG

An old standby among those who teach the early periods of literature—including satirical physiognomists such as Geoffrey Chaucer, would-be wizards such as John Dee, dramatists such as William Shakespeare and Molière, and mystics such as Jakob Boehme and Emanuel Swedenborg—is that of the analogy between the macrocosm and the microcosm. This notion holds that the appearance of an object corresponds both to its true nature and to some greater structure in the cosmos, the standard classroom example being the analogy of the parts of the human body to the command hierarchy of a ship, the government of a state, or even the design of the universe itself. Such comparisons illustrate that the head corresponds to the king, the God, or the captain, while the lower limbs and organs correspond to more utilitarian and less administratively engaged citizens, whether military guardians or rank-and-file workers. Underlying the macrocosm-microcosm similitude is naive pictorialism, an assumption that a given creature or object looks like or unambiguously signals what it does, what its role in the cosmos might be, and how it relates to larger processes or ideas. This assumption remained very much alive during the age of reason, unexpectedly flourishing in an empirically minded age in which scientists expected hands-on, eyes-open research to yield immediate insights into nature's laws. This highly semantic pictorialism influenced image-rich pop-culture traditions such as emblem books and physiognomy manuals as well as esoteric, high-tech, and cultivated pursuits such as chemistry, zoology, and cartography.

The signifying power of the insect image posed challenges while it opened opportunities for early entomologists. In addition to the swarm of entomologists mentioned in the opening paragraphs of this chapter, European virtuosi such as Italian Antonio Vallisneri investigated insect life through detailed drawings of nature's most diminutive creatures, suggesting that images carried a surplus of meaning. These individuals also introduced the new problem of scale by opening questions as to why the great Creator would enclose so much information in so inaccessible a vault as a mite's wing or a beetle's body. Cataloguers such as Johann Leonhard Frisch offered works such as the *Beschreibung von allerley*

*Insecten in Deutschland*, in which visual description ("Beschreibung") leads to expansive explanations and interpretations.[6] Both Lyonnet and Lesser mention an assortment of illustrator-scholars ("Henninius," "Johnston")[7] whom time has all but eclipsed but who also began their speculations and explorations with small-scale entomological portraiture. The status and the semantic power of the insect image underlie those great classification wars from which Carl Linnaeus and his system emerged as clear winners—controversies in which the advocates for various classification systems sought to develop compact characterizations of insect species that could balance the image, phenotype, and anatomy of insects against their functions, (genetic) heritage, and presumed significance for sacred as well as natural history.

Eager to reveal the wonders of creation, Lesser dodges the potential conflicts between insect form and function. He takes a supplementing approach in which behavior and meaning never clash, where marvelous facts are accumulated but seldom contrast with one another. Lyonnet seeks to shore up his master's fragile reputation by adding system and discipline to the analogy of nature—by asking how far scientists may go in the interpretation of insect images and by recasting the analogy of the observation and exegesis in the hope of making it consistent with modern science. Lyonnet is among the first to criticize what we, in our "digital" age, depreciate as "analog" representations—to question whether a straightforward correspondence between an object, its image, and its interpretation is always a good or obvious thing. Key to Lyonnet's project is the demand not only for accuracy in scientific illustration but for accuracy at particular scales, or the "patience to follow her [nature], step by step, in the delineation of an animal, so despicable in their [artists'] eyes, as an insect" (Lyonnet, 283–284). This formulation suggests that meaningful representation of insect phenomena is not as easy or spontaneous as Lesser might imagine but, rather, progressive and temporal, "step by step." Even the initial field or laboratory recording of insect anatomy involves more than a simple, timeless analogy of experience to universal design.

Lyonnet extends his critique to those false analogies that arise from unprocessed observation. Somewhat unfairly, he lashes out at Lesser's comparison of insect eggs to plant seeds and of insect wings to plants twigs, warning that a seemingly intuitive "analogy between insects and plants" leads to errors (Lyonnet, 298; see Lesser, 36).

Lyonnet vents equal contempt for folk and hagiographical tales such as the old legend that a spider imbibed by St. Francis during Holy Communion escaped from the saint's digestion unharmed (Lyonnet, 415, 439; see Lesser, 260). He even conducts a laboratory experiment to confirm or deny village wisdom about an antipathy between spiders and toads. Religious sentimentality especially offends Lyonnet, who scowls that bees dispose of their dead not for reasons of sanctimony but for reasons of hygiene (Lyonnet, 384). Secular analogies, too, come under satirical heat. Having observed the relation between gender and role in hymenopteran communities, Lyonnet refracts the political image of the beehive:

> Old prejudices are not so easily given up; these ideas of monarchical government have remained; not being able to make a king of this bee, they have made it a queen; and thus, this empire, which had been governed, for so many ages, by an uninterrupted succession of kings, has at last had the misfortune, to fall irretrievably under the distaff. After this disaster, I am afraid, that the monarchy of bees is hastening to its period, and that soon, when the royal authority shall have declined, the queen will be considered merely as a mother, her subjects, merely as a free people, and this well governed state, as nothing but a hive of bees and drones. (Lyonnet, 383)

Passages such as these, which spangle Lyonnet's annotations, function as hermeneutic stop signs—as limitations on the complexity of interpretations and as indications that evidence not only accelerates but also halts exegesis. Lyonnet grumbles at a passage in which Lesser applauds the creation of animals for the glory of God and the use of man, asking whether man might be "too vain, in believing, that everything was made of his use" and thereby encapsulating in an aphoristic question an extensive critique of the habit of analogy and of the hasty assumption that our species enjoys special access to the meaning of natural phenomena.

Fundamental to Lyonnet's critique of Lesser and of natural-supernatural analogies is the twin notion that (a) entomology, with its love of classification, is about identity and that (b) the diversity implied by the inventorying of identities sets a limit to the range and depth of any one analogy. When there are thousands of insects that *are*, specifically and emphatically, a few things, there are, by contrast, thousands of things that they *are not*. We learn from Lyonnet that most insects lack flesh and bones but that some, such as lobsters, have flesh. Such a mix of identifying attributes and kingdom-wide diversity limits analogies; an insect that has flesh but no skeleton is not a straightforward counterpart to standard flesh-and-bones creatures (Lyonnet, 303). "A most wonderful order prevails throughout Nature," exclaims Lyonnet, "composed of diversities and analogies without number" (Lyonnet, 307)—a loose use of the idea of infinity that suggests the existence of contrasting, limiting diversity for every candidate analogy. Inversely, God tends to use small numbers of gross morphological differences to identify his creatures, austerely relying on simple two-legged structure as an indication of human status (Lyonnet, 315).

At times, Lyonnet seems to take a perverse delight in limiting analogies by choosing bizarre comparisons. He develops, for example, a catachretical analogy between a Gordius worm and a cat gut violin string—an awkwardly mixed biological-musical analogy that is unlikely to sound out the depths of universal design. Another technique involves the development of exquisitely qualified comparisons in which the limits rather than the extent of analogy occupy the foreground. In one demonstration of this strategy, Lyonnet owns that most insects lack bones but then suggests that some parts of insect anatomy may compare to bones only at the level of function (Lyonnet, 301). Still another approach to the "semi-analogy" proceeds quantitatively. Lyonnet doubts, for example, whether a single bone in a slug constitutes a skeleton worthy of comparison to the scaffolding of vertebrate animals (Lyonnet, 302).

Lyonnet is a master of provocative anticlimax. In one of his great crescendos, he declares that almost everything found in larger animals appears in "traces" in insects, but, unlike Lesser, he uses that comprehensive comparison not to assert the unity of the cosmos but rather to limit the analogy of animals to plants (Lyonnet, 299). Lyonnet puts a new twist in the history of the design argument by substituting partial comparison for holistic, metaphorical analogy. Lyonnet, for example, disables bestiary lore. He quotes an anecdote from Frisch, reporting that the "Derester lardarius is so voracious, that though sometimes there is seen hanging from him a string of excrement, a yard long, he does not give over eating" (Lyonnet, 372–373), thus sketching the outlines of an analogical emblem of gluttony but stopping with offbeat particulars, with comment-free reports of novelty that erode the general meaning of the analogy. Lyonnet teases his reader with similarly brief, interruptive reports that ugly caterpillars yield beautiful butterflies, while ugly butterflies emerge from magnificent cocoons (Lyonnet, 343). Metaphors of development and emergence dissipate into compared inconsistencies.

Lyonnet's relish for inconsistencies is more than a peculiar taste. Details that modulate or qualify analogical interpretations of nature play a central role in Lyonnet's attempt to account for the role of time and of development in the making of emblematic meaning. It is easy enough to look at a stationary cocoon and develop a stable, pictorial analogy to the anticipation of the resurrection, but it is another matter altogether to take into account the entire life cycle of an insect and then figure out what it might mean. We learn not only that insects differ in their ways but also that even the metamorphic species evidence a diversity of approaches. Some merely hatch from eggs, while others undergo no less than three different kinds of transformations (Lyonnet, 336). Other insects occupy multiple habitats and display assorted dietary regimens during their fast-changing lives (Lyonnet, 308). Any allegorical or otherwise extrapolating approach to these multitasking creatures must take into account not only those phases of life that allow for convenient symbology but also all the other phases. Sixteenth-century illustrator Joris Hoefnagel comes in for special recrimination owing to his inattention to life-cycle issues:

> The plates are engraved with taste . . . [but] This collection cannot be of great use to the naturalist, because Hoefnagel

> did not follow his insects through their different changes, but contented himself with painting them in the state in which chance presented them to him, without observing either order or method. (Lyonnet, 280)

Hoefnagel specialized in brilliantly colored prints in which insects and other assorted organic products—whether fruits, flowers, or even rodents—appeared in visually pleasing but scientifically disconcerting arrays that seemed to combine curiosity cabinets and biological taxonomies with household decorating gewgaws for an effect that is pleasing yet dissatisfying (see Figure 1).[8] Hoefnagel's snapshot mentality conflicts with Lyonnet's drive to encompass the lifetime as well as the present structure of insects. By contrast, Lyonnet lauds Lesser, Jan Swammerdam, and Linnaeus for their ability to reconcile myriad individual differences and life cycle changes among insects (Lyonnet, 314). Nevertheless, Lyonnet's confession that the details of insects may not always line up with either biological classifications or allegorical meanings or roles in the design of nature represents a significant break from a science-driven theology in which general design and particular creatures coincide at the level of morphology—in which the signifying power of animal anatomy transcends the complications of time, change, and development.

Animating Lyonnet's critique of Hoefnagel (and many others) is an interest in the *process* of imaging and representation vis-à-vis intuitive theology. Exactly what is it that Hoefnagel is illustrating? The gross insect at full scale? Did he forget about a close-up sketching of its digestive system or dentition? What about a microscopic close-up of its follicles? For Lyonnet, all representations occur at specific scales; no eighteenth-century technology can represent the entire insect all at once, in holographic, wrap-around detail. Lyonnet chuckles at the duping of allegorically minded alchemists by an insect that appears to shimmer with gold. Closer inspection reveals this appearance to result from the layering of white and yellow materials of a very ordinary composition (Lyonnet, 342).

In another example, Sturmius's germ theory, in which the air abounds with vivifying particles, draws satire owing to absurdities arising from attempts to visualize such a busy universe (Lyonnet, 431–432). In an even more inventive critique of scientific method,

Figure 1: Joris Hoefnagel, *Flower Still Life with Insects* (1594). Courtesy of the Rijksbureau voor Kunsthistorische Documentatie (Netherlands). Note the decorative collage approach to biological illustration.

Lyonnet insinuates that scientific reports must pass a literary test, that of narrative probability. According to Lesser (215), Plutarch reports that bears cure indigestion with honey, a claim that Lyonnet rebuts (418) by asking a series of questions about the way in which this discovery was made and whether that process of discovery accords with any imaginable sequence of events. Lyonnet thus legislates a two-part requirement for the doing of science in a world dominated by process. On the one hand, science must remain intuitive. Esoteric theories and theories that draw their support from outside the range of perception—from beyond the domain of what John Locke calls "human knowledge"—fail owing to their irrelevance to an intra- and interreferential image-based discipline system in which phenomena can be compared to one another and can also signify larger theological ideas. On the other hand, the dynamic and flexible character of human perception requires scientists to recognize the limits of any one representation and to take into account whole series of observations over an extended period of time.

The two sides of Lyonnet's scientific semiosis—his simultaneous hope that scientific evidence will instantly mean a great deal for a wide range of disciplines and his insistence that every representation of experience suffers from definitive limits—modulates Lyonnet's approach to the beauty of nature. Among eighteenth-century design theologians, beauty was something more than an epiphenomenon. It was also a property of creation—an evidence of the artistic skill of what George Berkeley called, with a literary flair, "the Author of Nature." On one hand, Lyonnet denies Lesser's claim that humans will never match the subtleties of the divine artificer who made the multitudinous veins in tree leaves with an offhand note that this is all a matter of technology and that modern equipment now permits the production of plant skeletons that outdo the creator's handiwork (Lesser, 204; Lyonnet 425). On the other hand, Lyonnet follows Lesser's lead when it comes to occasional digressions on the wondrous beauty of plentiful nature (Lyonnet, 418), suggesting that nature's unique beauty remains material to physical theology.

## Made in the Image of God, Or Moving (Iconic) Pictures

In both Lesser and Lyonnet's theology we see a dramatic departure from previous versions of the argument from design. As developed by Aristotle, Thomas Aquinas, Isaac Newton, and a variety of virtuosi, the argument from design turns on an anthropocentric axle. Either humans' perception of beauty in the universe or a human-centered utilitarianism proves that an intelligent Creator has developed a system of nature that is profoundly favorable to human needs or expectations. "So Virtuous and so Noble a Design, / So Human for its Use, for Knowledge so Divine," declares Abraham Cowley's synoptic verse evaluation of the cosmos.[9] So the Enlightenment, despite having discovered the mind-numbing immensity of astronomical spaces, persisted in post-Ptolemaic efforts to position humanity at the center of God's plan. Lesser and Lyonnet pursue a heterodox approach to design. Rather than deriving design from an anthropocentric sense of nature's user-friendliness, these scientist-philosophers celebrate and discover cunning plans in the intractable *differences* between humans and insects.

The first step of this reversed strategy—this changeover from the pursuit of similarities, alliances, or commonalities to the applauding of divergences—is the inventorying of all those attributes that distinguish insects not only from humans but indeed from all other segments of the living creation. The twenty-first-century cult of diversity is nothing new for Lesser and Lyonnet, who confront readers with a book of nature that indexes harsh contrasts more often than it records affinities. Readers encounter insects with bizarre methods of reproduction; bugs that may multiply without a partner; borderline species that boggle the boundaries between plant, animal, and insect; anatomical features that proclaim the irreconcilable difference of insects from humans; and extravagant crawlers—some with more than sixteen hundred feet—that resemble nothing else in God's dominion (Lyonnet, 291–293, 295, 300, 304, 318). We learn about aphids whose male and female cohorts display dramatic phenotypical differences; we quietly hear about the absence of ears in offbeat grasshoppers and about their alternative means of sensing

(Lyonnet, 385); we recoil at the discovery that not even breathing is universal (Lyonnet, 323, 346). Lesser and Lyonnet display discontinuities among insects themselves, proffering, for example, a six-winged butterfly that has no counterpart in its four-winged tribe (Lyonnet, 320). This nonstop presentation of particularizing profusion drives an attack on the generalizing claims of science, for it calls into question the capacities and jurisdiction of the fundamental skill of biological classification. Noting the miraculous diversification of nature, Lyonnet contracts the boundaries of the taxonomy on which Linnaeus and others hoped to build systems:

> The author of nature, wishing as it were to shew that he is above the laws and rules he hath himself established, seems sometimes designedly to depart from them; hence it happens that however general the rules are on which a system is founded, there will always be found exceptions which will render that system imperfect in proportion to their number. Sometimes these exceptions are of so singular a kind, that it is impossible to foresee them, and nothing but experience can demonstrate them. (Lyonnet, 313)

"Designedly" departing from his own norms, God affirms his role as the manager of natural design by promulgating differences and churning up exceptions. Given the gigantic number of insect species known, dissimilarities enjoy a hefty numerical advantage over similarities in the variously designed universe.

Lesser and Lyonnet confront what might be called the "image of God problem." The Old Testament explains that God made man in his own image,[10] a claim that seems to situate "man" at a special station in the creation and thereby in the design of the universe. Admittedly, there are plenty of obvious anatomical and morphological similarities that affiliate humanity with most animals. Every dog, monkey, bear, and giraffe has eyes, a nose, a mouth, legs, and standard internal organs. Moving further afield—into insects, fish, and, worse, microscopic organisms—the census of creatures reveals that only a small minority bear what most anthropocentrically minded people regard as the image of the Creator. To deal with this problem while also celebrating the variety of creation and holding to their commitment to physical theology, Lyonnet undertakes an all-out campaign to redefine exactly what "image" it is that humans have, a campaign that goes far beyond anything in Lesser's writings. Lyonnet's beachhead in this campaign is the theory, familiar to readers of Laurence Sterne's *Tristram Shandy* (1759–1767), that the spermatic "animalcules" that impregnate women encapsulate complete (if miniature) persons—"homunculi," per the usage of early alchemists—that subsequently grow in the womb into full-sized human infants. Affirming that microscopes reveal no such miniature men or women in sperm and snapping that an animalcule "rather resembles a tadpole, consisting of nothing but a head and tail" (Lyonnet, 357), Lyonnet leaves behind the notion that otherwise unchanging persons simply swell into human scale. He imports into the study of human reproduction a developmental model like that which explains the metamorphosis of insects, per the emergence of butterflies from cocoons. With that, he recasts the human icon. The "image of God" becomes more of a process than a representation, while the gap between people and insects narrows. Lyonnet amplifies his arguments with a highly creative reductio ad absurdum, cautioning that if the "homunculus" theory is true, then the homunculi residing within spermatic animalcules must also contain the sperm that they will eventually use, which must, in turn, contain even smaller homunculi (of those children that the males will eventually sire). Those microscopic homunculi must, in turn, contain still smaller prototypic persons for a third future generation—and so forth, ad infinitum, until we arrive at infinitely small future beings housed in the infinitely small seeds of distant ancestors (Lyonnet, 357–359). Highlighting the function rather than the form or substance of the preimpregnation sperm depictorializes both the "image of God" and the associated anthropocentric design of nature while it emphasizes the processes that operate nature.[11]

Including function and process along with gross anatomy in the magazine of divine design allows Lyonnet to take another creative step by blurring the boundaries between similarities and differences. For example, Lyonnet discerns that caterpillars resemble other animals in their hairiness but cautions that caterpillar hairs differ from, say, mammal manes. Caterpillar hairs and cat hairs converge in function but diverge in structure and composition (Lyonnet, 404). So it is with miniaturization. Wondering whether insects possess blood, Lyonnet marvels that "it is not beyond the power of matter when in the hands of the divine Creator, to form in an insect however small, all the vessels necessary for performing the requisite digestions and filtrations to convert the aliments into blood" (Lyonnet, 406). Insect bodies perform functions identical to those in humans but at a scale so exquisitely tiny that the differences eclipse the similarities. Lyonnet is at his best when dealing with organisms that we would now describe as "extremophiles," creatures that live beyond what humans imagine the limits of "life as we know it." In a long narrative that, although it would leave an animal rights activist shuddering, inventively explores the transition zone between hard science to sensational wonder narrative, Lyonnet tells the tale of a perdurable beetle that defies every attempt to extinguish its life, whether by drowning, starvation, or a thousand other torments (Lyonnet, 347–349). This sturdy creature thrives in habitats, such as a vessel of wine, that occur within human experience but that reach beyond the boundaries of strangeness, it being inconceivable that a human being could survive for an extended period in a (giant) chalice of alcoholic beverages. There are limits: Lyonnet dismisses accounts of the taputa bird, an avian whose internal organs are allegedly composed of a mosaic of multitudinous worms, calling such a creature "absolutely impossible" (Lyonnet, 353)—that is, beyond the limits of any conceivable analogy to man, God, creatures, or any other known life forms. The members of the Salzburger sect and the French Protestants, on the other hand, not only existed and survived but flourished in their posteviction homes (see Lyonnet, 365), they, too, having been chosen by God as possessors of special durabilities—as beings similar to but also preternaturally different from their fellow citizens.

Lyonnet likes "extremophiles" because they are *explicable* wonders. Unlike the fabulous creatures found in the prodigy anthologies of Nathaniel Crouch and other ambitious publishers, real-life extremophiles lend themselves to scientific explanations that amplify our wonder at not only the artistry of the creator but also at the variety of—the *differences in*—the creator's devilishly divergent handiwork. While commenting on a section of Lesser's tome that bears the title "of some singular qualities in certain insects," Lyonnet snarls that a French explorer who has been touting American giant ants should "send some of those monstrous ants to Europe" (411) for inspection, in imitation of the empirically minded German illustrator Maria Sybilla Merian. Lyonnet himself confirms his speculative theory concerning the equal distribution of the soul across the bodies of some insects by repeatedly dividing an earthworm, his goal being the empirical demonstration that the vital force within this creature can, upon partitioning, reanimate multiple worm segments down to a very fine level of resolution (Lyonnet, 406–407). Such an experiment intones the similarity-and-difference theme. The same vitality that enlivens indivisible higher creatures asserts itself in surprisingly different ways among creatures for whom identity, even life itself, is flexibly distributed. Among the most remarkable of Lyonnet's anecdotes are those in which this entomologist relies on processes rather than on physical features to establish an apparent link between disparate parts of creation. Tarantula bites, which would seem to belong to entomology and perhaps to medicine, come together in a musical process—a cure through song and dance. According to Lyonnet, musicians must play various tunes on various instruments until one performance strikes an eligible nerve and sends the bite victim into a campaign of compulsive dancing. Once an effective tune is identified, the Terpsichore continues for several weeks, often at a pace of six to seven hours per day until medical and psychological stability return. Lyonnet considers several explanations for this cure, noting that some theories contain a little too much of "darkness and mystery," then opts for the most rational explanation: the human nerves can enter into a unison with certain tones and melodies, and this unison produces a purgative vibration ridding the body of toxins. Even here, however, Lyonnet finds too much mystification (Lyonnet, 434, 437–438). He relies on anecdotes about a quasi-medical process to create analogies between music, disease, nerves, and venom, but he calls attention to the gaps in the proposed explanation so as to remind readers that the reported phenomenon remains fundamentally mysterious and fundamentally enigmatic—fundamentally *different*.

## Scales, Numbers, Frames, Habitats

Discussions of universal design proceed in plurals. *Design* pertains to the arrangement and the relations of several parts; there is no such thing as a design that involves only one item. Even the standard thought experiment proposed in William Paley's *Natural Theology* (1802)—that of a solitary watch discovered along a road, the finding of which artificial object leads to the inference of the existence of a designer—involves multitudinousness. The design that characterizes the watch involves the interplay of multitudinous parts. Design, as the watch example suggests, is a matter of scale. When deducing the existence of a creator from an artful timepiece, should the observer attend to those many parts that range in size from a millimeter or two to a few centimeters; or should the viewer try to imagine the interaction of millions of molecules; or should the philosopher consider the contributions of metallurgists, glaziers, and merchants; or should a high-flying divine take into account the ability of a minute watch to estimate the time on Mars, Jupiter, and, indeed, the entire cosmos? Do all these designs concur, or do they announce themselves differently at varied scales?

The connections between science, scale, and design emerge early in Lyonnet's odyssey through Lesser. Despite his and Lesser's desire to see the vast universe in diminutive insects, Lyonnet prefers science on a local, regional scale:

> It would tend greatly to the advancement of Natural History, if those who publish on insects, would apply to the study of such insects only, as are to be found in the neighbourhood of their own place of residence. . . . Being limited to a small district, they would more easily discover what it contained, and this could not fail of making them find a great number of insects, which are still entirely unknown, and will continue so, as long as people content themselves, with making, in different places, vain and superficial investigations. (Lyonnet, 283)

A small-scale, local search allows for a manageable multiplicity that allows finite people to discover design—to uncover a portion of the "great number[s] of insects" without exceeding the limits of representation. Lyonnet calls for the representation of insects in their natural size and in accurate color so that small segments of divine design can be apprehended in detail as well as with reference to cosmic immensity. He errs on the side of smallness. He notes, for example, that microscopes reveal a level of natural design beyond human skill and imagination (Lyonnet, 279). Zoom lens in hand, Lyonnet studies such tiny phenomena as the speedy action of the butterfly tongue by way of setting a frame size that respects the scale of human sense organs and that allows for human interpretation. Lyonnet develops a kind of countersublimity in which the soaring Alps, mighty earthquakes, and assorted grandiose concepts that staggered eighteenth-century ode authors subside before astounding feats of nanotechnology. Peering down at the chutes from which spiders disperse their silk, Lyonnet waxes rhapsodic: "Who could have imagined, that the formation of a spider's web required such apparatus; or, that the papillæ of so vile an animal, was an object so worthy of admiration!" (Lyonnet, 394). Calibrating the time in which design evolves can also make God's artistry accessible. The quick life cycle of aphids, for example, should not lead researchers to believe that every insect lives, reproduces, and dies so speedily (Lyonnet, 334). Biologists who look for design need to explain the temporal scope as well as the physical size of the frames in which they enclose snapshots of God's sempiternal artistry.

Frames—the proper bracketing of aspects, views, and glimpses of experience—are key to Lyonnet's notions about design. Lyonnet praises the studies of French entomological superstar René Antoine Ferchault de Réaumur because Réaumur "hath detected them [insects] in their most secret actions" (Lyonnet, 287); the frame that Réaumur sets around his preferred segment of nature is rather more like a series of frames in a movie. He found a way to encapsulate insect action without portraying more heterodox elements than the average researcher can assimilate. German artist-biologist Maria Sybilla Merian draws an ovation owing to her sequential illustration of insect habitats in Hesse, Bavaria, Holland, and Surinam (see Lyonnet, 280)—for delivering one frame after another rather than trying to take in vast wholes (see Figure 2). Dutch engraver and botanical illustrator Jacob l'Admiral fares less well, owing to his sloppy selection of subject matter and his reluctance to limit the scope of his frames (see Figure 3):

> He [l'Admiral] proposes to represent each insect on the plant it uses for food: if he had spared himself this trouble, his book would not have been less valued by the learned. These superfluous ornaments serve but to divert the attention from the principal object; which is in some measure lost, when surrounded by so many accessory objects, greater than itself; and a treatise on insects, ornamented by so many plants, looks more like a botanical performance. (Lyonnet, 281)

Lyonnet never denies the utility of learning about insect dining habits, nor does he insinuate that plants are without their role in divine design. He pans l'Admiral for failing to limit the range of study to frames that can be readily perceived and processed, whether by disciplinary specialists or ordinary audiences. What Lyonnet relishes are small-scale epiphanies: inputs that barely pass over the boundary of detection. He offers a lovely passage in which the intuition of design emerges from the mass effect of tiny flapping wings—in which a buzzing sound arises from the collective input of individually inaudible wings, in which the frame surrounding design shrinks to the diameter of an ear (Lyonnet, 412). One of the longest of Lyonnet's notes studies ants that are not seen at all, that burrow underground and erect cavernous habitats in the most unusual and most limited of all frames—the blocks of earth under scientists' shoes (Lyonnet, 350).

One forward-looking way in which Lyonnet frames insects and segments design is the consideration of insects within those ecosystems to which they belong. The argument from design ultimately affirms that everything bears an important relation to everything else, but Lyonnet grapples with this huge idea by focusing on systems in which insects are foregrounded. Lyonnet expresses amazement and confusion over the astounding fertility of insects, noting that a common fly, if unhindered, could engender two billion youngsters by the third generation. "Let a person form to himself, if he can, an idea of the prodigious number of flies which at the end of a few years a single fly of this kind would produce, had not Providence taken care to limit the progress of such astounding fecundity" (Lyonnet, 321). The care of Providence turns out to be a true case of tough love—a combination of predation, disease, and environmental obstacles. Thoroughgoing optimists such as Gottfried Wilhelm Leibniz might have invited satire from the likes of Voltaire owing to uncritical assumptions about ours being "the best of all possible worlds," but Lyonnet dodges satirists' bullets by emphasizing the ugly side of an system—by applauding God for setting insects at the bottom of the food chain.

The literary result of such meditations is a kind of countersublimity, an enthusiasm for a no-nonsense design in which the ingenuity leading to the mammoth success of insect reproduction is undercut by a complementary ingenuity through which the creator preserves balance by deploying destructive forces in the interest of systematic balance. In the counterdesign idiom, appalling habits such as insect-on-insect cannibalism earn ovations.

> It is not only among other animals that insects meet with enemies; they destroy one another. The Formica-leo (Myrmeleon formicarium) devours ants, the Hemerobius perla and a great number of larvæ feed on all sorts of aphids; spiders eat flies, and are themselves killed by wasps, and other voracious flies. The tree bugs, various larvæ which change into beetles, and many beetles and flies devour caterpillars, pseudo-caterpillars, maggots, butterflies, and moths; some species of caterpillars eat one another. The ichneumon flies of many species destroy an infinity of larvæ by laying their eggs in them which produce young, that prey on the vitals of the animal which harbours them. The carnage is still greater among aquatic insects: of these there is hardly a species which is not, at some period of its life, a prey to some bolder or stronger insect. (Lyonnet, 323)

Figure 2: Maria Sybilla Merians, Plate 6 from *Metamorphosis Insectorum Surinamensium* (1705), depicting in detail the metamorphosis of a caterpillar local to the Surinam region. Public domain image courtesy of Wikimedia Commons.

Other cases of productive but limiting barbarity include the abandoning of eggs to the care of Providence; the failure of other species to provide help to the distressed young of other insects; the destructive laying of eggs in the bodies of rival species; and the quitting of the corpse that

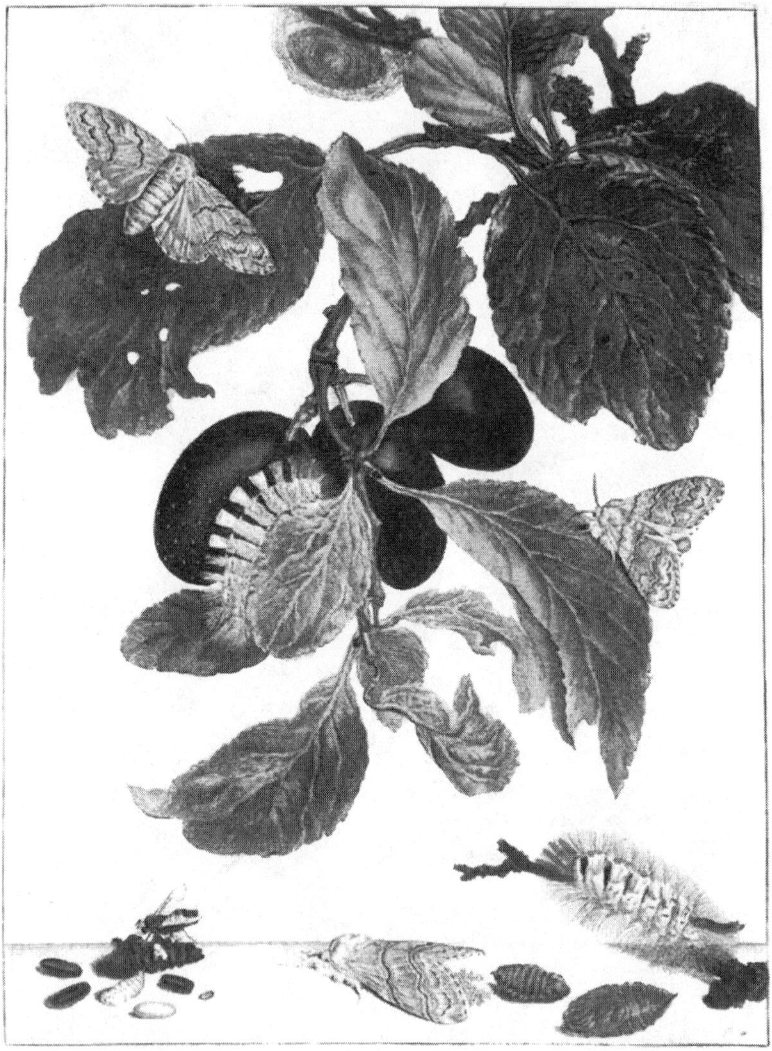

Figure 3: Jacob L'Admiral, plate from *Naauwkeurige Waarneemingen van veele Gestaltverwisselende Gekorvene Diertjes* (circa 1740). By permission of the Houghton Library of Harvard University. Note the degree to which the image of the vegetable food of the insects overwhelms the images of the insects themselves.

has supported them by ungrateful parasites searching for, if not greener pastures, then at least healthier bodies (Lyonnet, 323, 331, 333, 352, 366). In all these cases, the glory of design is proclaimed, in part, by a countervailing design that interrupts successful strategies and that greatly shrinks the frame—the ecosystem—in which a species may extend itself or be portrayed as a successful organism.

Design arguments tend to be monaural—to identify, for each natural phenomenon, one purpose, to regard the disclosure of that purpose as a sufficient statement about the role that the phenomenon plays in the grand design, and then to move ahead to the next phenomenon. Lyonnet takes a multichannel approach to design, ascribing to most creatures a primary purpose but then also identifying their secondary, collateral utility. Thus, "the seeds of vegetables are not destined merely for the preservation of the species, they are likewise destined for the nourishment of animals" (Lyonnet, 362). Secondary utility of this kind lends a divine patina to commercial exploitation of insects. Of silkworms, for example, Lyonnet exclaims, "Could it be supposed, that the gathering of animals so small, would become so considerable an article of commerce?" (Lyonnet, 423). The secondary utility of insects is also subject to the counterdesign mentioned above. The ingenious Creator, for example, outpaced greedy entrepreneurs by arranging not only for population regulation among silk-producing insects but also by sanctioning behavioral characteristics that limit the success of any insect-related enterprises. French entomologist Réaumur, Lyonnet reports, attempted to farm spider silk only to find that these predatory creatures so disdained one another that large-scale operations failed owing to mutual predation (see Lyonnet, 420–421). Less ferociously, ornamental butterflies can only ply (and beautify) those environments in which light, dry air permits their lacy wings to function (Lyonnet, 424). Barometric restrictions on butterfly motion epitomize what might be called "compound design": the felicitous interaction of one set of designs and purposes with another, here the interplay of butterfly anatomy with the behavior of gases. The design of nature thus hinges on its multiplicity—on the fact that several designs and teleologies run all at once, often to mutually productive results, albeit to the confusion of those who hope for a more straightforward teleology. For Lyonnet, then, the design of nature is less of an intrinsic part than an extrinsic, relational feature of God's creatures. The world of spiders and the world of commerce interact with one another, but neither contains that interaction in the way that, say, a ruminant animal contains a well-planned digestive system.

## Intelligent Design or Intelligent Perceptions

Lesser is a design-of-nature expert, but Lyonnet is an enthusiast for the *perceiving* of design. Lesser concentrates on the physical details of insects while attending to their behavior; Lyonnet stresses active perception, transitively *seeing* not only the organization of this or that species but also the interaction of designs. His gallery of nature is full of frames from which viewers assemble the big picture. Lyonnet takes every opportunity to amplify simple observations into *perceptions* and even *renderings* of nature. Thus, when Lesser suggests that righteous scientists should simply default to theism when passively observing design—"I will endeavor to dispose my readers to attribute to God, all those miracles that I shall lay before them" (Lesser, 25)—Lyonnet demands active worship:

> This is the proper end which a person ought to propose to himself in the study of the works of nature, which, without it, is nothing but vain curiosity. We commit an outrage on the Being of Beings, when we set ourselves to contemplate his wonders, without deigning to lift our eyes to their author. As every thing proclaims his greatness, and every thing bears the marks of his wisdom and infinite power, it is blindness not to acknowledge him, and it is criminal to acknowledge him without at the same time paying him the tribute of our worship and adoration. (Lyonnet, 289)

For Lesser, scientific discoveries imply artistry. A phenomenon would not be remarkable if it did not evidence design. Sound science requires a good attitude, specifically the inclination to attribute the wonders of nature to God. Lyonnet requires a much stronger effort, whether through the continuous lifting of the eyes to the Creator or the seeing of large designs in small phenomena. Lyonnet's active seeing pushes, prods, and enlarges the evidence that Lesser only shows. He routinely converts observation into revelation.

Forcing the perception and appreciation of divine design can involve overkill. Combing through Lesser's myriad pages of insect lore, Lyonnet selects and emphasizes the most unusual cases, highlighting the oddity rather than the regularity of design. He develops what might be called an "abilities-based" model of design in which the most compelling phenomena—those that "dispose" observers to credit God with proficient planning—are those that reveal unique capacities, that elicit function from form. Examples include insects with frightening predation techniques, bugs that deploy odor and chemical weaponry, creatures that manage disposable shells and that deal with aquatic environments, ultrastrong insects, and even spiders that deploy their surplus silk fibers as parawings for the purpose of airborne travel from one site to another (Lyonnet, 372–373; 378; 385; 401). Lyonnet compiles long inventories of phenomena that serve multiple purposes—phenomena in which functions outnumber forms (Lyonnet, 376). Endurance also counts among abilities. An alder-eating caterpillar whose metamorphosis requires twenty-two months emerges as a design superstar, not so much owing to its complexity as to its ability to outrun time's winged chariot (Lyonnet, 345). Lyonnet might deserve the sobriquet "the fiber philosopher," owing to his special interest in the astonishing variety and the countless uses of insect textiles and insect coiffeurs. Insect hair and insect fiber serve as the points of contact between the design of the individual insect and the many other designed systems in which it participates. Hair is more than dressing for Lyonnet; it compels observers to ask how the internal system of the insect contacts the external systems that compose the gigantic, complex divine plan.

The abilities comprising Lyonnet's abilities-based theology extend far beyond physical aptitudes. Lyonnet draws extensively on Lesser's catalogs of insect physical precocity, but he frequently introduces cognitive enhancements to the insect toolbox. Fundamental to Lyonnet's revision of Lesser's analogical theology is the introduction of options, whether insect choices with respect to behavior or philosophers' choices with respect to interpretation. Spiders, for example, exercise discretion with respect to their textile manufactures:

> Spiders have the power of spinning their threads, either fine or coarse, as they please, by drawing from their bodies, as many threads as the occasion requires, and joining them together: those which spread their nets in gardens, can even spin two sorts of threads, the one glutinous, the other not. (Lyonnet, 381)

At the very least, spiders enjoy the freedom and possess the ability to assess their setting when selecting the proper gauge of thread. Their capacities include the exercise of discretion. There are, of course, limits. Contrary to folklore, for example, silkworms may not select the color of their silk (Lyonnet, 382). Nevertheless, the operations of spiders and many other insects routinely surpass simple materialistic determination, with the result that observers must loosen their interpretations of those actions. Because spiders sometimes do *X* and other times do *Y*, arachnid hermeneutics must also vary. The meaning and the emblematic or analogical use of spiders must modulate. What appears strange or what seems to deliver moral meaning may dissipate semantically when understood biologically or when attributed to animal discretion. Lyonnet, for example, dilates on spider procreation, noting both spiders' bizarre mating procedures and the alarming fact that "the season of engendering" is the only time that spiders meet "without killing one another," adding that their otherwise cautious behavior seems less strange when understood with respect to the full spectrum of their seasonal actions. He allows that spiders give observers "a lesson" in "circumspection and care"—in assessment and thoughtful action (Lyonnet, 346). The moral lesson that spiders analogize is less a matter of fixed meanings appended to insects that always do the same deeds but rather a far more flexible message about thinking one's way through complex situations.

Both insect and interpreter make choices as Lyonnet's God-nature analogy evolves. Lesser titles his second chapter "Of the Use of Insects in Theology," but Lyonnet tweaks that title with a note in which he explains that, while Lesser sought to show that God made judicial use of insects "to raise us to himself," for example by inflicting a plague of locusts on the disobedient Egyptians, modern thinkers working from a mundane, secular platform should "endeavour to employ them for the same purpose" (Lyonnet, 424). Interested persons should employ discretionary, interpretative powers to extend the still indeterminate analogies that nature provides. Interpreters retain some options within the parameters that physical nature imposes. They are free, for example, to discern how much of an insect accomplishment is attributable to God and how much to chance, discretion, or external factors (see Lyonnet, 374). Lyonnet chides Lesser for denying reasoning powers to the brute creation, protesting that an omnipotent creator could easily bestow rudimentary logical capacities on insects (or any other creatures) and that insect behavior suggests some sort of thinking, yet he stops short of specifying how much ratiocination comes from insects, thus allowing for wide latitude in interpretation. Lyonnet leaves no doubt that he credits insects with the ability not only to choose courses of behavior but also to guide interpreters in the ascription of moral or religious meaning to their actions.

> We cannot but praise M. Lesser, for seeking, even in the conduct of insects, arguments to dissuade us from vice; but one would think, he did not perceive, that his zeal made him argue against his own principles, and that he cannot set in opposition what is praise-worthy in the actions of brutes, to what is blameable in those of men, without supposing, that they act like him, by some motive of reason. . . . One of two things must therefore be chosen; either not to compare man with the brutes, or to allow some degree of reason to these last. (Lyonnet, 375)

Any analogy that compares insects to humans or either insects or humans to God must include, somewhere in the chain of similarities, at least a few links to the laws of logic. Pure analogies—pictures of brute creatures that suggest moral meanings, per the emblem book tradition—remain only impressionistic. Modern moralizers should consider the processes that render nature eligible for service as the foundation of ethics and religion.

Lesser is the apostle of wonder, but Lyonnet is the bean counter of beauty. When Lesser marvels at the complexity and extensiveness of insect construction projects, Lyonnet reviews implementation plans and calculates per capita effort. "Roads of such laborious construction, would seem to require immense time from the ants which form them: but it costs them much less than one could easily believe. The regularity with which a vast multitude labour at the work, makes it go on rapidly" (Lyonnet, 350). What Lyonnet stumbles upon is not only a new idea of distributed intelligence but an equally innovative concept of distributed design. Whereas the traditional physical theology that Lesser cultivated focuses on one creator and then marvels that he could accomplish such a monumental task or could confer on so many creatures such diverse capacities, Lyonnet works from the ground up, suggesting that this massive project emerges from countless incremental efforts. His design emerges piecemeal, from crumbs, grains of sand, pollen, and specks of dung carried by billions of beetles, ants, and bees. This inversion of Lesser's top-down design theology—this bottom-up, beneath-the-grass-roots approach to constructing the universe—diminishes hermeneutic distance within the design argument. It is no longer the case for Lyonnet that discrete, objective creations such as fleas, aphids, and grasshoppers stand apart from an abstracted overview of creation, an overview that makes less use of creatures themselves than of the allegorical meanings that they transmit. In Lyonnet's world, insects continually and directly build the design that to some they seem only to signify. Old-style formulations such as "nature's bees teach us philosophical lessons about social order" collapse across the implied distance between morals and evidence. Insects participate directly in the manufacture of meaning.

For Lyonnet, variability, whether of behavior or of interpretative strategy, is a key indicator of both intelligence and design. Carrying even a tiny grain of earth in an orderly or purposive fashion indicates participation in and at least dim awareness of a rational plan; choosing how much or how little design to see in a phenomenon demonstrates mental talent. Intelligence is a partitive phenomenon. Comparing the usual regularity of insect behavior against insects' capacity to innovate in emergency circumstances tempts honest scientists "to allow them [insects] a portion of reason" (Lyonnet, 334). This partitioning and subdivision of intelligence is not only quantitative but also categorical; different types of intelligence may be divided in different ways among different animals. "Would the lion, for instance, attack with so much courage, if he were not conscious of the superiority of his strength? or, would the nightingale pass whole hours in singing, if it did not feel pleasure in the exercise of its voice?" (Lyonnet, 279). Aware of their attributes and abilities as befits their needs, the assorted animals aboard Earth's ark enjoy levels and aspects of intelligence that allow them not only to constitute but also to produce a diversely magnificent global design. In ascribing task-pertinent awareness to animals, Lyonnet passes another threshold. He not only requires the designer of nature and the philosophizing beholder of design to possess reasoning minds but he also requires the design components themselves to possess intelligence.

The twentieth- and twenty-first-century neofundamentalist notion of intelligent design may well be misnamed. Intelligent design as understood by conservative religious groups involves a centralized authority—an infinite, omnipresent, omnipotent, and omniscient divinity—that manages a universe filled with mindless materials and soulless creatures.[12] A term such as *intelligent design* would be far more aptly applied to the ideas of a humble annotator such as Pierre Lyonnet, who found intelligence in the integuments of the design itself—in the insects, birds, and beasts quietly engineering the myriad subsystems that fill out the sprawling plan of nature. By reducing reasoning and awareness into measurable quantities—by suggesting that a butterfly possesses a very small but not infinitesimal measure of the same intellectual powers that grace human beings—Lyonnet allows that the components of designed nature are indeed intelligent. Although now all but forgotten, Lyonnet and his copious endnotes to Friedrich Christian Lesser's work mark an important turn in the history of ideas concerning dispersed intelligence, distributed computing, neurology, artificial intelligence, animal rights, environmentalism, and process theology—ideas that enliven debates today. Combining an Enlightenment confidence in reasoning, experience, and empirical measure with a forward-looking understanding of the functions of intelligence, Lyonnet developed a theology simple enough to include ants, grand enough to claim the universe as its proper dominion, and yet sufficiently flexible to account for the full range of life forms, whether big or small. Lyonnet's is a universe in which the grand expresses itself in the minute and in which design is far more wonderfully complicated than his more famous Enlightenment counterparts imagined.

## Notes

1. Alexander Pope, *An Essay on Man* I:6. Accessed on *Representative Poetry Online* (http://rpo.library.utoronto.ca/poems/essay-man-epistle-i), November 24, 2015.

2. Accessed on *Bartleby.com: Great Books Online* (http://www.bartleby.com/297/154.html), 24 November 2015.

3. See, for example, Siegfried Rein, *Friedrich Christian Lesser (1692–1754): Pastor, Physicotheologe und Polyhistor* (Nordhausen: Friedrich-Christian-Lesser Stiftung, 1993) and also the online biography at the city of Nordhausen (http://www.nordhausen.de/allgemein/cblock_lang.php?CBlNr=11512).

4. For a full study of Lesser's insect-oriented theology, see Kevin L. Cope, "Tea at a Hexagonal Table? Gregarious Insects and the Outer Limits of Eighteenth-Century Sociability," in *La sociabililté en France et en Grande-Bretagne au Siècle des Lumières: L'èmergence d'un nouveau modèle de société*, eds. Norbert Col and Allan Ingram (Paris: Éditions Le Manuscrit, 2015), 265–288.

5. For the two versions of Pierre Lyonnet's life, see *The Gentleman's Magazine*, September 1789, 857–859, and *The Edinburgh Magazine: Or, Literary Miscellany*, vol. 10 (1789): 230–233.

6. See Johann Leonard Frisch, *Beschreibung von Allerley Insecten in Deutsch-Land: Nebst Nützlichen Anmerckungen und Nöthigen Abbildungen von diesem kriechenden und fliegenden inländischen Gewürme, zur Bestätigung und Fortsetzung der grüdlichen Entdeckung, so einige von der Natur dieser Creaturen heraus gegeben, und zur Ergäntzung und Verbesserung der Andern* (Berlin: 1720–1738).

7. Friedrich Christian Lesser with Pierre Lyonnet, *Insecto-Theology: Or, a Demonstration of the Being and Perfections of God, from a Consideration of the Structure and Economy of Insects . . . with Notes by P. Lyonnet* (Edinburgh: 1799), 286, 288. Citation of this work presents special challenges owing to its bifurcation into two sections produced by two authors. Henceforth, the work will be cited intratextually as "Lesser" when referencing material by Lesser and as "Lyonnet" when referencing Lyonnet's notes.

8. The very brief literature on Joris Hoefnagel includes Lee Hendrix, "Of Hirsutes and Insects: Joris Hoefnagel and the Art of the Wondrous," *Word and Image: A Journal of Verbal/Visual Enquiry* 11, no. 4 (1995): 373–390.

9. Abraham Cowley, *To the Royal Society*, stanza 8, The Abraham Cowley Text and Image Archive, accessed September 15, 2014, http://cowley.lib.virginia.edu/works/RoyalSociety.htm.

10. See Genesis 1:26.

11. The homunculus theory and the attendant accounts of animalculae provide Lyonnet with abundant opportunities to demonstrate his literary skill as a satirist. In two passages that rival the best religious satires of John Dryden or Voltaire, Lyonnet conducts an absurdist speculation on, first, the multiplicity of wasted souls lost in the act of procreation (millions of homunculi being expended to effect one fertilization) and, second, the possible answers from Catholics, Protestants, and other sects regarding the disposition of these souls in the afterlife (see Lyonnet, 363–364). "Here then for a member of the Church of Rome who should adopt the system of Leeuwenhoeck, the number of the Reprobate, who have never known good nor ill, becomes a thousand million times greater than that of those who

have become so by their own crimes; and yet the number of the Blessed is not encreased by a single individual. What a horrible idea!"

12. Not all contemporary redactions of the argument from design emerge from fundamentalist or conservative movements. Recently, for example, physicist and philosopher Owen Gingrich has devised an account of design that is reminiscent of Lyonnet's in its preference for a *purposive*, self-making universe over the more deterministic version put forth in the classic argument from design. See Owen Gingrich, *God's Universe* (Cambridge, MA: The Belknap Press of Harvard University Press, 2006), 115–117.

# An Apostate Maskil: The Effect of the Haskalah on Daniil Avraamovich Khvol'son

*Andrew C. Reed*

When the Jewish historian Jacob Raisin completed his work on the history of the Haskalah movement in Russia, he attached the following passage to the book's flyleaf:

> And the "Maskilim" shall shine
> As the brightness of the firmament …
> Many shall run to and fro,
> And knowledge shall be increased.[1]

This liberal play on the apocalyptic vision contained in Daniel 12:3–4 substitutes "Maskilim," the proponents of "Enlightenment," in place of the biblical "wise" or pious person.[2] Raisin's subtle alteration to the scriptural text reflects the monumental role that the maskilim played in the transformation of Russian Jewry in the nineteenth century. The term *maskil* (plural *maskilim*) referred to individuals who aligned themselves with the German *Aufklärung* and initiated a specifically Jewish movement known as the Haskalah.[3] Until recently, historians have focused on the events in Berlin, London, and Paris in their search for the entrance of Ashkenazi Jews into modernity.[4] The Haskalah has proven difficult to pin down as a coherent movement in European history because, as Shmuel Feiner argued, it lacked institutional coherence and ideological parameters.[5] The Haskalah is most often identified with German Jews, but, as is argued here, there were similar movements that developed in later decades that were equally transformational for Jewish communities in eastern Europe.

Scholars of the European Enlightenment now differentiate between enlightenments that occurred in various locations and decades to show that geography and chronology mattered and defined the issues that contributors took up as their priorities.[6] These efforts have bolstered the proliferation of books and articles situating Russia on the periphery of the European Enlightenment.[7] Following this trend, scholars of Russian Jewry have discovered new perspectives from which to examine the dramatic transformation of Jews within Russian boundaries through exposure to, and participation in, the Haskalah. Of particular interest here is Russia's encounter with newly acquired Jewish populations that forced upon nineteenth-century Russian rulers the issue of the incorporation of minority populations.[8] The program decided upon by Russian rulers reflected some Enlightenment principles, particularly the use of reason and the elimination of religious superstition that they so frequently associated with Jews and Judaism. While benevolent in their aims to expand education and application of reason among Jews, the program was driven by a utilitarian hope for greater usefulness to the empire.

The subject of this study is the early life of Daniil Avraamovich Khvol'son (born "Iosif Solomonovich Khvol'son") and his encounter with the Haskalah. Khvol'son (1819–1911) rose to prominence in Russian-Jewish society and reflected the shifting waves of government intervention with the Jewish community from 1819 to 1855.[9] Khvol'son was born in Vilna, modern Vilnius, educated in Breslau and Leipzig, and obtained a professorial post at St. Petersburg University. He defended Jews from the pernicious blood libel accusation and occupied a respected position among European intellectuals, including Abraham Geiger and Ernest Renan.

This sketch of his early life is also focused on the influential mentors and acquaintances with whom Khvol'son associated during his adolescent and university years. Khvol'son benefited greatly from mentors and scholars who valued the enlightened gaze of nineteenth-century scholarship and the principles of religious tolerance. By the 1850s, some observers viewed Khvol'son as one of the most successful products of a state-led Enlightenment project. His transition from poverty to renowned university professor illuminates three important developments within imperial policy related to the Jewish population during this period: the influence of German-Jewish education sponsored by the Russian state, the contested nature of Jewish communal life and religious developments, and the introduction of "expert Jews" (*uchenye evrei*) into the imperial bureaucracy. While Khvol'son's early life was somewhat exceptional given his humble beginnings, it illustrates perhaps better than any other Jewish biography the process by which the Nicholaevan government hoped to employ German educators to produce "enlightened" Jewish subjects for positions within the state apparatus.

Even before Russian authorities became involved, Jews in the Pale of Settlement—a region of Russia in which permanent Jewish residency was allowed but beyond which was generally prohibited—initiated an internal process of reform in some communities while others remained committed to the protection and continuation of more traditional communal forms. Feiner argues that as part of the Haskalah movement, maskilim adopted a new approach and understanding of historical time and the relationship between their current era and the past.[10] The modern period, often associated with the post–French Revolution period in European history, also signaled a major breakthrough for Jews when Napoleon attempted to incorporate them as citizens in postrevolutionary France. The position of Jews within European society was one of the most contested cultural battles during the eighteenth and nineteenth centuries, and Jews, like Christians, responded to that debate in various ways. As Adam Sutcliffe so clearly argued,

> Judaism was thus profoundly ensnared in the relationship between the Enlightenment and the Christian worldview from and against which it emerged. . . . Judaism during the Enlightenment can only be understood in the context of this relationship, and concomitantly, that the complexities clustered around Judaism are of central importance for a general understanding of the Enlightenment itself.[11]

If the core foundational values of the Enlightenment—tolerance, justice, and rationality—were at the center of the eighteenth-century political and social discourse, then it makes sense that Jews would understand their position as one on the brink of potential improvement. Maskilim of the first decades of the nineteenth century found root for internal reform movements aimed at education, language adaptation, and modernization of Jewish religious ritual and more generally, cultural modernization.

Adherents of the Haskalah composed a small (yet significant) group of Jews "who were conscious of being modern Jews, and the first to advocate a modernist transformational ideology."[12] For a select number of Jews within the Russian Empire, the legacy of the French Enlightenment provided the cultural seedbed for their assumption of values that separated "enlightened" Jews from their "uneducated" coreligionists in the Pale of Settlement. Baron Horace Ginsburg (1833–1909), the son of the liquor and bank magnate Evzel Ginsburg (1812–1878), provided the example for all other Russian Jews who sought to become maskilim. The younger Ginsburg "was carefully designed" to become the "ideal modern Jew."[13] For children of wealthy Jews, the path to enlightenment was relatively straightforward. Young Horace, due to his father's accumulated wealth after the Crimean War, visited relatives in Paris for an extended period at least once each year. While there, he participated in private music lessons, French instruction, Hebrew courses, and history classes led by accomplished French composers, poets, and historians. Those who followed the Ginsburg model were shipped off to Paris or other European cities to obtain continental Enlightenment education—a privilege afforded them by family wealth. When they returned to St. Petersburg (or elsewhere in the interior of the empire) they did so as Jewish elites who had a network of government and financial relations that secured opportunities for them to influence the future of Russian Jewry through philanthropy and lobbying.

For the vast majority of Russian Jews without monetary means to travel abroad, the pathway to education, along with the many benefits that resulted from it—language acquisition, access to university training, and inclusion in the wider world of Russian intellectual society—was less direct and required greater creativity. During the reign of Nicholas I (1825–1855), Russia attempted to revitalize the Jewish population to better contribute to the growth of the empire.[14] Efforts to employ Russia's Jews in new ways marked a rare occurrence of state-led reform (albeit limited) in the decade leading up to the 1848 revolutions in Europe. The limited reforms of Nicholas I's reign tend to be overshadowed in accounts of the nineteenth century by historians focused on the more ambitious reforms of his son, Alexander II. However, in the context of Russian-Jewish relations, the late 1830s and early 1840s marked a critical juncture because it was during this period that a select group of Jews were encouraged to begin qualifying for state service in new ways.

For maskilim in Russia, the period of Nicholas I and his official enlightenment policies served to bolster their hopes for the eradication of some of their more "obnoxious and arcane" traditions.[15] As Nathans argued, government officials like Nicholas I were "enlightened in the specific historical sense of using the power of the state to increase the productivity of the population by rationalizing, centralizing, and standardizing legal norms."[16] Although the specific aims of the reform efforts may have failed on the larger scale, they succeeded in their aim to create a pool of talented individuals within minority populations that later served as intermediaries between government and community, as seen in the case of Khvol'son. The development of minority groups that could be of use to the state mirrored the expanding state bureaucracy. By 1860, the number of state bureaucrats increased to nearly one hundred thousand, a remarkable transformation considering that about fifteen thousand were in the employ of the state at the turn of the century.[17] It was also during Nicholas's reign that figures of the "expert Jew" and "Jewish notables" (wealthy Jews with connections to the imperial bureaucracy) were linked to state policy and bureaucratic structures. In an increasingly diverse and expanding empire, minority populations attracted greater attention from the bureaucracy and demanded new methods for addressing their communal needs. More importantly, in an age of fear of insurrection, the tsar placed great hope in these minority middlemen to encourage further cooperation among his subjects and reduce rebellious factions. In order to build an efficient and loyal "enlightened bureaucracy," the state needed to educate those individuals according to the standards of science, enlightenment thought, and political ideas.[18]

Khvol'son was born on November 21, 1819, in Vilna, Russia.[19] The Khvol'son home was rich in Jewish wisdom, though less so in bread and other necessary provisions. According to one report, the family's four young children frequently retired to bed hungry, as all the Talmudic knowledge brought spiritual food but provided little for supper.[20] Khvol'son's mother was a seamstress and worked long hours to provide a meager income for the family. His father descended from a respected line of local Talmudists, and, in keeping with tradition and like many Jewish boys of his generation, young Iosif (Daniil) studied in the local *heder*, where he showed great promise.

Khvol'son's early Talmudic and Hebrew training came at the hands of Rabbi Israel Gintsburg and other well-respected teachers.[21] David Gintsburg (1857–1910), one of Khvol'son's students and strongest advocates late in life, published a *Festshrift* on the occasion of Khvol'son's eightieth birthday. In his contribution, Gintsburg reflected on Khvol'son's early years:

> Life was harsh to him as a child, he grew up in poverty, there was darkness all around him, but as soon as his conscience grew stronger, he began to struggle, straining in the strength of youth to achieve knowledge. . . . But he prevailed, and went out from the crucible a tried man, full of knowledge.[22]

Khvol'son was a product of his times; the influence of education and educational policies, both in their earliest forms and later as he pursued advanced degrees, placed him on his path in life. Despite the economic struggles of the Khvol'son family, young Iosif excelled in learning, drawing every bit of knowledge he could out of the local *melamed*. The *melamed*, or local teacher in the *heder*, was hardly a highly sought after position during the early decades of the nineteenth century. The experiences varied widely among the teachers in the early nineteenth-century *heder*. According to Shaul Stempfer's analysis of the *heder* in the Russian Empire, these Jewish institutions served a valuable role within the community by maintaining socioeconomic hierarchies that could not be maintained otherwise.[23] Jewish education equalized every male in the community because as young boys they would attend the *heder* together, and all of them were expected to study and learn to pray in Hebrew. The paradox, however, is that by allowing all young boys to participate in the tradition of learning, a natural division occurred between those who possessed a specific talent for learning and those who did not. Another aspect of this socioeconomic hierarchy reflected the broader division based on family wealth. Fathers who could afford to hire private tutors and instructors often did so to the great benefit of their sons. The *heder*, into which young boys entered around the age of three or four, served to train them for lives as scholars. Those who showed particular talent and aptitude advanced to further studies in the *yeshiva*. The requirements for working as a teacher of these young boys were minimal, salaries were notoriously meager, and many teachers were "highly unqualified and were neither learned nor creative."[24]

Khvol'son's seemingly limited exposure to subjects outside of the *yeshiva* meant that by his late teens, he was only able to speak Yiddish. Khvol'son's recounting of his educational situation to his family later in life painted a bleak image of his perceptions about the possibilities before him. Jews, who understood only their "*zhargon*," struggled to learn any language because they "did not know the foundations of grammar, and they had no dictionaries in their mother tongue."[25] While this image may be exaggerated, it reveals the aged Khvol'son's perception about his Jewish upbringing and the disadvantaged position that caused him to leave his native Vilna. For many Jews in the empire, education served as the surest ticket into Russian society. The Jewish Enlightenment, or Haskalah (as it related to education), entered into the imperial territories via a Russian state-driven effort to bring in German Jews, particularly German-trained rabbis, to improve Russia's Jewish population through the creation of Jewish schools that taught secular as well as Jewish subjects.

To meet the needs of the state, Nicholas I depended upon the Ministry of Education to further his aims. Nicholas's older brother, Alexander I, created the Ministry of Education (*Ministerstvo Narodnogo Prosveshcheniia*) in 1802 as part of the reorganization of the empire's bureaucratic structure—one of his first consequential acts as tsar. One of the major ambitions of Alexander I was the creation of a university system, noticeably absent in Russia at the beginning of the nineteenth century. Moscow University was founded in 1755, but the next half-century witnessed little innovation outside of that single institution. Alexander I was well aware of the need for Russia's modernization. As part of that modernization, new universities were established in Kazan, Kharkov, St. Petersburg, Vilna, and Dorpat (modern Tartu, Estonia).

An effective and modern university system depended upon an education system that prepared pupils for the demands of university life. Thus, between 1825 and 1849, the government set out on a widespread reform of elementary and secondary education. In 1833, Nicholas I appointed Sergei Uvarov (1785–1855) as the minister of education. Uvarov remained at the head of the ministry until 1849, when the reactionary Nicholas withdrew from reform. Uvarov is perhaps widely known today as the one who most succinctly summarized the Old Regime ideology of Nicholas's government in 1833. "Official Nationality," Uvarov argued, consisted of three pillars or principles: "Orthodoxy, autocracy, and nationality."[26] These three pillars provided a general platform for administering the empire, and it was in them that Uvarov grounded his efforts to draw the Jewish communities more closely into the Russian state by creating schools that aligned with the goals of the government.[27]

## The Haskalah in the Employ of the State

The Haskalah movement in the German lands produced a generational divide through the gradual migration and adoption of European ideas. During these years the Vilna community, like others with substantial Jewish populations, witnessed the intensification of the "culture war" over education.[28] Uvarov's plan sought to incorporate Jews into the Russian Empire by modernizing them and educating a small portion of the population, making them fit for civil service and providing a critical link to the traditional Jewish communities. The Jewish community in Riga sent a request to German acquaintances, bidding help in locating a German teacher and preacher to fill the post at the local school. The Riga Jewish community obtained government permission to conduct a search for such a figure in 1838. Ludwig Philippson (1811–1889), the editor of the weekly Jewish newspaper *Allgemeine Zeitung des Judentums*, suggested to twenty-four-year-old Dr. Max Lilienthal (1814–1882) from Munich that he apply straightaway for the position. A series of articles that the young Lilienthal sent Philippson in 1838 impressed him (also a moderate reformer) to the point that the editor sought to help the young rabbi find gainful employment. The rabbinical post benefitted from its location in Riga because the city contained a sizable German-speaking Jewish population. As such, Lilienthal continued to use German in his sermons and administrative responsibilities.[29]

It is important to understand Lilienthal's story if we are to make sense of his role in young Khvol'son's life. Lilienthal was the son of a relatively wealthy family in Munich. As a student he had excelled early on in his Talmudic training, and as a result he promised his dying mother (who died when he was ten years old) that he would become a rabbi. After completing his doctorate in Munich in 1837, Lilienthal worked for a brief time at the Royal Library as a researcher. During his childhood, the battle intensified between those who sought to preserve traditional Jewish ways of life and those who sought an assimilationist approach. In addition to his traditional Jewish education, private tutors exposed the young boy to the sciences.[30] This early training in sciences, regardless of the level of rigor, suggests that the Lilienthal family found value in the possibilities that a secular education provided when paired with his religious education.

When Lilienthal was hired for the position in Riga, he appeared to have been excited by the opportunity both for professional advancement and for the chance to help East European Jews. Whatever his perception of Jews in Russia, he was motivated to improve the Jewish condition and hopefully impart to them some of his learning and his experience. There existed among many German Jews a sense of superiority—evidenced by religious, social, and economic matters—over their neighbors to the east. Lilienthal was no exception. In his "My Travels in Russia," he wrote:

> I accepted this call at once, as Rev. I. N. Mannheimer, the renowned preacher of Vienna, had convinced me in a correspondence which I conducted with him, that something had to be done for the Russian Jews, who alone of all their coreligionists were

> behind the civilization of the age. The sphere of activity in such a vast empire flattered my youthful vanity, and hoping for the best results of my sincere endeavors—to raise millions of Jews to a higher standard—I asked the Russian ambassador in Munich for my passport.[31]

While this feeling would fluctuate at times, it remained a constant marker of Western superiority for many throughout the nineteenth century.[32] Evident in this passage and many others like it is the disdain of Eastern Jews not only because of their socioeconomic conditions but also because of their intellectual outlook. While this perspective drew upon a sense of superiority, it also motivated some of the secularly trained Jews to seek paths for improving their fellow Jews. In many ways, Lilienthal represented a certain strand of the Jewish Enlightenment, the Haskalah, which held at its core the values espoused by the wider European Enlightenment. The desire to improve oneself through education and moral refinement, modeled on the German idea of *Bildung*, lay at the heart of the Enlightenment program.[33] At the same time, it carried with it the added dimension of improving Jewish communal life. Many rabbis and scholars thereby discovered a public mission through their individual processes of gaining secular education.

Lilienthal, with his early tutorials in science, his rabbinic training in Munich and Fürth, and his doctoral degree from the newly founded University of Munich, was well positioned to spread Enlightenment thought to the Jews of Riga.[34] The attainment of the doctorate from Munich set Lilienthal apart from many of his contemporaries—even further so with respect to the Jews of the Russian Empire. Although there was a rich tradition of learning among Polish Jews who attained significant acumen in sciences by attending universities in the West in the sixteenth century, they remained a minority, even up to the beginning of the twentieth century.[35]

Even before he began teaching in Riga, the community asked Lilienthal to visit the Russian capital in hopes of gaining the ear of some high-level official and pleading their case. For the young Lilienthal, the thought of being sent on official business by the community to St. Petersburg fit well with his understanding of his role. The historical details get a bit muddled about how this unfolded, but needless to say, his initial reception was less spectacular than he had hoped. He met with Uvarov, the head of the Ministry of Education, who insisted that Lilienthal create a model Jewish school (along the lines of the German schools) that could then be used to encourage others to follow. From 1840 until 1845, Uvarov and Lilienthal formed a team that worked closely together to spread "enlightenment" to Russia's Jews. The program to improve Jews through education fit well with the imperial hope of bringing Jewish communities further within the scope of civil government and also with Lilienthal's aim to improve the training of his fellow coreligionists.

Almost immediately upon his arrival in Riga, the young doctor and rabbi evaluated the school and reported his progress to Uvarov. Lilienthal received direction from Uvarov to travel to the various posts and get a sense of the population's willingness to reform. Lilienthal was highly ambitious, if naively so, in his hopes of solving the Jewish question in Russia through educational reform. Lilienthal's hope was to gradually transform Jewish youth through improved schools and advanced learning, thereby opening avenues of assimilation for them into Russian society.

Although he anticipated unanimously warm reception across the Pale of Settlement when he visited the various cities, Lilienthal met staunch resistance in some places and a hero's welcome in others. In her memoirs of life in Brest in the 1840s, Pauline Wengeroff mentions specifically the excitement caused by Lilienthal's visit after 1840.[36] As the daughter of a well-to-do Jewish family, she noted that her brothers-in-law began collecting, reading, and discussing secular books instead of studying the Talmud. When Lilienthal visited the town, her father declared that he would be accompanying the young men to visit the rabbi. Her mother protested on account of Lilienthal's reputation and, by this point, his appointment as a government official responsible for Jewish education. Wengeroff noted that Lilienthal made it a point on such visits to gather around him the young men in the city and discuss with them their education, specifically their awareness of Western secular subjects and their knowledge of European languages

(Russian, German, and Polish).[37] At the same time, he also introduced the young men to philosophical and literary works popular among many German Jews, including those by Freidrich Wilhelm Joseph Schelling (1775–1854), Johann Wolfgang von Goethe (1749–1832), and Moses Mendelssohn (1729–1786).[38] The emphasis on Schelling is not surprising given Lilienthal's exposure to his ideas while at the university in Munich. Schelling resided in Munich from 1806 to 1841 and taught as a member of the philosophy faculty there. Goethe's influence is also not surprising, given his literary efforts to spread tolerance and Enlightenment among Germans.[39] Of the three writers included in this short list, the work of Mendelssohn, particularly his translation of the Bible into German, was the most important for this generation of young Jews.[40]

## From Vilna to Breslau

When he was eighteen years old, a good friend taught Khvol'son the Latin alphabet, which he practiced by observing Polish signs on the street. In order to continue his study of Latin letters, Khvol'son secured a German book and taught himself the foundations of German. From this humble beginning, Khvol'son's abilities with languages and texts became legendary, all the more so because he claimed that much of his learning came without specialized training until he attended the university. While such a stark portrayal of the man's lack of training should be accepted cautiously, it serves the Khvol'son myth well. How could a young man so pathetically trained and uneducated resist the opportunity to leave the community? Drawing upon his desire to learn German, and perhaps feeling the draw of a gradual yet significant Jewish exodus from traditional Polish/Baltic lands toward German-speaking regions, Khvol'son left Vilna in the early 1840s.[41] The historical record is vague about the timeframe for Khvol'son's departure from his hometown, though Cohen suggests Khvol'son was twenty-two years old when he left.[42] If Cohen's dating is correct, then the departure occurred sometime in late 1841 or 1842.

The importance of German-Jewish influence for Khvol'son, and for the Vilna Jewish community as a whole, was tremendous. For some in the community, the encroachment of secular ideas that funneled through Uvarov and Lilienthal's new schools threatened the very foundation of Jewish life, while others embraced the ideas as a moment of liberation. Khvol'son apparently found Lilienthal's ideas transformative to the point that he sought out the doctor on a visit to Riga. The decision to visit Lilienthal in Riga placed Khvol'son on a path from which he would never return, at least not as a religiously observant Jew. Though he left behind family and friends, Khvol'son was aided during his subsequent years abroad by several mentors who looked after his physical and intellectual wellbeing. Khvol'son's path out of the Vilna region coincided with efforts by the tsarist government under Nicholas I to bring Jewish educational structures under closer surveillance. In the early 1840s, the government, through the Ministry of Education, began identifying individuals who were open to cooptation, willing to employ their knowledge of Jewish networks and Judaism in the wider reform effort.

Khvol'son's journey from Vilna to Riga to Breslau was remarkable for several reasons. According to his grandson, he hiked on foot the entire journey, stopping at the occasional home or shop to ask for provisions.[43] At night he slept in the fields along the road. Khvol'son later reflected at times on this journey and often retold the many encounters he experienced along the way. In one self-deprecating instance, he recalled that a man he met along the road—when he discovered that the young Jewish boy was traveling alone—asked, "Are you not afraid?" Khvol'son noted that his immediate response was, "What does it mean to be afraid?"[44] Khvol'son remembered his younger self as ignorant and detached from the larger trends and movements in society, isolated within his small Jewish world. According to his grandson, Khvol'son's retelling of his story often included grateful mention of the many unknown individuals who provided occasional meals or provisions and small sums of money to help him on his way.

When Khvol'son arrived at Riga, he visited with Lilienthal, who was Khvol'son's senior by just five years. This meeting occurred while Lilienthal was heavily involved in the state-directed program to improve

Jewish schools. At the same time, he sought to find individuals who could potentially fill the categories of "useful" Jews fit for service in the empire. The order of events that led Khvol'son from Riga to Breslau are somewhat unclear. Whatever the context may have been, it is clear that Khvol'son depended upon a network of rabbis to facilitate his journey. Lilienthal provided a letter of recommendation on Khvol'son's behalf to the young, though already controversial, German rabbi Abraham Geiger (1810–1874) in Breslau.[45] The fact that Lilienthal recommended Khvol'son to his colleague in Breslau is significant for a number of reasons. First, it shows the dependence of Russian Jews upon their German coreligionists. This dependence took many forms, including but not limited to financial, religious, sociocultural, and political dependence. Second, the connection between Lilienthal—himself a product of German-Jewish culture—and Geiger was not limited only to a letter of recommendation. Rather, it suggested a broad project of bringing German-Jewish intellectuals and rabbis into the service of the East European Jews—with the anticipation of spreading Enlightenment. Thus, Lilienthal seems to have acted out of a sense of loyalty to the Russian government, or at least the minister of education, and an internal desire to improve a select few Jews who possessed desires for greater knowledge. The Haskalah project, then, was the result of internal Jewish motivations as well as external state-led initiatives.

In his effort to enjoin rabbis and teachers sympathetic to his cause, Lilienthal (under the direction of Uvarov) also asked Geiger to accept a position in the Russian Empire. In response to the request from Uvarov and Lilienthal, Geiger indicated he could not take up the post:

> There is still much that needs to be done in the Fatherland, which is the center of this progress. Would I not then be remiss in my duties if I were to leave here in order to give of my energies to another country, where at present only the after-effects of our own achievements can be felt?[46]

Geiger, like many Jewish intellectuals gazing to the East, believed fully in the German reform movement as central to the Haskalah. As fully committed supporters of improving the lot of Jews in German lands, these individuals maintained a hope that Christian society would soon open up fully to the emancipation of the Jews in every realm of life, if only Jews could eliminate those elements that prevented their full integration. Beyond the prescient hope for citizenship in German society, these individuals were also deeply tied to their familiar surroundings. This was, after all, the age of growing national identities, albeit loosely defined in the pre-1848 world. In his letter to Lilienthal, Geiger conceded, "I might as well admit—despite the fact that her authorities reject me because I am a Jew, I still love Germany."[47] Given the gradual, though not insignificant achievements of Jewish communities during the 1830s and 1840s in the German territories, Russia likely provided little incentive for those even remotely aware of the situation to their east.

The lack of positions available to well-educated Jews in their homeland drove some to consider working in the eastern empire. Further, as Geiger suggested in a letter to Joseph Naftali Dernburg on August 3, 1840, matters of "universal Jewish concern" were felt:

> Among those Jews who comprise the upper stratum of Jewry . . . [are] the Jews who reside among civilized nations, particularly Germany, and who will later be emulated and followed by those who now are still among the uneducated. That which goes on among the Jews living in the uncivilized countries, on the other hand, is of trifling importance only, even if it were to be of general import in those particular lands.[48]

The German-Jewish efforts for political, social, and religious emancipation in Germany were believed to be a model for Russia. Geiger understood that regardless of whatever minor achievements might be made in Eastern Europe, his mission and heart remained in his homeland. For Jews outside of Russia, there remained an abiding concern for their neighbors to the east, but many, like Geiger, recognized that without real and profound success in their struggles for emancipation in their own countries, they could do little to aid those in the Pale of Settlement. Although he rejected the Russian offer, Geiger did not abandon the Russian project altogether. As newly married and recently appointed to the Breslau rabbinate (assistant rabbi), he welcomed Lilienthal's recommendation to assist the young Khvol'son in gaining a position in a German university. Khvol'son was still untrained in classical languages—a prerequisite for his entrance into the German academy.[49] Geiger, an orientalist steeped in a number of languages, worked with Khvol'son on his language skills and within four years helped prepare him for university. The details of their relationship are unclear, though based on Khvol'son's comments and those of his family, it was a richly warm and positive one.

When his dissertation was published as a two-volume work in 1856, Khvol'son remembered Geiger and others who assisted him along the way. His acknowledgement of Breslau's rabbi, Abraham Geiger, illuminates the deep sense of respect and gratitude that Khvol'son possessed for the man. He gratefully acknowledged Geiger's efforts on his behalf:

> Finally, my heart urges me to express here my gratitude to a man who is in no way affiliated with this book, but to whom I have endless thanks, I mean the honorable, well-known, Dr. Geiger in Breslau. Many years ago I was in Germany, a country where I knew nobody and was known by no one, and I might have rotted intellectually and physically, that noble man took me in as a father, he sheltered and nurtured me physically and spiritually, and it is to him primarily that I owe great thanks that I have achieved the academic level which I now possess.[50]

The impact of Geiger's generosity is clear; he served Khvol'son at a time when the migrant student was "penniless" and destitute—actions that placed Khvol'son in his debt emotionally and temporally. At a time when Khvol'son felt orphaned in his new country, to have one whom he could respect and learn from proved critical to his success and helped set him on a course that he maintained for the rest of his life. Additionally, one of the lesser-recognized debts that Khvol'son owed his Breslau mentor was intellectual. Even after his dissertation was published, it is unlikely that Khvol'son fully understood the influence of Geiger on his future scholarship. Heschel highlights the continuation of Geiger's work by his student, but for Khvol'son the formative period with Geiger became an essential building block for his later life, perhaps even more than his homage quoted above suggests.[51]

Geiger was accepted as an assistant rabbi in Breslau in January of 1840 after a prolonged challenge from Orthodox rabbis and others, including Solomon Tiktin and his conservative congregants in the city. In late summer of the same year, he took up the post in Breslau, where he was responsible for religious education. Geiger was already well respected in intellectual circles (Christian and Jewish) for his doctoral dissertation, *Was hat Mohammed aus dem Judenthume aufgenommen?* (What did Muhammad receive from Judaism?).[52] In that text, Geiger challenged the idea that Islam was an original religion by suggesting that the theology of Islam developed out of rabbinic sources—particularly out of the rabbinic summaries and commentaries on biblical stories.[53] Geiger argued that the problem with the traditional perception of the rise of Islam and its foundations was that it placed Christianity as the center and external source that provided theological impetus behind the new religion. Geiger took issue with scholars and theologians who claimed "scientific" evidence and yet produced works that were deeply flawed and untrue to the historical context of early Christianity, Second Temple Judaism, and the advent of Islam. Thus, Geiger remained committed, as was Khvol'son later, to recast the three Abrahamic traditions as connected to each other through a common history and, to some extent, a common theological tradition.[54]

## Heinrich Leberecht Fleischer

Not only did Geiger provide material support and foundational knowledge for Khvol'son's academic career, he also introduced the young man to a number of Christian and Jewish scholars. Two of the most important contacts made by Khvol'son during this period in Breslau were a pair of renowned orientalists. The first was Franz Karl Movers (1806–1856), the famed Roman Catholic orientalist in Breslau who helped teach Khvol'son languages and encouraged his research. Khvol'son's first lessons in Arabic and ancient languages came from Movers. After Khvol'son completed his studies, reviewers of his work frequently commented that he maintained the high standard for scholarship that one came to expect from students of

Movers. The second, and perhaps the most important individual for Khvol'son's academic career, was the acquaintance of Heinrich Leberecht Fleischer (1801–1888). Fleischer was educated at Leipzig and Paris before returning to Leipzig in 1836, where he took up a post as a professor. Fleischer helped Khvol'son in many ways, not the least of which was to help secure his doctorate from his university. Khvol'son came to know of Fleischer through his two Breslau mentors, Geiger and Movers.

Initially the German school of orientalism depended upon the French school for its methods and, more importantly, for its training. While France led the charge in oriental studies in the early decades of the nineteenth century, it was eclipsed in the 1830s and 1840s by its German neighbors as more students who were trained in France took positions in central Europe. The leading French orientalist, Antoine Isaac Silvestre de Sacy (1758–1838), not only built up the French school of oriental studies but also proved critical for the transformation of the German school through one of his students, Heinrich Leberecht Fleischer.[55]

Fleischer, who later became Khvol'son's mentor and promoter, transformed the intellectual and professional expectations in the German universities from relatively weak philological skills to deep methodical research and rigorous linguistic training in languages like Chaldean, Persian, Syriac, Arabic, Aramaic, and Hebrew. As Schorsch argued in his short study of Fleischer's influence on the German orientalists, these scholars previously worked with theology departments, but during the 1840s they were housed within Philosophy faculties.[56] The move from theology to other faculties profoundly altered the scope of subjects and methodologies employed by orientalists, thus unbinding—at least partially—the Christian worldview from the study of Islamic and Jewish civilizations.[57] Under the intellectual guardianship of Fleischer, the Lutheran university at Leipzig became the flagship for Christians and Jews interested in studying ancient languages and cultures, not out of religious conviction but as subjects worthy of study on their own terms and, importantly, through their own sources. The increase in Jews who studied at the university during this period and in Jewish orientalists who, although not offered academic positions, conceived of their work in a scholarly way (e.g., Geiger and others) allowed the rabbinical seminaries in Breslau and elsewhere to provide an outlet for Jewish orientalists in German cities. Efron argued that Jewish orientalists, especially Geiger, "approached orientalism with a different set of assumptions and prejudices than Gentile orientalists" and that they tended to view Islam, the Quran, and Muhammad differently than their Christian counterparts.

For Geiger, Islam was an outgrowth of the very best form of Judaism, which valued above all else monotheism, revelation, and prophecy.[58] Islam became a way for Ashkenazic Jews in Germany to evaluate, and increasingly critique, the possibility of a more equal and peaceable relationship with the surrounding majority. With medieval Spain as their model, Jewish orientalists aimed to show where greater religious freedom (or at least indifference by the majority) contributed to an expansion of Jewish life and culture built on literature, philosophy, and education. Though Geiger criticized Muslims and their society at times, he also praised them for adapting Judaism as the model and basis of their religious texts and ideas.[59] Islam, he argued, adapted from the very best that Judaism had to offer and, though the relationship was not always congenial, exhibited extraordinary capacity for peaceful coexistence—something that Christian Europe largely failed to accomplish.

This rich tradition was well developed by the time Khvol'son began serious studies in the university. He would eventually become one of the central torchbearers of that scholarly heritage throughout the remainder of his long life. During Khvol'son's time in Breslau, he completed his work at the university, and under the supervision of Movers, he conducted an ambitious study of the Sabians, a non-Muslim group written about in the Quran and Arabic texts. Khvol'son first found interest in the Sabians after he read Maimonides's *Guide for the Perplexed*, even though the two differed in their understanding of who the Sabians were. For Maimonides, they were not a "people," while for Khvol'son they were a culturally identifiable group. The Sabians appear in a number of Arabic texts and were described variously as pagans, sometimes barbaric, but in other places they were understood by some to be culturally refined and deeply involved in philosophical and mathematical endeavors.[60] Khvol'son compiled an impressive number of texts about the community and provided a profound introduction and analysis of this group and their culture. Ultimately, Khvol'son concluded that the Sabians referred to in Quran should be seen as Mandeans who developed a Gnostic religious system. Likely prompted by Movers and Geiger, Khvol'son sent a draft of the first part of his work to Professor Fleischer in Leipzig. Fleischer received Khvol'son's text at the beginning of February 1850, and it was so well received in Leipzig that Khvol'son obtained the doctorate by February 20, 1850—even before Fleischer could see the rest of Khvol'son's work! Fleischer wrote to colleagues, "If God gives him health and he continues to work [he] . . . will soon rank among the top scholars of his nation (by which I understand Russians and not Jews)."[61] This positive reaction by the learned professor continued long after Khvol'son left for St. Petersburg and served as an enduring source of encouragement.

Khvol'son walked, quite literally, into this intellectual world perhaps unwittingly, but with a sincere longing (as many young Jews had during this period) for secular education and a greater awareness of the ideas and principles that influenced, and were in turn shaped by, his own Jewish heritage. Geiger was well connected to that world and served as an intermediary between traditional Jewish education and the German university to which Khvol'son was headed. In order to see Khvol'son's early work and its genesis in proper perspective, he must be viewed as a participant in the milieu of nineteenth-century German orientalism.

When Khvol'son submitted his dissertation work to Fleischer in 1850, he immediately gained the respect of that great scholar and placed himself, in large part due to their relationship, at the forefront of contemporary scholarship. After reading the complete dissertation manuscript, Fleischer is reported to have praised Khvol'son's genius in working with these texts. "You begin," he noted, "where others would end."[62] Fleischer's generous approval helped raise awareness of Khvol'son's ability as a scholar and of the promising future ahead. When it was finally published in 1856 in German by the Academy of Sciences in St. Petersburg, it extended to over seventeen hundred pages spread across two volumes. Khvol'son dedicated the work to Minister A. S. Norov "with sincere appreciation and heartfelt thanks."[63] In the first volume, Khvol'son provided an introduction to the Sabians and their culture along with his efforts to assign a date to many Sabian texts. The second volume amounted to the translation of a broad range of primary texts and transcriptions that he collected related to the Sabians.

Upon meeting Khvol'son, Fleischer, a busy scholar in his own right, decided to take the work on as an editorial project to help prepare the manuscript for publication. Fleischer edited the German mistakes and improved the overall presentation, although he did not alter Khvol'son's Arabic translations and transcriptions.[64] Khvol'son was indebted to Fleischer intellectually and acknowledged as much in a letter to his mentor dated 8 June 1850:

> I want to assure you that the manner in which you have treated me, which exceeded all my expectations, has instilled in me the firm resolve to relate to others exactly like you and to dispense as much blessing and joy as you do to those whom I will come in contact with. No one could be more solicitous and giving than you. I could never have imagined that you would revise my work with such care. You cannot possibly be more scrupulous with your own. The revision must have robbed you of so very, very much time.[65]

In perhaps the most fitting legacy of Fleischer's profound influence on Khvol'son, and other students, Khvol'son attempted to live up to such a promise, as his students and colleagues attested in the years preceding his death.

Fleischer became a lifelong promoter of Khvol'son and his work and sought to assist him in securing employment in St. Petersburg, where his obvious talents could be recognized. After meeting with Khvol'son in March of 1850, reviewing the entirety of his work, checking his textual translations, and considering the full import of his arguments, Fleischer submitted a letter of recommendation to Bernhard Dorn (1805–1881) in St. Petersburg. Dorn, a Leipzig connection of Fleischer's, was once a professor at Kharkov University but in 1850 was the leading orientalist in St. Petersburg, where he taught at the Institute of Oriental Languages and St. Petersburg University.[66] Fleischer also encouraged Dorn to consider publishing Khvol'son's work in St. Petersburg, which, in retrospect, was a strategic move on Khvol'son's part when it was finally published. Though Fleischer's letter did not place Khvol'son in a professorial appointment immediately, it certainly helped bring him to the attention of those who would later play a role in his career.

Through his connection with Geiger, Khvol'son was introduced to the German Enlightenment principles—and he became a disciple who espoused the values of pure reason and universal truths characteristic of the eighteenth-century movement. In order to understand the Jewish Haskalah and Geiger's reform movement, as well as the *Wissenschaft des Judentums* movement, these developments must be seen as part of the broader, earlier European Enlightenments in France, Germany, England, and elsewhere. Internally, while many maskilim agreed that transforming Jewish culture and life was essential in Germany and elsewhere if Jews were to achieve emancipation, the question of religious reform sparked heated debates within communities. The same was true of Jews in the Russian Empire. One of the major differences in the 1840s, particularly between German Jews and their Russian coreligionists, was the concerted effort of the government to speed religious reform along. Many Jews successfully integrated (at least moderately) into German society over the course of forty to fifty years. Russia sought to develop a similar program though the common belief that in Eastern Europe, the movement would not be organically derived from within the Pale of Settlement; rather it needed to be driven by government authorities.

Within Russia a small group of maskilim held firmly to the belief that Jewish existence in the empire was about to change for the better. Jews were beginning to live outside the Pale in greater numbers, and some were beginning to find access to economic and cultural resources. Jews needed to improve themselves through education and modernization. In so doing, proponents of the Haskalah argued, the state would then find a tremendous resource from which to draw Jews into its service. Central to this project was a reconceptualization of Jewish history that emphasized a consistent approach to reform and adaption across the entire spectrum of Jewish history. Within this movement for rewriting history, Khvol'son found the roots of his approach. Khvol'son understood that the modern age was, or at least should have been, very different from the age of the barbarians (in his mind, this meant roughly the tenth to fifteenth centuries). At the same time, Khvol'son, like Geiger, developed a deep interest in Islam, Judaism, and Christianity and sought to better understand their relationship theologically and historically.

## From the Ministry to the Church

For Khvol'son, many individuals (several of whom he acknowledged openly) aided his road to St. Petersburg. Likewise, his journey would not have occurred if it began ten years on either side of his departure from Vilna. The Russian imperial project that aimed to bring Jews into the service of the state apparatus found in Khvol'son one of its most successful participants, integrating into wider social and intellectual circles. The Ministry of Education, which jump-started the ambitious program, remained an important state institution involved in the reform process for the next half-century. It was through this path that Khvol'son was gradually brought into the state bureaucracy after he completed his doctoral work. Khvol'son was one of the individuals who clearly fit into the "useful" category because of his expertise in Jewish affairs. Although his path unfolded over decades, his faith in the system served to forever mark him as one among this generation of Jews who was encouraged to unite with the needs and functions of the state.

The opening of Russian policy toward Jews inaugurated by Sergei Uvarov just before 1840 until the mid-1850s allowed Khvol'son the opportunity to leave the empire and receive a German university education, including a doctoral degree. This was part of the Uvarov effort to create a class of intellectuals who could help elevate the Russian university to levels on par with their German competitors. Armed with a broad set of skills and knowledge, Khvol'son was then gradually incorporated into Russian culture in St. Petersburg. Khvol'son first arrived in the capital city after completion of the dissertation for which he received the doctoral degree from Leipzig University in 1850.[67] He immediately went to work within the Ministry of Education and acquainted himself with many St. Petersburg Jews. Within the Ministry of Education, Khvol'son was assigned to work on the committee for the supervision and censorship of Hebrew texts. The committee worked under the supervision of the state censor and belonged to a broad network of similar groups in the Pale of Settlement (including local departments in Vilna and Kiev). In the same way that Uvarov incorporated Lilienthal into his reform efforts, others brought Khvol'son within the purview of official bureaucratic structures—to the immense benefit of both parties.

Avraam Sergeevich Norov (1795–1869) was the head of the St. Petersburg Censorship Committee (*Glavnoe upravlenie tsenzury*), of which the division for Jewish publications was a part. Norov served in this role from 1850 to 1858 and jointly served as deputy minister of education for part of this period. In 1854, a year after the death of his predecessor, Shirinskii-Shikhmatov, in the Ministry of Education, Norov was appointed minister of education by Nicholas I.[68] As one of Uvarov's successors, Norov proved a critical figure for Khvol'son's incorporation into St. Petersburg academic circles and also the Ministry of Education. Norov was part of the gentry in prereform Russia, the son of a military officer and provincial authority. As a persistent promoter of literature and scholarship, Norov also associated closely with important scholars and intellectuals (as his frequent evening gatherings with figures like Vladimir Dal', A. N. Murav'ev, and others suggest).[69] Peter Weisensel characterized Norov as a good example of a large group of Russian bureaucrats in the decades leading up to the great reforms who were "those of less flashing brilliance" and who functioned as "transitional" figures between the two hallmark posts of "liberal" and "enlightened."[70] Highly functional in taking directives as a midlevel bureaucrat, Norov was figuratively crippled by ministerial responsibilities later when he occupied the position of minister of education (1854–1858).[71]

It is unclear when Khvol'son and Norov first crossed paths, though they were aware of each other by September 1850, when Khvol'son wrote Norov regarding his position in St. Petersburg.[72] Norov followed Khvol'son and the preparation of the manuscript of his dissertation closely while the young scholar worked in the offices of the Ministry of Education during his first years in St. Petersburg. Norov had clearly noticed the young scholar's intellectual prowess by 1856, when Khvol'son's dissertation was published in St. Petersburg. In a letter to an unnamed official at St. Petersburg University regarding a copy of *Ssabier und der Ssabismus* that he received,

Norov wrote: "having received from Your Excellency Mr. Khvol'son's essay, entitled 'Die Ssabier und der Ssabismus,' I ask you to take the trouble to express to the learned author of this remarkable work, my sincere thanks for giving me a copy."[73] There was much in the figure of Norov that Khvol'son likely found intriguing and worthy of emulation. In his own right, Norov published a series of works about the history of Orthodox religious sites.[74] Norov traveled to Egypt and Palestine in 1834 while on assignment from the Ministry of Internal Affairs, and the volumes that emerged from that trip stood him in good stead with Russian government officials because they found in him a crucial "expert bureaucrat" and scholar on all matters dealing with the Ottoman Empire.[75] In the years leading up to the Crimean War, Russian-Ottoman and Russian-Muslim relations were at a critical juncture.[76] Norov judged the relations between Christians and Muslims as hopeless: "Christianity and Islam are separated by a terrible gap, and who knows when it will be filled."[77] That Norov found his way to this conclusion, even when he offered laudatory praise to Islamic societies at times, suggests something of the nature of nineteenth-century understandings of religious perspectives of other faiths. At the same time, it offers some insight into why Norov was so impressed by Khvol'son's work in 1856, during which he attempted to bridge the two religious societies through scholarship.

Norov's kind, albeit somewhat distant, comment regarding the copy of *Die Ssabier und der Ssabismus* shielded their earlier personal relationship forged within the Ministry of Education before Khvol'son's conversion. Khvol'son and his twenty-six-year-old wife, Fanni Iakovlevna Khvol'son (1828–1883), chose to convert to the Russian Orthodox Church and were baptized on December 18, 1854.[78] The young couple had two sons who also converted at the same time: Orest Daniilovich (1852–1934), who later became the highly renowned physicist in late imperial and Soviet science, and Anatolii Daniilovich (b. 1854), who became a jurist in St. Petersburg.[79] Regarding his decision to convert, Khvol'son wrote in a letter to Heinrich Leberecht Fleischer (1801–1888), the well-known German orientalist and Khvol'son's *doktorvater* at Leipzig:

> A few days after receiving your letter of 5 November 1854, I began collating [the pages of my book],[80] which took me until New Year's Eve to finish. But what a chasm in between! I began

> the work as a Jew and finished as a Christian . . . ! As my first child lay dying from his circumcision, I made the initial decision to convert to Christianity, and after two years of vacillating the decision had ripened sufficiently to carry out. The pale face of my poor, wretched and sickly child admonished me constantly and thus fourteen days ago, my wife and I along with our two small children (the second is only ten weeks old and not yet circumcised) converted to Christianity. We would have preferred to become Protestants . . . but a variety of circumstances, which I cannot spell out here, prompted me to convert to the Greek [Orthodox] Church. Though different people may judge this step variously, God alone knows what was in my heart.[81]

This is the most complete statement offered by Khvol'son and is remarkable for many reasons. First, it suggests a fairly long gestation process for his decision, and yet the tone speaks to an almost exasperated frame of mind given the emotional tug of his son's condition. The statement about his desire to become a Protestant is intriguing because the same full rights would have been extended to him if he had followed that path. From this statement we might conclude that Khvol'son understood this decision as one of opportunity, even when he likely felt some guilt in abandoning his former religion. And yet, this short statement to his mentor is evidence that Khvol'son weighed the option over the course of several years, and only after a protracted period did he finally take action.

The Khvol'sons were among the last of 4,439 Jewish converts in 1854.[82] As a marker of the conversion and their new Christian identities, they adopted new names. Iosif Solomonovich Khvol'son became Daniil Avraamovich Khvol'son, while his wife remained Feofaniia Iakovlevna. The protopresbyter chief priest of the army and navy attested both baptisms. Khvol'son chose as his godfather (*vospriemnik*) the minister of education, Norov—hence the adoption of the patronymic Avraamovich after his baptism. Feofaniia chose as her godmother a highly respected and well-known figure in St. Petersburg society, none other than Tatiana Borisovna Potemkina (1797–1869), the wife of Aleksandr Mikhailovich Potemkin.[83] Potemkina, of noble birth (maiden name Golitsyn), often associated with the tsar and his family and was "well known for her piety and charity."[84] Potemkina's many philanthropic activities included contributions to the 1850 restoration of Sviatogorsk Monastery in eastern Ukraine, orphanages, poor houses, and Orthodox missions.[85] In their selection of Christian exemplars, the Khvol'sons linked themselves with the upper echelons of St. Petersburg society. In Daniil's case, Norov was instrumental in his entrance into the Ministry of Education and later St. Petersburg University. Feofania's choice, although perhaps not as personal, represented a conscious decision to emulate a familiar, extraordinary form of civic-mindedness among nineteenth-century Russian women. For the Khvol'son family, the choice to convert to Russian Orthodoxy brought with it many benefits; some occurred almost immediately. The Ministry of Education, likely at the behest of Norov himself, assisted Khvol'son in obtaining permission to remain in the city and procure a six-month lease of an apartment in St. Petersburg for his young family.[86]

Historically, religious conversion was messy business for religious and government officials—and for the newly converted. One leading theorist on conversion and national identity formation notes:

> In its most transparent meaning as a change of religion, conversion is arguably one of the most unsettling political events in the life of a society. This is irrespective of whether conversion involves a single individual or an entire community, whether it is forced or voluntary, or whether it is the result of proselytization or inner spiritual illumination. Not only does conversion alter the demographic equation within a society and produce numerical imbalances, but it also challenges an established community's ascent to religious doctrines and practices. With the departure of members from the fold, the cohesion of a community is under threat just as forcefully as if its beliefs had been turned into heresies.[87]

Religious conversion in modern Europe cannot be understood without placing it within the debates about minority emancipation and the attached discussions about broadening economic and political rights, nor should it be viewed as separate from a majority population's understanding of its own identity. How then do we understand Khvol'son's decision to seemingly abandon Judaism in favor of Christianity? The idea that conversion from one religion to another challenges the very foundations of imperialism is helpful here in placing Khvol'son and his conversion at the epicenter of a critique of religious identity—and therefore Russian identity—in the middle of the nineteenth century. Khvol'son's conversion, because his motivations are not clearly understood, remains problematic for Jews as well as Russians even today. Whether maligned or praised, Khvol'son as convert is a contentious topic because he represented a model of Russian life and identity that often crossed, rather than reinforced, existing legal, social, or religious boundaries.

Religious conversion was a tightly controlled process in Russia, suggestive not just of the bureaucratic network concerned with conversion but also of the importance of managing diverse communities and limiting the crossing of identity boundaries. Separating out the formulaic aspects from the true intentions or motivations can be challenging, as Stanislawski, Freeze, and Shainker have all argued.[88]

In many of the Russian cases, we have official documents submitted to the ober-prokurator of the Holy Synod and other bureaucratic institutions by witnesses commenting on the sincerity of the decision or other matters related to it. While many of these documents provide only scant details, on occasion they are rich in detail and meaning. One of the richest of these documentary troves is the file associated with German-Jewish Rabbi Levison. Vasilli Abram Levison (1814–1869), with whom Khvol'son's path crossed many times in the Ministry of Education and in their various bureaucratic and scholarly activities, has remarkable documentation of his conversion in 1839. The Levison files provide evidence of the types of petition that likely accompanied Khvol'son's own conversion years later. Friends and colleagues of Levison provided letters on his behalf, and Levison also submitted a lengthy letter about his desires and career goals.

In a July 1839 letter from the archpriest in Weimar (Stefan Sadinii) to the synodal Ober-Prokurator N. A. Protasov (1798–1855), there is a striking commentary on Jewish conversion and the process by which one convinced the necessary authorities that one was sincere. The letter is translated here at length:

On your Lordship's question concerning Rabbi Abraham Levison who wants to accept the Christian faith of the Greek Orthodox confession (*Grekorossiiskogo ispovedanie*)—who is he and is he sincere in his desire—in my opinion of his moral quality, I respond accordingly:

I have been acquainted with Rabbi Levison for about two years. The purpose of my acquaintance with him was to more closely familiarize myself with the teachings of the Talmud and other Jewish religious books, and from the beginning of this acquaintanceship he revealed to me many absurd Talmudic prescriptions and the impossibility of fulfilling them, and then also revealed to me, that as a Jewish teacher, he teaches things that are against his own convictions—and that he certainly resolved to become a Christian. His reading of Christian theological books and listening to the Jewish lectures of Christian professors in Germany have prepared him in advance for this decision. Now, this begs the question: Why did he not turn to the Lutheran faith? Although he studied Christianity through Lutheran theology books and because of this his conversion to Lutheranism ought to be expected: but he's viewed the multitude of parties in the Lutheran Church—their coldness to confessors and the lack of positions for scholars even for those of the Lutheran creed—and so he backed away from her even though his original intention was to join. Reading the *Pisem o Bogosluzhenii Pravoslavnoi Grekorossiiskoi Tserkvi* of Murav'ev and the short catechism for junior deacons of the Orthodox Church in German positioned him to turn to our church and maybe his appeal to me as much as anything contributed to the fact: In all the time of my acquaintance with him, the idea of becoming Christian and to be useful is his life, and because of this, I feel that his desire for conversion is sincere. With regard to his moral quality, he is in my observation an intelligent man, constant, sober, and as far as I know, honest. There is just one thing I will note: Since he studied Christianity mostly through the Lutheran theological books, it is not surprising that some of the rationalist ideas came

> into his head, so I advise he be mentored in the future as regards the Orthodox doctrine of Christianity, to pay attention to this weakness.[89]

Of note here are several important elements that speak to the nature of the conversion process and the ways in which personal conviction was measured. In seeking permission to convert and thus enter into Russian society, one needed to stake a personal claim as to why conversion was desired, but in cases in which added benefit might be contributed to state programs, those potential contributions needed to be systematically laid out as well.

In the archpriest's letter, his appeal to the superiority of the Eastern church to the Protestant confessions would not have fallen on deaf ears. As well, the archpriest's warning that even one so well prepared for conversion as Levison was still in need of continued supervision and mentoring to assure that any erroneous Protestant theology was replaced with "correct belief" is telling of the desire to protect the Russian church from Western theological teaching. For a Jew to become Protestant was acceptable for entrance into Russian society, but even more advantageous for those seeking career advancement would be full conversion to Orthodoxy. Underlying this effort was a belief that traditional Jewish religious rituals and practice were impractical in a modern nation-state and that Russia would only gradually dismantle the insularity of these communities.

The archpriest's letter of July 17, 1839, confirmed what Levison had written just a few days prior. In his own letter to Ober-Prokurator Protasov, Levison laid out in no uncertain terms his potential contributions to the Russian Empire. Levison's letter possessed a scholarly tone, characteristic of his writing in which he laid out his reasoning behind the decision. "I intend to devote my life to the spread of the church among the Jews," he began. He then suggested four areas in which his particular skills and talents might help accomplish this goal of converting Russia's Jews to the Eastern rite. Above all, he argued, who could deny the importance and direct lineage of the church from the "apostles and fathers of the Church" as the main source for church doctrine and practice. In claiming this, Levison established his desire to teach Jews this principle. Second, among those who historically helped attract the outsider or non-Orthodox (*inovertsy*) to the church was a trait "of tolerance, though not indifference." A third component used to show his possible contributions was his desire to see "state education . . . go hand in hand with the church." His fourth point is a blatant statement of his intentions, arguing for his specific ability to interact with and influence Russia's large Jewish population: "The main purpose of my life is that among the Jews living in the Russian Empire, who are more immersed in their Talmud, Mysticism, and Pharisaic delusions, to help position them for the adoption of Christianity."[90]

Levison staked out a position that would have made him particularly useful to the reform program, but he went further to show how he was unique and further outlined how he planned to accomplish his work. His intention was not to preach to the individual who does "not have any knowledge of Judaism" or only "belittles what the Jews think." His program was different, and he showed such by appealing to the notion of "expert Jews" and his desire to not work with the lowest class of Jews. Instead he would focus on the "the rabbis and Jewish scholars" and through scholarly means show that Judaism proved the "truthfulness of Christianity." Levison also appealed to historical precedence—in the form of Moses Mendelssohn and the German case—to show that much good would come from those enlightened individuals who wanted to improve Jews. "Mendelssohn did so much in favor of Christianity . . . [that] now thousands of Jews in Germany are turning to Christianity . . . [and] so much more can be done by the pure teachings of Christ about God."[91] The Levison model highlights the particular concerns about the German scholar entering into Russian society. It should be remembered that Levison was petitioning for membership in the Russian Orthodox community through conversion and also for access to the capital city as a semipermanent resident with a passport and legal rights equal to those of other subjects.[92] At the same time, he was a highly learned man who ambitiously sought a post in the university. Thus, Levison petitioned as a rabbi, but also as a "Doctor of Theology in Hebrew Law," thereby showing his credentials as well as his understanding of not just the books but also the culture. His delineation between the common Jewish folk and the rabbis and scholars suggests that his perception was, like that of the imperial bureaucracy, largely focused on changing the elite members of society as a means of gradually reforming the whole of it. This was a particularly German Haskalah approach to Jewish reform, which understood the importance of education that could then be disseminated to the lower classes.

## Interpreting Khvol'son's Conversion

Most scholars have understood Khvol'son's abandonment of Judaism as a move toward economic and professional prosperity. In part, this interpretation stems from the probably apocryphal statement about his want of an academic job in St. Petersburg. In nearly every secondary work that mentions Khvol'son, the following story is employed as evidence that his decision to convert was economically motivated. To the question "Tell us, Professor Khvol'son, were you baptized because of belief (*po ubezhdeniiu*) or because of coercion (*po prinuzhdeniiu*)?" he replied, "Yes, I was convinced it was better to be a professor in St. Petersburg than a *melamed* in Eyshishok" (a small village near Vilna).[93] From this statement, scholars have concluded that Khvol'son abandoned Judaism because he found opportunity to better his economic or social situation and obtain the longed-for professorship. Such a reading of Khvol'son's conversion is shortsighted and does not fully account for, or recognize, his concerted efforts to protect Jews afterward. However, when his conversion is seen within the broad context of his intellectual contributions to biblical scholarship and knowledge about Jews and Christians in interaction, such a view is far too simplistic.

Khvol'son battled for greater inclusion of religious minorities in the Russian imperial system. The effectiveness of his work on this front is difficult to assess because Russian Jews never fully acquired the same equality as Jews in other countries during his lifetime. However, his later work on first-century Christianity and Judaism left a lasting impact on both communities. In the final decades of the old professor's life, Jews celebrated his contributions to history and social issues, while Christians in Russia owed him great applause for his work on the translation of the Bible into Russian. In the end, Khvol'son's legacy is difficult to evaluate because he became what one scholar deemed a "good bad Jew," that is, one who apostatized and then used his newfound position among the majority to alleviate suffering and persecution of their former coreligionists.[94] In the end, Khvol'son was equally at home in Russian and Jewish society, though his conversion also marginalized him in both communities.

Indeed, Khvol'son was the very best example of the anticipated results of this imperial project. As a result of his cooptation into the state project, Khvol'son benefitted greatly when he received access to intellectual circles in St. Petersburg and obtained his academic post at the university. However, his was not solely a selfish decision. Rather, Khvol'son balanced his decision to embrace Christianity with his ongoing desire to find avenues toward greater toleration for Jews and alleviate the superstitions that led to devastating ends during the nineteenth century. Khvol'son was inspired by the German Enlightenment, particularly by the desire to employ scholarship and biblical criticism that he learned during his years in German universities, to enjoin the Jewish communities to the state project and thereby acquire the same level of equality with their Christian counterparts in the empire. As he sought to do so, he expected that some of the medieval superstitions that so plagued relations between Jews and Christians would be eradicated as reason and rationality replaced ignorance.

## Notes

1. Jacob S. Raisin, *The Haskalah Movement in Russia* (Philadelphia: Jewish Publication Society of America, 1913).

2. The passage in Daniel 12:3–4 reads: "And they that be wise shall shine as the brightness of the firmament; and they that turn many to righteousness as the stars for ever and ever. But thou, O Daniel, shut up the words, and seal the book, even to the time of the end; many shall run to and fro, and knowledge shall be increased." Raisin used the King James Version for his text.

3. The title "Haskalah" is derived from the Hebrew "le-haskil."

4. The historiography on the Haskalah in European cities is expansive, but a few key contributions stand out. Among the standard works, see Pierre Birnbaum and Ira Katznelson, eds., *Paths of Emancipation: Jews, States, and Citizenship* (Princeton: Princeton University Press, 1995); Michael A. Meyer, *The Origins of the Modern Jew: Jewish Identity and European Culture in Germany, 1749–1824* (Detroit: Wayne State University Press, 1967); Michael Graetz, "The Jewish Enlightenment," in *German-Jewish History in Modern Times*, ed. Michael Meyer,

vol. 1 (New York: Columbia University Press, 1996), 263–354; Jacob Katz, *Out of the Ghetto: The Social Background of Jewish Emancipation, 1770–1870* (New York: Schocken Books, 1978).

5. Shmuel Feiner, "Towards a Historical Definition of the Haskalah" in *New Perspectives on the Haskalah*, ed. Shmuel Feiner and David Sorkin (London: Littman Library of Jewish Civilization, 2001), 184–185.

6. Charles W. J. Withers, *Placing the Enlightenment: Thinking Geographically about the Age of Reason* (Chicago: University of Chicago Press, 2007), 8. Withers contested the assumption that the Enlightenment can be defined as a monolithic geographic and chronologic event. The central argument of Withers's work is that the Enlightenment must be viewed much more broadly to understand how "ideas of place, space, scale, and the 'traveling' nature of knowledge" perpetuated a set of common values. By doing so, the scope of "Enlightenment" is extended beyond its traditional borders. Thus, the Haskalah becomes one of the evidences of "traveling" ideas and even within this broad understanding there is room for differentiated Jewish responses and manifestations based on geography. See also Dorinda Outram, *The Enlightenment, New Approaches to European History*, vol. 7 (Cambridge: Cambridge University Press, 1995).

7. Simon Dixon argued that Russia belongs within this broadened understanding of "enlightenments." See Simon Dixon, "'Prosveshchenie': Enlightenment in Eighteenth-century Russia," in *Peripheries of the Enlightenment*, ed. Richard Butterwick, Simon Davies, and Gabriel Sánchez Espinosa, *Studies on Voltaire and the Eighteenth Century* (2008: 01), 229–249; Paul Dukes, "The Russian Enlightenment" in T*he Enlightenment in National Context*, ed. Roy Porter and Mikuláš Teich (Cambridge: Cambridge University Press, 1981), 176–191; Isabela de Madariaga, *Politics and Culture in Eighteenth-Century Russia* (London: Routledge, 1998), 215–283. One of the great classic works that most definitely accomplishes the task of shedding light on the Russian encounter with Enlightenment remains W. Gareth Jones, *Nikolay Novikov: Enlightener of Russia* (Cambridge: Cambridge University Press, 1984); as well as Roger Bartlett and Janet Hartley, eds., *Russia in the Age of Enlightenment: Essays for Isabel de Madariaga* (New York: St. Martin's Press, 1990), especially Marc Raeff's introduction to the volume. Russian language books that have taken up the charge to examine the Enlightenment during the second half of the eighteenth century include Aleksandr Kamenskii, *Pod seniiu Ekateriny: Vtoraia polovina XVIII veka* (St. Petersburg: Lenizadat, 1992); Vera Proskurina, *Mify imperii: Literature i vlast' v epokhu Ekateriny II* (Moscow: Novoe literaturnoe obozrenie, 2005). O. A. Omel'chenko, *Zakonnaia monarkhiia' Ekateriny II: Prosveschennyi absoliutizm v Rossii* (Moscow: Iurist, 1993) examines the legal developments under Catherine II, and was especially interested in placing the origins of the idea of "enlightened absolutism" to the German lands.

8. Simon Dixon, *Catherine the Great* (New York: HarperCollins, 2009), 309–310.

9. The transliteration of Khvol'son's name varies. It is often based on the German rendering, Chwolson or Chwolsohn. This study is bounded by Khvol'son's birth on one end and his acceptance of the university professorial post that he was awarded in 1855 on the other. Khvol'son and his family converted to the Russian Orthodox Church just before Christmas in 1854.

10. Shmuel Feiner, *Haskalah and History: The Emergence of a Modern Jewish Historical Consciousness*, trans. Chaya Naor and Sondra Silverston (Oxford: Littman Library of Jewish Civilization, 2004), 44–47ff.

11. Sutcliffe, *Judaism and Enlightenment*, 6.

12. Feiner, *Haskalah and History*, v.

13. Brian Horowitz, *Jewish Philanthropy and Enlightenment in Late-Tsarist Russia* (Seattle: University of Washington Press, 2009), 22.

14. The Russian government's adjustment to the newly acquired Jewish population following the partitions of Poland brought little change (if any) to Jews and their everyday lives. At the same time, Russian relations with Jews would be forever changed by this early encounter. The government's initial approach to the Jewish community was largely a continuation of Polish-Lithuanian Commonwealth allowance for a semiautonomous Jewish government that Jews had enjoyed previously. Although the early relationship between the Russian government and Jewish communities within its borders was one of ambivalence in the last quarter of the eighteenth century and the early decades of the nineteenth century, the policies revealed a concerted effort to control its subjects in the West more tightly.

15. Olga Litvak, *Conscription and the Search for Modern Russian Jewry* (Bloomington: Indiana University Press, 2006), 6–8. Litvak argued that although the Nicholaevan reign was encapsulated within Russian literary memory as the most anti-Jewish and hostile, such views did not reflect the understanding that the maskilim possessed at the time. For many, this era served as an opening up of opportunities for maskilim to enter into Russian society more organically and provided the means to develop a liberal Judaism that responded to the modern period.

16. Benjamin Nathans, *Beyond the Pale: The Jewish Encounter with Later Imperial Russia* (Berkeley: University of California Press, 2002), 31.

17. P. A. Zaionchkovskii, *Pravitel'stvennyi apparat samoderzhavnoi Rossii v XIX v* (Moscow: 1978), 67–71. Other key works on the workings of the Russian bureaucracy and ministers during this period include: Marc Raeff, Michael Speransky, *Statesman of Imperial Russia, 1772–1839* (The Hague: M. Nijhoff, 1957); Walter M. Pinter and Don Karl Rowney, eds., *Russian Officialdom: The Bureaucratization of Russian Society from the Seventeenth to the Twentieth Century* (Chapel Hill: University of North Carolina Press, 1980); and Daniel T. Orlovsky, *The Limits of Reform: the Ministry of Internal Affairs in Imperial Russia, 1802–1881* (Cambridge, MA: Harvard University Press, 1981).

18. Alexander Polunov, *Russia in the Nineteenth Century: Autocracy, Reform, and Social Change, 1814–1914* (Armonk, NY: M. E. Sharpe, 2005), 43.

19. A number of short encyclopedia articles exist related to Khvol'son. See for example, Iulii Gessen, "Khvol'son, Daniil Avraamovich," in *Evreiskaia entsiklopediia*, vol. 9, (St. Petersburg, Brokgaus-Efron, 1914), 584–587; "Khvol'son, D. A." *Biograficheskii slovar' professorov i prepodovatelei imperatorskago S.-Peterburgskago Universiteta za istekshuiu tret'iu chetvert' veka ego sushchestvovaniia 1869–1894*, vol. 2 (St. Petersburg: B. M. Vol'f, 1896), 305–307; D. E. Bertel's, "Daniil (David) Abramovich Khvol'son" in E. M. Zhukov, ed., *Sovetskaia istoricheskaia entsiklopediia* (Moscow: 1976), 559; P. N. Sen'ko, "Khvol'son, Daniil Abramovich," *Russkie tserkovnyi deiateli-chleny akademii nauk* (St. Petersburg: Izdatel'stvo "LANS," 1995); V. V. Grigor'ev, *Imperatorskii S. Peterburgskii Universitet v-techenie pervykh piatidesiati let' ego sushchestvovaniia* (St. Petersburg: V. Bezobrazova, 1870), 278–280; Ivan Troitskii, "Professor D. A. Khvol'son," *Zhurnal ministerstva narodnago prosveshcheniia*, n. 34 (1911), no. 8, otd. 4: 90–99.

20. E. A. Khvol'son, "D. A. Khvol'son, (Orientalist) 1819–1911, Zhivnennii put samouchni-potchetnogo chleni Akademii nauk," *Sankt-Peterburgskii filial arkiv—Rossiiskoi Akademii Nauk* (hereafter, *SPFA RAN*), f. 959, op. 1, d. 54, l. 3. This document is a short

handwritten manuscript (twenty-one pages) by Khvol'son's grandson, Evgenii Antonovich after Khvol'son's death. It is unclear when the document was originally written but it must have occurred sometime after the First World War as it references Khvol'son's declaration about the potential origins of war ten years before the war began. It is difficult to gauge the date of the text based on the paper or ink used to produce it.

21. Israel Cohen, *Vilna* (Philadelphia: Jewish Publication Society of America, 1992), 489. Cohen's work was originally published in 1943 as *Jewish Community Series*, Vilna.

22. David Gintsburg, "80-letie D. A. Khvol'son," *Novosti* (November 21, 1899).

23. Shaul Stampfer, *Families, Rabbis, and Education: Traditional Jewish Society in Nineteenth-Century Eastern Europe* (Oxford: Littman Library of Jewish Civilization, 2010), 163–164.

24. Ibid., 150. See also *Obshchestvo dlia rasprostraneniia prosveshchenie mezhdu evreiiami v Rossii, Sovremennyi kheder* (1912), 1–90. The accounts in *Sovremennyi kheder* are overly negative and carry much of the same doubt over the effectiveness of these educational institutions. Zhargon was used to represent the Yiddish language that many European Jews, including Khvol'son himself, grew up speaking. The same term was used by many who reflected on Khvol'son's upbringing and his limited linguistic capabilities early in life.

25. Stampfer, *Families, Rabbis, and Education*, 3–4.

26. Nicholas V. Riasanovsky, *Nicholas I and Official Nationality in Russia, 1825–1855* (Berkeley: University of California, 1959), vii.

27. Cynthia H. Whittaker, *The Origins of Modern Russian Education: An Intellectual Biography of Count Sergei Uvarov* (DeKalb: Northern Illinois University Press, 1984), 189–191; 202–207. Jewish intellectuals later reflected on the enlightenment program of Uvarov and the schools in I. Cherikover's entry for "Prosveshchenie" in *Evreiskaia entsiklopediia*, vol. 13 (St. Petersburg: Brokgaus-Efron, 1906–1913), 43–62. Based on the entry, the process of "enlightenment" was viewed by Jews as the product of secular education at all levels, from primary school through the university. This process began with reform-minded individuals that helped open the doors for state intervention into Jewish education.

28. Shmuel Feiner, *The Jewish Enlightenment* (Philadelphia: University of Pennsylvania Press, 2003), 367.

29. Iulii Gessen, "Ravinskie uchilishcha v Rossii," Evreiskaia entsiklopediia, vol. 13:258–263. The dependence on German among Baltic Jews is perhaps best noted by the fact that German was used as the language of instruction in the Vilna Rabbinical Seminary until the mid-1860s.

30. Bruce L. Ruben, *Max Lilienthal: The Making of the American Rabbinate* (Detroit: Wayne State University Press, 2011), 7. Ruben's book served as a much-needed updated look at Lilienthal's life. The other major work that scholars have depended upon is the 1915 collection of his writings, letters, and a fawning personal history by one of his students. See David Philipson, ed., *Max Lilienthal, American Rabbi: Life and Writings* (New York: Bloch, 1915). Philipson's book is important, however, because it contains personal letters and the extended essay by Lilienthal, "My Travels in Russia." Lilienthal's "My Travels in Russia" were composed in the mid-1850s and were serially published in The Israelite, in Cincinnati, Ohio, between 1855 and 1857. While it is an important record because it does provide insight to the experiences and the events of that formative period between 1840 and 1845 while he

was in Russia, it was recorded about ten years later and therefore may contain embellished elements, as Lilienthal was wont to do on occasion.

31. Max Lilienthal, "My Travels in Russia," in Max Lilienthal, American Rabbi: Life and Writings, ed. David Philipson (New York: Bloch, 1915), 159.

32. David Fishman also provides an example of non-Jews who maintained the same disdain for the parts of the Russian Empire. See David Fishman, *Russia's First Modern Jews: The Jews of Shklov* (New York: New York University Press, 1995), 47. Fishman notes that the German Christian Julian Schlegel—an official delegate visiting the Russian Empire—wrote specifically about the backwardness and uncultured nature of the area around Shklov, but found particular delight in the comfort and extravagant nature of one of the wealthy homes. For a larger discussion of Enlightenment commentaries on eastern Europe, see Larry Wolff, *Imagining Eastern Europe: The Map of Civilization on the Mind of the Enlightenment* (Stanford: Stanford University Press, 1994).

33. Ruben, *Max Lilienthal*, 20. See chapter one of Ruben's book for the larger discussion of Bildung as a part of the nineteenth-century German education psychology. For more on the meaning of Bildung see David Sorkin, *The Transformation of German Jewry, 1780–1840* (Oxford: Oxford University Press, 1990).

34. Ibid., 11–12. Ruben's discussion of the implications of a university education and the connection between the Haskalah and secular studies is one of the most coherent in the secondary literature. Ruben suggests that Lilienthal may have been only the third Jew to study at the University of Munich, which was founded in 1826.

35. David Fishman, Russia's First Modern Jews, 6:24–28.

36. Pauline Wengeroff, *Rememberings: The World of a Russian-Jewish Woman in the Nineteenth Century*, trans. by Henny Wenkart, edited with an afterword by Bernard D. Cooperman (Bethesda: University Press of Maryland, 2000).

37. Ibid., 74–75.

38. Deborah Hertz, *How Jews Became Germans: The History of Conversion and Assimilation in Berlin* (New Haven: Yale University Press, 2007), 48–49.

39. For an introduction to Goethe and his writing about Jews, see Paul E. Kerry, *Enlightenment Thought in the Writings of Goethe: A Contribution to the History of Ideas* (New York: Camden House, 2001), 177–192.

40. Mendelssohn's *Sefer Netivot Hashalom* was published between 1780 and 1783. Informally, the work was known as the "Bi'ur."

41. Abraham Geiger, Max Wiener (ed.), *Abraham Geiger and Liberal Judaism: The Challenge of the Nineteenth Century* (Cincinnati: Hebrew Union College Press, 1981), 17.

42. Israel Cohen,Vilna, 433.

43. *SPFA RAN*, f. 959, op. 1, d. 54, l. 4. This story is also mentioned briefly in Lucy S. Dawidowicz, *Golden Tradition* (Syracuse, NY: Syracuse University Press), 335.

44. *SPFA RAN*, f. 959, op. 1, d. 54, l. 4.

45. Iulii Gessen, "Khvol'son, Daniil Avraamovich," in *Evreiskaia entsiklopediia*, vol. 15 (St. Petersburg, 1906–1913), 584–587. Khvol'son joined Geiger in Breslau, where Geiger had recently founded a school for the study of religion and Hebrew philology. Iulii Gessen (1871–1939) was born in Odessa and grew up under the tutelage of prominent Odessa figures such as Simon Dubnow and Ahad Ha'am, among others. He was a devoted socialist, historian, and also a contributor to the Society for the Promotion of Enlightenment among Jews of Russia (OPE) and the Ethnographic Society. He was also a major

contributor to the Evreiskaia Entsiklopediia. Gessen is mentioned throughout this work as he was one of the major compilers of information about Khvol'son (he lived in St. Petersburg/Leningrad from 1895 or 1896 until the end of his life. He was a transmitter of the Khvol'sonian legacy to the younger generation. Gessen developed a personal interest in the work of Khvol'son in the early twentieth century as a result of the blood libel issue that both men wrote about at length.

46. Abraham Geiger, *Abraham Geiger and Liberal Judaism: The Challenge of the Nineteenth Century*, compiled with a biographical introduction by Max Weiner, trans. Ernst J. Schlochauer (Philadelphia: Jewish Publication Society of America, 1962), 110–111.

47. Ibid., 111.

48. Ibid., 87. See also *Allgemeine Zeitung des Judentums*, XVIII, no. 22, 258.

49. Ilia Troitskii, "Pamiati professora Daniila Abramovicha Khvol'sona 23 Marta 1911," *Tserkovnyi Vestnik*, no. 14–15 (April 7, 1911), 430.

50. Daniil Avraamovich Khvol'son, *Die Ssabier und der Ssabismus* (St. Petersburg: Buchdruckerei der Kaiserlichen Akademie der Wissenshaften, 1856), xxi.

51. Susannah Heschel, *Abraham Geiger and the Jewish Jesus* (Chicago: University of Chicago Press, 1998), 219–221. Heschel argues that Khvol'son was "one of the most unusual figures to extend Geiger's arguments."

52. Abraham Geiger, *Was hat Mohammed aus dem Judenthume aufgenommen?* (Baden, 1833). This work, originally a prize-winning essay, was republished in 1902. F. M. Young, *Judaism and Islam* (Madrasa: M.D.C.S.P.C.K. Press, 1898). This was republished as *Abraham Geiger, Judaism and Islam* (New York: Ktav, 1970). This is a reprint (with new introduction by Moshe Pearlman) of the 1898 edition.

53. For a more detailed description of this work, see Heschel, *Abraham Geiger*, 30–31, 51–75.

54. However, one ought not forget that both men understood Judaism to be the most important contributor to both Christianity and Islam. It was Judaism that gave the material out of which to two other traditions developed and Jews were unique in the world because of their intellectual and spiritual achievements. For Khvol'son, "Kharakteristika semiticheskikh narodov," *Russkii Vestnik* 97 (1872): 423–475.

55. Although nothing came of it, de Sacy attempted to help Fleischer gain a position in St. Petersburg upon completion of his (Fleischer's) studies.

56. Ismar Schorsch, "Converging Cognates," 6.

57. John Efron, "Orientalism and the Jewish Historical Gaze," in *Orientalism and the Jews*, ed. Ivan Davidson Kalmar and Derek J. Penslar (Lebanon, NH: Brandeis University Press, 2005), 80–93.

58. Ibid., 84.

59. Geiger promoted this idea first and foremost in his essay, which later became his dissertation that examined the Jewish contributions to the Islam and its foundations.

60. The earliest identifiable descriptions of the Sabians appeared sometime during the tenth century, though Khvol'son and others suspected that there were indeed missing manuscripts and texts that could reveal more if they could be recovered. The Sabians were also of interest to Maimonides—and we can see evidence that Khvol'son read Maimonides and drew some of his insights from him, particularly in regards to the great philosopher's translations of texts. See Sarah Stroumsa, *Maimonides in his Portrait of a Mediterranean Thinker* (Princeton: Princeton University Press, 2009), 84–86. Stroumsa shows how Maimonides

understood the Sabians as a "milla" comprised of various peoples who existed around the time of Abraham and possessed a fully functioning religious group. See also Jonathan Elukin, "Maimonides and the Rise and Fall of the Sabians: Explaining Mosaic Law and the Limits of Scholarship," *Journal of the History of Ideas* 63, no. 4 (October 2002), 619–637.

61. As cited in Ismar Schorsch, "Converging Cognates: The Intersection of Jewish and Islamic Studies in Nineteenth Century Germany," *Leo Baeck Institute Year Book* 55, no. 3 (September 2010): 18.

62. E. A. Khvol'son, "D. A. Khvol'son, (Orientalist) 1819–1911, Zhivnennii put samo-uchni-potchetnogo chleni Akademii nauk," *SPFA RAN*, f. 959, op. 1, d. 54, l. 9.

63. Khvol'son, *Die Ssabier und Ssabismus*, vol. 1, front matter dedicatory page.

64. Schorsch, "Converging Cognates," 18–19.

65. Ibid., 19. I draw upon Schorsch's translation as these letters from Khvol'son are unavailable to me at this time. Schorsch indicates the letter is contained in the Royal Library Copenhagen, Fleischer papers, Chwolson file.

66. Dorn was later elected to the Russian Academy of Sciences and as director of the Asiatic Museum in St. Petersburg.

67. *SPFA RAN* f. 959, op. 1, d. 12, l. 1.

68. Norov was familiar with the position of minister before his ascension because he covered for the oft-ill Shirinskii-Shikhmatov at State Council meetings and affairs between 1850 and 1853. In 1853, Nicholas I named Norov as acting minister.

69. Peter R. Weisensel, *Prelude to the Great Reforms: Avraam Sergeevich Norov and Imperial Russia in Transition, Minnesota Mediterranean and East European Monographs, A Modern Greek Studies Yearbook Supplement,* no. 4 (Minneapolis: University of Minnesota, 1995), 66.

70. Ibid., ix.

71. Ibid., 70–71. Norov was literally crippled early in his military career when he was wounded at the Battle of Borodino, which resulted in his left leg being amputated. He was fitted with a wooden prosthetic for the rest of his life.

72. Otdel Rukopisei—Rossiskaia natsional'niia biblioteka St. Petersburg (hereafter, OR RNB), f. 531, d. 416, "Khvol'son, D. A. pis'ma A. S. Norovu," September 18, 1850.

73. *SPFA RAN* f. 959, op. 1, d. 57, l. 1 "Pis'mo velikogo kniazia Konstantina Norovu A. (S vyrazheniem blagodarnosti za prislannuiu rabotu Khvol'sona, D. A.)" (May 15, 1856).

74. See, for example, the republished volume, *Avraam Sergeevich Norov, Puteshestvie k semi tserkvam upominaemym v apokalipsise* (St. Petersburg: Tip. III ontel'nenniia Sobstvennoi e. i. v. kantseliarii, 1847; reprint St. Petersburg: Tip. P. P. Soiskin, 1890; Moscow: Indrik, 2005). His other volumes included *Puteshestvie po Egiptu i Nubii v 1834–1835* (St. Petersburg: Tip. III ontel'nenniia Sobstvennoi e. i. v. kantseliarii, 1835); *Puteshestvie po Sitsilii v 1822 g.* (St. Petersburg: Tip. A. Smirdina, 1828); and *Puteshestvie po Sviatoi Zemle v 1853 g.*, 2 vols. (St. Petersburg: Tip. A. Smirdina: 1838).

75. Wiesensel, *Prelude to the Great Reforms*, 22–31.

76. Robert Crews, "Empire and the Confessional State: Islam and Religious Politics in Nineteenth-Century Russia," *The American Historical Review* 108 no. 1 (2003): 50–83; Stephen K. Batalden, "Musul'manskii i evreiskii voprosi v Rossii epokhi Aleksandra i glazami shotlandskogo bibleista i puteshestvennika," *Voprosy Istorii* (2004): 46–63.

77. Norov, *Puteshestvie po Egiptu i Nubii v 1834 i 1835 gg.*, 1:375. Khvol'son and Norov discussed Egypt and the Holy Land in a series of letters written between 1854 and 1859, see

OR RNB f. 531, d. 631, "Khvol'son, D. A., orientalist, pis'ma Avraamu Sergeevichu Norovu, 1854–1859, Die Erbauer der Piramiden."

78. Fanni's maiden name was Cohn.

79. *SPFA RAN* f. 959, op. 1, d. 28, l. 1 (January 22, 1855).

80. The book referenced here is the published version of his dissertation, *Ssabier und der Ssabismus*, published in St. Petersburg in 1856.

81. As cited in Ismar Schorsch, "Converging Cognates," 19. This letter (dated January 29, 1855) from Khvol'son to Fleischer is housed in the Royal Library Copenhagen, Fleischer papers, in a separate file related to Khvol'son.

82. Ellie Shainker, "Imperial Hybrids: Russian-Jewish Converts in the Nineteenth Century," PhD diss., University of Pennsylvania, 2010 (ProQuest 3414113), 4.

83. *SPFA RAN* f. 959. op. 1, d. 27, l. ll.1–2.

84. Joe Peschio, *The Poetics of Impudence and Intimacy in the Age of Pushkin* (Madison: University of Wisconsin Press, 2012), 18.

85. *Russkii biograficheskii slovar'* XIV, 646–647; Robin Wheeler, *Palmer's Pilgrimage: The Life of William Palmer of Magdalen* (Bern: Peter Lang, 2006), 100.

86. *SPFA RAN* f. 959, op. 1, d. 28, l. 1.; other letters from Norov to the Minister of Finance Petr Fedorovich Brok (1852–1858) with regard to Khvol'son include those found in RGIA f. 571, op. 3, d. 35, l. 1–2 (June 1855); also, from the same file l. 4 a letter to the Department of Various Taxes and Fees (Departament raznykh podata i sborov') regarding Khvol'son. These communications with the Ministry of Finance and its internal departments highlight, first and foremost, the potential for immediate economic and residential benefits for Jews who converted.

87. Gauri Viswanathan, *Outside the Fold: Conversion, Modernity, and Belief* (Princeton: Princeton University Press, 1998), xi.

88. Michael Stanislawski, T*sar Nicholas I and the Jews: The Transformation of Jewish Society in Russia, 1825-1855* (Philadelphia: Jewish Publication Society of America, 1983), 141-48; ChaeRan Freeze, "When Chava Left Home: Gender, Conversion, and the Jewish Family in Tsarist Russia," in *Jewish Women in Eastern Europe, Studies in Polish Jewry* 18 (2005); and Ellie Shainker, "Imperial Hybrids: Russian-Jewish Converts in the Nineteenth Century," PhD diss., University of Pennsylvania, 2010. Proquest (3414113).

89. RGIA f. 797, op. 9, d. 25232, ll. 16–17. Delo Kantseliarii Ober-Prokurora Sviateishago Pravitel'stvuiushchago Sinoda, "O zhelanii evreev Levisona primet' pravoslavnuiu veru."

90. RGIA f. 797, op. 9, d. 25232, l. 9.

91. RGIA, f. 797, op. 9, d. 25232, ll. 11–12.

92. In both the Khvol'son and Levison documents there is reference to that secondary (though perhaps not less significant) condition that they also be permitted to live in St. Petersburg without further undergoing registration processes and applications other than would normally be required.

93. Semen Reznik, "Krovavyi navet v rossii istoriko-dokumental'nye ocherki," *Vestnik* 24 (November 23, 1999), 1. Available online at http://www.vestnik.com/issues/1999/1026/koi/resnik.htm (accessed February 10, 2013). Most of the summaries of Khvol'son's statement leave out the original question, Reznik provides the original question and provides a slightly different answer. He suggests that Khvol'son replied "Of course, out of belief. He was convinced that it was better to get the salary of a professor in St. Petersburg than starve

in the Pale of Settlement." These words are quoted in many summaries of Khvol'son. While they are attributed to him, it remains unclear when or where he uttered the phrase. The most common version of the quote (the one included here) is from Lucy S. Dawidowicz, *The Golden Tradition: Jewish Life and Thought in Eastern Europe* (Syracuse, NY: Syracuse University Press, 1996; orig. New York: Holt, Reinhart, and Winston, 1967), 335.

94. Shulamit S. Magnus, "Good Bad Jews: Converts, Conversion, and Boundary Redrawing in Modern Russian Jewry, Notes toward a New Category," in *Boundaries of Jewish Identity*, ed. Susan A. Glenn and Naomi B. Sokoloff (Seattle: University of Washington Press), 133.

# The Discourse of Civil Religion in M. M. Kheraskov's *Numa Pompilius*

*Andreas Berg*

Civil religion was not a well-developed theme in eighteenth-century Russian thought, in part due to the still-powerful influence of Orthodoxy but primarily due to the lack of consistent engagement with classical literature and early-modern juridical sources.[1] A lack of attention to civil religion, however, does not mean that there was no notion of religion that derived its strength from its civic significance. To the contrary, the unprecedented religious reforms ushered in by the Petrine revolution have shown that it was impossible to think of religion and its truth claims without also subjecting them to the test of public utility. The contribution of Mikhail M. Kheraskov (1733–1807) to this theme was quite important because he attempted to combine the notion of common good with that of individual spiritual rebirth, thus overcoming the threat that an overly utilitarian understanding of religion posed to personal transcendence. Not only did Kheraskov strike a new chord in his own national context, but he also extended the discourse of civil religion beyond its usual spheres of application in Western European enlightenments. Lack of consistent attention to Kheraskov's religious thought is particularly unfortunate given that he has long been recognized as a "central figure of the literary scene" in eighteenth-century Russia.[2] Although Kheraskov rose to national prominence because of his epic poems, his novels were popular and influential as well.[3]

Kheraskov's masonic novel, *Numa Pompilius, or Flourishing Rome* (1768), a subject of attention in Russian and Anglophone scholarship for its literary, political, and ethical content, has not yet been analyzed in terms of its religious significance. I argue that the key theme of the novel is the process of instituting a civil religion and that without a grasp of this process, the richness of one of Russia's most important eighteenth-century texts would remain underappreciated. Perhaps N. K. Piksanov came closest to noting the importance of a political understanding of religion when he characterized the genre of Kheraskov's novel as a *Staatsromane*, a political treatise written in fictional form to serve as advice to the sovereign and the intellectual elite.[4] If that is the case, then it is necessary to focus not only on the way in which politics and religion intersected throughout the narrative but also, and perhaps more importantly, on the actual content of Kheraskov's advice.[5] Kheraskov did not seem to be interested in suggesting small-scale reforms or alterations of existing arrangements of the state. Rather, he was interested in giving advice regarding one foundational change that made all future changes possible. His main concern was to show that religious sensibility had a critical role to play in the move from rudeness to civilization, a move considered almost synonymous with the move from a state of near-perpetual warfare to one of civic peace.

The theme of civic peace, when presented as advice, is of course indebted to Fénelon's *Adventures of Telemachus* (1699), which exercised a particular influence in Russia. All eighteenth-century Russian fictionalizations of how an individual progressed in virtue in consequence of instruction from a superior mind were, at least in some way, conscious imitations of the archbishop's novel. *Numa Pompilius* was not an exception. However, though Kheraskov was influenced by the idea of a moralizing novel that intertwined character and kingship, his novel framed very different problems. Unlike Fénelon, Kheraskov attended to the genesis of religious institutions, religion's status in regards to truth ascertained individually, and the need for toleration. While these were themes relevant to Fénelon's theological works, they were of peripheral value to the pedagogical intentions of Telemachus. In fact, one of the things taught to Telemachus was that "a king ought to be subject to religion, and without ever attempting to subject it to his regulation."[6] Notwithstanding his Quietist leanings,

Fénelon was a firm supporter of the established Catholic doctrine, as evinced by his voluminous attacks against Jansenism. Kheraskov was much freer, in that he was not writing to defend Orthodoxy but religion; therefore, he could take the much more radical position of imagining the possibility of religious norms emerging by royal fiat. Kheraskov could set aside his confessional commitments not only because of their perceived deficiencies but also because he was interested in the emergence of religion as distinct from its subsequent confessional differentiation.

Unlike Western European intellectual contexts, which contained discourse on civility before the development of Enlightened modes of thought, Russian culture was not introduced to the issue of historical progress in a substantive sense until the wake of its modernization in the first quarter of the eighteenth century. Whereas Western humanist-trained intellectuals were consistently exposed to a classical, especially Roman, understanding of the civilizing process, their pre-Petrine Russian counterparts simply did not have the relevant repertoire at hand to orient them to probe into the conditions necessary for the emergence of socio-political institutions. This problem was further compounded by the fact that from around the Renaissance onwards, it was at least theoretically possible for Western authors to discuss religion in its nondoctrinal functional sense, provided that sufficient dissimulation was in place. In Russia, however, religion was usually synonymous with Russian Orthodoxy and, therefore, could not be easily isolated as a discrete topic open to judgment based on its political value. Thus, for instance, Machiavelli could scrutinize the effectiveness of religion as a political force and, to some extent, lament the decay of its civic role because he could turn to ancient Roman social engineering as a basis for his discussion of present challenges. The determination of the objective worth of religion was possible because the very idea of change and reform could be measured and evaluated against the deeply charged backdrop of Roman political thought, which cut across the Western European confessional divide. Nonetheless, by the time *Numa Pompilius* was published, the Russian reading public was sufficiently saturated with works about Roman history to be able to understand Kheraskov's way of appropriating antiquity.[7]

In focusing on the foundational myth of the Roman state contained in the story of how King Numa transformed the Romans from predators to farmers, Kheraskov proposed classical history as an intellectual space in which contemporary problems in religion and the spiritual life of the individual could be articulated.[8] One such problem was the interrelationship among religion, the sovereign, and the citizens at a time when traditional confession was ceasing to completely satisfy the religious sensibilities of the Russian educated elite. As attested by the subsequent growth in Freemasonry and its attendant mystical worldviews, Orthodoxy failed to bridge the gap between the desire for personal moral progress and loyalty to the institutions of the state, resulting in a fracturing of Russian religious culture.[9] Kheraskov showed that progress in politics was largely dependent on the development of personal mores, which were, in turn, shaped by manmade religious institutions; in doing so, he voiced sentiments common to both humanism and the Enlightenment but hitherto almost absent from the Russian reading public.[10] Although M. J. Okenfuss was partly correct in highlighting barriers to proper assimilation of the classical corpus in Russia, Kheraskov's consistent preoccupation with the classical corpus does not in any way suggest a failure of humanism among the Russian literati, especially in religious matters.[11]

In terms of its attempt to rethink the role of religion in the state, the closest analogy to Kheraskov's *Numa Pompilius* is Mikhail M. Scherbatov's unfinished utopian novel, *Journey into the Land of Ophir* (1783–1784). The latter work also sought to conceive of a *Polizeistaat* in which religion, cleansed of superstition, played a prominent civic role in the moral formation of the citizens. Moreover, Scherbatov shared Kheraskov's interest in showing that the aims and structure of civil religion differed considerably from the function of Russian Orthodoxy. Indeed, Scherbatov's novel was much more forthright in its condemnation of Orthodoxy as a religion that unnecessarily "exhausted the mind and the body" through useless ceremonies.[12] Thus, there was a consensus between the two works in terms of their conclusions regarding religion: first, that Russian Orthodoxy could not continue to occupy the same privileged role in society without further reform and, second, that it was permissible to seek Western European precedents in order to improve the citizens' spiritual well-being. Religion, then, was not only conceived as a totalized outlook informing a person's attitude to secular occurrences but was also opened up to critical scrutiny.

Despite these important similarities, there are crucial differences that further underscore the originality of Kheraskov's thoughts on religion. Scherbatov promoted a religion with an overwhelmingly utilitarian character. Although peace and goodwill were the cardinal virtues promoted by the citizen-priests of the land of Ophir—evidenced by their distaste for any sacrifice other than a "pure heart"—the citizen-priests were also given wide-ranging policing powers.[13] Even though it was conceivable for a citizen to hold religious notions that superseded the content of the state religion, private beliefs were not meant to be the subject of public discussion. Therefore, it was not clear whether an individual participated in civic religious forms to become a better citizen or whether participation was merely a normative duty expected of all citizens. The fact that Scherbatov made a point regarding the severe penalties imposed on those who did not participate in the state cult suggests overeagerness to rely on the government's punitive apparatus to maintain social conformity.[14] This reliance on the state contrasted considerably with Kheraskov's vagueness about how the compulsory nature of Numa's religion was to be maintained. It seems as though Numa engineered the rites in such a way that they would, in themselves, appear to the Romans to be worthwhile pursuits.

Moreover, the complete lack of mystical undertones in Scherbatov's account of religion raised questions as to whether there was any meaningful role for spirituality in his conception of the state. This perspective was evident in Scherbatov's complete denial of revelation. Ophir religion was based entirely on a teleological affirmation of God's existence.[15] Scherbatov obviously presented an Enlightened view of religion in a general sense, especially when compared to some of the irrational practices of revelation-based faiths; however, such curtailing of the transcendent threatened the very possibility of human autonomy. In comparison, Kheraskov made sure to combine the etatist implications of civil religion with its metaphysical source, which was foreclosed to any political control. If the truths of religion were derived solely from the truths of science, then the state, as the controller of knowledge, would necessarily act as an arbiter of the meaning and the content of belief. Scherbatov seemingly assumed that recognition of facts of nature could lead to reverence of the creator without the need for the citizens to cultivate a philosophical sense of wonder regarding the inexhaustible intricacy of life. Without the possibility of the intellect humanizing the brute conditions of nature, any religious sentiment that was sourced solely in nature would have to depend on the punitive arm of the state for its existence. This view was varied considerably from Kheraskov's firm commitment to a spiritual horizon that greatly exceeded the dictates of any political arrangements. Numa's absolutist establishment of a new religion was counteracted by his sense of subservience to aspects of wisdom that could never be adequately reflected in the institutions of the state.

For these reasons, Scherbatov can be thought of as someone who wanted to extend the authority of the *Polizeistaat* into the realm of the spiritual, whereas Kheraskov wanted to find rational means for its containment. That is, Scherbatov represented an Enlightened tradition, which continued to see the state as the only conduit for reform. In that sense, although in some respects he was religion's critic, Scherbatov framed his views about religion well within the terms of reference that sustained Peter the Great's understanding of the central role of the state in the lives of its citizens. In contrast, Kheraskov envisaged an Enlightenment that sought to harmonize the responsibility of the state in fostering civic virtue with the right of individuals to engage in spiritual self-fashioning. This difference was crucial, because it ultimately reflected the possibility for individuals to choose alternative forms of the Enlightenment. Stated somewhat differently, Kheraskov represented a shift in Russian society away from delegating to the state the authority to develop solutions to all crucial problems. Reengagement with idealized Roman antiquity was particularly useful in this regard because its Stoic elements combined (a) inward cultivation of virtue as an aspect of individual responsibility with (b) a sober recognition of the irreplaceability of governance. Kheraskov showed considerable acumen in thinking that religion was a crucial topic, because it simultaneously inhered within individual subjectivity and institutions and, therefore, was not to be monopolized by either.

The crucial aspect of humanism that Kheraskov addressed and projected in his *Numa Pompilius* regarded the nature of civil religion as the ancients understood it. For Roman historians such as Livy and Plutarch, the idea of a civil religion implied a religion that originated through legislation a sovereign enacted to inspire loyalty and reverence for the laws that made communal life possible. There was an element of deliberate deceit, a noble lie intending to rechannel people's credulity in a way that would enable them to become virtuous citizens. For that reason, the Romans did not believe there was much hypocrisy in the existence of a state cult, insofar as its underlying truth was the degree to which it bound citizens together and to their patria.[16] For Numa's political, social, and even agricultural reforms to take hold, they had to be shown to be of divine origin and their acceptance had to be seen as a normative part of the political existence of any citizen. Livy's account of Numa's role in establishing Rome as a viable political unit placed the invention of new religious rites as the cornerstone of the civilizing process, as the historian understood it:

> By these means the whole of the population of Rome was given a great many new things to think about and attend to, with the result that everybody was diverted from military preoccupations. They now had serious matters to consider; and believing as they now did, that the heavenly powers took part in human affairs, they became so much absorbed in the cultivation of religion and so deeply imbued with the sense of their religious duties, that the sanctity of an oath had more power to control their lives than the fear of punishment for law-breaking. Men of all classes took Numa as their unique example and modelled themselves upon him, until the effect of this change of heart was felt even beyond the borders of Roman territory.[17]

Attention to the sacred, minimization of violence, and the imperative of an oath were all key ingredients of civic life, which figured largely in Roman political praxis. In fact, according to Cicero, the Latin term *religio*, from which the word religion was derived, means a correct observance of rites on the presumption that piety is reducible to a law-like discharge of prescribed duties to the gods.[18] This definition, of course, squares up well with Livy's description, insofar as individuals were shown to be preoccupied with scrupulous attention to their religious obligations while, at the same time, seeking to enact what they had sworn to do. Neither of these duties was qualitatively different from the type of behaviors necessary for the functioning of a well-regulated public sphere; in that sense, they represented virtues normally found in a community. The reason civil religion could achieve these things, whereas the more irrational forms of earlier religions could not, was that a state cult was explicitly framed by ethical norms, which formed the object of worship as distinct from the gods.[19]

Plutarch's Life of Numa generally agrees with Livy's account, except for two details of crucial significance for Kheraskov. First, Plutarch showed that Numa was possibly a devotee of Pythagorean doctrines, from which he derived knowledge of how to transform human society.[20] Second, Plutarch discussed whether Numa could have been "honoured with a celestial marriage" to Eegeria, a deity of wisdom.[21] Although Plutarch doubted the veracity of the marriage, he considered it plausible that Eegeria "should not dislike or disdain the company of a wise and holy man." Plutarch made a point of suggesting that Numa was anchored in an esoteric tradition that shaped his political behavior, especially in regard to religion. These are important details for acquiring a more sophisticated understanding of civil religion, because freedom to experiment with or to create religious forms was made possible by Numa's commitment to mystically derived truths, which could not be compromised. In *Numa Pompilius,* Kheraskov made an even stronger case for the reformist will of the sovereign by suggesting that real truth did not necessarily inhere in institutions or in dogma, thus making it permissible to modify them for political ends.

It is on the basis of such reasoning that Kheraskov composed his own account of King Numa's reforms, albeit with due respect to the eighteenth-century notions of civility and to his own mystical leanings. By Russian standards, Kheraskov was so well acquainted with the relevant Roman sources that he was confident in his capacity to alter the received versions of the story without distorting its classical origin. Consequently, the alert reader would, on the one hand, imbibe in a strongly humanistic understanding of religion and, on the other, appreciate how such an understanding could point toward a new way of thinking about personal spirituality. What I want to do now is follow up on Kheraskov's explanation of how civil religion was established, its purpose to result in progress, and to what extent it still retained the idea of a theistic God. If for the Romans there was no irresolvable conflict between deceit and the positive result of a peaceful society, for Kheraskov there was the added imperative to link human capacity to create religious institutions with a belief in metaphysics. It was not that the content of Christian revelation had to be directly equated with the discourse of civil religion and, by implication, with the products of reason. It was sufficient for Kheraskov to show that revelation in general could act through entirely artificial religious norms.

The thorny issue of providence needs to be detailed further because it underscored the extent of Kheraskov's seemingly contradictory prioritization of reason *and* mystical intuition. Eighteenth-century Russian readers, who were quite alert to the use of providence as a justification for political changes, palace coups, and even success on the battlefield, were presented with the possibility that God's will was not necessarily a plausible explanation. Insofar as Numa enacted religious reforms through which Romans felt accountable to a higher power, it could be said that it was human engineering that hid behind the hand of the divine. In qualified terms, such engineering hinted that the political had considerable autonomy from traditional theological interpretations of history. This recognition of autonomy was precisely the point behind civil religion, insofar as the latter served to solve specifically political problems with minimal dependence on dogma. The fact that providence was characterized as something that could be believed in without it necessarily being the real cause of events, at least tacitly, called for a reexamination of historical causality. In this case, Numa acted as a rational agent with knowledge about using natural human anxieties as motivations for action.

However, while Kheraskov was indeed casting doubt on traditional conceptions of an interventionist God and demarcating space for human reason, he was also conscious of the need to conform human existence to reality as it appeared to a purified intellect. In other words, Kheraskov envisaged the possibility of a qualitative transformation of society brought on by individuals who had mastered contemplative praxis. As will be discussed subsequently, it was wisdom that interrupted the established course of history by acting through its adepts, such as Numa. Plutarch himself gave some credence to such an increase in the role of active human participation in the workings of the divine by distinguishing between Numa's creation of religious rites by *fiat* and Numa's possible adherence to Pythagorean doctrines. So, although Numa did display considerable political authority, it served as a medium to express a higher reality accessible only to the mind. Obviously, in his defense of a noetic reality, Plutarch could not possibly have been concerned with the Judeo-Christian notion of providence. Yet, his reference to Numa's marriage to wisdom could be read in eighteenth-century terms as an alternative understanding of how the divine could act upon the world. Kheraskov's Numa derived the content of his politics from his exposure to wisdom as a distinct entity that actively guided his understanding of what was true and necessary.

It might appear that Kheraskov rethought the operations of providence simply by way of restricting the number of individuals through whom providence could act and that he, accordingly, reworked Plutarch's narrative to allow for a more decisive role of wisdom in the affairs of humanity. However, Kheraskov's intentions were significantly more substantive than that. Kheraskov was able to adapt Plutarch's emphasis on Numa as wisdom's favorite to present a larger argument suggesting that existing institutions were not necessarily reliable conduits of divine will. If God was more likely to intervene via his select believers, who, unlike the prophets, held on to the more practical aspects of reason, then religious arrangements could be modified at will without incurring the charge of impiety, so long as these modifications were not inconsistent with a transcendental vision of the truth. This is precisely what Numa proceeded to do upon obtaining the advice of Nymph Egeria. The religious forms that were created were entirely temporal in nature, yet they were sanctioned by something that was superior to the political. Simply put, only through those who were wise and could act as wisdom's receptacles would social conventions become reflective of the divine and become imbued with teleology. In the absence of someone as wise as

Numa, Romans could have carried on with their warlike ways indefinitely for lack of anyone with superior knowledge to initiate progress.

The fact that Kheraskov primarily relied on the amorphous term wisdom instead of God increased the anxiety regarding whether God could be reached without strenuous intellectual activity. Given the inherent flexibilities of the fictional genre, Kheraskov could have made the pagan story of king Numa more palatable to Christian sensibilities, but he has elected not to do so. He likely consciously chose not to in order to subvert simplistic notions of providence and to apportion much greater responsibility to humans for the moral state of society. When the nymph revealed herself to Numa in all her transcendent glory, she characterized herself and her role in such an ambivalent way that the very notion of a God became rather distant. Despite her potency, Egeria had to bluntly tell Numa that she was not fully divine:

> Do not combine divinity with the creature, the priestess replied. I am not a goddess, but my essence is superior to that of humanity. Virtuous Numa, know me now as the nymph Egeria. I talked to you in the guise of a priestess, I have guarded your heart from the passions afflicting it and protected your soul from temptations. The gods have desired to reward your virtues and have chosen you to rule over the Roman kingdom.[22]

Wisdom was shown to have a hand in making someone virtuous. Yet, if wisdom is not conflated with any notion of a God, then human agency becomes decisive. This Platonic reading of *sophia*, which places the onus on the inquiring mind to love the latter through knowledge, aligns with what has been argued so far regarding the primacy of the human pursuit of understanding. As an expansion of this analogy, it might be said that a philosopher-king was only as good at ruling as he was at cognizing the world of forms. In other words, the ruler's political authority intrinsically depended on his or her commitment to loving wisdom. One may also note Kheraskov's passive language. Egeria only guarded Numa's heart while the gods have only chosen Numa without constantly directing his actions. Real effort in seeking virtue and knowledge was, as will be seen, entirely up to Numa. A more freethinking reader could even infer, albeit somewhat against the grain, that if wisdom was the main medium through which improvement was possible, God was not too active in the arena of history.

However, it would be wrong to think that wisdom's middling status gave the legislator a right to manipulate religious sentiments solely as an act of political expediency because of the credulity of the common people. Kheraskov implied that religious reform could only be enacted by a king who was not skeptical about the existence of God. The sovereign had to immerse himself in an extended process of self-improvement—which resulted in the attainment of virtue—and take seriously the aspects of reality not reducible to the senses. Numa had to be presented as different from other Romans, to justify his right to initiate radical reforms. To that end, Kheraskov characterized Numa as someone completely dedicated to a life of virtue and knowledge:

> His spare hours Numa dedicated towards an inquiry into the sacred mysteries of the Divine, gaining knowledge of the true pathways of virtue, the eradication of vain thoughts which secretly infect the heart with flattering flaws; disregard for the enticements of false happiness and the beguiling attractiveness of wealth. Without doing this, Numa would not be wise.[23]

Such use of time was meant to contrast greatly with the way Numa's fellow citizens occupied themselves. The underlying distinction in kinds of activities was existential and determined by the reality in which they were undertaken. That is, in mildly Platonic terms, Kheraskov distinguished between a reality that could only be inhabited if it was explored and a reality that was merely experienced. Numa was called wise because of this turning away from the accepted view of how one should live and what one should live for. The subtle combination of otherworldliness and wisdom in the character of Numa has, therefore, left little room for a cunning manipulation of circumstances solely for the purpose of achieving or maintaining power. At the same time, however, Kheraskov made a point of showing that Numa acquired wisdom and its accompanying virtues through his own efforts, thus prioritizing the imperative of human will in all undertakings. The fact that Numa was able to overcome his specifically human imperfections without directly invoking any deity to help him justified the possibility of politics as a predominantly human discourse capable of solving peculiarly human problems.

It may be thought that such an idealized image of Numa implied that Kheraskov was writing well within the bounds of advice literature. This is true up to a point, and influences of this genre can be detected in *Numa Pompilius*. Yet, if religion is seen as the core theme of the work, then Kheraskov's intentions can be interpreted as quite original. The reason the emphasis on wisdom is so important is that, as will subsequently become clear, wisdom indicated how an alternative understanding of religion could come into being. Instead of sourcing religion to a moment of prophetic inspiration that, by the standards of Enlightened sensibilities, usually suggested rudeness, Kheraskov opted for the more ambitious task of showing how religion could be the product of a rational human attempt to consciously mediate divine truths. Society did not need just any kind of religion to progress. What it needed was a religion that was, itself, progressive. Had Numa spent his time solely contemplating mysteries, without also seeking to attain virtues, it would be difficult to call him wise because of the danger that readers might think he was misanthropic.[24] Individuals incapable of transforming themselves as substantively as Numa did—through participation in civil religion—would nevertheless be able to attain some of the same virtues, albeit without having the understanding of their transcendent origin.

It was precisely on account of the virtues Numa developed in solitude that he was elected king of the Romans. This fact allowed Kheraskov to attend to the moral state of the fledgling Roman kingdom on the eve of Numa's reforms. When Roman dignitaries approached Numa with the offer of kingship, he was tilling the fields. Even though he was of aristocratic lineage, Numa had willingly chosen a rustic life with his elderly father, away from the corrupting effects of power. Such distance from society did not imply a hatred of the people. To the contrary, Numa was practicing virtues necessary for a future polity. First, Numa devoted himself to productive labor, which was imperative for the material well-being of society. Second, he recognized the force of duty regarding his father—a duty that, in turn, formed the basis of justice. These virtues are usually taken for granted on account of their normativity. Yet, Kheraskov referred to an imagined time when these virtues were not universally accepted and even were almost seen as an embarrassment. Consequently, when Numa appeared to the dignitaries in clothes covered in dust and with farming implements in his hands, he realized how uncouth he must have looked to vain and idle men.[25] The disparity in values was so greatly felt that Numa had to explain that it was his acceptance of physical work that enabled him to become morally upright and to be of genuine use to his father.[26] Given that the sense of the common good was almost absent among the Roman ruling elite, legitimate questions could be raised as to whether Rome had a society and whether Rome was not, in fact, more akin to a violent state of nature.

The task, then, was to institute a type of religion that would replicate some aspects of Numa's personal moral progress, but in the population at large and without the aid of philosophy. Romans had religious institutions prior to Numa's ascension to the throne. However, Kheraskov implied that the institutions were primarily characterized by idolatry and opulence. The only exception was the cult of the Vestal Virgins, wherein Egeria was disguised as a priestess. The distinguishing characteristic of this cult was that it did not depend on imagination to win the allegiance of the people; instead, it relied on promoting practical morality:

> Its custodians did not dishonour the goddess' altar with collections of people's wealth. Moderation is wondrous in these individuals who have positioned themselves as intermediaries between God and the people. Virtuous living, useful advice, care of the ill and of the poor, are their primary concerns and because of this, their temple has become a refuge for virtuous people. To that end, this temple lacks proud ostentatiousness and does not sparkle with gold and expensive stones which vanity and despicable weakness usually devote to divinity and which covetousness and false humility seek to gather. Yet, virtue, being always immaculate and moderate, must not offer anything else to God except a pure heart and a spirit inflamed by love.[27]

Kheraskov singled out moderation as a virtue that could free individuals from vain pursuits and allow them to become empathetic toward others. This perspective is not as trite as it may sound, because Kheraskov also made a point of suggesting that worship was reducible to philanthropic activity. In other words, the content and the purpose of this religious institution did not exceed the natural needs of ordinary people. The few virtuous souls who participated in this cult may have, like Numa, experienced the more esoteric aspects of wisdom. However, the individuals who sought help from the practitioners of the cult could derive benefit from action without knowing the causal links connecting it to knowledge.

It is possible to see how moderation operated on two different but connected levels. On the one hand, the custodians of the cult moderated their pride, as evinced by the simplicity of their institutional arrangements. That is, they did not give in to the predatory mores of the larger society and use wealth as an expression of power. It is assumed that if offerings were made, they were disposed of in ways that were diametrically opposed to the social interactions of a warlike society and given away freely to those in need. On the other hand, those who turned to the cult for help did not seem to expect anything more than a tangible amelioration of their sorry circumstances through human effort, unless they pleaded for a miraculous intervention of the divine. In the latter case, idolatrous assumptions about the way God aided the needy were moderated in favor of direct engagement with human empathy. Indeed, although Kheraskov stated that the custodians were the intermediaries between God and the rest of the people, he did not explain how this was possible, given that the custodians' function in society did not include any supernatural elements. Far from being an inconsistency, the characterization of the custodians as intermediaries reflects Kheraskov's belief in virtue as something that is in itself divine, especially at a time when virtue was not yet considered to be a universal social norm.

The cult of the Vestal Virgins was, therefore, a blueprint for the development of a more all-encompassing religion that would bridge the gap between morality as understood by Numa and as practiced by the Romans. The way to bridge this gap was to humanize religion in a way that served human ends. The behavior of the custodians and the devotees of the Vesta cult exemplified how this was possible. Especially important in this regard was the absence of animal sacrifice, which indicated a reliance on a completely different type of transaction between individuals and God.[28] At least indirectly, sacrificial bloodletting sanctified ordinary violence because it upheld cruelty as a normative ingredient in human interactions with higher powers. Instead of sacrifice, the custodians related to God by attending to the needs of others and, in doing so, establishing a community that did not rely on force for its cohesion. Religion could become the foundation of a polity only by prioritizing reciprocal human relationships based on moral obligation. This did not necessarily mean that there was no room for legal compulsion, but it did mean that law had to aim at defending duties that were intrinsically rational and that could be accepted as such without coercion. To that end, it was not incidental that Kheraskov singled out love as the only offering that could be made to God, based on the assumption that the only thing religion could hold sacred was a principle of relationality in which all human interactions could be anchored.

Underscoring the allusion to a state of nature that pitted individual wills against one another in the absence of higher authority, Kheraskov had nymph Egeria tell her protégé that Rome needed a single ruler to pacify ongoing feuds.[29] This circumstance resulted from needing to legitimate absolute rule and using it to transform society so that a religious bond was necessary. Egeria intimated what kind of challenge Numa would face, describing the Romans as warlike, with cruel hearts and with minds "immersed in the depths of ignorance."[30] The crucial point is that for Egeria, a rational belief in God was implicated in the concern for the common good and submission to authority. Numa knew how idolatrous the Roman religion was at the time and misunderstood it to mean that existing religion had to be suppressed, leaving the people without any guidance. In responding to this concern, Egeria announced a definition of civil religion that simultaneously gave considerable scope to the reformist zeal of the sovereign but avoided subverting belief:

> I do not ask for this. I am not advising to demolish the sacred temples, said the Nymph. Such an alteration will startle feelings which have not yet been put into order. These establishments are

> necessary until such a time as when the truth guarded within these precincts will emerge and shine brighter than the sun to all quarters of the universe. Leave for the time being, idolatrous priests and their rites. However, in order to maintain this kind of faith, do not lessen the glory of the gods who constantly gaze upon your deeds. In order to attract your people to prayers and to divine service, you can invent different rites which are more harmonious with divinity and with nature. Neither stones nor perishable things constitute the law. Rather, it is composed of good deeds, humility and love of humankind. Think about this Numa and return to your abode. [31]

What Kheraskov was suggesting was quite radical and inconsistent with the received definition of civil religion. Namely, Numa was asked to reform and to make up religious rites, not merely to soften manners. A natural order of things and a transcendent God could be revealed through human engineering. In other words, it was insufficient for the divine to reveal itself prophetically. What was needed was a rational reconstruction of revelation through human labor. At this point, the significance of Egeria's personification of wisdom and of Numa's characterization as wise can be clarified. Wisdom, here, implied nothing less than an active use of reason in domains where it was previously excluded. It was something that in itself was beyond the range of ordinary human experience. In the paradox Kheraskov attenuated, to reach certain natural truths regarding the human condition, reason had to actualize them through imposture if necessary.

Nevertheless, it might seem as though Kheraskov settled for the understanding of civil religion conceived by Rousseau. Firstly, Numa was likened to an extraordinary person, a perspective aligning with Rousseau's view of the legislator as nearly godlike in his creative power.[32] Secondly, Numa intended to foster moral consciousness in the Romans, which harmonized with Rousseau's view that salvation was achievable in social terms through the enactment of moral duty.[33] Yet, there is one major difference that makes it difficult to conceive of Kheraskov as merely a follower of an already-existing civil religion discourse. What Kheraskov added to this discourse, and what signified an enduring aspect of Russian religious thought, was the firm belief that a human being was a partner, a participant in the creative forces that formed reality. From that perspective, far from indicating a narrowing or a retreat of religion into the realm of the political, Kheraskov's understanding of civil religion extended religious thinking into the very heart of society, albeit in a new key. It was not that Kheraskov gave in to the secularizing tendencies of his age. Rather, it is more correct to presume that he used the relatively liberal climate of Catherine the Great's first years on the throne to attempt an alternative synthesis of personal spirituality and politics. This synthesis was driven by the notion that the sovereign had almost absolute responsibility for the moral state of the citizens, on the condition that the sovereign was conscious of a metaphysical underlay to reality, an underlay he was beholden to.

This conclusion might be erroneously interpreted to mean that temporal authority was to be unlimited, thus justifying the type of Russian *polizeistaat* to which Enlightened mystics such as Kheraskov were reacting. Insofar as *Numa Pompilius* functioned as advice literature to rulers, it would be more correct to view the novel as simultaneously extending in some areas and severely limiting in others the power of the monarch. The key argument that Kheraskov proposed was that mores, as understood and practiced by the majority of citizens, were largely determined by the sociopolitical institutions to which individuals owed allegiance. Therefore, it is not surprising that on the eve of Numa's ascension to the throne, Rome was in the grip of one dominant type of social organization, namely, predatory warfare. This, in turn, predetermined the individual character of the Romans. The contrast between a laboring Numa and the indolent Roman elite was very much a contrast between two types of humanities as they emerged from two vastly different forms of social conditioning. Consequently, if a ruler possessed goodwill combined with reason, then his or her capacity to effect substantive change in the internal state of the subjects could be substantial. Arguably, such sentiments are partly responsible for the masonic penchant for the panegyric, insofar as the production of the panegyric was anchored in a belief that at least some of the prelapsarian bliss could be recovered if the attention of the ruler could be oriented toward it.[34]

The extension of monarchical power into matters of religion was based on the notion that the monarchy was the institution most responsible for the formation and upkeep of popular mores. Indeed, on the surface, there seems little disagreement between Peter the Great's enforced integration of Russian Orthodoxy into the state's autocratic structure and Kheraskov's prioritization of the religious role of the absolute ruler. In reality, there an insurmountable difference between Orthodoxy's status as an appendage of a bureaucratic apparatus and Kheraskov's blueprint of how religious life could be rethought. That difference posed a fundamental limit to political authority as such. Kheraskov was quite sensitive to the fact that the content of civil religion ought to include only those aspects of spirituality deemed necessary for communal life to be possible. That is, the inherently political nature of religion as conceived by Egeria was not presented as circumscribing the entirety of spiritual existence. This point is, of course, very much at odds with the cameralist reform of Orthodoxy, which aimed at making the sovereign directly responsible for the salvation of the citizens.[35] Russians were presented with a state that claimed to satisfy all of their spiritual needs, so long as they believed their primary duty was to act patriotically in the nation's interests.[36] In effect, by providing a counter-narrative regarding how a ruler could alter the religious sentiments of the citizenry, Kheraskov was suggesting that transcendent truth could not be implicated into politics and that, consequently, spiritual becoming was a strictly individual pursuit in which the state could not exercise its authority.

One can detect how Kheraskov carefully distinguished between the expansive and outward-looking civil religion on the one hand and a concentrated and inward contemplative praxis on the other. It is important at this point to recall that the prelude to the formation of a new Roman religion was signified by Numa's ascetic separation from the normative activities of his compatriots into a domain that privileged physical and, most crucially, intellectual labor. This distinction suggests that if there is a religion higher than a civil one, then it cannot have originated in the authority of the sovereign. In contemplating the mysteries, Numa was subject to the transcendent, which he cultivated within his own person. Thus, Kheraskov positioned his readers to think of the absolute necessity of freedom or, at least, noninterference from external authorities as a precondition to a substantive self-relation. In fact, it seems as though the ascetic focus on what he deemed to be most valuable in life implied that beyond the practical worldly significance, spiritual development was an intimately personal process foreclosed to direct institutional mediation. Therefore, a religion legislated for the polity was preceded by a set of private experiences of the divine, which were radically different from the predominantly communal and temporal character of civil religion.

In light of this reasoning, it would make more sense to see *Numa Pompilius* as Kheraskov's critique of how religion in post-Petrine Russia was largely conflated with the dictates of the state. The fact that many mid- to late-eighteenth-century Russians were turning to alternative religious forms that prioritized the role of the individual implied that the domineering role of the state was perceived to be a threat to the spiritual integrity of the person.[37] It is at this point that the polemical intentions driving Kheraskov's nuanced distinction between civil religion and wisdom can be better appreciated. In brute terms, Kheraskov was advising his audience not to think of the outward features of religion—no matter how revered or saintly they appeared to be—as beyond critical inquiry. In that sense, the religion as practiced by the Romans prior to Numa's becoming king could be interpreted as a very indirect attack against some of the enthusiastic practices of the Orthodox Church. Kheraskov's characterization of Numa's new cult as closer to nature and as conducive to peace is inherently at odds with the totalizing claims of any revealed religion that has appeared thus far in the course of human history. Orthodoxy's many superstitious rituals—especially those of folk extraction; its proclaimed status as the only true religion, resulting in civic discord; and its veneration of saints known for military exploits—contrasted greatly with Numa's intention to found a religion that was peaceful, practical, and congruent with natural reason.

Kheraskov and like-minded Westernized Russian intellectuals would have supported, in principle, attempts to modernize Orthodoxy and to align some of its aspects with the interests of the Russian state. The sticking point was the immense authority that the church continued to claim for itself in worldly and spiritual affairs while remaining deeply inimical to individual queries regarding its efficacy.[38] Consequently, paradoxical as it may sound, Peter the Great's reshaping of the Russian religious landscape did not proceed far enough in terms of sanctifying moral postures necessary for political flourishing and minimizing the prevalence of some of its more divisive and irrational features. When nymph Egeria allayed Numa's fears that social progress required that existing temples be imbued with new content, she was in effect pointing toward the possibility of reforming the content of Orthodoxy rather than displacing it altogether. However, it could also be said that Peter's reform of Orthodoxy went too far in that it reaffirmed what, in Voltairean terms, represented the infamous dependence of the church, as the monopolizer of other-worldly truth, on the punitive apparatus of the state. Indeed, as Anthony Pagden noted, one of the concerns of Enlightened intellectuals was the possibility that a church subservient to the state would become even more reactionary, resulting in a "double form of oppression."[39] Thus, it was crucial for Kheraskov to equate law with love of humankind in order to minimize future conflict over interpretations and observance of dogma.

Ultimately, then, *Numa Pompilius* can be read as a plea to Russia's governing class to recalibrate the interrelationship between church and state and to rectify some of the more glaring side effects of Peter the Great's religious reforms. Of course, in taking a somewhat conjectural approach to history, Kheraskov did not specify what policies the state should pursue, instead preferring to provide a general blueprint for the essential purpose of religion in a polity. At the level of practicality, what Kheraskov may have been proposing was a lessening of surveillance of individual beliefs, especially those held by the Russian Westernized elite. Greater trust in the ability of individual citizens to direct their own inner life required the freedom to experiment with, to read about, and to discuss non-Orthodox spiritual traditions. Clearly, *Numa Pompilius* was itself an example of a nondoctrinaire inquiry into spirituality that bypassed traditional authorities. However, although the novel was the first work of its kind in Russia—followed later by others—on its own it could not respond to all of the moral needs of its readers. In fact, Kheraskov's increasing preoccupation with the unmediated experience of the divine was the main motivator behind his huge literary output and determined his interest in fostering a culture dedicated to serious reading, reflection, and self-improvement. In other words, the nascent Russian intelligentsia needed a guarantee that its members could concern themselves with their own inner well-being, as Numa did, without the threat of external intervention—be it on the part of the church or the state.

It is obvious that the type of spirituality Kheraskov promoted was very much informed by his idealized version of the meaning and purpose of Freemasonry. This influence is particularly apparent when some of the ideas in *Numa Pompilius* are compared to the ideology and civic activities of the Russian Rosicrucians.[40] However, I have avoided discussing the Masonic aspects of the novel in order to highlight the political implications of an Enlightened approach to mystical spirituality, especially in relation to personal autonomy. What Kheraskov seemingly suggested was that the genuine freedom an individual could enjoy for the purposes of his or her own *bildung* required a considerable degree of social engineering. In other words, the public sphere had to be governed by enforceable religious norms aimed at the development of politically oriented virtues only, leaving the more transcendent and nonpolitical aspects of spirituality entirely up to individual choice. There was, in effect, a mystical religion for the intellectual elite, far exceeding the practical demands of society, and there was another religion, which was civil and obligatory to all citizens. It seems Kheraskov believed that these distinct features of religious consciousness could coexist peacefully so long as they were kept apart and societal reform was undertaken by someone who was firmly committed to wisdom in its unadulterated form. It might seem that Kheraskov was naïve to hope for a society in which humane interactions between citizens could stand in for religion, but it must be remembered that his view entailed a rather sober assessment of the many failings of organized religion. *Numa Pompilius,* while broadly utopian in character, looked to neither a past golden age nor a future paradise. Instead, it foregrounded the possibility of a new beginning, at least in regard to religious institutions. That is why Kheraskov could combine a hope for better politics with a realistic assessment of the need to transform the inner dispositions of the citizens through law and ritual.

As mentioned, *Numa Pompilius* was one of Kheraskov's early works, and it preceded his major poetical pieces, which established his literary importance. Given the overwhelmingly religious orientation of some of Kheraskov's epic poetry, some readers might query why his epic poetry was not the subject of the present analysis. The problem is that as a writer, Kheraskov's worldview was becoming increasingly mystical, giving more weight to human interiority at the expense of political considerations. This, of course, was a major development in the history of Russian humanism and a chapter in the constellation of Russian Enlightenments. Yet, precisely because of his deepening commitment to mysticism, Kheraskov saw no reason to add anything more to the civic aspects of religion as it was discussed in *Numa Pompilius.* Kheraskov's epic poem *Vladimir Reborn* (1785) is a telling example of how mystical spirituality of the person almost completely eclipsed the politics and religion of state. Though this focus does not necessarily mean that Kheraskov no longer believed in a rational religion of the state, it does mean that he became more preoccupied with individual *bildung,* undertaken without exclusive reliance on religious institutions. In addition, it must be remembered that in the latter part of her reign, Catherine the Great no longer positioned herself as seeking advice from her subjects, thus making it less likely for writers and thinkers to seriously engage with political discourse.

*Vladimir Reborn* was very loosely based on the story of how Prince Vladimir converted eastern Slavic tribes from paganism to Byzantine Orthodoxy in the tenth-century. The possibility of discussing the political implications of choosing a particular faith and of the faith's impact on the nascent Russian polity would not have been lost on Kheraskov's contemporaries. The fact that a fundamental shift—such as resulting from a change of faith—was effected by a ruler could not be seen except through the prism of Peter the Great's modernizing efforts. Thus, Kheraskov did have at his disposal the rudiments of a narrative through which he could have continued his analysis of how the aims of politics and religion intersected in the mind of an ambitious ruler. Tempting as it may have been for Kheraskov to subject the history of the Russian dark ages to the test of Enlightened civility, he did something else. Simply put, instead of showing how religion improved society and made civic life possible, Kheraskov detailed the spiritual rebirth of a single individual without explicating its sociopolitical implications. Instead of narrating the thorny path of a polity transfigured via institutionally anchored virtues, Kheraskov squarely focused on how mystical insight improved the inner state of the individual, specifically that of Vladimir.

Kheraskov did not treat Vladimir as a historical figure but, rather, as an example of a personhood that prioritized self-introspective praxis. In fact, in the preamble to the poem, Kheraskov intimated that his work was an allegorical record of spiritual progress.[41] Kheraskov's foregrounding of individuality over external religious infrastructure is particularly evident in his belittling of the role of the Russian Orthodox Church in Vladimir's self-transformation. Even after Peter's secularizing policies, Orthodoxy remained the state confession and, at least in part, derived its privileged status from the fact that its emergence in Russia was almost contemporaneous with the emergence of the Russian state. At no point throughout *Vladimir Reborn* was there an indication that the confessional uniqueness of Orthodoxy related at all to personal spiritual development. In fact, the very words *church* and *Orthodoxy* rarely appear in poem, even though Vladimir's fame rested on introducing Byzantine religiosity into Russia. Instead of religious dogma being the conduit through which Vladimir discovered virtue, Vladimir's discovery of virtue was influenced by the wisdom of another individual: Elder Cyrus, who represented Orthodoxy. Though reflective of the Pietist leanings shared by many late-eighteenth-century Russian intellectuals, displacement of institutional authority by individual virtues was quite radical. The worth of a religious institution, no matter how ancient, depended on individual saintliness for its justification.[42] Therefore, perceptive readers were likely to query whether organized religion could be eliminated altogether in favor of the free associations of intellectuals seeking personal improvement.

Without sophisticated philosophical terminology (which was germinal in Russia at the time) and about a decade before the flowering of Russian mystical culture, in *Numa Pompilius* Kheraskov was able to express a very complex Platonic approach to wisdom in terms that help explain Kheraskov's reconfiguration of faith and politics. Beyond the merely literary significance of the description of Numa as wise, holding conversations with wisdom personified was an alternative understanding of how knowledge was possible. In stark opposition to the popular Enlightened notion that reason was individual and reducible to a set of cognitive capacities, Kheraskov described wisdom as participation. That is, the intellect was not wise merely because of its inner content. Rather, the intellect was wise because it was in the proximity of wisdom as something extrinsic to its individuality. When seen from this highly metaphysical perspective, it might be the case that Kheraskov did not feel threatened by the possibility of an irresolvable conflict between products of human reason and religious truth. What Kheraskov was implying was that if reason could become an object of appropriate reverence, the civil religious norms could not distance the citizens from God because the former did not, strictly speaking, originate from human subjectivity. Thus, although it was possible to say that certain aspects of religion were consciously created by a person, the capacity to create these aspects was greater than the intellect that wielded the capacity. Consequently, Kheraskov pointed to the freedom to isolate and discuss important problems in humanistic terminology and, at the same time, evinced thought patterns that would be developed further after Russian intellectual culture matured in the following century.

## Notes

1. This does not mean that individual Russian thinkers were exposed to foreign legal thought. In fact, Peter the Great's reform of Russian Orthodoxy was informed by an array of juridical sources. See James Cracraft, ed., "Feofan Prokopovich," *The Eighteenth Century in Russia* (Oxford: Clarendon Press, 1973), 76. The original version of this paper was presented in the very friendly environment provided by the *British Society for Eighteenth-Century Studies* annual conference at St Hugh's College, Oxford in 2016. I particularly wish to express my gratitude to Professor Paul Kerry for his keen interest in my presentation at that conference. I also wish to thank the editorial team, especially Professor Brett McInelly, as well as the peer reviewer for helpful commentary which made the present article possible.

2. Isabel de Madariaga, *Russia in the Age of Catherine the Great* (London: Phoenix, 2003), 330.

3. Nikolai K. Piksanov, "Masonskaia literatura," *Istoriia russkoi literatury v 10 t. T. IV: Literatura XVIII veka Ch. 2* (Moscow: Izd-vo AN CCCR, 1947), 74.

4. Ibid., 79. Kheraskov has written other novels based on classical themes focusing on the need for virtue in a polity, but he did so without attending to the institutional side of religion as much as he did in *Numa Pompilius*. See his *Kadm i Garmonia* (Moscow: Univer-

sitetskaia tipografia u N. Novikova, 1789) and *Plydor, syn Kadma i Garmonii* (Moscow: V Tip. I. Zelennikova, 1794).

5. Cynthia Whittaker, in her outstanding study of political dialogue between writers and rulers in eighteenth-century Russia, made a brief comment regarding *Numa Pompilius* and Kheraskov's hopes for a new society. See her *Russian Monarchy: Eighteenth-Century Rulers and Writers in Political Dialogue* (DeKalb: Northern Illinois University Press, 2003), 144. Additionally, in one of the most detailed and subtle of contemporary essays on the history of the Numa Pompilius and the theme of civil religion in Western thought and literature, Mark Lilla only mentioned Kheraskov's novel in a footnote. This misunderstanding of Kheraskov's authorial intentions is particularly unfortunate because much of what the essay says on the efficacy of religious sentiment accords well with the content of *Numa Pompilius*. See Lilla's "Numa Pompilius and the Idea of Civil Religion in the West," *Journal of the American Academy of Religion* 72, no. 4 (2004), 888. One of the most recent Anglophone discussions of Kheraskov's *Numa* has misinterpreted the text's politico-religious implications as predominantly panegyric in character. See Dragana Grbić, "*Telemachus*: Dositej Obradović's Last Wish. The Serbian Reception of Fénelon," *Fénelon in the Enlightenment: Traditions, Adaptations, and Variations*, ed. Christoph Schmitt-Maaß, Stefanie Stockhorst, and Doohwan Ahn (Amsterdam: Rodopoi, 2014), 246.

6. Fénelon, *Telemachus* (Cambridge: Cambridge University Press, 1994), 305.

7. Charles Rollin's *Histoire romaine depuis la fondation de Rome jusqu'à la bataille d'Actium* (Paris, 1738) was translated into Russian prior to the publication of *Numa Pompilius*. See *Rimskaia istoria. Ot sozdania Rima do bitvy Aktiiskia toest' po okonchanie Respubliki* (St. Petersburg: Sanktpeterburgskaia Imperatorskia Akademii Nauk, 1761–1767). At the same time, there was also a translation of Plutarch's Lives, including that of Numa. See *Zhtiia slavnyh v drevnosti muzhei pisannye Plutarhom* (St. Petersburg: Tip. Suhoput. kadet. korpusa, 1765).

8. Elise Wirtschafter noted that the language of civic humanism was appropriated by Russian writers for the purposes of political critique. This, of course, is particularly true of writers such as Kheraskov, who turned to classical themes. See Elise Wirtschafter, *The Play of Ideas in Russian Enlightenment Theater* (DeKalb: Northern Illinois University Press, 2003), 4.

9. Rafaella Faggionato convincingly argued that a very intense experience of religious anxiety and alienation from traditional Orthodoxy forced many educated Russians to turn to an Enlightened form of mysticism. See her *A Rosicrucian Utopia in Eighteenth-Century Russia: The Masonic Circle of N.I. Novikov* (Dordrecht: Springer, 2005), 129.

10. This can be seen in terms of a heightening attention to the development of self-consciousness as a key ingredient of progress. In a very perceptive remark made regarding Kheraskov's poetical works—and can be directed to *Numa Pompilius* as well—Ol'ga M. Goncharova argued that Kheraskov's authorial intention was to return to the self, its genealogy and its being. See her *Vlast' traditsii i novaia Rossia v literaturnom soznanii vtoroi poloviny XVIII veka* (St. Petersburg: Izd-vo RHGI, 2004), 91.

11. Max J. Okenfuss, *The Rise and Fall of Latin Humanism in Early-Modern Russia: Pagan Authors, Ukrainians and the Resiliency of Muscovy* (Leiden: Brill, 1995). Okenfuss's overall argument was that humanism failed to properly percolate in Russia. This assertion is true in the formal sense of classical studies but there was not an absence of humanistic thinking.

12. Mikhail M. Scherbatov, "Puteshestvie v zemlu ofirskuiu," *Izbrannye trudy* (Moscow: ROSSPEN, 2010), 223.

13. Ibid., 208–209.

14. Ibid., 208.

15. Ibid., 221–222

16. For a complex treatment of Livy's ideas on political religion, see W. Liebeschuetz, "The Religious Position of Livy's History," *The Journal of Roman Studies* 1, no. 2 (1967): 48.

17. Livy, *The Early History of Rome*, Books I–V of *The History of Rome from Its Foundation*, trans. A. De Selincourt (London: Penguin, 1971), 1.19.

18. Sarah F. Hoyt, "The Etymology of Religion," *Journal of the American Oriental Society* 32, no. 2 (1912): 128.

19. Edna M. Hooker, "The Significance of Numa's Religious Reforms," *Numen* 10, no. 2 (1963): 129.

20. Plutarch, *Lives*, Volume I of Loeb Classical Library, trans. Bernadotte Perrin (Cambridge, MA: Harvard University Press, 1914), 333. See also K. R. Prowse, "Numa and the Pythagoreans: A Curious Incident," *Greece & Rome* 11, no. 1 (1964): 39. Plutarch's Platonist leanings may have compelled him to perpetuate the story that Numa was under the influence of Pythagoras, even though this could not possibly have been true.

21. Plutarch, *Lives*, 319.

22. Mikhail M. Kheraskov, *Numa Pompilii, ili protsvetauschii Rim*. Izdanie chetvertoe (Moscow: Vol'naya Tipografiia M. Ponomareva, 1809), 2–3.

23. Ibid., 13.

24. Tatiana V. Artem'eva interpreted Numa as an archetypal natural man imbued with virtue. See her outstanding *Ot slavnogo proshlogo k svetlomu buduschemu: Filosofiia istorii i utopiia v Rossii epohi Prosveschenia* (St. Petersburg: Aleteiia, 2005), 380.

25. Mikhail M. Kheraskov, *Numa Pompilii*, 4.

26. Ibid., 5.

27. Ibid., 10.

28. Ibid.

29. Ibid.,14.

30. Ibid., 29.

31. Ibid., 79.

32. John T. Scott, "Politics as the Imitation of the Divine in Rousseau's *Social Contract*," *Polity* 26, no. 3 (1994): 496.

33. Fred H. Willhite, Jr., "Rousseau's Political Religion," *The Review of Politics* 27, no. 4 (1965): 508.

34. Stephen Baehr convincingly argued that "the search for heaven on earth became a central theme in Russian culture" and was not impeded by eighteenth-century modernization. See his *The Paradise Myth in Eighteenth-Century Russia. Utopian Patterns in Early Secular Russian Literature and Culture* (Stanford: Stanford University Press, 1991), 15. It needs to be added that, for Baehr, the utopian possibilities of a search for a heaven on earth could be applied to praise, to censure, or to advise Russian rulers, depending on the intentions of the particular writer as well as on the political climate in the country.

35. Marc Raeff, "The Well-Ordered Police State and the Development of Modernity in Seventeenth and Eighteenth Century Europe: A Comparative Approach," *The American Historical Review* 80, no. 5 (1975): 1229.

36. Ibid.

37. Douglas Smith, *Working the Rough Stone: Freemasonry and Society in Eighteenth-Century Russia* (DeKalb: Northern Illinois University Press, 1999), 6.

38. It is important to remember that throughout the eighteenth century, the Holy Synod of the Russian Orthodox Church had the right to oversee literature that contained religious themes. Although the church's demands to suppress or ban certain publications often went unheeded, the church retained considerable influence and was regularly consulted regarding manuscripts prior to publication. The Holy Synod was concerned with maintaining its monopoly over spiritual literature, which is why it was wary of non-Orthodox ideas. See Gary Marker, *Publishing, Printing, and the Origins of the Intellectual Life in Russia, 1700–1800* (Princeton: Princeton University Press, 1985), 213–214.

39. Anthony Pagden, *The Enlightenment and Why It Still Matters* (Oxford: Oxford University Press, 2015), 81.

40. Baehr noted the presence of nascent masonic themes in *Numa Pompilius*; these themes were articulated in much greater depth in Kheraskov's later works. See his *The Paradise Myth*, 100.

41. Mikhail M. Kheraskov, "'Vladimir Vozrozhdennyi' in Kheraskov" in Kheraskov, M. M., *Tvoreniia M. Kheraskova, vnov' ispravlennyia i dopolnennyia. Chast' II* (Moscow: V Universitetskoi Tipografii, 1797), VIII.

42. Ibid., 122.

# George Whitefield, John Wesley, and the Rhetoric of Liberty

*Glen O'Brien*

## Introduction[1]

George Whitefield died on September 30, 1770, during an attack of asthma and was widely mourned throughout America. Five years later, a Revolutionary chaplain and several officers opened his casket in Newburyport, Massachusetts. They removed his clerical collar and wrist bands, cut them into strips, and distributed the pieces among the soldiers, thus taking Whitefield with them into battle.[2] That Whitefield's clerical insignia could somehow embolden American troops in their fight against perceived tyranny is an indication of the high regard in which he was held in America and of his iconographic status during the American Revolution.

Superficially, Whitefield seems an unlikely candidate for such a status. A priest of the Church of England who always preached in full clerical dress and was an enthusiastic supporter of the Hanoverian monarchy seems hardly the type to be appropriated by the republican cause. Whitefield died before the American Revolution, but he very closely identified with America and American interests during his seven preaching tours there. This contrasts with the more negative attitude toward the American cry for liberty on the part of Whitefield's friend John Wesley. Whitefield was an American personality in a way that Wesley was not. This chapter will attempt to compare and contrast the views on political liberty of these two Methodists in the hope of shedding further light on our understanding of the religious aspects of the Revolution.

In addition to the colonists seeing the British administration as a threat to hard-won liberties guaranteed under the crown, there was also what Mark Noll calls "a deep vein of religiously charged discourse" consistently mined by colonists in their move toward independence.[3] The connection between Christian theological convictions and the Whig conception of government was very strong and provided fertile soil for revolutionary ideas. Republican ideas flowed from religion into politics and not always the other way around, as is often supposed. As Noll notes, "Rather than a rhetoric of republican civic humanism spreading out into the religious backwaters of colonial society, the religious backwaters may have been rising to carry republicanism where its leading theorists had not intended it to go."[4] Similarly, Nathan Hatch in *The Sacred Cause of Liberty* argued that in the "civil millennialism" of New England, a link existed between evangelical religion and the politics of liberty. "In picturing the struggle of liberty versus tyranny as nothing less than the conflict between heaven and hell, the clergy found their political commitments energized with the force of a divine imperative and their political goals translated into the very principles which would initiate the kingdom of God on earth."[5]

The current interest in the global and transatlantic dimensions of the American Revolution suggests a need for further investigation of its religious aspects, particularly among Methodists. Mapping these two leading Methodists' responses to the "language of liberty" on both sides of the Atlantic can contribute to such an investigation.

## George Whitefield: Accidental Revolutionary

In two books rehearsing essentially the same argument, *Preaching Politics: The Religious Rhetoric of George Whitefield and the Founding of a New Nation* and *The Accidental Revolutionary: George Whitefield and the Creation of America*, Jerome Dean Mahaffey argues that the "logic template" of New Light revivalism in George Whitefield's preaching of the new birth prepared the way for the American Revolution.[6] The "choice of a new identity" entailed in Whitefield's message of the new birth provided an identity not based on traditional ties of kinship or denominational allegiance but, rather, on an experience of personal transformation. The introduction of choice in religion "paved the way for republican politics, a political system of self-government through representatives chosen by the people."[7] In the message of the new birth, a person was either in the family of God or out of it; now, whether or not one was "in the family" depended upon one's attitude toward political liberty.[8] On the one hand, Whitefield was Whiggish in opposing Anglican hegemony in America. On the other hand, he praised and supported the Hanoverian kings. According to Mahaffey, Whitefield created a third alternative and evolved into "a spiritual statesman for the republican ideology, championing the privileges of the people within the bounds of monarchical authority."[9]

Mahaffey's work borrows heavily from other scholars, makes several unsubstantiated claims, and is stronger in its rhetorical observations than its theological ones.[10] Nonetheless, his broad argument is supported by Harry S. Stout's authoritative biography *The Divine Dramatist*.[11] Stout sees Whitefield's libertarian rhetoric growing to "a revolutionary pitch" and asserts that "from its first expression" the rhetoric of liberty in British America was identified with Whitefield. "As Americans moved ever forward in their great 'experiment in liberty,' the name Whitefield would continue to lead them and be identified with their quest."[12] In the challenge of bringing thirteen distinct colonies together in a sense of united purpose, perhaps nothing was more significant than the personality of Whitefield and his ability to forge a corporate American identity. The itinerant nature of intercolonial evangelism had earlier pointed toward an emerging national consciousness. As Noll observed in relation to Gilbert Tennant, to read newspaper reports of the evangelist's intercolonial preaching tours led people to begin to think of themselves as American Christians rather than, for example, New Jersey Presbyterians.[13] Whitefield's contribution to such an identification was even more significant than Tennant's because of his greater celebrity.

In spite of contributing to this new American identity, Whitefield frequently expressed loyalty to the Crown. Early in his career he responded to an anonymous 1744 pamphlet, "Observations upon the Conduct and Behaviour of a Certain Sect, Usually Distinguished by the Name of Methodists," which had accused Whitefield of fomenting sedition and compared him to those who had beheaded Charles I. This was a particularly highly charged accusation in the context of a feared Jacobite invasion of England. Whitefield replied to this in two separate letters to the bishop of London, "An Answer to the First Part," (March 1744) and "An Answer to the Second Part of an Anonymous Pamphlet" (August 1744).[14] In these he steadfastly asserted his, and all Methodists', firm loyalty to the king and membership of the established church.[15] For his own part he expressed his willingness to pray for the king "surrounded by popish enemies," even on pain of death.[16]

In 1745 Whitefield publicly supported and recruited for the Louisbourg expedition, which saw colonial troops under the American commander George Pepperell capture a French-built fort in Nova Scotia on June 16. This was the largest expeditionary military force ever assembled in America up to that time. They marched under a slogan provided by Whitefield: "If Christ leads, never fear." During the American Revolution, soldiers continued to march under this motto, with a sense that Whitefield was with them.[17] The Louisbourg expedition can be seen as marking the beginning point of Whitefield's status as an American icon. If Americans could unite again successfully like they did during the Great Awakening, where denominational barriers meant little so long as one was "born again," then they could also set aside their differences to unite in politics and war.[18]

In response to the failed Jacobite invasion of England, Whitefield's sermon "Britain's Mercies and Britain's Duties" was preached at the New Building in Philadelphia on Sunday, August 24, 1746.[19] In it he showed support for the Hanoverians and rejected the Stuart claims on the basis that Catholicism (and thus the French) represented "arbitrary power" over "liberty."[20] Whitefield's rhetoric is situated in the wider view of history that saw "the struggle between Protestants and Catholics as one battle in the larger war between liberty and arbitrary power."[21] The "horrid plot" of the popish pretender, "first hatched in hell, and afterwards nursed at Rome," was designed to bring Britain into "vassalage to the see of Rome."[22]

> Besides, was a popish pretender to rule over us, instead of being represented by a free parliament, and governed by laws made by their consent, as we now are, we should shortly have had only the shadow of one, and, it may be, no parliament at all. This is the native product of a popish government, and what the unhappy family, from which this young adventurer pretends to be descended, has always aimed at. Arbitrary principles he has sucked in with his mother's milk.[23]

John Wesley and George Whitefield took differing views on the legitimacy of war, with the latter approving of wars fought for a holy cause. For example, Whitefield saw the Seven Years' War as a holy war against the anti-Christian powers of Rome in order to protect English civil and religious liberties.[24] His *Short Address to Persons of All Denominations Occasioned by the Alarm of an Intended Invasion, in the Year 1756* (1756) was written in the expectation of a French invasion of England and became a bestseller.[25] Just as God had confounded the builders of the Tower of Babel, so he stood ready to confound those whose aim to establish "universal monarchy" was perceived as only another such tower.[26] The French had broken the 1748 Treaty of Aix-la-Chapelle, and so the British could be sure that their prayers for victory could be answered.[27] In Whitefield's thinking, war with France was in defense of Britain's "civil and religious liberties," which made it a "just and righteous cause"[28] against "France, and Rome, and Hell."[29]

John Wesley, though he shared the same anti-Catholic stance, usually expressed an in-principle opposition to armed military conflict between professedly Christian nations. In Sermon 22, "Upon Our Lord's Sermon on the Mount Discourse the Second," Wesley recalls how the pagans once observed of the early Christians, "See how these Christians love one another!" and how they could not say the same in his day, with "Christian kingdoms . . . tearing out each other's bowels, desolating one another with fire and sword! These Christian armies that are sending each other by thousands, by ten thousands quick into hell!"[30] There were some wars, however, that he considered more legitimate than others, and he did indicate willingness in 1779 to contribute Methodist manpower to a proposed militia designed to defend England against another feared French invasion.[31]

One area of close agreement between Wesley and Whitefield was their shared belief that the British people under both George II and George III were, in respect to their civil and religious liberties, the freest people on earth. It was inconceivable to Whitefield that anyone, however critical of the present government, could possibly prefer a French to an English government, or a "popish Pretender, born, nursed, and bred up in all the arbitrary and destructive principles of the court and church of Rome, to the present Protestant succession . . . of Hanover."[32]

In the 1760s, the new political climate in New England recognized Whitefield as "a champion and fellow spirit."[33] After successfully defeating French "tyranny" in the Seven Years' War, the switch to British "tyranny" was not too great a stretch. The Stamp Act was passed in March 1765 partly to recoup the expense of the Seven Years' War, and American colonists saw this as a threat to their liberty. No longer would France and Rome be seen as the major threat to liberty—now Parliament would fill that role. In 1764 Whitefield warned Samuel Langdon and other ministers in Portsmouth, New Hampshire, "I can't in conscience leave the town without acquainting you with a secret. My heart bleeds for America. O poor New England! There is a deep laid plot against your civil and religious liberties, and they will be lost. Your golden days are at an end. You have nothing but trouble before you. . . . Your liberties will be lost."[34] He perhaps had in mind rumored plans to end colonial self-government and establish an Anglican episcopacy in America. The Stamp Act was seen as a partial fulfilment of this prophecy. When Benjamin Franklin addressed the House of Commons in 1766 to explain American grievances, Whitefield accompanied him to London, offering friendly support and praising his performance in defending American liberty. When the Stamp Act was finally repealed on March 16, Whitefield gave thanks to God.[35] Some American colonists saw Whitefield's disputes with Archbishop Thomas Secker over control of the Bethesda College project in Georgia as another example of British tyranny trampling upon American religious liberties.[36]

Whitefield's American identity placed a strain on his relationship with the established church from which he drew his priestly orders. When six Methodists were expelled from Edmund Hall, Oxford, on March 11, 1768, for using extemporary prayers, Whitefield was given a pretext for commenting on American affairs, in particular the threat of the appointment of an Anglican bishop in America, accusing the church of functioning as "a society for propagating Episcopacy in foreign parts."[37] For the bishops to countenance this unfair treatment would only increase colonial prejudice against the establishment of episcopacy "from Quebec down to the two Floridas."[38] Some of his Church of England colleagues saw this as an identification with the rebels of British America—and they were right. There is perhaps a note of special pleading in Whitefield's reminding the vice chancellor of the loyalty of the Methodists to the Crown, assuring him that "every additional proselyte to true Methodism, is an additional loyal subject to King George the Third" and that Methodists remained what they had always been: "steady, invariable friends to the Protestant succession in the illustrious house of Hanover."[39] Or perhaps Whitefield genuinely believed that the Americans could achieve their hoped-for liberty by remaining connected to a constitutional monarchy.

One area of stark difference between Wesley and Whitefield was their views on the legitimacy of slavery. In his 1740 "Letter to the Inhabitants of Maryland, Virginia, North and South Carolina," Whitefield issued a plea for the "poor negroes" who were treated worse than dogs. "Whether it be lawful for Christians to buy slaves, and thereby encourage the nations from which they are brought, to be at perpetual war with each other, I shall not take it upon me to determine; but sure I am it is sinful; when bought, to use them as bad as, nay worse, than brutes."[40] He urges upon slave masters that they teach their slaves the Christian faith, for the slaves were also sinners and had just as much reason to be saved as white people.[41] Though Whitefield stood at the forefront of those who argued for the humane treatment of slaves, his ownership of slaves, his acceptance of the institution, and his argument for its legalization in Georgia remain problematic and self-serving.[42]

In 1747 Josiah Smith wrote from Charleston, South Carolina, that Whitefield's supporters had subscribed two hundred pounds sterling "to purchase and improve with Negroes a very good plantation."[43] Whitefield wrote to the trustees of the orphan house on December 6, 1748, concerned about its precarious financial condition, "Had a negroe [*sic*] been allowed, I should now have had a sufficiency to support a great many orphans, without spending above half the sum which hath been laid out. . . . Georgia never can or will be a flourishing province without negroes be allowed."[44] Given this pecuniary motive, one wonders what Whitefield would have thought of his friend John Wesley's claim thirty years later that no slaver ever purchased a slave out of a motive of mercy, but only ever to make money.[45]

Along with Indepnedence architects, Whitefield, "the forgotten founding father," failed to see the contradictions between the rhetoric of freedom and the continuance of slavery.[46] Wesley, on the other hand, explicitly pointed out the irony of slaveholders crying out for liberty while "ten thousand negroes in the American colonies" were enslaved.[47] In *Thoughts upon Slavery* (1774), Wesley responded to those who claimed that it was necessary to purchase slaves in order to furnish plantations with labor, arguing that while it may be necessary to that end, the end itself is not necessary. It would be better for land to remain uncultivated forever than to be worked on by slaves. White men were just as able to work the land as black men, which Wesley says he himself proved by his and others' hard manual labor in Georgia. If slavery was necessary for the "trade, wealth, and glory" of the nation, it would be better for England to have no wealth at all than to procure it through villainy and the "tears, and sweat, and blood, of our fellow-creatures."[48]

Whitefield's final days occurred around the time of the Boston siege on March 5, 1770, when five Bostonians were shot by British troops during a riot. By this time, the English priest with an American heart had become a symbol of liberty. Whitefield arrived in Philadelphia in early May, still grieving over the event. Among Whitefield's last words, written a week before he died, were his lamentations about the British government's attempt to dissolve the Massachusetts charter. "Poor *New England* is much to be pitied. *Boston* people most of all. How falsely misrepresented! What a mercy that our Christian charter cannot be dissolved."[49] Whitefield died, in the words of Stout, both "a Pauline evangelist and an American patriot."[50]

## "Fear God and Honour the King": John Wesley's Rhetoric of Liberty

John Wesley's defense of the poor, his admiration for the common sense of the ordinary person, and his emphasis on religious societies dedicated to self-improvement might suggest Whig politics. He was, in fact, a political conservative with a passionate commitment to the principle of submission to the divinely instituted authority of the Crown. Though Wesley claimed no special expertise in the area of politics, he did write a considerable number of political tracts and expressed very strong political opinions.[51] Wesley's political writings are not heavily theological, but they consistently reject, on historical and pragmatic grounds, John Locke's social contract theory, with its idea that nations should only govern by the consent of the governed.[52] While biblical themes lie in the background of Wesley's political writings, the arguments themselves are based more on political theory and on notions of natural law than on explicitly theological grounds. In fact, Wesley states in *Thoughts upon Slavery* that he developed his argument against slavery by "setting the Bible out of the question."[53] Slaves have the right to rebel against any system that takes away their natural right to liberty, "which they have as much right to as the air they breathe."[54] David Hempton sees Wesley's political conservatism as based not only on an amended Toryism but also on his appreciation for the liberty enjoyed by "free-born Englishmen."[55]

American Methodists have sometimes taken encouragement from the idea that their founder was some kind of protodemocrat and a champion of natural rights. Such a view reads Wesley the way Mahaffey reads Whitefield, as "an accidental revolutionary." Recent scholarship has made this view increasingly untenable.[56] It was the principle of natural rights and human liberty that was most securely preserved in the Hanoverian dynasty. It was this principle, rather than the idea of divine right, that led Wesley to insist on "honouring the King."[57] Wesley held a "constitutional Toryism" that saw the Glorious Revolution as the true beginning of English liberty and made room for the checks and balances placed on the power of the Crown by Parliament.[58] Wesley stood not in the tradition of individual liberty so much as in the tradition that ran from Richard Hooker to Edmund Burke, which asserts an organic unity between the Crown, the Parliament, and the people.[59]

Wesley's fear of English radicalism undergirds all of his political tracts. Both John and Charles Wesley frequently compared the American Revolution with the English Civil War and were fearful that a revolutionary storm beginning in America would soon spread to England.[60] The American troubles were being fomented by those at home who wanted to overthrow the Crown. The colonists were but pawns in a game, unaware that they were being played by the malevolent forces of revolution there.[61] Wesley wrote to his brother Charles in October 1775 that he was in danger of losing his love for Americans, or at least for their leaders. "The bulk of the people both in England and America mean no harm; they only follow their leaders, and do as they are bid, without knowing why or wherefore."[62]

As Bernard Bailyn made clear, it was difficult in the eighteenth century to conceive of "sustained opposition to constituted authority as anything other than the work of parties [which] were believed naturally to degenerate into conspiratorial juntas whose aim in the end could only be the overthrow of the existing government."[63] In such a context, Wesley's outlook was certainly not unusual. During the American Revolution, differences in the conduct of the war in a newly media-saturated culture divided households and led to civic unrest and violence at home. John Wesley was only one of many who responded to widespread popular criticism of the government as disloyal and even treasonous. Rather than being seen as an "arch-Tory" out of step with political realities, Wesley should be seen as holding views typical of a large sector in the wide public debate on the American question.

For their part, the patriots in America also discerned a conspiracy, but one of an opposite kind. Robert Middlekauff attributes to "the character of their Protestantism" the view of "the children of the awakened," that "an evil plot against their liberties had been hatched in a corrupt and faintly 'Catholic' England."[64] The roots of the conflict lay in a conspiracy between ministers of state and their supporters to overthrow the British Crown both in England and America—thus severely limiting, if not annihilating, English liberties.[65]

In 1768 several people died during a civil uprising in response to the denial of a seat in Parliament for radical MP John Wilkes. Wesley responded to this event in *Free Thoughts on the Present State of Public Affairs* (1768).[66] There were riots in the streets as mobs called for justice. They cast the king and Parliament as despots and destroyers of liberty, while revering Wilkes as a champion of civil liberties.[67] For Wesley, however, the king and Parliament represented the best method of securing and maintaining genuine liberty, and Wilkes and his radical followers were the surest way of destroying it. In 1767, the Townsend Acts had placed a tax on a number of commodities in the American colonies—including tea, glass, and paper—which led to a colonial boycott of British goods. Resentment rose further until 1768, when troops were deployed to Boston to put down rioters protesting trade regulations. Wesley showed considerable sympathy for the Americans when he asserted, "I do not defend the measures which have been taken with regard to America: I doubt whether any man can defend them, either on the foot of law, equity, or prudence."[68]

In *Thoughts upon Liberty* (1772), Wesley asserts that the desire for liberty is a rational instinct belonging to all, and that it would be hard to find any people more desirous of it than Britons who had always resisted foreign invasion.[69] Wesley divides liberty into two basic types: religious and civil. Religious liberty, like reason, is endowed by the Creator and is the right of every person—yet it is a liberty that nations have often labored to remove from their citizens.[70] Wesley sets forth a long report on the deprivation of religious liberty in Britain beginning with the days of Mary Tudor. The Act of Uniformity, the Act against Conventicles, and the ejection of ministers from their livings are cited as evidence of English religious intolerance, pointing out that it was no better in Scotland.[71] However, Wesley is careful to note that the situation had been very different under the Hanoverians, who had been true to the word of George I: "I tell you, while I sit on the English throne, no man shall be persecuted for conscience sake."[72] Indeed, Wesley was convinced that there was no other nation in the world that enjoyed such religious liberty as England, where one was free to choose any religion or none.[73] The current cry for liberty could not, therefore, have religious liberty as its object, for no one had been deprived of it.

What then of civil liberty defined as "liberty to enjoy our lives and fortunes in our own way; to use our property, whatever is legally our own, according to our own choice"?[74] Wesley argues as follows: Foreign kings may demand the life of their subjects without cause, but this cannot happen in England, where no one is in danger of losing their civil liberty unless they act contrary to the law. Those who cry for their liberty have no other fetters than those in their imagination.[75] The present unrest and cry for liberty lies in the poisonous propaganda of pamphleteers such as "Junius" and others who, in attacking the king's ministers in the press, attack the king himself. The Parliament's support of the king and a loyal army are all that are preventing the radicals from having their way.[76] Remove the redcoats, and the Parliament would soon be set upon by the mob.[77] Wesley proposes the rather draconian measure of enacting a law making it a capital crime to perpetrate lies designed to breed dissension between the king and the people.[78]

Wesley's concept of liberty as something guaranteed by the Crown may well lie behind the initial sympathy he demonstrated for the American cause. He also had a strong affection for America and Americans; this affection can be traced back to his time spent in Georgia from 1735 to 1738.[79] In June of 1775, Wesley wrote to the Earl of Dartmouth, secretary of state for the American colonies and a friendly evangelical, and the following day Wesley wrote essentially the same letter to the Prime Minister Lord North, outlining his concerns about the American situation.[80] Wesley felt that the Americans had some cause for complaint but pleaded ignorance on the political matters at the heart of the dispute. He was bound, he admitted, to take a conservative stance, being "a High Churchman, the son of a High Churchman, bred up from my childhood in the highest notions of passive obedience and non-resistance." Describing the Americans as "an oppressed People" who had "asked for nothing more than their Legal Rights," he warned that a war with Americans could not easily be won since they were "calm, deliberate Enthusiasts" for liberty. They fought not only for this but also for their wives and children. Such a force would always have the advantage over those who fought merely for pay. He concluded his appeal with a warning to "remember King Charles I," bringing to mind the specter of the

English Civil War, never far beneath the surface of Wesley's fears over radical politics.

This conciliatory and sympathetic attitude toward the Americans and their cause was replaced in 1775 in Wesley's *A Calm Address to Our American Colonies*, probably the best known of John Wesley's political tracts and usually considered the primary source for ascertaining his views on the American Revolution. A Loyalist pamphlet published in September 1775, only a short time after the hostilities at Lexington and Concord, it defended the right of Parliament to tax the American colonies, pointed the Americans to the liberties they already enjoyed under the Crown, and ended with an exhortation to "fear God and honour the king." Up to nineteen editions appeared, with 100,000 copies circulated, within its first year its publication.[81] The bulk of *A Calm Address* was borrowed (plagiarized, said Wesley's detractors), from Samuel Johnson's *Taxation No Tyranny*, published the same year.[82] Johnson was not bothered but delighted by this borrowing. On February 6, 1777, he would write to Wesley, referring to *A Calm Address* as "your important suffrage to my argument on the American question. To have gained such a mind as yours may justly confirm me in my own opinion."[83] In fact, Wesley did Johnson a favor by turning his flowery prose into a more readable style, thus effectively spreading the government's position to a wider audience.

Lord North's government was also delighted, knowing that Wesley, by this time seventy-two years of age and one of the best-known men in England, was heard gladly by many. The government purchased the entire first edition and circulated it to every church in London.[84] The overall argument of *A Calm Address* is that the English Parliament had the rightful power to tax the American colonies and that the inhabitants of British America remain obligated to submit to the king's authority. The colonies were established under royal charters and had no more right to establish their own legislature than the multitudes in England—who had no vote—had a right to establish their own Parliament.

What is to account for Wesley's change of tune in *A Calm Address*? Frank Baker suggests a reaction on Wesley's part to the increasingly militant pro-American discourse in Britain.[85] Wesley himself attributed his change of heart to his reading of Johnson's *Taxation No Tyranny*, stating that "as soon as I received more light myself I judged it my duty to impart it to others."[86] Holland sees Wesley's strengthening support of the king as influenced by the discussions at the Leeds Conference of August 1–3, 1775, in which a group of preachers urged a separation from the Church of England.[87] But this can only be a supposition.[88] Perhaps more significant than all of these suggestions is that the king's Proclamation of Rebellion on August 23, 1775, declared that anyone aiding or abetting the Americans would be considered treasonous. This tended to put a damper on the more diverse discussion of the situation that had prevailed earlier. Wesley could not now show sympathy for the Americans without the possibility of an accusation of treason.[89]

Though *A Calm Address* caused quite a stir, and many responses appeared in the British press, its direct impact in British America was likely to be minimal. In October 1775, Wesley told Thomas Rankin, his assistant in America, "I had written a little tract upon the subject before I knew the American ports were shut up."[90] The oft-repeated claim that Methodists destroyed copies when they reached America in order to protect themselves from the charge of being Loyalist is built on very little evidence and has perhaps gained credence because of its appearance in Robert Southey's influential biography of Wesley.[91] On October 20, 1775, Wesley wrote to Thomas Rankin that there were those who "would willingly burn me and it together."[92] It should be remembered, however, that he is referring here to people in England—not to the American colonies. Apart from this, there appears to be no further evidence for the "burning of the pamphlets" story, and in fact the claim is directly refuted by Wesley's own reference to the closing of the American ports and his inability to "send it abroad as I designed."[93] No copies of the original *A Calm Address* could have been burned in America by Methodists or anybody else since none ever reached there.

The following year, 1776, Wesley published *Some Observations on Liberty Occasioned by a Late Tract*, a response to Richard Price's *Observations on the Nature of Civil Liberty*. In it Wesley rejected Price's claim that there could be no liberty without independence. British subjects already had perfect liberty under the Crown.[94]

Wesley lauded Price as "a man of uncommon abilities" who had produced "a masterpiece of its kind" and had written accurately and with a sincere desire to serve the subjects of the British Empire. Nonetheless,

Wesley wished to add a few further thoughts on the subject.[95] This polite beginning hardly masks the fact that Wesley considered Price's work a "dangerous tract . . . which if practiced would overturn all government and bring in universal anarchy."[96]

Wesley's single aim in replying to Price was to determine whether the American cry for liberty was just or unjust. Wesley was insistent that the colonists already had perfect liberty under the Crown and that what they were actually claiming was independence, wishing "no longer to own the English supremacy." At first they hid this intention but now they had made it plain, and Englishmen applaud them for it.[97] For Wesley, the greater the share the people had in government, the less liberty existed. The most civil and religious liberty is available under a limited monarchy, less under an aristocracy, and least of all under a democracy.[98]

Wesley's anti-American rhetoric reached a high point in his *Calm Address to the Inhabitants of England* (February 1777). After this his responses were more muted, in order to calm the people's fears about French Catholic aggression in the event of an American victory. Even as early as December 1775, Wesley seemed willing to admit defeat. The war had been expensive and was not likely to resolve; it was better to let the Americans have their independence.[99] War had proven unavoidable, and the time had now come to reassure people that England and Ireland were still safe from their enemies. Claims that England was facing financial ruin were countered in an attempt to encourage the populace.[100] The entry of the French into the war caused particular concern, and Wesley noted fear and panic among the people not seen since the days of the Glorious Revolution.[101] After contact with the Loyalist Joseph Galloway, Wesley grew concerned about the way the war was being conducted and published three pamphlets critical of the British military command.[102] As the war continued, Wesley said less about it and seemed to retreat to the refuge of Providence. God, it seemed, was cleansing both sides of the conflict, sweeping away the wicked with the broom of destruction.[103] From 1780, Wesley began to turn his discourse away from the war itself and toward anti-Catholic activity, fearing that French involvement in the war might lead to a Catholic-backed revolution in England.[104] Wesley grew increasingly disillusioned with the conduct of the Parliament, and in 1783 he expressed the wish to his brother Charles that the king would act the despot and rule his own country rather than defer to a prime minister who could not get things right.[105]

## Conclusion

Wesley and Whitefield both supported the Hanoverian dynasty as a guarantee of religious and civil liberty and because of their genuine affection for George II and George III, with a corresponding rejection of the claims of the Stuarts. Wesley and Whitefield also shared the conviction that French Catholic aggression represented tyranny and the threat of arbitrary power. Their differences over the American rebellion were more speculative, at least in regard to Whitefield, whose death in 1770 precludes anything beyond speculation. It is quite possible that Whitefield might have supported the American Revolution, given his love for Americans and his heartfelt sympathy for their grievances. It could be argued, on the other hand, that for all of his support for the American cause, Whitefield never lost a corresponding loyalty to the Crown. It may be that, like Wesley, when complaint over injured liberties was replaced by the cry for independence, Whitefield, if he had lived to see the day, might have turned against the Americans in a similar fashion. James Habersham, Whitefield's good friend and the cofounder of Bethesda College, stands as a good example of one who opposed British administration in America and supported the colonial cause yet drew the line at independence, remaining a Loyalist after war was declared.[106]

However, where Wesley saw the cry for independence as unmasking a hidden plot to overthrow the king not only in America but also at home in England, Whitefield did not express alarm at developing colonial discontent but rather remained a warm advocate for the Americans, supporting them in all of their grievances. Even though they opposed the Sugar Act and the Stamp Act, rejected an Anglican episcopacy in America, and deeply resented British troops in the streets of Boston, Whitefield never took the Americans to task for disloyalty. He never publicly forsook loyalty to the Crown (in 1770 at the opening of his beloved Bethesda College in Loyalist Georgia, he urged a hearty "Amen" to the governor's toast to the king),[107] yet he never came close to accusing the Americans of being pawns in a plot to overthrow the king or the Parliament.

Whitefield was much more ready to support "holy wars" in the cause of liberty than Wesley was. Beginning with the Louisbourg Expedition and through the Seven Years' War and the Jacobite rebellion, Whitefield used his considerable rhetorical powers to enlist supporters of liberty in order to resist tyranny and arbitrary power by military means. When the discourse switched in the Revolutionary period from French to English tyranny, it would be easy to see how Whitefield might have supported the American cause. Certainly his heroic and iconic status during the war, albeit posthumously, demonstrates that Americans saw him as on their side of the conflict.

While both Wesley and Whitefield felt the threat of French, and therefore Catholic, tyranny, Wesley preached no enlistment sermons and tended to be more damning of wars between professedly Christian nations. After 1775, he consistently maintained that the Americans already had perfect liberty under the Crown and that they had become the "dupes of designing men" who sought not only an American war but another English civil war. When the war finally ended, Wesley remained somewhat bitter toward American leaders and was never fully reconciled to the new situation. When Princeton's John Witherspoon, a signer of the Declaration of Independence, was invited to England for a fund-raiser, Wesley could not offer support.[108] Once independence from Britain was secured, Wesley could do no less than urge the Methodists to render due submission to the established government. Yet there is a note of caution, perhaps even suspicion, in his advice to Thomas Coke in 1789: "I wish you to obey 'the powers that be' in America; but I wish you to understand them too."[109] This cool distance from Americans stands in sharp contrast to Whitefield's emotional, even gushing attachment.

The rhetoric of liberty rings somewhat hollow in light of the existence of slavery in the American colonies and its continuance into the new republic. Whitefield's purchase and use of slaves, even though accompanied by advocacy for their humane treatment, was driven by the financial needs of the Bethesda Orphanage and was clearly a blind spot in his thinking. Wesley, on the other hand, whose *Thoughts on Slavery* was the first significant non-Quaker treatises on the topic, saw clearly the inconsistency of Americans crying for liberty while justifying slavery and exploited this logical lapse for his own rhetorical purposes in opposing it.

On his seventh and final voyage to America, in 1769, Whitefield, motivated by a growing sensitivity to the tension between Britain and its American colonies, turned to a study of constitutional histories of England and the theme of liberty. In the wake of the Stamp Act and with British troops en route to Boston, Whitefield headed in a decidedly Whiggish direction, with the colonial patriot cause ever closer to his heart. He died an American patriot in 1770, and it seems unlikely that in the few short years that followed he would have backed away from his political commitments. Faced with a choice between England and America, Whitefield may well have chosen America, his colonial identity proving even stronger than his allegiance to the Crown. Usually when Wesley and Whitefield are compared and contrasted, scholars focus on the differences regarding absolute predestination and unconditional election. Certainly this theological difference placed considerable strain on the two men's relationship, both privately and in the public sphere, but there were also political differences. If Whitefield had lived to take a stand on the American Revolution, the differences between these two famous Methodists regarding the foundations of genuine liberty may well have thrown even the heated controversy about predestination into the shade.

## Notes

1. An earlier and shorter version of this chapter was presented as a paper at the George Whitefield @ 300 Conference held at Pembroke College, Oxford, June 25–27, 2014. I would like to thank the Oxford Centre for Methodism and Church History at Oxford Brookes University, the Wesley Summer Seminar at Asbury Theological Seminary, and the Summer Wesley Seminar at the Centre for Studies in the Wesleyan Tradition, Duke Divinity School, all of whom provided resources for the writing of this article and the larger project of which it is a part. I am also grateful to Booth College for the provision of study leave.

2. Jerome Dean Mahaffey, *The Accidental Revolutionary: George Whitefield and the Creation of America* (Waco, TX: Baylor University Press, 2011), 172. Such veneration of Whitefield's relics continued after the Revolution. Methodist circuit rider Jesse Lee descended into Whitefield's vault in 1789 and removed the coffin lid so he could gaze on

his remains and handle his skull before praying for a similar anointing on his own ministry. Leroy M. Lee, The Life and Times of Jesse Lee (Louisville, KY: John Early, 1849), 246, cited in Mahaffey, *Accidental Revolutionary*, 172. When the Baptist minister David Marks visited the vault in 1834, he described the coffin as "one third full of black earth. Out of which projected a few bones. The skull bone was detached from the rest and turned over." Jon Butler, *Awash in a Sea of Faith: Christianizing the American People* (Cambridge, MA: Harvard University Press, 1990), 188. The disturbed state of his remains suggests frequent reverential handling over time. Indeed his skull was removed and two hundred replicas were made for public display. Mahaffey, *Accidental Revolutionary*, 172.

3. Mark A. Noll, *Christians in the American Revolution* (Vancouver: Regent College Publishing, 2006, reprint of 1977 edition), 25–27.

4. Mark A. Noll, *America's God: From Jonathan Edwards to Abraham Lincoln* (New York: Oxford University Press, 2002), 83.

5. Nathan O. Hatch, *The Sacred Cause of Liberty: Republican Thought and the Millennium in Revolutionary New England* (New Haven: Yale University Press, 1977), 54.

6. Jerome Dean Mahaffey, *Preaching Politics: The Religious Rhetoric of George Whitefield and the Founding of a New Nation* (Waco, TX: Baylor University Press, 2007); Mahaffey, Accidental Revolutionary.

7. Mahaffey, *Accidental Revolutionary*, 37.

8. Ibid., 169–170.

9. Ibid., 101–102. Mahaffey also argued that when Whitefield spoke of the gift of the Spirit as "the common privilege" of all believers, he was drawing on the concept of natural rights found in Locke's Treatises on Civil Government, borrowing a political belief to explain a religious idea. Ibid., 89, 102. This seems to be drawing a somewhat long bow, and Mahaffey asserts rather than demonstrates that link.

10. His theological missteps in Preaching Politics include mistranslating *ordo salutis* as "way of salvation" rather than "order of salvation" (Mahaffey, *Preaching Politics*, 64), misrepresenting both Calvinism and Arminianism (ibid., 79), and describing regeneration as a continuum (ibid., 77–78). The term dispensational doctrine on page 91 seems anachronistic. Mahaffey's description of the colonial setting lacks nuance by assuming a uniformly negative attitude toward the British administration. He does not seem to do justice to the Loyalist sentiment that existed among non-Anglicans (though he does concede a degree of Loyalist sentiment when discussing Thomas Paine's *Common Sense*, ibid., 231–243). His claim that Americans uniformly converted from Tories to Whigs is altogether too neat. His account of the fear that the appointment of an Anglican bishop would open the door to the arbitrary power of the papacy does not seem to take into account the anti-Roman sentiment that existed among Anglicans themselves. It seems highly unlikely that Whitefield ever questioned the concepts of divine right to rule and of hereditary succession, yet Mahaffey asserts this idea without providing support for it (ibid., 232). The work is marred by several non sequiturs, including the idea that Thomas Paine, in adopting a ministerial tone in *Common Sense*, donned "the rhetorical robes of George Whitefield" (ibid., 240–241).

11. Harry S. Stout, *The Divine Dramatist: George Whitefield and the Rise of Modern Evangelicalism* (Grand Rapids, MI: William B. Eerdmans, 1991).

12. Stout, *Divine Dramatist*, 219.

13. Noll, *Christians and the American Revolution*, chap. 2.

14. George Whitefield, "An Answer to the First Part," and "An Answer to the Second Part of an Anonymous Pamphlet," in *The Works of the Rev. George Whitefield* (London: 1771), 4:123–140; 141–169, hereafter referred to as Whitefield, *Works*.

15. Whitefield, *Works*, 4:129, 132–313.

16. Ibid., 129.

17. Stout, *Divine Dramatist*, 195–196.

18. Ibid., 252.

19. Whitefield, *Works*, 5:79–93.

20. Mahaffey, *Accidental Revolutionary*, 107–115.

21. Hatch, *Sacred Cause of Liberty*, 76. For a wider range view of how the rhetoric of Catholic conspiracies informed political ideas in early America, see Owen Stanwood, *The Empire Reformed: English America in the Age of the Glorious Revolution* (Philadelphia: University of Pennsylvania Press, 2013).

22. Whitefield, *Works*, 5:82.

23. Ibid., 5:83.

24. Mahaffey, *Accidental Revolutionary*, 129–130.

25. George Whitefield, "A Short Address to Persons of All Denominations Occasioned by the Alarm of an Intended Invasion, in the Year 1756," in Whitefield, *Works*, 4:263–274.

26. Ibid., 4:267.

27. Ibid., 4:267–268.

28. Ibid., 4:268.

29. Ibid., 4:274.

30. John Wesley, "Upon Our Lord's Sermon on the Mount: Discourse the Second," in Albert C. Outler, ed., *The Works of John Wesley: Sermons I*, 1–33 (Nashville, TN: Abingdon, 1984), 1:507–508.

31. John Wesley to the Methodist Societies, October 24, 1779, *The Letters of the Rev. John Wesley, A.M.*, ed. John Telford, 8 vols. (London: Epworth Press, 1931), 6:360, hereafter cited as *Letters* (Telford); see also John Wesley to Thomas Webb, May 25, 1782, *Letters* (Telford), 7:123–124; John Wesley to Ann Loxdale, July 24, 1782, *Letters* (Telford), 7:130–131.

32. Whitefield, "Short Address," in Whitefield, *Works*, 6:271.

33. Stout, *Divine Dramatist*, 255.

34. William Gordon, *The History of the Rise, Progress and Establishment of the United States*, 2nd ed., 3 vols. (New York: Samuel Campbell, 1794), 1:102, cited in Elis Sandoz, *Political Sermons of the American Founding Era*, Vol. 1, 1730–1788 (Indianapolis: Liberty Fund, 1991), 121.

35. Mahaffey, *Accidental Revolutionary*, 160–161.

36. Ibid., 166–167.

37. George Whitefield, "A Letter to the Reverend Dr. Durell, Vice-Chancellor of the University of Oxford. Occasioned by the expulsion of Six Students from Edmund Hall," (April 12, 1768), in Whitefield, *Works*, 4:311–41 (esp. 325–126).

38. Ibid., 4:326.

39. Ibid., 4:335–336.

40. George Whitefield, "A Letter to the Inhabitants of Maryland, Virginia, North and South Carolina," (January 23, 1740), in Whitefield, *Works*, 4:37.

41. Ibid., 4:39–41.

42. Stout, *Divine Dramatist*, 100–101, 258, 272c273. See Glen O'Brien, *'Freedom in the Atlantic World: John Wesley and George Whitefield on Slavery,' Wesley and Whitefield? Wesley versus Whitefield?*, ed. Ian Maddock (Eugene, OR: Pickwick, 2018), 161–182.

43. Ibid., 198.

44. Whitefield, Letter DCCXIV "To the Honourable Trustees of Georgia," December 6, 1748, in Whitefield, *Works*, 2:208–209.

45. John Wesley, "Thoughts upon Slavery," in *Works*, ed. Thomas Jackson, 3rd ed., 14 vols. (London: Wesleyan Methodist Book Room, 1872; reprint, Grand Rapids: Baker Book House, 1979) 11:71–72, hereafter referred to as Wesley, *Works* (Jackson).

46. Stout, *Divine Dramatist*, 198–199.

47. John Wesley, *Some Observations on Liberty Occasioned by a Late Tract* (London, 1776); Wesley, *Works* (Jackson), 11:90–118.

48. Wesley, "Thoughts upon Slavery," in *Works* (Jackson), 11:72–74.

49. George Whitefield, Letter MCCCCLXV, "To Mr. R - K - n. Portsmouth, New Hampshire," September 23, 1770, in Whitefield, *Works*, 3:426.

50. Stout, *Divine Dramatist*, 287.

51. I have drawn some of the material in this section from Glen O'Brien, "John Wesley's Rebuke to the Rebels of British America: Revisiting the 'Calm Address.'" *Methodist Review* 4 (2012): 31–55.

52. David Hempton cited without bibliographical detail in E. Atiba, "The Rhetoric of Liberty: John Wesley and the Polemics of the American Revolution," honors thesis, Duke University, 1996, 69.

53. Wesley, "Thoughts upon Slavery," in *Works* (Jackson), 11:70.

54. Ibid., 11:68.

55. Ronald H. Stone, *John Wesley's Life and Ethics* (Nashville, TN: Abingdon Press, 2001), 173, citing David Hempton, *The Religion of the People: Methodism and Popular Religion, c. 1750–1900* (London: Routledge, 1996), 82.

56. Jason Vickers sets out a very helpful survey on the changing views of Wesley's political philosophy—from those like Maldwyn Edwards and William Warren Sweet, who saw him as a High Church Tory, to those like Bernard Semmel and Leon E. Hynson, who saw him as a Whiggish champion of liberty in a second-stage development of his thinking. Jason E. Vickers, "Honouring the King: The Politics of Divine Right," chap. 3 in *Wesley: A Guide for the Perplexed* (London: T & T Clark, 2009), 60–82. For his own part, Vickers argues for an essential unity to Wesley's political thought based on what he calls Wesley's "covenantal Arminianism." Ibid., 108–110.

57. Hempton, *Religion of the People*, 80–82. Theodore Jennings also stresses Wesley's commitment to principles over party in portraying him as a champion of human rights and a forerunner to liberation theology. Theodore W. Jennings, *Good News to the Poor: John Wesley's Evangelical Economics* (Nashville, TN: Abingdon Press, 1990), 200.

58. Vickers, "Honouring the King," 60–82; Theodore R. Weber, *Politics and the Order of Salvation* (Nashville, TN: Abingdon, 2001), 149–151.

59. Weber, Politics and the Order of Salvation, 30.

60. John Wesley to Thomas Rankin, April 21, 1775, *Letters* (Telford), 6:147–148; John Wesley to Charles Wesley, June 2, 1775, *Letters* (Telford), 6:152–153. Charles Wesley, 'Hymns on Patriotism,' 23, lines 67–72, cited in Donald S. Baker, "Charles Wesley and the American War of Independence," *Proceedings of the Wesley Historical Society* 34 (1964): 161.

61. John Wesley to Thomas Rankin, August 13, 1775, *Letters* (Telford), 6:173.

62. John Wesley to Charles Wesley, October 17, 1775, *Letters* (Telford), 6:179.

63. Bernard Bailyn, *The Origins of American Politics* (New York: Vintage, 1970), 36.

64. Robert Middlekauff, *The Glorious Cause: The American Revolution, 1763–1789* (New York: Oxford University Press, 2005), 146.

65. Bailyn, *Origins of American Politics*, 10–13.

66. *Letters* (Telford), 5:370–388; Wesley, "Thoughts upon Slavery," in *Works* (Jackson), 11:14–33. Wesley's "Thoughts upon Liberty" (1772) and "Thoughts Concerning the Origin of Power" (1772) also arose out of the Wilkes controversy.

67. For recent biographies of Wilkes, see J. Sainsbury, *John Wilkes: The Lives of a Libertine* (Aldershot, UK: Ashgate, 2006); Arthur H. Cash, *John Wilkes: The Scandalous Father of Civil Liberty* (New Haven: Yale University Press, 2007); Peter D.G. Thomas, *John Wilkes: A Friend to Liberty*(Oxford: Oxford University Press, 1992)."

68. John Wesley, "Free Thoughts on the Present State of Public Affairs," in *Works* (Jackson), 11:24.

69. John Wesley, "Thoughts upon Liberty," in *Works* (Jackson), 11:34.

70. Ibid., 11:37–38.

71. Ibid., 11:38–40.

72. Ibid., 11:40.

73. Ibid., 11:40–41.

74. Ibid., 11:41.

75. Ibid., 11:42.

76. According to Lutnick, "George III and the North ministry had very little trouble managing Parliament between 1775 and 1782. The King's measures were so certain of passing through the House of Commons with a handsome majority that he could afford to ignore popular opinion." Solomon Lutnick, *The American Revolution and the British Press 1775–1783* (Columbia: University of Missouri Press, 1967), viii.

77. Wesley, "Thoughts upon Liberty," in *Works* (Jackson), 11:43–45.

78. Ibid., 11:45.

79. Zele maintains, however, that Wesley's views of America and Americans were negatively affected by his time in Georgia. "For Wesley, the map of America that existed in his mind was of a large Georgia colony covering the entire eastern seaboard. Wesley understood that larger cities existed in Boston, Philadelphia, and New York, but when he wrote about the American environment or residents, he was almost always describing Georgia." Adam Scott Zele, "John Wesley's America" (PhD diss., Duke University, 2008), 339–340. Wesley's time in Georgia is usually seen negatively and in terms of failure. For an important revisionist account in a more positive light, see Geordan Hammond, *John Wesley in America: Restoring Primitive Christianity* (Oxford: Oxford University Press, 2014).

80. John Wesley to the Earl of Dartmouth, June 14, 1775, *Letters* (Telford), 6:155–160; John Wesley to Lord North, June 15, 1775, ibid., 160–164. J. C. D. Clark uses Wesley's letter to Lord Dartmouth to demonstrate how English politics were polarized concerning support or rejection of the king's actions. J. C. D. Clark, *The Language of Liberty 1660–1832: Political Discourse and Social Dynamics in the Anglo-American World* (Cambridge: Cambridge University Press, 1994), 297.

81. It first appeared in Bristol, but it is the second edition, published in London shortly after, that appears in the Jackson edition of Wesley's *Works*. This second edition

carries a slight amendment. The statement "Our sovereign has a right to tax me . . . whether we have votes for Parliament-men or no" is softened by the addition of a footnote on page 21 that qualifies the king's right to tax his subjects—"That is, in connection with the Lords and Commons." I have consulted the London edition printed by R. Hawes, in Dorset-Street, Spitalfields, 1775, though I reference the version in the Jackson edition of Wesley's *Works* in this article for the convenience of readers. The circulation figures are drawn from Sandoz, *Political Sermons*, 410.

82. Samuel Johnson, *Taxation No Tyranny: An Answer to the Resolutions and Address of the American Congress* (London, 1775).

83. Samuel Johnson to John Wesley, January 6, 1776, in Sandoz, *Political Sermons*, 424. Raymond argues that Johnson probably encouraged Wesley to publish a popular edition and even suggests that the pamphlet was "produced at the urging of the government," but admits there is no proof of this. Allan Raymond, "'I Fear God and Honor the King': John Wesley and the American Revolution," *Church History* 45 (September 1976): 321–322. Wesley certainly had greater appeal to the masses than Johnson.

84. Sandoz, *Political Sermons*, 424.

85. Frank Baker, "The Shaping of Wesley's 'Calm Address,'" *Methodist History* 14 (1975): 4–5.

86. John Wesley, "A Calm Address to the Inhabitants of England," in *Works* (Jackson), 11:80.

87. Lynwood M. Holland, "John Wesley and the American Revolution," *A Journal of Church and State* 5 (1963): 201.

88. Allan Raymond believes that Holland confuses dates and "should be used with great caution." Raymond, "I Fear God and Honor the King," 316.

89. Frederick V. Mills Jr., "New Light on Methodists and the Revolutionary War," *Methodist History* 28 (1989): 60.

90. Richard P. Heitzenrater, *Wesley and the People Called Methodists* (Nashville, TN: Abingdon Press, 1995), 262. Also John Wesley, Letter to Thomas Rankin, October 20, 1775, *Letters* (Telford), 6:182.

91. Robert Southey, *The Life of Wesley and the Rise and Progress of Methodism*, ed. Maurice Fitzgerald, 2 vols. (London: 1925), 2:244. Riggs also makes this claim. Riggs, "John Wesley and the American Revolution Reconsidered," undated (c. 1976) typed manuscript, 3, Frank Baker Papers, Rare Book, Manuscript and Special Collections Library, Duke University, box 7. Riggs is citing Thomas Walter Herbert, *John Wesley as Editor and Author* (Princeton: Princeton University Press, 1940), 106–107.

92. John Wesley to Thomas Rankin, October 20, 1775, *Letters* (Telford), 6:182.

93. Wesley, "A Calm Address to Our American Colonies," in *Works* (Jackson), 11:129. The American ports were closed on July 20, 1775, as a result of a decision of the Continental Congress of July 4–6.

94. Price was a nonconformist of Arian persuasion who became a leading figure as a result of the success of this pamphlet. He declared that all civil government originates with the people and has only their happiness in view. Magistrates are trustees or deputies of the people engaged to bring that happiness into effect. Richard Price, *Observations on the Nature of Civil Liberty, the Principles of Government, and the Justice and Policy of the War with America* (London, 1776), 6–7.

95. John Wesley, "Some Observations on Liberty," in *Works* (Jackson) 11: 90.

96. Wesley wrote these words on Thursday, April 4, 1776, the day he began to write "Some Observations on Liberty." W. Reginald Ward and Richard P. Heitzenrater, *The Works of John Wesley*, vol. 23, *Journals and Diaries VI* (1776–1786) (Nashville, TN: Abingdon Press, 1995), 8, hereafter referred to as Ward and Heitzenrater, *Journals and Diaries.*

97. Wesley, "Some Observations on Liberty," in *Works* (Jackson), 11:92.

98. Ibid., 11:105.

99. John Wesley, Letter to Christopher Hopper, December 26, 1775 *Letters* (Telford), 6:199.

100. John Wesley, "A Serious Address to the People of England, with Regard to the State of the Nations" (1778), in *Works* (Jackson), 11:140–149.

101. John Wesley, entries for March 1–4, 1778, Ward and Heitzenrater, *Journal and Diaries*, 6:76.

102. John Wesley, *An Account of the Conduct of the War in the Middle Colonies. Extracted from a Late Author* (1780); *An Extract from a Reply to the Observations of Lieut. Gen. Sir William Howe, on a Pamphlet entitled, Letters to a Nobleman* (1781), *An Extract of a Letter to the Right Honourable Lord Viscount H[ow]e on his Naval Conduct in the American War* (1781).

103. John Wesley to Christopher Hopper, October 25, 1780, *Letters* (Telford), 7:36–37.

104. John Wesley to the Printer of the Public Advertiser, January 12, 1780, *Letters* (Telford), 6:370–373; John Wesley to the editors of the Freeman's Journal, March 23, 1780, *Letters* (Telford), 7:3–9; and March 31, 1780, *Letters* (Telford), 7:3–16.

105. John Wesley to Charles Wesley, April 4, 1783, *Letters* (Telford), 7:173–174.

106. I am thankful to Frank Lambert for making this observation when this chapter, at the time a research paper, was first presented at Pembroke College, Oxford. See Frank Lambert, *James Habersham: Loyalty, Commerce and Politics in Colonial Georgia* (Athens: University of Georgia Press, 2015). See also Lambert's influential *Peddler in Divinity: George Whitefield and the Transatlantic Revivals* (Princeton: Princeton University Press, 1994).

107. Stout, *Divine Dramatist*, 274.

108. John Wesley to Brian Bury Collins, March 11, 1784, *Letters* (Telford), 7:214.

109. John Wesley to Thomas Coke, September 5, 1789, *Letters* (Telford), 8:163–164. It is possible of course that "the powers that be" here refers to the Methodist hierarchy, but in my view it seems unlikely, since Coke and Asbury were officially equal in authority—though clearly Asbury's actual authority far exceeded that of Dr. Coke, who was often seen by American itinerants as an inconsistent and bumbling meddler in their affairs.

# The Enlightenment in the Historical Imagination of Evangelical and Awakened Protestants in Europe, Britain, and North America, c. 1750–1850

*Andrew Kloes*

In the first volume of his encyclopaedic interpretation of the history of the Enlightenment, Jonathan Israel remarked how the "rationalization and secularization" of intellectual life that had been inaugurated by the Enlightenment must be recognized as "one of the most important shifts in the history of man."[1] Its significance for Western cultural development lays in how it had succeeded in calling into question in the minds of many Europeans, from the Atlantic Coasts of New England and Great Britain to the Ural Mountains of Russia, the "veracity of the Bible and the Christian faith."[2] According to Israel, the primary intellectual engine of the Enlightenment was its radical wing, which "whether on an atheistic or deistic basis, rejected all compromise with the [Christian] past [of Europe];" denied all orthodox beliefs concerning creation, providence, miracles, life after death; and "refused to accept that there is any God-ordained social hierarchy."[3] Israel's analysis follows a long historiographical tradition of conceptualizing an essential antithesis between the official orthodoxy of most ancient, medieval, and early modern Christian churches in

Europe and the anthropology and cosmology of many Enlightenment-era thinkers.

Two of the most trenchant antecedent analyses of the developmental history of European philosophy and Christian theology during the era of the Enlightenment were written by distinguished émigré scholars from Germany and the Soviet Union: Ernst Cassirer, who taught at the Universities of Berlin and Hamburg before moving to Columbia University, and Isaiah Berlin, who spent the entirety of his academic life at the University of Oxford. Philosophers by training, Cassirer and Berlin independently advanced the bold historical thesis that the numerous commonly referred to simply as "the Enlightenment" all had one single common denominator: the repudiation of the historic orthodox doctrine of original sin and the entire systems of Christian doctrine that were built upon it.

Cassirer and Berlin observed that the rejection of the traditional confessional Catholic and Protestant understandings of the doctrine of sin (hamartiology), once had profound implications for virtually every other area of Christian belief, especially the doctrines of God (theology proper), mankind (anthropology), and salvation (soteriology), and thereby had introduced a major caesura into European religious and intellectual history. As Cassirer remarked in his 1932 standard work, *Die Philosophie der Aufklärung*:

> The idea of original sin was the common opponent against which all of the different philosophical movements of the Enlightenment united together. On this subject, Hume stood on the side of the English deists and Rousseau locked arms with Voltaire. The common pursuit of this goal, towards which the entire Enlightenment strove, seemed to transcend, at least for a time, all of the abiding disagreements concerning the particular means by which this outcome was to be achieved.[4]

In a subsequent section, Cassirer turned his attention to the results of this move within academic theology.

> The rejection of the dogma of original sin was the characteristic hallmark of the basic direction of the theology of the Enlightenment, especially as it developed in Germany, where it had its most

> important proponents. These Enlightened theologians all regarded the idea of an historical original sin, the consequences of which had been inherited by future generations of humanity's first parents, as absolutely absurd and an affront to the most foundational laws of logic and ethics. . . . While the controversy over the dogma of original sin in France led to the sharpest separation between religion and philosophy, eighteenth-century German Protestants demonstrated that they were capable of essentially transforming their faith through incorporating contemporary trends in philosophy, whereby they either destroyed or abandoned the historical tenets of Protestantism.[5]

Such observations were part of Cassirer's larger imagination of European religious history since the end of the Middle Ages as a perpetually evolving conflict between what he referred to as the "humanism, Pelagianism, and religious universalism" of the Renaissance and the Enlightenment, and the "biblical Christianity, Augustinianism, and religious exclusivism" of the Reformation.[6]

In 1968, Berlin published his famous essay on "The Counter-Enlightenment," in which he recognized two general types of opposition to the Enlightenment: religious and romantic.[7] According to Berlin, religious opposition to the Enlightenment came from those who opposed both "the proclamation of the autonomy of reason and the methods of the natural sciences based on observation as the sole reliable method of knowledge," and the concomitant "rejection of the authority of revelation, sacred writings and their accepted interpreters, tradition, prescription, and every form of non-rational and transcendent source of knowledge."[8] Berlin observed how:

> What the entire Enlightenment has in common is denial of the central Christian doctrine of original sin, believing instead that man is born either innocent and good, or morally neutral and malleable by education or environment, or, at worst, deeply defective but capable of radical and indefinite improvement by rational education in favourable circumstances, or by a revolutionary reorganisation of society.[9]

Berlin then examined how "the powerful reaffirmation of the Pauline and Augustinian doctrine of original sin was the sharpest single weapon in the root and branch attack on the entire Enlightenment," which, in his view, had been most significantly led by the French Roman Catholic intellectuals Joseph de Maistre, Louis Gabriel Ambroise de Bonald, and François-René de Chateaubriand.[10]

I begin this essay by rehearsing the well-known historical interpretations of the Enlightenment that have been advanced by Cassirer, Berlin, and Israel so that I may place into historiographical context the following discussion of how certain Protestant intellectuals writing between 1750 and 1850 comprehended the same changes in Western intellectual life and cultural consensus. Spanning the mid-eighteenth to the mid-nineteenth centuries was a series of popular religious developments throughout Protestant communities on both sides of the Atlantic, known as the "First and Second Great Awakenings" in America,[11] the "evangelical revival" in Great Britain,[12] the "Erweckungsbewegung" in German-speaking Europe,[13] the "opwekking" in the Netherlands,[14] the "réveil"[15] in French-speaking Europe, and similar names in Scandinavia.[16] The Protestant intellectuals whom I will discuss here are those who were recognized as prominent leaders in these movements, which I will hereafter refer to synonymously as evangelicalism and awakened Protestantism.

When these individuals spoke of "religious revivals" and "awakenings," as having occurred or needing to occur, they implied through their invocation of such notions a particular historical verdict, apart from which those terms were meaningless. This rhetoric reflected their subjective perceptions, indeed, their theological judgments, in which they measured the contemporary conditions of religious life in their societies against either earlier, idealized historical periods or a purely ideal state of religious affairs. Of course, as an academic discipline, history lacks both the methodological resources and the interpretative vantage point to judge as to whether or not either an awakening (or an enlightenment) actually took place, but through studying how such terms were used, history can provide insights into the mentalities of the members of religious communities during a period of significant cultural change.

It is important to recognize that there were many abiding differences between those Protestants whose religious beliefs and activities constituted these contemporary, largely analogous, religious movements. However, I will argue that it is possible to observe a fundamental commonality between those modern British, continental European, and North American Protestants, who were eager to affirm the doctrinal inheritance of the ancient creeds and the Reformation confessions. This commonality is to be found in the highly similar ways in which they imagined history and thereby conceptualized their religious identities in relation to a particular historical metanarrative. I will discuss this historical metanarrative through a comparative analysis of how such Protestants imagined history as a progressively unfolding cosmic struggle of spiritual warfare between the devil and the people of God. In this view of history, successive periods were distinguished by the degree of divine or diabolical superintendence of historical development that transpired under the mysterious providence of God.

In his insightful history of historiography in Western culture, written in exile from Germany as a refugee professor at the New School for Social Research in New York City, the philosopher and future University of Heidelberg professor Karl Löwith regarded the belief that spiritual warfare was going on behind mundane history as one of the quintessential aspects of what he called "the biblical view of history":

> Seen in the perspective of the world's history, Jesus Christ is the founder of a new sect; seen with the eyes of faith, he is the *Kyrios Christos* and thereby the Lord of history. While the lords of the history of the world are Alexanders and Caesars, Napoleons and Hitlers, Jesus Christ is the Lord of the Kingdom of God and therefore of a secular history only in so far as the history of the world hides a redemptive meaning. The particular stories of the world are but indirectly related to the narrow but universal history of salvation and in themselves incommensurate with it. Merely as a background and as empirical instruments in God's dealing with man are empires and world-historical persons drawn into the orbit of the biblical perspective of history

> in the Old and New Testament. Behind the visible figures and happenings, mysterious powers are invisibly working as *archontes* or primary agents (Romans 13:1 [ἐξουσίαις]; 1 Corinthians 2:8 [ἀρχόντων]). Since Christ these powers are already subjected and broken, but still they are powerfully alive. Invisibly, history has fundamentally changed; visibly it is still the same, for the Kingdom of God is already at hand, and yet, as an *eschaton*, still to come.[17]

Löwith originally published these ideas in English in 1949 as *Meaning in History*, a work that was translated into German in 1953 as *Weltgeschichte und Heilsgeschichte.*

I will argue that during the century of Western cultural transition to modernity (circa 1750–1850) awakened Protestant intellectuals in continental Europe, Britain, and North America drew upon the theological resources of their Protestant traditions to formulate a new imagination of history, one whose leitmotif was supernatural spiritual warfare between the devil and the people of God. Such an understanding of history was integral to how they thought of their religious identity as the righteous opponents of wickedness. I will demonstrate how such Protestants perceived the Enlightenment, the French Revolution, and subsequent revolutions to be works of the devil, to which God was responding, or to which God would soon respond, in two interrelated ways: through executing a punitive judgment on the wicked and through bringing about a religious revival for the preservation of the righteous true church. They believed that this is what God had done earlier in European history at the time of the Reformation. This distinctive evangelical Protestant imagination of history clarifies how awakened Protestantism was an intrinsically modern development that arose in multiple Protestant contexts during the century of Europe and North America's "transition to modernity." The historiographical concept of a "transition to modernity" during this time was formulated by the late University of Bielefeld professor Reinhart Koselleck and the other contributors to the multivolume work, *Geschichtliche Grundbegriffe: Historisches Lexikon zur politisch-sozialen Sprache in Deutschland*, to describe related developments in many areas of Western culture during the century from 1750 to 1850.[18]

Evangelical historical imagination was highly ecclesiocentric and Western Eurocentric and might be cursorily sketched as follows: the sending into the world of God the Holy Spirit in Jerusalem on Pentecost originated the church. The devil opposed the church from its beginning through the persecutions that he initiated through the officials of the pagan Roman Empire; however, God preserved the church through them. During its first several centuries the early church adhered to right beliefs and practices, but during late antiquity and in the early medieval period, the church progressively began to succumb to a new attack from within as the devil succeeded in corrupting it more and more by false teaching. The adulteration of the Christian message attained its apogee in late-medieval Western Catholicism. Then in the early sixteenth century, God empowered the Reformers to revive and awaken the church through recalling it to the true and original Christian message that it had heretofore mostly forgotten. Operating through the Roman Catholic Church and its political supporters, the devil tried to crush the Reformers, but God would not permit them to be overwhelmed. Unsuccessful, the devil adopted a new strategy seeking to undo the church through the promotion of unbelief and antipathy toward historic Christian doctrines in the Enlightenment and then through the nascent anthropocentric atheism and secularism associated with the most radical phases of the French Revolution. Then in the early nineteenth century, in the aftermath of the chaos of a quarter century of European wars that God had sent in judgment, God brought about a time of religious revival by empowering a generation of leaders, as at the Reformation, whose mission it was to awaken, rebuild, and enlarge the church. Such was the story that evangelicals in Britain, continental Europe, and North America liked to tell to make sense of their place in the history of Christianity and to explain their religious identity in relation to those earlier Christians whom they admired.

I examine Protestant articulations of this interpretation of history over the century spanning 1750 to 1850, from its inchoate beginnings to its more fully developed formulations. Of course, it would be hazardous to forget that this was a period of considerable changes. It would be an ahistorical approach to this material to overstress continuities across the whole of the period from 1750 to 1850. Following Koselleck and his collaborators, what I wish to do in this essay is to trace how this interpretation of history first appeared, and then progressively became more detailed and developed among awakened Protestant intellectuals. Herein, we may also observe a significant transformation of the target of Protestant polemic and Protestant self-understanding as the people of God vis-à-vis the devil. From the time of the Reformation through the early eighteenth century, all Protestants from Saxony to the Cévennes to New England commonly denounced the papacy as antichrist and satanic, but beginning around 1750, evangelical Protestants began more and more to attribute the work of the devil in the world to the Enlightenment and its perceived offshoot, "the Revolution."[19]

## Protestant Anti-Enlightenment Polemics in Europe and North America

In 1748, August Wilhelm Friedrich Sack, the royal chaplain to Friedrich II of Prussia, whom the king had made a member of the Prussian Royal Academy of Science, published an apologetic work entitled *Vertheidigter Glaube der Christen* (*The Faith of Christians Defended*), in which he declared in the language of 2 Peter 3:3 that the church was now living in the "last days," in which the "degeneration of morals had spread in all directions and advanced against almost all humility and innocence."[20] According to Sack, there was at this time "a huge herd of non-believers and so-called free-spirits, who have risen up among us, who publicly speak scornfully of religion and virtue, and especially of the teaching and person of Jesus Christ, which they seek to befoul with the most outrageous blasphemies and mockeries."[21]

A world away in colonial New Jersey in 1758, the New England theologian Jonathan Edwards, who had just been appointed the president of the College of New Jersey (modern-day Princeton University), was revising a series of sermons that he had preached in 1739. These sermons were published posthumously in Edinburgh in 1774, in London in 1788, and in New York City in 1793 as *The History of Redemption on a Plan Entirely Original: Exhibiting the Gradual Discovery and Accomplishment of the Divine Purposes in the Salvation of Man; Including a Comprehensive view of Church History and the Fulfilment of Scripture Prophecies.*[22] In commenting upon "the opposition that Satan has made against the Reformation," Edwards singled out the rise of "Deism among Protestants in England," accusing Deists of being worse than the heretical "Arians and Socinians," because unlike the aforementioned so-called heretics, Deists "wholly cast off the Christian religion and are professed infidels" who "deny the Bible, all revealed religion, and believe that God has given mankind no other light to walk by but their own reason."[23]

At this same time, in England, John Wesley—who, in addition to being the leader of the Methodists, was an ordained Church of England priest and Fellow of Lincoln College in the University of Oxford—wrote in a December 9, 1758, letter to Calvinist antagonist Augustus Toplady that "no single person since Mahomet has given such a wound to Christianity as Dr. [John] Taylor. They are his books, chiefly that upon Original Sin, which have poisoned so many of the clergy, and indeed the fountains themselves—the Universities in England, Scotland, Holland, and Germany."[24] In order to provide "an antidote against that deadly poison which has been diffusing itself for several years through our Nation, our Church, and even our Universities" (by which he meant Taylor's popularization of unorthodox interpretations of the Christian scriptures), Wesley published in 1757 one of his longest works, *The Doctrine of Original Sin: According to Scripture, Reason, and Experience*. The stated aim of this work was to oppose "the open Deism" and the "barefaced infidelity" that "saps the very Foundation of all Revealed Religion," and which had thereby called into question the necessity of the incarnation of Christ and the atonement.[25]

This set of concerns prevailed too in the Kingdom of Denmark-Norway, where in 1757 the "awakened"[26] pro-chancellor of the University of Copenhagen (and former bishop of Bergen in Norway), Erik Pontoppidan, published a booklet entitled *Impartial Reflections on the Natural Causes of the Numerous and Powerful Earthquakes and on the Unusual weather, Within and Without Europe, Which We Have Heard so Much About*, in which he concluded, from the same texts in 2 Peter as Sack, that the appearance of so many "foolish mockers" of religion signalled that the church was now living in the last days.[27] Pontoppidan believed that the aforementioned abnormal meteorological and seismological events (especially the Lisbon earthquake on All Saints' Day, 1755) comported with the prophecies written in Zechariah 14 and ought to, therefore, be regarded as the "warnings and signs of the times."[28] These "prophesied the evening of the world" and anticipated the eschatological return of the God Israel to Jerusalem, whom Pontoppidan equated with the return of Jesus, according to Acts 1.[29] The following year Pontoppidan published *The Power of Truth to Defeat Atheistic and Naturalistic Unbelief; Depictions of Various Historical Examples of Mockers of Religion, Who Either Repented and Gave Honour to God, or Who Met a Horrific End*, which Pontoppidan wrote to encourage his readers to persevere in their faith and to not be troubled by certain challenges to Christian faith that were philosophical or theological in nature.[30] *The Power of Truth* consisted of detailed accounts of how eighteen former "atheists, naturalists, freethinkers, and Epicureans" (nine Germans, six Frenchmen, two Englishmen, and one Dane), who had lived in the sixteenth, seventeenth, and eighteenth centuries, had "awakened from their unbelief,"[31] professed faith in Jesus Christ, and died in the joy of the Lord. More grimly, Pontoppidan included accounts of three others (one Frenchman, one German, and one Italian), whose acceptance of the Christian message or commitment to unbelief remained ambiguous at the time of their death, and of six others (two Frenchmen, two Dutchmen, one Dane, and one German), who, immediately after their deaths, he believed, began to experience "the eternal punishment of the damned."[32]

During the American Revolution, James Sayre, an American loyalist residing in British-defended New York City in 1779, discovered a small book entitled *God's Thoughts of Peace in War, Published in these Turbulent and Trying Times, for the Consolation of the Afflicted and the Awakening of the Careless and Profligate*. This work had been published first in London in 1759 as an English translation made from *Die göttlichen Gedanken des Friedes im Kriege*, which was written by Carl Heinrich von Bogatzky, a student of August Hermann Francke, and published in Halle in 1758 during the Seven Years' War.[33] Not long after the major American victory in October 1777 at the Battle of Saratoga, Sayre remarked in his preface to his republication of Bogatzky's pastoral booklet that he found a striking "resemblance between the state of things which gave occasion for the author's writing it and that attending our own nation and country."[34] Sayre reaffirmed Bogatzky's view that:

> Our lot is cast in such times, when both the temporal and spiritual judgments of God walk through the earth, yet amidst the general coldness and supinity, they are attended to by very few, such that God must call not only to the careless and sinners, but likewise to many teachers, *Awake thou that sleepest*, Ephesians v. 14. For the general population, and even some teachers, lie in a deadly lethargy without a single thought about their souls, and the salvation of them.[35]

According to Sayre and Bogatzky, Germany and America had fallen into this state of divine judgment because they had lost their faith and morals.

> Our Protestant church . . . has exceedingly sinned; the general population makes little account of God and his word, and few, very few, walk worthy of the evangelical religion. The spirit of free-thinking and naturalism, which in our time has pervaded so many places with such fatal infection, I omit; but how bare-faced do whoredom, adultery, drunkenness, and other abominations stalk among us . . . and how do the rich and powerful oppress the poor![36]

Because the people had not been "awakened by the thunder of God's preached word," Bogatzky claimed that in response, God had sent the Lisbon earthquake in 1755 and the Seven Years' War in 1756 to awaken Europe to repentance.[37]

Another who blamed England, in particular, for the rise in perceived unbelief and hostility toward Christianity in eighteenth-century Europe, just as Edwards and Wesley had, was the Lutheran chaplain at the Charité hospital in Berlin, Johann Heinrich Friedrich Ulrich. In his lengthy 1781 work, *Geschichte der Christlichen Kirche für christliche Leser aus allen Ständen* (*A History of the Christian Church for Christian Readers from all Social Standings*), Ulrich contended, in a chapter he bluntly entitled "The Enemies of Christianity," that the restoration of Charles II in 1661 was the year when "unbelief ascended the throne."[38] According to Ulrich, not long thereafter "there appeared in the midst of Christendom a great host of atheists, those indifferent to religion, and deists," the dissemination and popularization of whose ideas continued "until approximately 1730, when the single most important period in the history of unbelief began."[39] Ulrich had in mind here literary activities of Johann Christian Edelmann, Julien Offray de la Mettrie, Claude Adrien Helvétius, David Hume, Viscount Bolingbroke, Denis Diderot, Jean-Jacques Rousseau, and Voltaire, among others.

Thirteen years after Ulrich published his history, Abigail Adams, whose husband was John Adams, the then vice-president and future second president of the United States, composed a March 10, 1794, letter in Boston in which she confided to an acquaintance with young children her concerns with how "in the rising generation, [there is] a want of principle."

> This is a melancholy truth. I am no friend of bigotry; yet I think the freedom of inquiry, and the general toleration of religious sentiments, have been like all other good things, perverted, and, under that shelter, deism, and even atheism have found refuge.[40]

The publication that year in the American and British capitals of, respectively, Philadelphia and London of Thomas Paine's *The Age of Reason; Being an Investigation of True and Fabulous Theology*, which had already appeared in Paris the previous year as *Le Siecle de la raision, ou Le Sens commun des droits de l'homme*, greatly amplified such concerns among many in the new republic.[41]

In German-speaking Europe, the new bogeyman was not Paine, but Immanuel Kant. During the French Revolutionary Wars, Frankfurt-am-Main was sacked by French forces twice, in 1792 and 1796, and heavy financial indemnities of millions of guilders were on both occasions imposed upon the former Free Imperial City. In response, the minister of the city's Reformed congregation, Gottfried Menken, published in 1795 and again in 1797, a booklet entitled *Üeber Glück und Sieg der Gottlosen* (*Regarding the Felicity and Victory of the Godless*). Menken's message and tone had much in common with the one Bogatzky had given to the residents of Halle, and that Sayre had repeated to the loyalists in New York: the Enlightenment had engendered unbelief in Europe. In Frankfurt, in particular, this unbelief engendered ungodliness, and ungodliness invited the wrath of God.

> In such an evil age, in which, among a perverse people, error passes for the truth, and the truth is taken for error and foolishness, one is not able to know what actually is virtuous; that is, what is it that is laudable in God's sight and what is loathsome to him and what distinguishes between the two. Because men are now striving after a false ideal of human worth, one which they have created for themselves, and because of the impact that the energetic forces of Hell are having everywhere, most people are no longer able to realise that through the philosophy of their age, they have been robbed of the truth, and thereby, they have been robbed of God and of virtue.[42]

Referring to the reception with which three of Kant's major works, *Kritik der reinen Vernunft* (*The Critique of Pure Reason*, 1781), *Kritik der praktischen Vernunft* (*The Critique of Practical Reason*, 1788), and *Die Religion innerhalb der Grenzen der bloßen Vernunft* (*Religion Within the Limits of Reason Alone*, 1793) were met, Menken exclaimed:

> How swiftly and triumphantly has the anti-Christian teaching of Kant spread throughout Germany! How unbelievably swiftly and with what unbelievable obedience has enlightened Germany bowed itself under the blasphemous and despotic imperatives of this philosophical pope?[43]

While Ulrich and Menken were haranguing some of the most prominent citizens of the Republic of Letters from their pulpits in Germany, Timothy Dwight—Jonathan Edwards's grandson, his successor as minister of the parish church in Northampton, Massachusetts, and the president of Yale College from 1795 to 1817—had begun to make the same types of criticisms in New England.

Thus far, I have taken a chronological approach in tracing the historiographical development of the evangelical imagination of history by discussing the earliest interpretations of the Enlightenment that were written from this perspective. Toward the turn of the eighteenth to the nineteenth century, Protestant intellectuals began to write more and more detailed interpretations of modern history as a cosmic struggle between the devil and the people of God. Thus it becomes both possible, and more profitable, to shift to a thematic approach to their development of this idea.

Awakened Protestants held a thoroughly organic view of how God had created society to function. They ultimately believed the foundation for human flourishing (in every sphere of life), was obedience to the will of God, which was revealed most clearly and fully in the word of God. In light of these religious convictions, they imagined the devil as working through the Enlightenment to undo the orderliness of Christian societies in Europe and North America by undermining those religious beliefs upon which the common good was based. Without adherence to these beliefs, in both the church and in society at large, awakened Protestants believed that the world would descend into the social chaos they witnessed in both the French Revolution and the European revolutionary movements of 1848. In the two remaining sections of this essay, I will first discuss examples of how awakened Protestant intellectuals perceived the devil to be fomenting opposition to orthodoxy through the philosophy and theology of the Enlightenment. Then I will discuss what these scholars conceived of as the deleterious social consequences of the eclipse of orthodox beliefs and how they saw the devil unraveling the fabric of society through the ideas of the Enlightenment.

## The Enlightenment Imagined as the Devil's Assault on Orthodoxy

In a November 28, 1781, Thanksgiving worship service for the French and American victory at the Battle of Yorktown, Timothy Dwight preached a sermon to his western Massachusetts congregation in which he articulated his meta-narrative view of Western history since the sixteenth century.[44] This history was essentially the result of how "the Most High supported his cause in the world," and how "the devil supported his own cause also, and opposed that of the Deity."[45] Within this framework, Dwight considered the "pretended miracles, spectres, witches, and other abuses of human credulity" of late medieval Catholicism to have been a "branch of the Satanical system" that had hindered and obscured the clear proclamation of the Christian message. While "God had given a fatal blow," against this system through superintending the "revival of learning" that yielded the Reformation, Satan and his minions soon thereafter corrupted this new academic impulse for deceptive purposes.[46]

> The first efforts of learning and reasoning [the Reformation] were made in the cause of truth; the second [the Enlightenment] in that of error. Evil beings found themselves necessitated to adopt a new method in their controversy with the Most High, and urged by policy, as well as necessity, began to change their former weapons, power, pretended miracles, and extraordinary interpositions, for schemes of sophistry and literary deceit.[47]

Opposition to the Enlightenment as an inherently anti-Christian movement was a recurrent theme throughout Dwight's works. In responding to the Boston pastor Charles Chauncy's 1784 work, *The Mystery hid from Ages and Generations, made manifest by the Gospel-Revelation*, which taught soteriological universalism, Dwight published a poem in classical epic style, *The Triumph of Infidelity*, in which he portrayed Chauncy as but the latest in a series of intellectuals since "the reign of Charles II"—the same event that had been regarded by Ulrich as a pivotal moment for the development of Western religious culture—whom Satan had raised up in Europe to deceive the world after "Luther and Calvin had given great injuries to infidelity."[48] Following reports that public atheism was rampant among the students at Harvard College, and that students in Princeton had celebrated the burning of a Bible, Dwight vigorously reiterated his opposition to certain seventeenth- and eighteenth-century English and French philosophers in two sermons based on Colossians 2:8 ("Beware, lest any man spoil you through philosophy and vain deceit, after the tradition of men, after the rudiments of the world, and not after Christ"), which he preached at the 1797

Yale College baccalaureate services and published as *The Nature and Danger of Infidel Philosophy*.

The evidence appears to be strong that provocatively blasphemous acts by students at Harvard, Princeton, and other American colleges really did happen (e.g., Williams College students in western Massachusetts purported administering the Lord's Supper to dogs).[49] Similarly, William Mundt's 1995 University of Utrecht doctoral dissertation mentions that certain professors and students at the University of Wittenberg allegedly conducted a funeral service and burial of the Bible on January 1, 1800, to celebrate the beginning of a century of Enlightenment.[50] In any case, the actual historicity of these events is far less significant than how evangelicals in New England and Germany at the time believed reports of such stories to be true because of their conviction that the Enlightenment was of the devil and caused people to behave hostilely toward Christianity. Supernaturally oriented visions of history with many similarities to Dwight's were independently advanced during the early decades of the nineteenth century by four continental European scholars: Nikolaj Frederik Severin Grundtvig, the Danish Lutheran bishop and pioneering Norse philologist and folklorist; Claus Harms, the Kiel pastor; Isaac da Costa, the aristocratic poet and Jewish convert to the Dutch Reformed Church; and August Tholuck, the University of Halle professor and member of the supreme consistory of the Protestant State Church in Prussia. These scholars saw the cosmic struggle between the devil and the people of God as aggregately composed of how this conflict transpired within the lives of many individuals.

Grundtvig, whom the University of Aarhus professor of church history Poul Georg Lindhardt later characterized as "an orthodox Bible Christian, really a phenomenon in Denmark in 1811,"[54] also spoke about his personal religious life as a spiritual battle with the devil. "When Satan seizes me in his serpent's teeth and in the darkness of the night cruelly slaps me, there is no help in either knowledge or art; only thy [God's] Word is not in vain, for that alone can bind him."[55] Such imagery also shaped Grundtvig's philosophy of ministry. Near the end of his long life (1783–1872), Grundtvig reflected on his struggles with theological rationalism in the 1820s:

> I had fallen into deep thought concerning the bewildering state of affairs in which the unlearned members of Christ's church had fallen. It was unthinkable that nearly all the learned theologians claimed that the origin, contents, authenticity, and proper interpretation of the Bible was highly doubtful, and that the cardinal doctrines concerning the Trinity and Christ's divinity and atonement were not to be found in the Scriptures. . . . I could see how Christian youth and lay people were in dire straits, since I myself with all my Bible knowledge, could not, prior to my church-historical knowledge, find a means to silence their Satanic witness.[56]

The same year that Grundtvig's historical study appeared, Claus Harms, the Lutheran pastor in Kiel, made similar historical and theological interpretations of the Enlightenment in conjunction with the tercentenary of the Reformation.

Harms symbolically promulgated ninety-five new theses on the "rationalist" spiritual crisis that he then saw plaguing the church in Germany. In a deliberate echo of Luther's first thesis from 1517, Harms began (thesis 1), "When our Master and Lord Jesus Christ says: 'Repent!' he wants men to conform their lives according to his teaching; he, however, does not conform his teaching to men, as many now do, according to the changes of the spirit of our age (2 Timothy 4:3)."[57] Harms inveighed that "reason" had become the "pope of our times," an "antichrist that has been placed in God's place," and that (thesis 27) just as the ancient Israelites had fallen into idolatry through rationalistic theology, modern German Protestants were guilty of religious novelty and of "creating God in man's own image (Isaiah 44:12–20)."[58] According to one of Harms's mid-twentieth-century interpreters, the University of Kiel professor of church history Gottfried Ernst Hoffman, he was emphatic that Lutherans needed to repent, in Hoffman's words, "from deforming Christian doctrine and ethics to suit human standards" (theses 1–8), "from the false morality of the rationalists and abuse of the notion of an autonomous conscience" (theses 9–24), "from the false teaching of the rationalists and the abuse of the notion of autonomous reason (theses 25–49), "from the practice of arbitrary exegesis and the rationalistic abuse of the Bible" (theses 50–62), "from rationalistic worship" (theses 63–74), and from ecclesiastical union with Calvinists on rationalistic foundations (theses 75–91).[59] Five years after the publication of Harms's theses in Kiel, there appeared in Leiden a booklet written in much the same theological tenor, whose title invoked the same biblical imagery as had Harms's first thesis.

Following his completion of doctorates in law (1818) and in philosophy (1821) at the University of Leiden, the young Sephardi Jew Isaac da Costa was baptized into the Dutch Reformed Church in 1822 at age twenty-four. The following year, he authored one of the most important early works of the Dutch Protestant Awakening, *Bezwaren te den Geest der Eeuw* (*Objections to the Spirit of the Age*).[60] Da Costa prefaced his work with two New Testament quotations pertaining to spiritual warfare from Ephesians 6:12 and 2 Corinthians 11:14, and one regarding watchfulness against false teaching from 2 Peter 2:19:

> For we do not struggle against flesh and blood, but against the rulers, against the authorities, and against the powers of this world, AGAINST THE DARKNESS OF THIS AGE, against the evil spiritual beings in the heavens.
>
> Satan himself changes into an angel of light.
>
> They [false teachers] promise them [their auditors] freedom, while they themselves are servants of depravity.[61]

Hereafter, da Costa, with great verve, embarked on a wide-ranging cultural analysis of how he perceived the satanic spirit of the age to be operating in various dimensions of European life, through chapters entitled "Religion," "Morality," "Tolerance and Humanity," "Belles-Lettres," "Scholarship," "Constitutions," "Social Status," "Public Opinion," "Education," and "Freedom and Enlightenment." Throughout, da Costa commented critically upon the writings and reception of Schelling, Fichte, Kant, "the devilish Voltaire," "the unashamed Rousseau," "the awful Diderot," Helvétius, Lord Byron, the Welsh communitarian Robert Owen, and other unnamed "German neologians," "English Radicals," and "sophistic French and German free-thinkers."[62] Many of the concerns voiced by da Costa, Harms, Grundtvig, and Dwight were echoed by August Tholuck, whose academic works were thematically opposed to the Enlightenment in the form of theological rationalism.

In 1817, August Tholuck traveled from his native Silesia to Berlin to matriculate as a theology student at the newly founded university in the Prussian capital, having previously studied Arabic and Persian at the University of Breslau. For his gymnasium thesis, Tholuck had written an essay entitled "The Superiority of the Oriental World over the Christian,"[63] in which he extoled Islam as a religion and social system. Soon after moving to Berlin, he became deeply committed to Protestantism through an experience of religious awakening that he had while participating in a Bible study group with Baron Hans Ernst von Kottwitz—a devout member of both the Moravian Brethren and the Berlin chapter of the Christianity Society (Christentumsgesellschaft).[64] Tholuck described his new sense of personal devotion to Jesus after his spiritual conversion in his highly popular, semiautobiographical epistolary novel, *Die Lehre von der Sünde und vom Versöhner, oder die wahre Weihe des Zweiflers*, which was published in six German editions between 1823 and 1839. It was then published in English—in London in 1836 and in Boston in 1854—as *The Doctrine of Sin and of the Redeemer and the True Consecration of the Skeptic*:

> For everything in you that longs for redemption, Jesus has come as a Redeemer. He has redeemed your heart and your reason, your body as well as your soul; he has redeemed you and the natural world that is all around you. He has redeemed you, not only by his death, but also by his resurrection; he not only redeemed you by living for you, but now he sits at the right hand of God for you; he redeemed you not only by his deeds, but by his word; not only by his humanity, but equally by his divinity; he redeemed you by his eternity as well as his life in time.[65]

With its quotations of classical Greek and Latin texts in the original languages, numerous unexplained allusions to figures from classical literature, citations from the ancient church fathers, and seventeenth-, eighteenth-, and early nineteenth-century Western philosophy, Tholuck's prose was written for the leisure reading of a highly educated audience.

Tholuck explained the origins of rationalism by invoking the same historical metanarrative of cosmic spiritual warfare that other Protestant intellectuals had in their anti-Enlightenment polemics. In the preface to the novel based on his own experience of religious awakening, Tholuck insisted that the early nineteenth-century religious revivals in Europe were comparable in significance to the Reformation, as they both were the work of Christ himself. In both of these instances, Christ opposed the work of Satan by reawakening the church after the alleged near disappearance of the gospel in both late-medieval Catholicism, the Enlightenment. Writing in 1823, Tholuck declared that while at the end of the eighteenth century "the prince of darkness had cried with mocking laughter 'all is finished' over all the earth," Christ "resurrected the Church" in the early nineteenth century, which began, "a struggle of spirits in the religious sphere such as there has perhaps never been since the days of the apostles."[66]

Between 1831 and 1833, Tholuck published thirteen historical studies of Christian apologists from England, Scotland, France, and Germany in the *Literarischer Anzeiger*, an academic theology journal that he edited in Halle.[67] According to Tholuck, the central theme that ran through all these reviews was that the Enlightenment had been an intellectual movement advanced by "unruly spirits," whose "insolence and unbelief" had "first poisoned England, then France, and finally Germany."[68] Yet all throughout these dismal years, God repeatedly raised up pastors and theologians "to wield the sword of the Spirit [Ephesians 6:17] against such enemies of Christianity."[69] In a further development of his interpretation of the intellectual history of the eighteenth century, Tholuck published in 1838, *Abriss einer Geschichte der Umwälzung, welche seit 1750 auf dem Gebiete der Theologie in Deutschland statt gefunden* (*An Outline of the Catastrophe Which has Occurred in German Theology Since 1750*).[70] Opening with an argument that resembles the thesis of William Wilberforce's 1797 book, *A Practical View of the Prevailing Religious System of Professed Christians, in the Higher and Middle Classes in this Country; Contrasted with Real Christianity* (which had been translated into German, Dutch, and French in 1807, 1817, and 1821, respectively), Tholuck contended that

> In France, but no less so than in Protestant England, unbelief has become dominant in the upper classes, while from sometimes pure and other times impure motives, it has been the clergy, who, with varying degrees of skill, have taken up the defense of Christianity. To the contrary, in Germany since the middle of the preceding century, unbelief in the foundational truths of Christianity developed chiefly among the clergy, who did not recognize that this tendency is undermining the very foundations of our ecclesiastical institutions.[71]

Tholuck then proceeded to trace the various streams of intellectual influence that had acted upon the German professoriate and pastorate from the philosophy of Christian Wolff, to English deism, to French naturalism and atheism, to what he considered the rationalistic biblical exegesis of Johann Semler. Tholuck concluded that such historical analysis summarized "the transition from the era of faith in the German church to the era of its denial," and yet, he still held out hope "that one day the history would be written of how faith overcame all these expressions of doubt in academic dress."[72]

Awakened Protestant scholars believed that the theological challenges introduced by the Enlightenment were so lamentable not only because of how they obscured divine truths, but also because of the concomitant detrimental changes in Western political and economic life that they precipitated. In the following section, I will discuss how awakened Protestants imagined the work of the devil in certain societal developments that they regarded as harmful and attributable to the Enlightenment. Above all, these were centered in the phenomena of revolution.

## Revolution Imagined as the Satanic Fruit of the Enlightenment

Dwight took for his aforementioned Thanksgiving sermon from Isaiah 59:18–19. He expounded the text, "the Lord will repay the islands their due" with respect to the recent British military defeats, not only in America, but also in India in the Second Anglo-Mysore War and on the high seas in the Fourth Anglo-Dutch War, as signs that God was punishing "the sins of Great Britain," which, by this time, were "in degree enormous, and in multitude innumerable."[73] In a scathing critique of the relationship between colonial imperialism and domestic consumerism, Dwight fulminated that the British people had become motivated by a spirit of national and individual selfishness to pursue exploitative political and economic policies against non-Western peoples for their own enrichment and indulgence. Dwight saw this selfishness, which he considered intrinsic to mankind in its fallen state, as having become greatly intensified through a precipitous decline in public morals throughout the eighteenth century—the root cause of which had been unbelief in Christianity prompted by the Enlightenment. In Dwight's view, the British people had been the first to fall for such diabolical deceptions, and this had led them to commit the sins for which God was now, in 1781, rebuking them. Dwight's American auditors and readers found this concept important, since at the time of their national independence, they had to consciously reject the godlessness of the Enlightenment—or likewise be corrupted and come under similar divine judgment.[74]

Twenty years later, in 1801, Dwight published *A Discourse on Some Events of the Last Century*, which together with his posthumously published 1822 "Letters on Religion in New England" contained Dwight's most systematic and detailed historical reflections on the problem of infidelity in Europe and America.[75] Underneath the cosmic spiritual warfare, Dwight attributed the rise of infidelity in Europe since 1750 to the sinfulness that had been motivated and facilitated by "excessive wealth." This wealth came from trade and colonization, which he asserted had "generated enormous luxury, the multiplied enjoyments of which have become not only the ruling objects of desire, and the governing motives of action, but in the view of a great part of the inhabitants, the necessary means of even a comfortable existence."[76] Returning to a withering, theologically grounded, condemnation of consumerism, Dwight lamented how "voluptuousness and splendour . . . engross men in public and private stations, in the university, the camp, the shop, and the desk, as well as the court and the cabinet," and how to "satisfy the universal demand for pleasure, the mines of Golconda [on the eastern coast of India] are ransacked, the caverns of Mexico emptied, and the mountains of Potosi [in present-day Bolivia] transported across the ocean."[77] Dwight bemoaned, "to a mind, to a nation, dissolved in sloth, enervated by pleasure, and fascinated with splendour, the Gospel is preached and heaven presented in vain."[78] Having had their consciences inoculated through such idolatrous consumerism, Europeans and Americans became, in Dwight's view, unable to recognize the false and anti-Christian teachings that "lowered the spirit of the Bible to the corrupt taste of man, lessened the distinction between virtue and vice, and rendered the terms of salvation convenient," whereby the people who were so influenced "became Infidels without knowing it."[79] Such thinking permeated every class of society; "from lofty philosophical discourse," infidelity had "descended through all the intervening gradations [of media] to the newspaper paragraph."[80]

Like many of his contemporaries, Dwight did not believe that it was possible to have a moral society without religion and saw in the extraordinary public violence of the French Revolution, in the executions in Paris, and in "the ravages of La Vendee, Nants, Toulon, and Lyons," confirmation that unbelief had led to moral chaos.[81] "Infidelity is hostile to all public and personal happiness," and "without the influence of Religion, political freedom can never be long enjoyed."[82] Dwight concluded that revolution had proven itself to be the telos of infidelity and exhorted resistance to the Enlightenment in the young American republic—both for the sake of temporal well-being and for eternal welfare.

Just as Dwight had connected "infidelity" directly to the outbreak of the French Revolution in 1789, so too had Tholuck perceived a direct link between unbelief and revolution. Immediately upon receiving news of the revolutionary uprising that had broken out in Paris in February 1848, which inspired similar disturbances in Berlin in March 1848 that forced King Friedrich Wilhelm IV to briefly flee from the city, Tholuck, in his capacity as university chaplain, preached a strong antirevolutionary sermon at Halle based on Psalm 46: "Nations are in uproar, kingdoms fall; God lifts his voice, the earth melts. The Lord Almighty is with us; the God of Jacob is our fortress."[83] Tholuck thundered, "What Europe has long anticipated with great trepidation has now come to pass." Tholuck then linked "the spiritual and intellectual contamination that has spread to us from France over the past one-hundred and fifty years," that is, since 1700, with the "horrific" French invasions of Germany during the Napoleonic Wars, to how French now wished to "menacingly unfurl their red flag over our heads."[84]

Tholuck continued that no political revolution could ever bring about the just society that those on the barricades righteously desired, because the cause of all injustice in the world did not lie in political systems, but in the sinfulness of the human heart. Prophesying that the revolution would bring nothing but disaster, Tholuck warned his auditors:

> The people of Europe will now have to accept with blood and tears the doctrine that a tyrant resides just as much in the hearts of the people as he does in the heart of the prince, as long as the Spirit of God has not sanctified them both; no democratic constitution, no worker's organization, no kind of education, no human endeavour whatsoever can bring man peace, as long as the holy breath of God-given religion has not yet put to death the poisonous worm in the heart of man that eats away at all peace: selfishness. Topple thrones, scatter crowns, and break the scepters of tyrants, but as long as the worm of selfishness within you has not been put to death, instead of one tyrant standing before you there will be one-hundred thousand and your final state will be worse than it was at first. Europe's peoples will first have to learn these lessons practically, with tears, before their liberal institutions are able to make them happy.[85]

Such criticism of the Enlightenment as the satanic harbinger of revolution, summarily sketched by Dwight and Tholuck, was most fully developed by two ardent antirevolutionary thinkers: Guillaume de Groen van Prinsterer, Dutch aristocrat and parliamentarian; and Friedrich Julius Stahl, University of Berlin professor of law and Jewish convert to the Lutheran Church.

On November 8, 1845, Groen delivered his first of fifteen lectures on how the French Revolution had shaped the subsequent course of European intellectual, social, and cultural history to a small number of his close friends and colleagues, whom he had invited to his home in The Hague.[86] By the age of twenty-three, Groen had already earned two doctorates, in classics and in law, from the University of Leiden—with Latin dissertations on Plato and the Byzantine Emperor Justinian I. In these Saturday evening discourses, which he hosted regularly throughout the winter of 1845–1846, Groen reflected upon more recent European history—advocating the ideological vantage point that he described as his "Christian-historical perspective," and endeavouring to demonstrate the existence of "a necessary and natural link" between "unbelief and revolution."[87] With such poignant rhetoric, Groen referred to how, in his view, "the rejection of the Gospel" and the "denial of the living God" in European intellectual and political life had inevitably resulted in a state of affairs in which great "confusion, injustice, and slavery" prevailed everywhere "revolutionary principles" were ascendant, and to how such shifts could not be fully perceived apart from a worldview that was informed by Christian faith.[88] A year later in 1847, these informal lectures were published in Leiden as *Unbelief and Revolution.*

Groen shared the conviction of many other evangelical Protestant intellectuals that the intellectual, religious, and political aspects of modern European culture that they found offensive to the Word and ways of God were most clearly explained and contextualized within a cosmic imagination of history as the progressive unfolding of the spiritual warfare between the devil and the people of God. Groen bewailed how without the spiritual protection supplied by fidelity to Christian orthodoxy, Christian Europe had become de-Christianized under a hail of "fiery darts from the evil one [Ephesians 6:16]." He bemoaned how by 1847 the continent had become full of an evil comparable, in Groen's eyes, to Jesus's parable in Matthew 12:45 of the man who was possessed by seven evil spirits.[89]

Groen began his discourses with a clear definition of his terms: "By Revolution I do not mean one of the many events whereby a government is overthrown. Nor do I merely mean by it the storm of upheaval that has raged in France. Rather, by Revolution I mean the entire inversion of the general spirit and mode of thinking that is now manifest in all Christendom."[90] The leitmotif of these lectures was that all of life existed as a great moral binary that was constituted by the fundamentally contradictory ideas and actions, which, Groen argued, flowed necessarily and without exception from either obedience or disobedience to Christ. "Unbelief has no outlet except for the principle of Revolution."[91] The bulk of Groen's book was comprised of his analysis of how unbelief had historically manifested itself in the respective cultural spheres of religion and politics, and how unbelief in these two primary domains of public life had mutually reinforced each other. In drawing these connections, Groen systematized the evangelical Protestant anti-Enlightenment polemic to a heretofore-unprecedented degree.

According to Groen, the first cause of the Revolution had been its rejection of the texts of the Old and New Testaments as authoritative divine revelation, such that human reason became epistemologically privileged above any other source of truth or manner of recognizing truth. Groen saw the elevation of reason as having produced metaphysical skepticism towards any truth claim that could not be known by reason. He concluded that those who refused to submit themselves to the authority of the Bible either became pantheists, "like Hegel"[92] in his attempts to comprehend the world spirit apart from personal revelation; or, when they were intellectually consistent and honest with themselves, they became atheistic materialists, "like Claude Adrien Helvétius or Julien Offray de la Mettrie."[93]

Groen further discerned that disbelief in the scriptures inherently generated challenges to pre-Enlightenment notions about the nature of political legitimacy and sovereignty. Confidence in the biblical worldview, in which God was not only the ultimate source of all religious truth but the ultimate origin of all sovereign authority, crumbled with the growth of unbelief in the scriptures. This was then replaced by the belief that the people, as the nation, were themselves ultimately sovereign, as well as by the resulting corollary belief that having the assent of their collective will was the ultimate criterion of political legitimacy. In lengthy reflections on the numerous shifts in French political history between the French Revolutions of 1789, 1830, and 1848 (in the second edition), Groen perceived a cyclical pattern of radicalism inspired by notions of popular sovereignty that created chaos that led to dictatorship, which became replaced by liberalism after the people rejected the dictators. Dictatorships then returned to radicalism as utopian desires were not fulfilled, thereby recapitulating "the incessant revolutionary cycle."[94]

Groen further contended that the popularization of the idea of popular sovereignty and the epistemological exaltation of rationality each depended upon and supported the other. "If anyone in the Netherlands before 1750 had suggested that the Christian and historical law should be discarded in favour of implementing ideas that had only just been thought up by a few so-called philosophers, there would have been a universal outcry against this."[95] Yet as religious beliefs about the identity of mankind and mankind's relationship to God and the universe changed over the ensuing decades, new revolutionary paradigms of political order became publicly plausible. Groen also argued that the revolutionary political paradigm reinforced unbelief and hardened hearts against orthodox Christianity. Once people came to believe that the nation is ultimately sovereign and that people are autonomous—literally, that they are the source of their own laws—it became difficult, if not impossible, for them to simultaneously believe that God is the Lord Almighty. Through such analysis, Groen provided a more holistic and sustained critique of the Enlightenment from an orthodox Protestant perspective than had any other previous commentator.

In 1860, Groen remarked how, because of the similarities between their antirevolutionary political and cultural stances, some were beginning to call to him "le Stahl de la Hollande," in reference to the University of Berlin professor of law Friedrich Julius Stahl.[96] Stahl had been born to an Ashkenazi Jewish family in Bavaria and was the grandson of Abraham Uhlfelder, the leader of the Jewish community in Munich during the time of its emancipation.[97] In 1819, following his religious conversion and baptism into the Lutheran Church at age seventeen, Stahl commenced his university studies in law. He became a lecturer at the University of Munich in 1826, and at the age of thirty he became a professor at the University of Würzburg before moving to posts in Erlangen and Berlin.[98] Stahl dated his own personal religious awakening to his years as a professor in Erlangen when he became acquainted with Christian Krafft, the Erlangen theology professor and pastor of the local Reformed congregation, whom he praised as "the man who built up the Church in my Bavarian fatherland, the most apostolic man I ever met in my life . . . [who] caused throughout the whole land a spring to bloom whose fruits will ripen in eternity."[99]

On May 8, 1852, Stahl delivered an address in Berlin entitled "*Was ist die Revolution*?" in which he answered this question in many of the same ways that other Protestant polemicists had, with a unique emphasis placed on revolution as the harbinger of the apocalyptic appearance of the antichrist.

> Revolution means the specific political teaching, which since 1789, has been transforming the nations' ways of thinking and has been shaking the institutions of public life throughout the world. Does one inquire as to what lies at the heart of the Revolution? The answer is this: The Revolution is the establishment of all of public life and relations according to the will of man, rather than according to God's order and acts of providence. According to Revolutionary thinking, all authority and power is not from God, but rather is from human beings, from "the people." According to Revolutionary thinking, the goal of societal life is not adherence to the holy commands of God and the fulfilment of his plans for the world, but is instead the satisfaction of mankind's licentious desires.[100]

Stahl saw the development of revolutionary thinking as an incremental historical process that had begun with the Enlightenment and finally flowered into the nascent communist movement; according to Stahl, the latter's categorical rejection of private property was merely the logical extension of the rejection of God's propositional truths and God's moral absolutes to a rejection of God's providential ordering of human beings into different social and economic circumstances.[101] When Martin Luther pondered the meaning of 2 Thessalonians 2:3–4 in his 1545 tractate *Wider das Papsttum zu Rom, vom Teufel gestiftet* (*Against the Papacy in Rome that has been founded by the Devil*), it appeared as self-evident to him that this text was prophesying about the earthly Vicar of Christ.[102]

> Do not let anyone deceive you in any way, for that day [the return of Jesus] will not come until the rebellion occurs and the man of lawlessness is revealed, the man doomed to destruction. He will oppose and will exalt himself over everything that is called God or is worshiped, so that he sets himself up in God's temple, proclaiming himself to be God.

Three hundred and seven years later, however, Stahl asserted that "what was foretold about the man of lawlessness" was perfect prophesy of "the essence of the Revolution and rationalism," which constituted "perhaps the final stage in the development of the battle between the spirits of light and the spirits of darkness."[103]

## Conclusion

In the foregoing pages, I have attempted to show that many awakened Protestant intellectuals in the modern West retained strong beliefs about the influence of God and evil spirits upon human affairs, beliefs which were grounded in a biblically derived historical imagination.[104] This is contrary to Max Weber's characterisation of modernity as, "*die Entzauberung der Welt*," and his concomitant assertions that "with the progress of science and technology, man has stopped believing in magic powers, in spirits and demons; he has lost his sense of prophecy and, above all, his sense of the sacred," and that "reality has become dreary, flat and utilitarian, leaving a great void in the souls of men which they seek to fill by furious activity and through various devices and substitutes." Indeed, it has been the aim of this study to demonstrate that what awakened Protestants regarded as the alarming and bewildering trends in theology and philosophy—which Cassirer, Berlin, and Israel described as deep breaks with historically orthodox Protestant beliefs—did not so much drive them toward adopting secular beliefs, as much as such trends compelled them to attempt to make sense of such developments within the available conceptual categories of their religious framework. This they did primarily through conceptualizing the Enlightenment as a particularly ignoble and baleful historical epoch in a larger historical metanarrative, in which the central dynamic in history, from the creation of the world to the end of the world, is the struggle between the devil and the people of God. These attempts furnish examples of how fostering a particular kind of historical consciousness informed religious self-understanding and identity formation for certain modern Protestants in Europe, Britain, and North America after the Enlightenment.

# Notes

1. Jonathan I. Israel, *Radical Enlightenment: Philosophy and the Marking of Modernity, 1650–1750* (New York: Oxford University Press, 2001), vi.
2. Ibid., 4.
3. Ibid., 11–12.
4. Ernst Cassirer, *Die Philosophie der Aufklärung* (Tübingen: J. C. B. Mohr-Siebeck, 1932), 188.
5. Ibid., 212–214.
6. Ibid., 182–185.
7. Isaiah Berlin, "The Counter-Enlightenment," in *The Dictionary of the History of Ideas*, ed. Philip P. Wiener (New York: Charles Scribner's Sons, 1968), 2:101.
8. Ibid., 101.
9. Ibid., 110.
10. Ibid.
11. Thomas S. Kidd, *The Great Awakening: The Roots of Evangelical Christianity in Colonial America* (New Haven: Yale University Press, 2007).
12. G. M. Ditchfield, *The Evangelical Revival* (London: University College London Press, 1998).
13. Erich Beyreuther, *Die Erweckungsbewegung* (Göttingen, Germany: Vandenhoeck and Ruprecht, 1977).
14. Fred van Lieburg, ed., *Opwekking van de natie: Het protestantse Réveil in Nederland* (Amsterdam: Verloren, 2012).
15. Alice Wemyss, *Histoire du Réveil, 1790–1849* (Paris: Les Bergers et Les Mages, 1977).
16. Kaj Baagø, *Vaekkelse og wirkeliv I København og omegn I første halvdel af det 19. århundrede* (Copenhagen: Gad, 1960); Alv Johan Magnus, *Veirydder med gnagsår, Hans Nielsen Hauge og vekkelsen som forandret Norge* (Ottestad: Prokla-Media, 1996); Jacob Peter Bang, *De stora väckelserörelserna: en historisk och psykologisk framställning* (Stockholm: Svenska kristliga studentrörelsen, 1926).
17. Karl Löwith, *Meaning in History* (Chicago: University of Chicago Press, 1949), 187–188.
18. Melvin Richter, "Appreciating a Contemporary Classic: The Geschichtliche Grundbegriffe and Future Scholarship," in *The Meaning of Historical Terms and Concepts: New Studies on Begriffsgeschichte*, ed. Hartmut Lehmann and Melvin Richter (Washington, DC: German Historical Institute, 1996), 10.
19. Luc Racaut, "Religious Polemic and Huguenot Identity," in *Society and Culture in the Huguenot World*, ed. Raymond Mentzer and Andrew Spicer (New York: Cambridge University Press, 2002), 39.
20. August Wilhelm Friedrich Sack, *Vertheidigter Glaube der Christen* (Berlin, 1773), 3–4.
21. Ibid., 4.
22. George Marsden, *Jonathan Edwards: A Life* (New Haven: Yale University Press, 2004), 193–194.
23. Jonathan Edwards, *The History of Redemption* (New York: T. J. Swords, 1793), 462.

24. John Wesley, "Letter to Augustus Toplady, 9 December 1758," in *The Letters of Rev. John Wesley*, ed. John Telford (London: Epworth Press, 1931), 4:48.

25. John Wesley, *The Doctrine of Original Sin* (Bristol: E. Farley, 1757), iv–v.

26. Burkard Krug, "Erik Pontoppidan," *Biographisch-Bibliographisches Kirchenlexicon*, ed. Friedrich Wilhelm Bautz (Berlin: Verlag Traugott Bautz, 1994), 7:830–831; Johan Fredrik Lampe, *Bergens Stifts Biskoper Og Praester, Efter Reformationen* (Christiana: Gammer Meyers Boghandel, 1895), 1:20.

27. Erich Pontoppidan, *Die Kraft der Wahrheit den atheistischen und naturalistischen Unglauben zu besiegen. In verschieden historischen Beyspielen solcher Religionspötter vorgestellt, welche sich entweder bekehrt und Gott die Ehre gegeben oder auch ein Ende mit Schrecken genommen haben*, trans. Christian Gottlob Mengel (Leipzig: Friedrich Christian Pelt, 1757), 69.

28. Erich Pontoppidan, *Unvorgreifliche Bedenken über die natürliche Ursache der vielen und starken Erdbeben, und des ungewöhnlichen Wetters, welches man seit einziger Zeit so wohl in als außer Europa vernommen hat*, trans. Christian Gottlob Mengel (Leipzig: Friedrich Christian Pelt, 1757), 69–71.

29. Ibid., 71.

30. *Sandheds Kraft til at overvinde Den Atheistiske og Naturalistiske Vantroe: Forestillet i adskillelige Historiske Exempler paa saadanne Religions-Spottere, som enten have vendt om og givet Gud Ære, eller og taget en Ende med Forskrekkelse*. In her summative analysis of Pontoppidan, Karen Larsen commented that he "possessed the good qualities of pietism without its extremes and was imbued with the devotion to learning characteristic of the Enlightenment." Karen Larsen, *A History of Norway* (Princeton: Princeton University Press, 1948), 338.

31. Pontoppidan, *Die Kraft der Wahrheit*, 32.

32. Ibid., 347.

33. "Art. 30," *The Monthy Review, or Literary Journal* 20 (1759): 93.

34. Carl Heinrich Bogatzky, *God's Thoughts of Peace in War, Published in These Turbulent and Trying Times, for the Consolation of the Afflicted and the Awakening of the Careless and Profligate*, ed. and trans. James Sayre (London: 1779), i.

35. Ibid., 1.

36. Ibid., 24.

37. Ibid., 27.

38. Johann Heinrich Friedrich Ulrich, *Von der Reformation bis auf unsre Zeiten, vol. 2 of Geschichte der Christlichen Kirche für christliche Leser aus allen Ständen* (Frankfurt: Johann Philipp Reiffenstein, 1782), 521.

39. Ibid., 522.

40. Abigail Adams, "To Mrs. Smith, 10 March 1794," in *Letter of Mrs. Adams, The Wife of John Adams*, ed. Charles Francis Adams (Boston: Wilkins, Carter, 1848), 366–367.

41. Eric R. Schlereth, *An Age of Infidels: The Politics of Religious Controversy in the Early United States* (Philadelphia: University of Pennsylvania Press, 2013), 45–76.

42. Gottfried Menken, *Über Glück und Sieg der Gottlosen* (Frankfurt, 1795), 6.

43. Ibid., 26.

44. Timothy Dwight, "A Sermon Preached at Northampton on the Twenty-Eighth of November 1781: Occasioned by the Capture of the British Army Under the Command of Earl Cornwallis" (Hartford: Nathaniel Patten, 1781).

45. Ibid., 5–6.

46. Ibid., 6.

47. Ibid., 7.

48. Kenneth Silverman, *Timothy Dwight* (New York: Twayne, 1969), 81–87; [Timothy Dwight], *The Triumph of Infidelity: A Poem* (Printed in the World: 1788), 9.

49. Brooks Mather Kelley, *Yale: A History* (London: Yale University Press, 1974), 115.

50. William F. Mundt, *Sinners Directed to the Saviour: The Religious Tract Society Movement in Germany, 1811–1848* (Zoetermeer: Uitgeverij Boekencentrum, 1995), 71.

51. Nikolaj Grundtvig, *Uebersicht der Welt-Chronik vornähmlich des Lutherischen Zeitraums*, trans. Johann Volkmann (Nuremberg: Raw'schen Buchhandlung, 1837), iii.

52. Grundtvig, *Uebersicht der Welt-Chronik*, 389.

53. Ibid., 379–388.

54. Poul Georg Lindhardt, *Grundtvig: An Introduction* (London: SPCK, 1951), 19.

55. Tryge R. Skarsten, "Rise and Fall of Grundtvigianism in Norway," *The Lutheran Quarterly* 17 (1965): 126.

56. Ibid., 128–129. By most definitions of evangelicalism, Grundtvig's adoption of what he called his "church-historical knowledge" turned him into something other than the evangelical that he had previously been. In a July 31, 1825, sermon, in which he first articulated that the solution he had come to regarding his aforementioned biblical-theological difficulties was that they could simply be bypassed through putting one's faith in the words of the Apostle's Creed and Christ's self-testimony in the sacraments alone. "Thus," in Grundtvigianism, "the Christian's firm foundation is not to be found in the Bible, but wherever a congregation gathers around God's spoken word at baptism and Holy Communion." Anders Pontoppidan Thyssen and Christian Thodberg, "A Brief Biography," in *N.F.S. Grundtvig: Tradition and Renewal*, ed. A. P. Thyssen and C. Thodberg, trans. Edward Broadbridge (Copenhagen: Det Danske Selskab, 1983), 12.

57. Claus Harms, "Thesen zum Reformationsjubiläum 1817," in *Ausgewählte Schriften und Predigten*, ed. Gottfried Ernst Hoffman (Flensburg: Ch. Wolff, 1955), 1:211.

58. Ibid., 211–214.

59. Ibid., 210–225.

60. Friedrich Wilhelm Bautz, "Isaac da Costa," *Biographisch-Bibliographisches Kirchenlexicon*, ed. Friedrich Wilhelm Bautz (Berlin: Verlag Traugott Bautz, 1993), 1:1138–1139; Bart Wallet, "Het Réveil als joodsche Hervorming," in *Opwekking van de natie: Het protestantse Réveil in Nederland*, ed. Fred van Lieburg (Hilversum, The Netherlands: Verloren, 2012), 186–199.

61. Isaac da Costa, *Bezwaren tegen den Geest der Eeuw* (Leiden: L. Herdingh and Son, 1823), iii–iv. Translated from Costa's Dutch New Testament citations; capitalization in the original.

62. Ibid., 10, 13–14, 21, 23, 87.

63. Philip Schaff, "Friedrich August Gottreu Tholuck," in *The New Schaff-Herzog Encyclopedia of Religious Knowledge*, ed. Samuel Jackson (Grand Rapids: Baker, 1953), 11:420–421.

64. Leopold Witte, *Das Leben Doktor Friedrich August Gottreu Tholuck's* (Leipzig: Velhagen and Klasing, 1886), 1:113.

65. August Tholuck, *Die Lehre von der Sünde und vom Versöhner, oder die wahre Weihe des Zweiflers* (Hamburg: Friedrich Perthes, 1830), 72–73.

88. Ibid.
89. Ibid., 178–179.
90. Ibid., 5.
91. Ibid., xi.
92. Ibid., 198.
93. Ibid., 228.
94. Ibid., 271.
95. Ibid., 28.
96. Abraham Klink, "Groen van Prinsterer en Stahl," in *Groen van Prinsterer in Europese Context*, ed. Jan de Bruijn and George Harinck (Hilversum: Verloren, 2004), 55.
97. Edgar Feuchtwanger, "The Jewishness of Conservative Politicians: Disraeli and Stahl," in *Two Nations: British and German Jews in Comparative Perspective*, ed. Michael Brenner et al. (Tübingen: Mohr Siebeck, 1999), 224.
98. Wilhelm Füßl, "Friedrich Julius Stahl," in *Biographisch-Bibliographisches Kirchenlexicon*, ed. Friedrich Wilhelm Bautz (Berlin: Verlag Traugott Bautz, 1995), 10:1130–1135.
99. Cited in Philip Schaff, *The Creeds of Christendom with a History and Critical Notes* (London: Harper and Brothers, 1919), 1:554.
100. Friedrich Julius Stahl, *Was ist die Revolution? Ein Vortrag auf Veranstaltung des Evangelischen Vereins für kirchliche Zwecke am 8. März gehalten* (Berlin: Wilhelm Schultze, 1852), 4.
101. Ibid., 7–8.
102. Martin Luther, "Wider das Papsttum zu Rom, vom Teufel gestiftet," *D. Martin Luthers Werke: kritische Gesammtausgabe*, ed. Karl Drescher (Weimar: Hermann Böhlau Verlag), 54:215.
103. Stahl, *Was ist die Revolution*, 12–13.
104. Cited in Daniel Bell, "The Return of the Sacred: The Argument about the Future of Religion," in *Bulletin of the American Academy of Arts and Sciences* 31 (1978): 30.

66. August Tholuck, "Vorwort zur ersten Auflage," in *Die Lehre von der Sünde und v Versöhner Die Lehre von der Sünde und vom Versöhner, oder die wahre Weihe des Zweifl* (Hamburg: Friedrich Perthes, 1854), v–vii. While Tholuck welcomed the earlier signs religious Awakening in Germany, he nonetheless maintained a critical stance towards wl they actually signified. Emphasizing his belief that true spiritual awakening entailed m than concurrence to doctrine, Tholuck rhetorically mused: 'The doctrines of orthodox Chr tology and praise for our historic faith are once again heard from our pulpits and univers lecterns; but is this the same as hearing the proclamation that our redeemer who had die now alive again? If here and there a prince or other ruler comes forward to defend Chri anity, is he not often acting this way for political reasons and not out of his concern for gospel?

67. August Tholuck, "Ueber Apologetik und ihre Litteratur," in *Vermischte Schrif grösstentheils apologetischen Inhalts* (Hamburg: Friedrich Perthes, 1839), 1:149–373.

68. Ibid., 347, 362.

69. Ibid., 347.

70. August Tholuck, "Abriss einer Geschichte der Umwälzung, welche seit 1750 dem Gebiete der Theologie in Deutschland statt gefunden," in *Vermischte Schriften grösst theils apologetischen Inhalts* (Hamburg: Friedrich Perthes, 1839), 2:1–147.

71. Ibid., 1.

72. Ibid., 147.

73. Dwight, "A Sermon Preached at Northampton," 13.

74. Ibid., 34.

75. Timothy Dwight, *A Discourse of Some Events of the Last Century, Delivered in Brick Church in New Haven, On Wednesday, January 7, 1801* (New Haven, 1801); Timo Dwight, "Letters on the Religion of New England," in *Travels in New-England and New-* (New Haven, 1822), 4:364–462.

76. Dwight, *A Discourse of Some Events*, 22.

77. Ibid.

78. Ibid.

79. Ibid., 25.

80. Ibid., 26.

81. Dwight, "Letters on the Religion of New England III," 383.

82. Ibid., 385.

83. Leopold Witte, *Das Leben Doktor Friedrich August Gottreu Tholuck's* (Leip Velhagen and Klasing, 1886), 2:439–440.

84. Ibid., 2:440.

85. Ibid., 2:440–441. In a metaphor that shows great sympathy and compassion for downtrodden in Europe, those for whom, ostensibly, the uprisings where meant to up Tholuck could also look at the March Days and see that "there are being driving alon the whirlwind that is now blowing through the peoples, little flowers and fine grains of g and holy ideas—the mask of the devil, on which the wicked desires of mankind lies, sho not deter us from recognizing that under it is the face of an angel."

86. Joris van Eijnatten and Fred van Lieburg, *Niederländische Religionsgeschi* (Göttingen: Vanenhoeck and Rupprecht, 2011), 302–303.

87. Guillaume Groen van Prinsterer, *Ongeloof en Revolutie: Eene Reeks van Histori Voorlezingen* (Leiden: S. and J. Luchtmans, 1847), v.

# Tale of the Comet: Enlightenment Discourse, the Salem Witch Trials, and the Undoing of Puritan Orthodoxy

*Douglass Madison Furrh*

The Enlightenment saw the ascension of the merchant class and their correlative ideologies of capitalism and modern science. Indeed, "the development of capitalism . . . demanded a behavior whose rational orientation required ever more information."[1] Commerce, as Jürgen Habermas observes, caused the merchant class to need reliable information to conduct profitable trade, and as a result, seventeenth-century bourgeoisie made ever-more sophisticated attempts to decipher the natural world for their own self-interest. The ascension of Enlightenment ideologies resulted in a culture war throughout the Western world that reverberates into the present day. Often, this conflict manifested itself in the natural world and in the varying interpretations that the contrasting worldviews of orthodoxy and rationalism produced.

The cultural fault lines these antagonistic ideologies generated roiled the Massachusetts Bay Colony in the late seventeenth century. Although evidence of this conflict can be observed throughout the literature of the period, from providential historiographies to captivity narratives and jeremiads, this chapter will focus on the appearance of the Great Comet of 1680 and the subsequent influx of Newtonian physics and Cartesian philosophy that are observable in the literature produced by both theocrats and merchants in the colony. These two distinct applications of scientific methodology—one adhering to the supernaturalism of the colonists' forefathers, while the other increasingly relied on the precepts of rationalism—caused a schism in Puritan intellectual thought that fractured the political stability of the colony, leading to the Salem witch trials, the expulsion of the Mathers from Harvard College, the subsequent secularization of its curriculum, and the emergence of a formidable and enduring nature-based theology in the colony.

The effects of the comet on the literature and politics of Puritan New England are seen in the work of Sir Isaac Newton. In the foundational text of modern science, *Philosophiae Naturalis Principia Mathematica* (1687), Newton commends the observations performed by an unnamed Puritan at Harvard College. On November 18, 1680, the faint and unusual light of an approaching comet first appeared to the keen eye of "a young man . . . at *Boston* in *New England*."[2] The twenty-two-year-old Puritan, who was the son of a wealthy merchant, was peering through the telescope at the Harvard Observatory. In his observations, the recent graduate spotted a celestial oddity "in the middle between two small stars . . . in the southern hand of [the constellation] Virgo." The young Bostonian was at the observatory again the following morning, where he recorded his observation that at 4:30 a.m. the comet "was distant from Spica about 2 [degrees] towards the northwest."[3] "The observer in *New England*" returned again and again over the next several weeks, meticulously recording his observations.[4] The nebular light moved mysteriously through the unchanging firmament, frightening many of his fellow colonists. But the twenty-two-year-old Bostonian was more concerned with precise measurements than dogmatic superstitions.

The Great Comet of 1680, due to it traveling toward the sun and the subsequent melting of its tail, grew ever brighter until, by late November, "the tail appeared 30 [degrees] long, and directly opposite the sun, extending itself to the planet Mars."[5] The celestial nomad continued its flight over the Massachusetts sky and "in the month of *December*, just after it had been heated by the sun, did emit a much longer tail, and much more splendid, than in the month of *November* before, when it had not yet arrived in perihelion."[6] To Sir Isaac Newton, the comet had appeared as two separate entities. However, "the observer in *New England*" had seen it differently. The unsigned "Observations of a Comett" (1681), which tracked the comet's orbit about the sun, was read at the Royal Society meeting on April 13, 1681. Newton, who was then president of the society and present at the meeting, wrote in *Principia* (1687) that the observations "are better which were made by taking the position of the comet to the fixed stars by *Montenari*, *Hooke*, *Ango*, and the observer in *New England*."[7] The "anonymous person alluded to by Newton in the *Principia* as having made such good observations of the comet of 1680" was Thomas Brattle.[8]

Increase Mather, one of the most famous Puritan ministers of the day, also observed and wrote about the comet. Mather awakened in the middle of the night and took his son Cotton, who had just turned eighteen, to Clark's square, where they saw the comet with its massive tail stretching across the eastern horizon. Awestruck by "the fearful sight and great sign in Heaven," the forty-one-year-old Increase Mather's "belly trembled, [his] lips quivered."[9] He knew that God "had placed the Stars in heaven, to be for signs as to events that in ordinary course of nature should come to pass."[10] William Bradford's "hidious & desolate wilderness" of the American frontier was extended to the unintelligible firmament.[11]

For the next four years, comets and their meaning became Increase Mather's obsession. He spent countless nights "pouring over histories and encyclopedias," and in January 1681 he delivered the sermon "Heaven's Alarm to the World" at the North Church in Boston.[12] For Mather, the "blazing star" was an "awfull sign of desolation . . . hanging over the City, menacing the ruin thereof."[13] The comet meant societal declension and God's wrath. Accordingly, Mather told his congregation that "fearful sights are called signs in the scripture . . . in that they are signs that the Lord is coming forth out of his holy habitation to punish the world for their iniquityes."[14] Mather, espousing the traditional Puritanical orthodoxy that God spoke to his followers through augural signs in nature, demanded: "*Reformation! Reformation!*"[15] Nature as emblem translated seamlessly to demands for social reform.[16]

Mather, like his forefathers, embraced science not as a rationalist seeking to understand cause and effect but as a minister intent on using natural science to document God's providence at work in the material world. The result was one of Mather's most respected literary accomplishments,

*Kometographia* (1683). It is a massive treatise that attempts to link the appearance of every comet throughout the assumed five-thousand-year history of the planet "and the remarkable occurrences of Divine Providences, which have attended them."[17] The subtitle of *Kometographia* clearly states the nature of Mather's ambitious project: "The Nature of Blazing Stars Is Enquired Into: With an Historical Account of All the Comets Which Have Appeared from the Beginning of the World unto This Present Year . . . and the remarkable events Which Have Followed in the World."[18] For example, Mather argues that a comet that appeared in the year AD 56 foreshadowed that "the Emperor Claudius died, bloody Nero succeeded, who murdered . . . an infinite number of Holy Martyrs."[19] According to Kenneth Murdock, Increase Mather "accepts some of the newest scientific tenets, and his attempt to combine them with his religious views results in a position held by others for a century after him, and not wholly abandoned to-day."[20] For Increase Mather, a natural effect was the result of a supernatural cause. A link between the invisible world and natural science was forged in the colony.

Based on their observations of and experiences with this one comet, Mather and Brattle authored two dramatically different documents—documents that give evidence of a rift in colonial science and how it was performed. Mather and Brattle emerged as the leading practitioners of two conflicting approaches to science in the Massachusetts Bay Colony. Although Mather's treatise overshadowed Brattle's terse, anonymous, and largely forgotten observations, Brattle's work is evidence of rationalist thought on American soil. Over the course of the next several decades, these seeds grew into one of the most formidable forces in the political life of the colony.

As Newtonian physics, Cartesian philosophy, and a more intense scrutiny of the natural world became central to the literature of the colony, comets were demystified and brought into the arena of rational thought. Consequently, Puritan intellectual discourse underwent a paradigm shift. By the early eighteenth century, Puritan "scientific work show[ed] greater reliance on the argument from design, and less on the decipherment of religious emblems in the natural world."[21] As Puritans investigated the natural world, their belief in natural causation was fortified. As a result, divine determination—in which God intercedes and overrides the laws of nature to alter the natural course of events—began to lose its stronghold on intellectual thought in the colony. The natural progression of the scientific investigation of nature was the demystification of the supernatural. This in turn resulted in a struggle for the colony's systems of power—a struggle that began in earnest with the Salem witch trials, led to the erection of the Brattle Street Church, and culminated with the Mathers' expulsion from Harvard.[22] The introduction of rationalism set off a chain of events that pushed the colony to the brink of dissolution. The placement of comets within a scientific context was a major blow to the orthodoxy. Indeed, the disparity between Increase Mather's jeremiads and Brattle's observations were harbingers of political conflict.

## "No Room for Providential Control": Science and the Harvard Curriculum

The ideas associated with the Enlightenment had reached New England by 1671, as "books by followers of Descartes . . . became the most popular texts" at Harvard College.[23] Rene Descartes "raise[d] a new philosophy, free from all occult ideas and based only on human consciousness and experience, ranging from the direct mental apprehension of God to observation and experiment in the physical world."[24] In fact, "Descartes divides reality into *cogito,* 'I think', the only domain about which certain information can be obtained, and the world 'outside myself', which I am compelled to doubt. The separation he introduced between *res cogitans* and *res extensa* . . . deprived visible nature of the spiritual value it was allotted in earlier natural philosophy" so that "Cartesian mechanistic philosophy saw nature not as an animated principle, but as no more than a mechanism that satisfies the laws of particle physics."[25] Descartes "devised so effective a cosmic mechanism that it left no room for providential control."[26] Indeed, there was a dramatic shift in the "cognitive structure of science" by which Newton, Descartes, and Robert Boyle, among others, mechanized our view of the world as "teleological explanations of natural phenomena were replaced by explanations in terms of mathematical, mechanical laws."[27] These early Enlightenment ideas were used in the education of Brattle and of Mather's son, Cotton. Cartesian logic, Newtonian physics, and divine providence, once translated from the interpretation of celestial bodies, were the core ideas under dispute during the infamous witchcraft trials of 1692.

Although it is vital to look into the socioeconomic, gender, and racial issues at work in the witchcraft accusations, what is perhaps more significant is how Cotton Mather and other theocrats drew on this social discord for their own political advantage—eventually leading to their demise.[28] The Salem witch trials, there is little doubt, were caused by the clergy trying to maintain control at a time when the colony was in the midst of the political and social turmoil evidenced by King Phillip's War, the dissolution of the colony's charter, and an increasingly merchant-oriented demographic.[29] At the heart of the Mather-Brattle debate around the Salem witch trials was experimental philosophy and its role in the ideological framework of the Massachusetts Bay Colony.[30]

Relations of power—and, especially, the relation of science to religion—were shifting, and Cotton Mather did everything possible to isolate his flock from a new discourse, or at least confuse the nature of that discourse, which subordinated religious dogma to rational thought. In 1689, with his father abroad and therefore with a responsibility to oversee the North Church, Cotton, who "possessed more power, and wielded greater influence, perhaps, than any other individual ever did in Massachusetts," made a political bet against the "inward belief" of his father as he attempted to document witchcraft at work in the material world.[31] Increase had had his comets, but Cotton's documentation of the supernatural in and about the colony spread his fame, and infamy, in far greater circles than his father had ever known as the younger Mather turned his gaze from the firmament to the colonists.

For several years, colonists had been "turning their backs upon the public worship," and Mather turned to the time-tested strategy of fear and divine providences to return people to the pews.[32] According to the younger Mather, witches were sent by the "singular Providence of God" so that "many other[s], even some scores, of young people, awakened by the picture of Hell," would be "brought home to the Lord . . . and admitted unto our Church."[33] To this end, he published his first book, *Memorable Providences relating to Witchcrafts and Possessions* (1689), in which he pursued witchcraft specifically to rid the colony of the "sensual Sadducees, [who] count it their wisdom to credit nothing but what they see and feel."[34] Explicitly showing his disdain for experimental philosophy, Mather continued: "How much this fond opinion has gotten ground in this debauched Age is awfully observable; and what a dangerous stroak it gives to settle men in Atheism, is not hard to discern."[35] If Mather could document—as in the case of the Goodwin children in 1689, in his works concerning Salem in 1692, and again in the aftermath of the Salem trials with the case of Margaret Rule in 1693—the existence of the "being of Angels either good or evil," he would prove how the invisible world affects the material realm. By extension, he would disprove Cartesian philosophy and the ideas associated with the early Enlightenment, in which the "main business of natural philosophy is to argue from phenomena without feigning hypotheses and to deduce causes from effects."[36] In its place he could reassert the old philosophy that "God's Providence" permits "Satan and his Instruments to Molest His children, not in the Estates only, but in their Persons and their Posterity too."[37]

Accordingly, Mather began visiting the house of John Goodwin and his six children in the summer of 1688. Although four of the children were "afflicted" at different times and with different symptoms (e.g., "Unaccountable stabbs and pains"), his book concentrates on the case of the eldest daughter, Martha, who was then thirteen.[38] The twenty-five-year-old Mather took Martha to live in his house, where he conducted "experiments [that] were often enough repeated."[39] Mather, relying on his own "Ocular Observation" as testament of substantial authority, consciously decided to continue operating in the sphere of Aristotelian science, where he, like his father before him, simply worked to confirm postulated causes—namely, God's providence at work in the material world.[40] And so Mather, in his own home, began to conduct a number of "experiments" that would have—had they not led to the execution of the Irish-Catholic laundress who cared for the children—been mere frippery.

Among the superstitious, it was a widely held belief that witches were not able to recite the Lord's Prayer, so "an experiment was made, whether she could recite [it]."[41] "Tho clause after clause was most carefully repeated to her," young Martha "could not possibly avoid making Nonsense of it."[42] The experiments did not stop there. Mather brought in several other texts, including "my Fathers *Remarkable Providences*" and his "Grandfather Cottons Catechism called *Milk for Babes*," which predictably brought "hideous Convulsions on the Child if she look't into them."[43] On the other hand, Martha could read very well "a Quakers Book" and "a Book that pretends to prove, that there are no Witches."[44] Happy with the results of his experiments, Mather notes, "I hope I have not spoil'd the credit of the Books, by telling how much the Devils hated them."[45] As bizarre as these experiments seem, they reveal two sobering facts: that Cotton Mather was keenly aware of then-current scientific thinking that attempted "to prove, that there were no witches" and that the execution of an Irish-Catholic laundress troubled him little, if at all.

Cotton Mather was well versed in the ideas of the Enlightenment, as his Harvard education and renowned personal library attests, but he was unprepared to reconcile these two epistemologies. Increase and Cotton Matter did to scientific discourse what they had done to all other narrative structures that informed and fueled their power: they warped it and grafted it into the Old Testament myths in order to usurp the Israelites' claim to be God's chosen people and further validate the covenant. This method had yielded the divines unchecked power throughout the colony's history. The fact that Cotton Mather would stop at nothing to protect his reading of the scriptures—and the political capital that interpretation provided—from empiricism is evident in his conclusion in *Memorable Providences*: "God is therefore pleased . . . to suffer Devils sometimes to do such things in the world as shall stop the mouth of gainsayers, and extort a Confession from them."[46] Further, his willingness to hang innocents in defense of his ideas is evidenced when he writes: "But I resolv'd after this, never to use but just one grain of patience with any man that shall go to impose upon a Denial of Devils, or of Witches."[47] Mather continues, "I suppose the Instances of this direful thing are seldom, but that they are not never we can produce very dismal Testimony."[48] The still-youthful Mather was poised to lead Puritan orthodoxy into the eighteenth century, but the ideas of the Enlightenment stood in his way. Science was usurping the power of the theocracy, and the best way to stop it was to attack the philosophical roots that sought to limit the influence of invisible spirits on this world.

## "The Doer of All the Hard Things": Cotton Mather and the Executions at Salem

Cotton Mather's role in the witch trials is mystifyingly still disputed even though Mather himself stated that "the mad people thro' the Countrey . . . reviled mee, as if I had been the Doer of all the hard Things, that were done, in the Prosecution of the Witchcraft."[49] Mather's influence on the August executions is undeniable. On August 19, 1692, George Jacobs Sr., Martha Carrier, the Reverend George Burroughs, John Willard, and John Proctor were carried in a cart through the streets of Salem. "A very great number of spectators" awaited the arrival of the accused at Gallows Hill, where they were to witness the third round of executions ordered by the Court of Oyer and Terminer.[50] Mather, mounted on horseback, rode confidently about, knowing that "the councellors of the province," who were "of [his] own father's nomination," had a close eye on the proceedings.[51] "Mr. Cotton Mather . . . and Mr. Sims, Hale, Noyes, Chiever, &c." were all in attendance.[52] Brattle, the merchant and astronomer, was among the crowd.[53]

As previously stated, it was a long-held superstition that witches could not recite the Lord's Prayer without error, and the recitation was often used "as a tryal of their guilt."[54] Each of the accused "said they were innocent," but it was the "very puny man," George Burroughs, who took the drama from crescendo to silence when he ascended the ladder toward the noose that was to take his life.[55] Standing near the ladder's top step, Burroughs, who "was regarded with confidence by his neighbors and looked up to as a councellor," delivered his final sermon.[56] The tension was palpable as Burroughs, short in stature but renowned for strength, "made a Speech for the clearing of his Innocency, with such Solemn and Serious Expressions, as were to the Admiration of all present."[57] "Mr. Burrough[s]," writes Samuel Sewall—who was one of the judges who had convicted and sentenced Burroughs and the others—"by his Speech, Prayer, protestation of his Innocence, did much move unthinking persons."[58] Burroughs recited the Lord's Prayer with "composedness" and "fervency," and his speech "drew Tears from many (so that it seemed to some, that the Spectators would hinder the Execution)."[59] However, "the humane feelings which were manifested at the execution" were adroitly stemmed by Cotton Mather.[60] Still on horseback, Mather declared: "The Devil has often been transformed into an Angel of Light."[61] Mather's words "somewhat appeased the people and the Executions went on."[62] Then "Mr. Mather said they all died by a Righteous Sentence."[63] After Burroughs was hanged, he was unceremoniously cut down and thrown into a two-foot-deep hole between some rocks. His body lay entangled with those of Martha Carrier and John Willard, where "one of his Hands and his Chin, and a Foot of one [of] them" protruded from the piteous grave.[64] Samuel Sewall, in the margin of his diary for August 19, wrote, "Dolefull Witchcraft!"[65] This moment haunted Mather in the decades that followed, for his actions went unforgiven by many in the colony—especially those of the merchant class.

## "As Experience Teaches": Thomas Brattle's Letter

Shortly after Brattle learned that his "Observations of a Comett" had been read at a Royal Society meeting, he took part in the reverse migration, as did many young colonists, as he "very much imprv'd himself in his Studies and by his Travels abroad."[66] In fact, Brattle spent nearly eight years in England, from 1682 to 1689.[67] While abroad, Brattle not only kept the company of Sir Robert Boyle, the "doyen of the new, experimental science" and the father of modern chemistry, but also became well acquainted with Sir Christopher Wren, the principal architect of St. Paul's Cathedral, and John Flamsteed, the royal astronomer.[68] Brattle's "abilities earned him the praise and respect of the most important English scientists of the era and he brought back to his provincial home a scientific and philosophical expertise unknown in the colony."[69] Brattle's presence at the center of the scientific community at the dawn of the Enlightenment prepared him for his repeated confrontations with the increasingly antirationalist Cotton Mather.

Until the fall of 1692, the discourse concerning witchcraft had been monopolized by the conservative branch of the colony's theocracy, and the results had been disastrous. "By October it seemed as though the bonds of society were dissolving; nineteen persons had been hanged, one had been pressed to death, and eight lay condemned; a number had fled, but their property had been seized and they were beggars; the prisons were choked, while more than two hundred were accused and in momentary fear of arrest."[70] Those awaiting trial in prison were, according to Governor Phips, "in great misery by reason of the extream cold and their poverty, most of them having only spectre evidence against them."[71] A growing group of outraged citizens believed the actions of the court were simply beyond reason.

On October 8, 1692, Brattle's "A Copy of a Ms. Letter, Giving a Full and Candid Account of the Delusion Called Witchcraft" was "circulated through the proper quarters in manuscript."[72] After October 8, the unfolding of events became frantic. Brattle's letter was written on the evening before the session of the General Court. On or about the eighth of October, Governor Phips "began to feel alarm lest he should [b]e called to account in England."[73] Although a chorus of voices protested the court's reliance on spectral evidences—including those of the Reverend Samuel Willard and even Increase Mather after his return from England—Brattle's letter portrays the ideological divisions that had developed in the late seventeenth century and marks the advent of rationalism as a political force within the colony. The letter checked theocratic power, leaving the colonists to consider that "ages will not wear off that reproach and those stains which these things will leave behind them on our land." Mather well knew "that these methods [of the Salem judges] will utterly undoe poor N[ew] E[ngland]."[74] Perry Miller states that Brattle's letter was the first document in New England "that step[ped] outside of the scheme of the jeremiad."[75] Indeed, Brattle stepped well outside the jeremiad because he was deeply concerned with cause and effect in examining the unscientific methods employed by the judges. He mocked the judges' provincial understanding of early Enlightenment discourse, writing: "The reasonable part of the world, when acquainted herewith, will laugh at the demonstration, and conclude that ye said S[alem] G[entlemen] are actually possessed, at least, with ignorance and folly."[76] In the same paragraph, Brattle assails the ludicrousness of the judges' methodology: "I suppose his Honour never made the experiment, whether there was not as much virtue in his own hand . . . to cure the touch."[77] When defendants stood on trial, they were often ordered to touch the "afflicted children," or the accusers, and if the children did not immediately come out of their fits, the defendants were then instructed by the court to "grasp hard, harder yet," after which the children would finally recover. Brattle observes, "the reason is very good, because that a touch of any hand, and process of time, will work the cure; infallibly they will do it, as experience teaches."[78] Brattle "condemn[s] this method of the justices . . . as it is sorcery, and a superstitious method" because "we have no rule for [it], either from reason or religion."[79]

Brattle—who constructs an argument in a fashion that was to become commonplace at Harvard over the next several decades—then scoffs at the court for thinking "they are so well instructed in the Cartesian Philosophy, and the doctrine of *effluvia*."[80] The absurdity of the Salem justices' understanding is recounted by Brattle. In a futile attempt to satisfy the need of cause and effect, the judges explained that the concept of effluvia consisted of "venemous and malicious particles" that "were ejected from the eye . . . [and] return to the body from whence they came, and so leave the afflicted persons pure and whole." This process was the means, the judges rationalized, by which the specters from the invisible world could have an impact on persons in this world. Brattle concludes, "I must confesse to you that I am no small admirer of Cartesian Philosophy; but yet I have not so learned it. Certainly this is a strain that it will by no means allow of."[81] The delineations between the physical and invisible worlds had been utterly confused by the judges.

Brattle dissects these proceedings with a confidence derived from his beliefs in Cartesian philosophy, which asserts that God "is wholly perfect and veracious" and therefore does not deceive us.[82] In a telling passage, he relates the words of "a wise and good Judge" who said "that they know not but that God almighty, or a good spirit, does give this information to these afflicted persons."[83] Brattle, again applying Cartesian philosophy, writes: "I make answer thereto, that it is neither almighty God, nor yet any good Spirit, that gives this information; and my Reason is good, because God is a God of Truth; and the good Spirits will not lye."[84] And just as the veracity of God is trustworthy, the duplicity of the devil is not. Brattle informs the court "that the witches' meeting, the Devill's Baptism, and mock sacraments, which they oft speak of, are nothing else but the effect of their fancye, depraved and deluded by the Devill, and not a Reality to be regarded or minded by any wise man."[85] Brattle's words echo those of Descartes in *Meditations* (1641). "We may question," Descartes asserts, "that some malignant demon, who is at once exceedingly potent and deceitful, has employed all his artifice to deceive me. . . . For, in fine, whether awake or asleep, we ought never to allow ourselves to be persuaded of the truth of anything unless on the evidence of our reason." Descartes concludes: "And it must be noted that I say of our reason, and not of our imagination or of our senses: thus . . . we may very distinctly imagine the head of a lion joined to the body of a goat, without being therefore shut up to the conclusion that a chimaera exists; for it is not a dictate of reason."[86] The inhabitants of the colony were getting a first-class education in the precepts of Cartesian philosophy: that which scientific inquiry deciphers through repeated experiments is given to us by a veracious God; delusions, which have no cause or effect in reality, are attributed to the devil. According to this Cartesian logic, the judges are the ones who should repent for having listened to the devil. Brattle says, "I build my faith on God's testimony and if I practice upon it, this my practice is properly built on the word of God"; those who are "informed by the Devil and act thereupon," he writes, are cause for "a lamentation."[87]

Brattle then directs his criticism at Cotton Mather. Addressing the lucidity and sincerity of the condemned at Salem, Brattle writes: "They protested their innocency as in the presence of the great God, whom forthwith they were to appear before: they wished . . . that their blood might be the last innocent blood shed upon that account. With great affection they intreated Mr. C. M. to pray with them."[88] Significantly, Brattle uses the phrase "Mr. C. M."—a direct reference to Cotton Mather. Meanwhile, in the conclusion to Mather's *Wonders of the Invisible World*—his defense of the witchcraft trials—Mather includes a series of four "*Curiosities*," in which he echoes Brattle's diction concerning "innocent blood" and the "stains . . . on our land."[89] In *Wonders*, Mather writes: "If a Drop of Innocent Blood should be shed, in the Prosecution of the Witchcrafts among us, how unhappy are we! . . . But on the other side, if the Storm of Justice do now fall only on the Heads of those Guilty Witches and Wretches which have defiled our Land, How Happy!"[90] It is noteworthy that this allusion to Brattle's letter appears near the end of Mather's nearly three-hundred-page book. Due to the nature of the printing press, last-minute additions could only come at the end of a document in the form of an addendum. Mather had been working on *Wonders* since August and was forced to hurriedly append this defense against Brattle's argument. Further, that Mather felt it necessary to address Brattle's letter, even as Phips was urging him to finish *Wonders*, demonstrates that the impact of his letter on the decision to end the trials is greater than scholars have previously granted.

## "Fenced with Iron": Cotton Mather's *Wonders* (1693)

With the tide of sentiment turning against the men who had orchestrated the trials, an emergency meeting was called in Sewall's house. According to Sewall, on Thursday, September 22, "William Stoughton, Esqur., John Hathorne, Esqur., Mr. Cotton Mather, and Capt. John Higginson, with my brother St., were at our house speaking about publishing some Trials of the Witches."[91] "His Excellency, the Governor [Phips], [had] laid his positive commands upon" Cotton Mather to undertake the task. Accordingly, Mather "composed and published [his] Book, entitled, *The Wonders of the Invisible World*" in which his "*Observations*" into the "*Nature, the Number, and the Operations of the Devils*" was a clever and sadistic way to turn the ideas and methodologies of natural science against the very men who "credit[ed] nothing but what they see and feel."[92] Indeed, Mather claimed that there were "unintelligible circumstances," that people were "tormented by invisible hands," and that "a thousand preternatural things [happened] everyday before our eyes."[93] *Wonders* was Mather's attempt to clothe the residual ideas of providences in the emergent rhetoric of early-Enlightenment discourse. However, even Mather was concerned that such an attempt would persuade readers abroad. The section titled "The Author's Defence" indicates Mather was acutely aware that an author who wrote about witches "at such a Time, had need be Fenced with Iron, and the Staff of a Spear."[94] "To send abroad a Book," Mather worried, "among such Readers, were a very unadvised Thing, if a man had not such Reasons to give, as I can bring, for such an Undertaking."[95] His reasons, however, proved threadbare.

In *Wonders*, the irrationality of Cotton Mather's argument is easily gleaned in his treatment of the Reverend Burroughs—the man he had made certain was hanged in the August executions. Mather again slanders Burroughs, portraying him as "a King in Satans Kingdom" on such absurd "evidence" as his ability "for extraordinary Lifting."[96] And Burroughs was not the only victim of Mather's slanderous document. "This Rampant Hag, Martha Carrier" was apparently a "Queen of Hebrews" because a "well-kept Cow, which without any known cause quickly fell down and Dy'd . . . [and] they could guess at no natural reason for."[97] Rather than operating within the ideas of the age, Mather had obdurately pitted himself against them. Mather was well aware that he was pervasively censured, as he admits in his diary: "The cursed *Reproaches* with which this unworthy, ungodly, ungrateful People, do load [loath] not only myself, but both my *Fathers* too."[98] Mather's *Wonders* was "a reviled book" even in its author's estimation.[99] Indeed, "everything that Mather wrote can be seen as a call to defend the old order of church authority against the encroachment of an increasingly secular world. As an apologist for the 'old New England way,' there is no doubt that Mather left himself open to attack."[100] In fact, even "after His Excellency (with their Majesties' approbation as is said) had put a stop to the executions," Mather continued undaunted in defending the old order of the church.[101]

In September 1693, well after the close of the trials, Mather again brought a young woman, Margaret Rule, to live in his home under the pretense of possession. This time the merchants became more organized and, according to Mather, sent "spies . . . to report about town that she was not afflicted."[102] Robert Calef, "the Weaver (though he presumes to call himself Merchant),"—as Mather derogatorily referred to him—was "with some others . . . drawn by curiosity to see Margaret Rule, and so much the rather because it was reported Mr. M[ather] would be there that night."[103] Calef, who is credited with authoring *More Wonders of the Invisible World* but "was furnished with materials for his work by Mr. Brattle," attended the supposed possession of the young woman and turned a skeptical eye on the proceedings.[104] Calef, addressing the reader, writes: "If the bigots willfully and blindly reject the testimonies of their own reason . . . it is no more than I expected from them, but . . . if you are willing to distinguish truth from error . . . I shall not miss my aim."[105] Calef makes clear that Mather was capitalizing on the accusations for political gain: "Mr. Cotton Mather, having been very forward to write books of witchcraft, has not been so forward either to explain or defend the doctrinal part thereof."[106] Further, Calef portrays the Mathers not as divines but as sexual deviants. According to Calef, the Mathers "rub'd her breast" and "when they did it in the right place she could fetch her breath, and by that they knew" she would come out of her fit.[107] Cotton Mather denied this charge, claiming that he "rubbed Rule's stomach, her breast not being covered."[108] Further, Mather "stayed alone with her in her room half an hour," while she would only drink "rum."[109] As a result of Calef's account, Mather, in a letter to Calef, complained that the "people believe a smutty thing of me."[110] Mather had Calef "brought before their Majesties' justice, by warrant, as for scandalous libels," but Mather did not appear at the court, "upon which [Calef] was dismissed."[111] After the publication of *More Wonders*, the feud spilled over to Harvard College. Calef, Brattle, and others, armed with the beliefs and practices cultivated and honed through commercial and scientific activities, effectively unmasked the fear-based ideology of the theocrats. Indeed, "the development of capitalism . . . demanded a behavior whose rational orientation required ever more information."[112] This ability to systematically gather, process, and scrutinize information was put to use by an organized group of merchants to end this final episode of supposed witchery and to assume control of Harvard.

## Conclusion

Increase Mather, in one of his last acts as president of Harvard College, "ordered the wicked book," Calef's *More Wonders*, "to be burnt in the college yard."[113] Further, the younger Mather complained that Brattle "scornfully styles *his* President a reverend Scribbler.—A moral heathen would not have done as he has done."[114] The ideological feud, first seen in the discourse about the Great Comet of 1680 and begun in earnest at Salem, directly resulted in the Mathers' permanent exclusion from Harvard. In contrast, less than a year after the trials concluded, on May 8, 1693, Brattle was elected as treasurer and tutor at the college. Brattle "continued in that Post 20 years & ten days."[115] The feud begun at Salem became more acrimonious as the factions fought bitterly over control of Harvard, which had hitherto been the lifeblood of educating the colony's theologians; the victors would control the intellectual direction of the colony.

Cotton Mather's frustrations at being excluded from the affairs of the College are repeatedly expressed by the reverend in the years that follow: "Oh! For a wise, a meek, an humble, and a patient Conduct, under the Venome and Malice which the disaffected Rulers of our Colledge, treat me withal!"[116] At the death of John Leverett, Mather hoped to seize an opportunity: "The sudden Death of that unhappy Man, who sustained the Place of President in our College, will open a Door for my doing the singular Services to the Best of Interests. Indeed his being within a Year of myself, loudly calls upon me, to live in a daily Expectation of my own Call from hence."[117] That these factions solidified through time and that rationalist thought was at the core of their dispute is evident in many of Mather's diary entries from the early 1700s. After learning that he would not be offered the presidency of Harvard College, Mather wrote: "The perpetual Envy, with which my Essays to serve the Kingdome of God are treated among them, and the Terror that Satan has of my beating up his Quarters at the College, led me into the former sentiment. The marvellous Indescretion, with which the affairs of the College are carried on, led me into the latter."[118] The gates of Harvard, and the control of the intellectual direction of the colony, were forever closed to Mather.

Meanwhile, Cartesian philosophy became more firmly entrenched in the Harvard curriculum in 1693 as William Brattle, Thomas's younger brother, introduced *Compendium Logicae secundum Principia D. Renati Cartessi* (1693).[119] The reintroduction of Cartesian philosophy almost immediately after the trials concluded and the fact that it was reintroduced by the brother of the trials' most vocal critic and in the same year Thomas Brattle was elected treasurer of Harvard suggest that those in power at Harvard recognized Brattle's contributions in bringing the trials to a close. Further, Thomas and William Brattle and John Leverett transformed "Harvard College from a divinity school into a secular institution" as they educated a class of early eighteenth-century Puritan intellectuals who subsequently embraced science in their analysis of the world around them.[120] For example, Thomas Brattle's star pupil, Thomas Robie, was measuring the "diameter of the Sun and Planets with the Moon . . . calculated from the latest Observations by Sir Isaac Newton's Rules."[121] Brattle, Robie, and others at Harvard were observing solar and lunar eclipses, measuring distances in the heavens, and explaining meteor showers.[122]

In stark contrast to Brattle's and Robie's work, Mather, in *The Christian Philosopher* (1721), uses Newton's law of universal gravity for religious ends. Mather writes, "A *Ton* Weight on the surface of the Earth, raised Heaven-wards unto the height of one Semidiameter of the Earth from whence, would weigh but one quarter of a ton."[123] Mather expands on Newton's law, stating: "At three Semidiameters from the Surface of the Earth, it would be easy for a man to carry a *Ton*, as here to carry little more than an hundred Pounds. At the distance of the *Moon*, which suppose to be sixty Semidiameters of the Earth, 3600 Pounds weigh but *one Pound*; and the Fall of Bodies is but sixteen Foot in a whole Minute."[124] Mather is obviously drawing on the algebraic equation $F = G\frac{m_1 m_2}{r^2}$ where $F$ is the force, $G$ is the gravitational constant, $m$ is the mass of each body, and $d$ is the distance that separates the two masses. In other words, two bodies attract each other "with a force inversely proportional to the square of its distance."[125] Mather concludes: "The further you fly toward *Heaven*, the more . . . you must *lessen*. . . . *Defamations* particularly will be Things by which you must be *lessn'd*." Mather adds, "But *my Friend*, if you were near *Heaven* as you ought to be, you would make *light* of them; you would bear them wonderfully!"[126] For the duration of his life, Mather directed his intellectual energies toward forming "an Enchiridion of the liberal Sciences, which might enable persons easily to attain them: and at the same time, consecrate the whole Erudition unto the Designs of Piety."[127]

Although the ultimate result of the Puritans' merging of scientific and religious ideologies eventually weakened Puritanism, for a brief period during the late seventeenth century science and religion commingled within the intellectual landscape of the colony. The result was the loss of twenty-one innocent lives at Salem, a subsequent struggle for control of Harvard, a splintering of the previously unified colony, and the emergence of a formidable and enduring nature-based theology in the colony. The fundamentally superstitious interpretation of the natural world, which had been propagated by the Puritan orthodoxy throughout the seventeenth century, shifted toward an empirical investigation of nature. In the merging and purging of scientific discourse and religious commentaries, the nascency of a uniquely American ideology can be seen.

## Notes

1. Jürgen Habermas, *The Structural Transformation of the Public Sphere: An Inquiry into a Category of Bourgeois Society* (Cambridge, MA: MIT Press, 1994), 36.
2. Sir Isaac Newton, *Mathematical Principles of Natural Philosophy and His System of the World* (Berkeley: University of California Press, 1966), 516.
3. Ibid., 516.
4. Ibid., 518.
5. Ibid., 520.
6. Ibid., 522.
7. Ibid., 518.
8. Francis Bailey, *Supplement to the Account of the Reverend John Flamsteed, the First Astronomer-Royal* (London: Glavard College, 1837), 725n. Raymond Stearns, in *Science in the British Colonies of America* ( Urbana: University of Illinois Press, 1970), sums up Brattle's contribution: "Independently [Brattle] recognized the fact that a comet which disappeared

at perihelion into the glare of the sun's rays and reappeared on the other side of the sun was one and the same comet. His observations were valuable to Newton because . . . they helped him to determine the orbital elements of a comet moving in an ellipse" (p.153). Brattle's observations helped "Newton test Kepler's three laws, to work out the law of gravitation, and to write the great Principia" (153).

9. Increase Mather, "Heaven's Alarm to the World, or, A Sermon Wherein Is Shewed, That Fearful Sights and Signs in Heaven Are the Presages of Great Calamities at Hand" (Boston: John Foster, 1681), in *Sabin's Dictionary of Books relating to America* (1997), 13.

10. Ibid., 3.

11. William Bradford, *History of Plimouth Plantation* (2008), http://www.gutenberg.org/files/24950/24950-h/24950-h.htm.

12. Michael G. Hall, *The Last American Puritan: The Life of Increase Mather, 1639–1723* (Middleton, CT: Wesleyan University Press, 1988), 159.

13. Increase Mather, "Heaven's Alarm," 16.

14. Ibid., 13.

15. Ibid., 16.

16. See *The Massachusetts General Court: Provoking Evils* (1675) for an example of how declension, reformation, and the divines' ability to decipher the natural world were used as a means of social control. Everyday behaviors, such as "rudeness in youth," leaving "the public worship before it be finished," and "common swearing and cursing," were reasons that "the righteous God hath . . . given commission to the barbarous heathen to rise up against" the Puritans. God's providence and the doctrine of declension, as wielded by Puritan divines, confuses cause and effect in order to exert social control.

17. Increase Mather, *Kometographia* (Boston: Printed by S.G. for S.S., 1683), in Sabin's Dictionary of Books relating to America (1997), ix.

18. Ibid., frontispiece.

19. Mather, *Kometographia*, 38.

20. Kenneth Ballard Murdock, *Increase Mather, the Foremost American Puritan* (New York: Russell and Russell, 1953), 146–147. Concerning the use of declension and emblematic interpretations of natural phenomena in contemporary America, consider the Reverend Franklin Graham's response to the devastating hurricane Katrina. Graham argued that New Orleans was punished by God, as it "is one wicked city . . . known for Mardi Gras, for Satan worship. It's known for sex perversion. It's known for every type of drugs and alcohol and the orgies and all of these things that go on down there in New Orleans."

21. Clark A. Elliott and Margaret W. Rossiter, *Science at Harvard University: Historical Perspectives* (Bethlehem, PA: Lehigh University Press, 1992), 32.

22. Thomas Brattle greatly shaped the intellectual development of the colony. He founded the Brattle Street Church in 1699 outside the authority of the colony's theocratic powers.

23. David Levin, *Cotton Mather: The Young Life of the Lord's Remembrancer, 1663–1703* (Cambridge, MA: Harvard University Press, 1978), 48.

24. Sir William Cecil Dampier, *A History of Science and Its Relations with Philosophy and Religion* (Cambridge: Cambridge University Press, 1944), 148.

25. Thijs Weststeijn, *The Visible World: Samuel Van Hoogstraten's Art Theory and the Legitimation of Painting in the Dutch Golden Age* (Amsterdam: Amsterdam University Press, 2008), 330.

26. Ibid., 162.

27. P. M Harman, *Metaphysics and Natural Philosophy: The Problem of Substance in Classical Physics* (Sussex, UK: Harvester Press, 1982), 1.

28. See Mary Norton's *In the Devil's Snare* for an illuminating analysis of the social pressures that drove the accusations; these pressures included socioeconomic factors, ergotism, political instability, and hysteria.

29. "Puritan New England had been in deep trouble since the late 1670s. The threat of Indian wars, French imperialism, rising commercialism, and rapid growth causing an increasingly pluralistic society combined to eat at Puritan assurance in their divinely ordained role as 'New English Israel.'" (Rick Kennedy, *Aristotelian and Cartesian Logic at Harvard: Charles Morton's Logick System and William Brattle's Compendium of Logick* [Publications of the Colonial Society of Massachusetts, 1995], 91–92. It was in this state that the orthodox Puritan might have felt he was living in "a collapsing world" (Kennedy 91).

30. Evidence of the feud can be seen in a number of documents from 1692 and well into the eighteenth century. For example, on the frontispiece of Gospel Order Revived, the anonymous author(s) complained in the "Advertisement [that] The Reader is desired to take Notice, that the Press in Boston is so much under the aw of the Reverend Author, whom we answer, . . . that we could not obtain of the Printer there to print the following Sheets, which is the only true Reason why we have sent to Copy so far for its Impression." The authors are listed as being "Sundry Ministers of the Gospel in New England," but several sources, including Sibley's *Biographical Sketches*, attribute the piece to Thomas Brattle. A noteworthy product of this feud was the struggle of the "manifesto men" in forging some semblance of a public sphere in the colony as the theocrats resisted "the principle of publicity [being turned] against the established authorities" (Habermas, 56).

31. John Langdon Sibley, *Biographical Sketches of Graduates of Harvard University, in Cambridge, Massachusetts*, vol. 3, 1678–1689 (Cambridge, MA: Charles William Sever, 1967), 18; Cotton Mather quoted in Robert Calef, *More Wonders of the Invisible World, in Narratives of the Witchcraft Cases, 1648–1706, ed.* George Lincoln Burr (New York: Charles Scribner's Sons, 1914), 335.

32. Massachusetts General Court, "Provoking Evils (1675)," in *Five Hundred Years: Exploring American Traditions*, ed. Scott Casper (Boston: Simon and Schuster, 2000), 36–39.

33. Cotton Mather, *Diary of Cotton* Mather (New York: Frederick Ungar, 1911), 160–161.

34. Cotton Mather, *Memorable Providences, relating to Witchcrafts and Possessions, in Narratives of the Witchcraft Cases, 1648–1706*, ed. George Lincoln Burr (New York: Charles Scribner's Sons, 1914), 95.

35. Ibid.

36. Isaac Newton, "The Argument for a Diety," *The Portable Enlightenment Reader*, ed. Isaac Kramnick (New York: Penguin Books, 1995), 96.

37. Colton Mather, *Memorable Providences*, 96.

38. Ibid., 99.

39. Ibid., 113.

40. Ibid., 94.

41. Ibid., 103.

42. Ibid.

43. Ibid., 113.

44. Ibid., 112–113.
45. Ibid., 113.
46. Ibid., 95.
47. Ibid., 123.
48. Ibid., 131.
49. Mather, *Diary*, 151.
50. Samuel Sewall, *The Diary of Samuel Sewall* (New York: Farrar, Straus, and Giroux, 1973), 294.
51. Mather, *Diary*, 148.
52. Sewall, *Diary*, 294.
53. Brattle's letter, titled "A Copy of a ms. Letter, Giving a Full and Candid Account of the Delusion Called Witchcraft, Which Prevailed in New England; and the Judicial Trials and Executions at Salem, in the County of Essex, for That Pretended Crime, in 1692," specifically refers to the events that took place at the August executions.
54. Calef, *More Wonders*, 350.
55. Sewall, *Diary*, 294; Levin, *Cotton Mather*, 221.
56. Sibley, *Biographical Sketches*, 326.
57. Calef, *More Wonders*, 360.
58. Sewall, *Diary*, 294.
59. Calef, *More Wonders*, 360.
60. Sibley, *Biographical Sketches*, 332.
61. Calef, *More Wonders*, 361.
62. Ibid., 361.
63. Sewall, *Diary*, 294.
64. Calef, *More Wonders*, 361.
65. Sewall, *Diary*, 94. On January 14, 1697, Sewall had John Willard read the following as Sewall stood in front of his fellow church members: "Samuel Sewall sensible of the reiterated strokes of God upon himself and family; and being sensible, that as to the Guilt contracted upon the opening of the late Commission of Oyer and Terminer at Salem (to which the order for this Day relates) he is, upon many accounts, more concerned than any that he knows of, Desires to take the Blame and shame of it, Asking pardon of men, And especially desiring prayers that God, who has an Unlimited Authority, would pardon that sin." He was the only member of the Court of Oyer and Terminer to offer a public apology.
66. John Leverett, *John Leverett's Diary, 1707–1723*, p. 96, Papers of John Leverett: An Inventory 1652–1724, 1730, Box 8, Harvard University Archives.
67. For more on Brattle's relationship with Boyle and his period abroad, see Rick Kennedy, "Thy Patriarchs' Desire: Thomas and William Brattle in Puritan Massachusetts" (doctoral dissertation, University of California, Santa Barbara, 1987).
68. Michael Hunter, *Robert Boyle Reconsidered* (Cambridge, England: Cambridge University Press, 1994), xi.
69. Kennedy, "Thy Patriarchs' Desire," 38–39.
70. Brooks Adams, *The Emancipation of Massachusetts: The Dream and the Reality* (Boston: Houghton Mifflin, 1962), 397.
71. Sir William Phips, "Letters of Governor Phips to the Home Government, 1692, 1693," in *Narratives of the Witchcraft Cases, 1648–1706*, ed. George Lincoln Burr (New York: Charles Scribner's Sons, 1914), 200.

72. Perry Miller, *The New England Mind from Colony to Province* (Cambridge, MA: Harvard University Press, 1953), 197.

73. Adams, *The Emancipation of Massachusetts*, 398.

74. Thomas Brattle, "A Copy of a ms. Letter," in *Collections of the Massachusetts Historical Society, for the Year 1798* (Boston: Johnson Reprint Co.), 79, 75.

75. Perry Miller, The New England Mind from Colony to Province, 196.

76. Brattle, "Letter," 64.

77. Ibid., 62–63.

78. Ibid., 63.

79. Ibid.

80. Ibid. Brattle's letter, along with his role as a tutor at Harvard from 1693 to 1713, resulted in an entire generation of intellectuals who became members of the Royal Society and wrote scientific inquiries in the tradition of Brattle's letter. One example of the subsequent inquiry is Isaac Greenwood's *A Brief Account of Some of the Effects and Properties of Damps* (Boston: Royal Society, 1729). Also see Brattle's *Eclipse of the Moon 5 April 1707, Observed at Boston* (Boston: 1707).

81. Brattle, "Letter," 63.

82. Rene Descartes, *Discourse on the Method of Rightly Conducting the Reason, and Seeking Truth in the Sciences*, trans. John Veitch (Chicago: Open Court, 1913), 43.

83. Brattle, "Letter," 73.

84. Ibid., 73.

85. Ibid., 77–78.

86. Rene Descartes, *The Meditations and Selections from the Principles of Rene Descartes*, trans. John Veitch (Chicago: Open Court, 1927), 27.

87. Brattle, "Letter," 73.

88. Ibid., 68–69.

89. Ibid., 69, 79.

90. Cotton Mather, *The Wonders of the Invisible World, in Narratives of the Witchcraft Cases, 1648–1706*, ed. George Lincoln Burr (New York: Charles Scribner's Sons, 1914), 248.

91. Sewall, *Diary*, 297.

92. Mather, *Wonders*, 152, 209; Mather, *Memorable Providences*, 95.

93. Mather, *Wonders*, 267.

94. Ibid., 210.

95. Ibid.

96. Ibid., 216, 220.

97. Ibid., 243. Disturbingly, Carrier was accused by neighbor Benjamin Abbot, who "gave testimony [that] . . . Carrier was very angry with him, upon laying out some land near her husband's" (Mather, *Wonders*, 241–242).

98. Mather, *Diary*, 175.

99. Ibid., 153.

100. Ronald Gottesman, ed., *The Norton Anthology of American Literature* (New York: Norton, 1979), 4.

101. Calef, More *Wonders*, 328.

102. Ibid.

103. Cotton Mather, *Some Few Remarks upon a Scandalous Book, against the Government and Ministry of New-England, Written, by One Robert Calef. Detecting the*

*Unparrallel'd Malice & Falsehood, of the Said Book; and Defending the Names of Several Particular Gentlemen, by Him Therein Aspersed & Abused* (Boston,: T. Green, 1701), 35; Calef, *More Wonders*, 324.

104. George Lincoln Burr, ed., *Narratives of the Witchcraft Cases, 1648–1706* (New York: Charles Scribner's Sons, 1914), 292.

105. Calef, *More Wonders*, iii.

106. Ibid., 388.

107. Ibid., 94, 95.

108. Ibid., 335.

109. Ibid., 313.

110. Correspondence of Cotton Mather quoted in Calef, *More Wonders*, 335. The Mathers, working through several of their church members, responded with *Some Few Remarks upon a Scandalous Book against the Government and Ministry of New England, Written by One Robert Calef.*

111. Calef, *More Wonders*, 329.

112. Jeurgen Habermas, *Structural Transformation*, 36. Commerce, according to Habermas, caused the merchant class to need reliable information to conduct profitable trade; as a result, seventeenth-century bourgeoisie produced and relied upon letters and fledgling news reports as well as almanacs in ever-more sophisticated attempts to decipher the natural world for their own self-interest. Further, these early forms of communication were instrumental in the formation of the public sphere. It is relevant that Brattle published one of the first almanacs in the colony. See Thomas Brattle, "An Almanack of Coelestial Motions of the Sun and Planets, with Their Principal Aspects, for the Year of the Christian Aera 1678; Being in Our Account the Third After Leap-Year and from the Creation, 5627, the Vulgar Notes of Which Are . . . Calculated for the Longitude of 315.gr and 42.gr.30. min of North Latitude" (photocopy of the original in the Watkinson Library, Hartford, CT, 1954). It is this type of activity and orientation with the natural world that made the growing merchant class of seventeenth-century New England adversaries of the providential interpretations espoused by many of the Puritan divines.

113. Burr, *Narratives of the Witchcraft Cases*, 293. Also see Josiah Quincy, *The History of Harvard University, Volume 1* (Cambridge, 1840), in which Mather "enumerates the great lights Cambridge and the College had formerly enjoyed; and reminds them of the many countries and places, which, after possessing a faithful ministry, had become, through 'young profane mockers, and scornful neuters, overgrown with thorns and nettles, so that the glory of the Lord had gradually departed.' Mercy forbid that such things should be verified in Cambridge" (129).

114. John Sibley, *Biographical Sketches*, 492.

115. John Leverett, The Papers of John Leverett: An Inventory 1652–1724, 1730, Harvard University Archives.

116. Mather, *Diary*, 474.

117. Ibid., 723.

118. Ibid., 749.

119. See Rick Kennedy, "The Alliance between Puritanism and Cartesian Logic at Harvard, 1687–1735," *The American Enlightenment*, ed. Frank Shuffleton (Rochester: University of Rochester Press, 1993), 3–26.

120. Leverett, *Diary*.

121. Thomas Robie, "An Ephemeris of the Coelestial Motions, Aspects and Eclipses, etc. for the Year of the Christian Era, MDCCX" (Boston: 1710), in *Early American Imprints* (1985), 1.

122. See Thomas Robie, "A Letter to a Certain Gentleman Desiring a Particular Account May Be Given of a Wonderful Meteor That Appeared in New England, on Decemb. 11, 1719." Robie attributes the meteor to natural causes in an attempt to assuage the public's fear of a providentially directed calamity. Also see Thomas Brattle, "An Account of Some Eclipses of the Sun and Moon, Observed at Cambridge, in New-England."

123. Cotton Mather, *The Christian Philosopher: A Collection of The Best Discoveries in Nature, with Religious Improvements* (Gainesville: Scholar's Facsimile and Reprints, 1721), 91.

124. Ibid., 91.

125. Newton, Mathematical Principles, 193.

126. Mather, *Christian Philosopher*, 91.

127. Mather, *Diary*, 570.

# “The Glorious Liberty of the Children of God”: Moral Agency and Human Liberty in Samuel Clarke’s Newtonian Theology

*Jonathan D. Pike*

In the wake of Isaac Newton’s *Principia* (1687) and the Glorious Revolution (1688), latitudinarian clerics clung to the order revealed in Newton’s universe as a mainstay and pattern for social stability. Foremost among these clerics was Newton’s most trusted and devoted disciple, Samuel Clarke (1675–1729), who argued for the existence of an active and ever-present Deity constantly supporting and upholding the framework of the universe. Clarke’s conception of God emphasized his freedom and the attribute of rationality that the Creator shared with his special creation, humankind. Clarke used this Newtonian conception of God and understanding of his attributes to assert that humans enjoyed an essentially unhindered free will, as opposed to Augustine’s teaching of original sin. For Clarke, this meant that human beings, because of their rationality, were in a position not only to choose but to be accountable for what they chose. He argued that individuals were intended to use their God-given endowment of free choice to emulate the order revealed in both nature and scripture, thereby increasing their capacity and likeness to God’s own liberty.

This chapter outlines the basis and extent of Clarke’s thoughts regarding human freedom as supported by the Newtonian perspective, as conveyed through Clarke’s lectures, sermons, and correspondence.

The excellent monographs by Margaret C. Jacob and David Nicholls[1] have been of particular help in framing the flow of Newton's influence on latitudinarians in theological, social, and political thought, such as Clarke.[2] The greater emphasis, it must be stated, has been placed on the relevant primary sources. In terms of Clarke's oeuvre, his Boyle lectures and correspondence with Leibniz are of particular interest, but his sermons garner the greater attention in this analysis; although relatively few sermons will be discussed, they are fully consonant with the theology and tone of Clarke's wider work.[3] Other notable scholars who helped me increase my understanding of Newton and Clarke and their context are Thomas Pfizenmaier, Ezio Vailati, Eric Schliesser, Sean Greenburg, John Gascoigne, John H. Gay, and Peter Harrison.[4] While much of the scholarship acknowledges Clarke's capable and argumentative genius in both his Boyle lectures and correspondence with Leibniz, this chapter will highlight the late patristic origins of his concern about free will, as well as draw heavily on his all-too-often neglected sermons on the matter, with the goal of offering a more substantial perspective of his views.

Clarke has largely been underreviewed in historical theology and in historical narrative generally.[5] Such was not the case in his own time. Gascoigne commented that for an entire century, Clarke's reputation was "renowned not only within Britain but throughout Europe".[6] Nicholls quoted Voltaire's description of "the illustrious Clarke" as "a man of unswerving virtue and a gentle disposition." Voltaire even placed Clarke alongside Newton, Locke, and Leclerc as "the greatest thinkers and finest writers of their age"—he was "a real reasoning machine".[7] However, Clarke's career was overshadowed (and indeed kept that way) by what were perceived as heterodox views relating to the Thirty-Nine Articles of Religion for the Anglican faith, particularly in regard to the articles' doctrine of the trinity.[8] While not uncommon, his views were taken to be outside of orthodoxy. Moreover, due to Clarke's intellectual and political proximities, the careful airing he gave his views was prominent and scrutinized accordingly.[9] Pfizenmaier stated that this deeply held perception guaranteed Clarke "a lasting place in the backwaters of theology.[10] Even so, Clarke had a unique voice and an "abiding preoccupation with the moral dignity of humanity based on the possibility of free will,"[11] which had a long-lasting impact on the eighteenth century. This perspective is well worth understanding, by both theologians and historians, in order to capture the spirit and frame of mind that inhabited the revolutions of that singular century.[12]

A very brief and relevant summary of Clarke's first Boyle lecture will be given. Then a sampling of his sermons will be discussed to demonstrate his preoccupation with engaging the early source of doubt concerning the capacities of human free will and to present his understanding of the nature of free will in relation to moral agency and human liberty.

## Clarke's Newtonian God

In his Boyle lectures of 1704 and 1705, Clarke gave "A Demonstration of the Being and Attributes of God" and argued for "the Unchangeable Obligations of Natural Religion and the Truth and Certainty of the Christian Revelation."[13] The Boyle lectures had become by the dawn of the eighteenth-century "a podium for latitudinarian thought and for Newtonianism."[14] Jacob has pointed out, however, that because of the particular Newtonian bent of the lectures beginning in 1692, "only Samuel Clarke . . . possessed the technical skill necessary to comprehend the *Principia*, and at the time of his lectures he was on intimate terms with Newton."[15] Among Clarke's multiple contentions in 1704 were that God, "the Self-Existent Being" and "Original Cause," is "Infinite and Omnipresent," "One," and "an Intelligent Being."[16] The third claim, that of an "Intelligent Being," is most significant for understanding his argument in relation to the free will of humankind.

Claims that Clarke made in the lecture highlight more explicitly God's capacity to act, including the "Power of Creating Matter . . . [as well as] an Immaterial Cogitative Substance, indued with a Power of beginning Motion, and with a Liberty of Will or Choice."[17] For Clarke, these creative powers instigated the free will of the human soul, expressly providing for a conception of God's capacity "to endue a Creature with Freedom or Liberty of Will."[18] Clarke did not ask, since it was already known, "Where the Seat of Liberty [i.e., God] is: but whether there be at all in Man any such Power, as a Liberty of Choice and Determining his own actions; or, on the contrary, his Actions be all as necessary as the Motions of a Clock."[19] This rhetoric perfectly encapsulates Clarke's insistence that the framework of connections—or the constellation that argues for the reality of God's freedom—be understood, maintained, and even coupled with a clear conception of human free will.

Clarke insisted on the relationality of rational creatures with their Creator, deriving therefrom the idea that the principal measure of accountability for sin or righteousness correlated with each person's capacity for "Free Choice," according to his or her measure of rationality. "It has indeed," Clarke wrote, "been sometimes taught, that Liberty is a great *Imperfection*; because it is the Occasion of all Sin and Misery. But, if we will speak properly, 'tis not Liberty that exposes us to Misery, but only the Abuse of Liberty"—its "Corruption and Depravation."[20] He went on to explain that simply because "Liberty makes Men *capable* of Sin", that does not make liberty an imperfection; for "by the same Argument, Reason and Knowledge, and every other Perfection . . . even Existence it self, will be proved to be an Imperfection."[21] Instead, Clarke asserted that "the more Perfect any Creature is, the more perfect is its Liberty: And the perfectest Liberty of all . . . can never by Ignorance, Deceit or Corruption, be byassed or diverted from Choosing, what is the Proper Object of Free Choice, the greatest Good."[22] Here, Clarke sought to reassure that a voluntary God could be depended on; Clarke went so far as to state that it is "therefore as impossible and Contradictory, to suppose *his Will* should *Choose* to do any thing contrary, to justice, Goodness or Truth; as that *his Power* should *be able*, to do any thing inconsistent with Power."[23] In keeping with his purposes, Clarke asserted that these same principles of morality were by extension "the State of good Angels, and of the Saints in Heaven."[24] For "the Creator of all things, who himself governs all his Actions by these Rules . . . cannot but require the same of all his reasonable Creatures."[25] For Clarke, this shared rationality (or capacity for intelligence) was "the true Ground and Foundation of all Eternal Moral Obligations"—a consistent standard, which God required of himself and also of "all Subordinate Intelligent Beings."[26] As such, this celebrated lecture, "A Demonstration of the Being and Attributes of God," provides the framework for understanding Clarke's consonant sermons on the same subject, but more expressly focused on humankind.

## Clarke and Human Liberty

The seminal derivative of Clarke's God of "perfect freedom," which Clarke introduced through his Boyle lectures, was that humans, by sharing in the divinity of rationality, were also free. And just as God voluntarily supported the universe, so did each person voluntarily conform to or break from God's laws. Conformity to the laws of God meant peace and harmony. Breaking from God's pattern led to dissolution and preventable pain. Ultimately, commensurate eternal rewards hinged on this basic capacity to choose, whereby God could judge according to his omniscience. Clarke's perspective on human liberty emphasized a human free will derived from that of the divine, an increasing capacity or becoming, and a just accountability.

At the end of the *Principia*, Newton had speculated briefly on where the animal capacity to "move at command of the will" originated, citing "a certain very subtle spirit, . . . the vibrations of this spirit being propagated through the solid fibers of the nerves from the external organs of the senses to the brain and from the brain into the muscles." At this point Newton abruptly ended this thought (and the *Principia*) with a single sentence: "But these things cannot be explained in a few words; furthermore, there is not a sufficient number of experiments to determine and demonstrate accurately the laws governing the actions of this spirit."[27] Where Newton left off, neuroscience would later continue; however, Clarke sought to establish a bulwark of support surrounding the path that led to this new shoreline of knowledge. The path would provide the proof for autonomy and accountability, while the shoreline marked the unknown physical cause for the veritable/perceptible capacity of the will.

Free will, or "liberty," as Clarke most often referred to it, was a phenomenal observation, the reality of which no one could doubt without making God a tyrant, the author and purveyor of injustice, misery, and decadence. Clarke argued that the very nature of God would not allow such voluntary associations except those that were becoming of God. God was God by virtue of his volition to do good. Good is coexistent with God—all of the attributes of God are coexistent and eternal as God. Therefore, God cannot but be himself. However, this leads to the question of God's liberty. For if God simply *is*, then it follows that he *cannot choose* otherwise. Is this free? Clarke argued that it is free, not because God cannot choose otherwise but because it is not his character to do so; furthermore, human beings are free in the same way through their natural (i.e., God-given) endowment of rationality.

According to Clarke, rationality is key to the character of God and to his creatures thus endowed.[28] To act contrary to reason is to act against God and our own special creation by him, making us less than we *are*. God is never less than he *is*, so where does the human propensity to be less come from? In a series of sermons, Clarke addressed these questions and principles.[29] These sermons lend insight regarding the exact nature of Clarke's system. The relationship between matter and freedom is not the focus of this research, as this relationship has been discussed at length by Gay.[30] Rather, I am expositing Clarke's views on human free will as it is derived from the proportionally shared attribute of rationality with God. I will offer a brief contextualization of the deep and early theological debate surrounding free will, after which I will detail Clarke's views.

## Clarke's Divergence from Augustine

To realize the full import of Clarke's defense of Newtonian science by advocating an essentially unhindered human free will via divine endowment, some theological context must be established. That context most relevantly begins with Augustine (AD 354–430), Bishop of Hippo in North Africa.[31] Augustine argued that humans did indeed possess "free choice of the will" but that through the "original sin" of Adam and Eve, free will became compromised. Thereafter, human free will, in the words of one prominent Protestant theologian, was "loaded"—it contained "an inbuilt tendency to sin"—and each human being shared in the sin of Adam.[32] Individual freedom *to do good* was nonexistent, at least insofar as the specific endowment of God's grace was necessary for any *good* desire or action, and communal penance was required. As a gifted polemic, Augustine defeated his opponents, most prominently

Pelagius, through a lengthy debate that continued even after they were excommunicated and banished by Pope Innocent I.[33] Even if Clarke was not aware of the specifics of that early debate, he was cognizant of the historical backdrop and his break with the orthodoxy that had prevailed. In a sermon titled "Of the Grace of God," Clarke declared that "there is no one Question in the whole System of Divinity, which has raised greater Controversies in the Church of God, than That concerning the Extent of the Grace of God and the Power of Man."[34] Clarke went on to indicate in the same sermon a tacit awareness of those earlier "controversies," quite arguably those in relation to Augustine and Pelagius: "Whether therefore They who in Antient Times were represented as Deniers of the Grace of God, were rightly charged with so doing or no, does not certainly appear; because the Ground of that charge, was only their asserting the Freedom of the Will of Man."[35]

Clarke framed this "Antient" discussion and debate concerning the "one Question" through juxtaposing the two primary positions in his own assertion. Clarke stated that those who asserted "the Freedom of the Will of Man" were judged by "their Adversaries . . . to infer a Denial of the Sufficiency of the Power or Grace of God, yet perhaps They Themselves saw no [such] Consequence of [asserting] it."[36] Clarke was giving those so accused the benefit of the doubt, but, according to Clarke, the accusers were actually guilty in the opposite extreme: "However That be," he continued, "others, in the contrary extreme, that they might be sure not to ascribe too little to the Efficacy of the Divine Grace, have supposed men to have no natural Powers at all of Acting or Willing, no use of the original Faculties given them at their Creation, no Liberty of Will or Freedom of Choice, in matters of Morality and Religion."[37] Clarke was displaying a prescient knowledge of the nuance and seeming paradox pregnant in this "Antient" debate and its eventualities.

The claim that those who believed humankind to possess "no Liberty of Will or Freedom of Choice, in matters of Morality and Religion" is important to the demonstration of Clarke's prescience. It was not that Augustine, or Calvin (as the furthest extremity), denied the existence of free will; but they held that the will was incapable of choosing God (or good) without God's express assistance or allowance, and furthermore, that there existed in humankind through hereditary sin "a serious bias . . . toward evil."[38] Clarke stated that through this conception of the doctrine, "they have consequently . . . introduced an absolute Necessity or Fatality upon Men's Actions. From whence it follows, in the next step of deduction, (though This indeed they are not so willing to see;) but in Truth it does necessarily and unavoidably follow; that God Himself, and not Man, will be the Author of Sin."[39] For Clarke, these competing positions were indicative of the ultimate extremities produced in polemic that he was seeking to bridge: man gains salvation of himself; or, people have nothing to do with the petition of God's grace and are therefore mere spectators of their own salvation (or damnation), regardless of their choices—that is, a nonexistent, unrecognized, or superfluous grace versus a theory of grace that not only compromised the God-given rationality of man but was irresistible in its power once offered.

## Clarke's "Moral Agent" Position

Clarke's argument contains neither of these extremes. Rather, Clarke was earnestly seeking the harmony that ought to be possible between a free agent and a law. For example, Clarke stated that if the argument rested solely on the assumption that it was "unworthy" of God's power "to do anything ineffectually or to permit Any Act of His to be resisted by the power of frail and mortal Men," without question such an assumption would indeed be correct. However, Clarke claimed an exception to this assumption, for "in Moral matters, where whatever is not done voluntarily and without Compulsion, is not done at all; the case is very different."[40] Morality, Clarke taught, is inextricably linked to autonomy in choice:

> For in these matters, to influence a Moral Agent with such an Efficacy as cannot be resisted, is entirely to destroy the Morality of the Action, to take away the whole Nature of Virtue and Vice, and to make all Reward or Punishment impossible or unjust. . . . It would altogether be unworthy of [God] to exercise That Power; because it would be a subverting of his whole Design, in creating rational and intelligent Beings at all.[41]

He continued his sermon by describing the mien of the desired harmony between God's power and the moral autonomy of God's creatures, giving a particularly sharp rebuff (akin to that in his Boyle lecture)[42] to purely deistical conceptions toward the end:

> Moral Agents, must be influenced only by Moral Motives; by Reason and Argument, by Persuasion and Conviction, by Hopes and Fears. The Efficacy therefore of the Grace of God, can consist only in laying before men strong Arguments for their Conviction, and giving them sufficient Helps and Assistances to overcome whatever would hinder them from acting according to such conviction. Any other influence than what is of this moral nature; any influence that amounted to force, and could not be resisted; far from being truly efficacious to make Men good and virtuous, would on the contrary make it as impossible for them to have any Virtue or Goodness at all, as it is that a Clock or a watch should be virtuous and praise-worthy.[43]

Clarke's strong defense of the moral agency afforded to humankind was a theological statement that struck at the heart of determinism and predestination, and here Clarke proclaimed the full freedom of the human will to choose according to the sufficient grace of arguments and assistance, far short of an overwhelming abandon of inhibition.

In another sermon, "Of the Liberty of Moral Agents," Clarke went further to assert that freedom, far from being merely static, was in fact contingent on proportional knowledge, which in turn was contingent on adherence and conformity to Christ's doctrine in practice. Clarke explained the text for his sermon in terms similar to Christ's admonition to his disciples. Clarke stated:

> If ye will be truly my Disciples, ye must not only profess by a sudden perswaision to be convinced of the Truth of what I say, but ye must so retain and steddily adhere to my Doctrine, as to conform your Lives and Practices thereto. . . . And by such Practice, you will continually attain a more and more perfect *Knowledge* of the Truth; and *That Knowledge* will secure to you the greatest and most desirable *Freedom* in the World.[44]

Choice and capacity could thus be increased by faithfully living the doctrine of Christ.

Clarke was careful, though, to distinguish between the "mere *physical* or *natural* Liberty" that mankind shares on the instinctual level "with the savagest Lyon" and "the meanest insect": "For They also do what they will, and go and come as they please, and follow the instinct, and gratify all the Appetites of Nature."[45] So, while humans retain "that Liberty which is common to Man with every living Creature," Clarke maintained that humans are raised to a higher status and accountability through their rationality, the status of a moral agent: "But the Liberty of a *Moral* Agent and of a *rational* Being, implies something more. It implies a Liberty of doing what is *Right*; a Freedom of hearkning [*sic*] to what *Reason* dictates, and a Power of executing what the unprejudiced and improved *Understanding* judges to be fit; fit and reasonable, fit for Him who is a rational Person, fit for any *Other* rational Person in *His* place, to do."[46] The latter part of Clarke's statement contains a significant concept that will have a long-lasting social and political impact; however, the point here is that Clarke was declaring the full capacity of humans to not only think rationally but to act accordingly. An understanding of the critical status of a moral agent to Clarke's system of thought is crucial to understanding Clarke's interpretation of Newtonian science and the Christian religion.[47]

## Sin and Clarke's Moral Agency

Clarke's conception of the moral agency of humankind changes the Augustinian assumptions of the nature of sin and sinners. In "Liberty of Moral Agents," Clarke described "the vitious Libertine," who is "blinded with Ignorance and Prejudice."

> His understanding is darkned with false Representations, and his Will bribed perpetually with deceitful Allurements; while he loves the dominion of Sin, and takes pleasure in the Practice of Unrighteousness, and silences the Voice of Reason and Conscience; he fancies himself Master of the most unbounded Liberty, and yet at the same time is really in bondage to the most unreasonable Service.[48]

Clarke had no qualms in stating that "more *usually*, they [libertines] not only are in Captivity to Sin, but *feel also and know* themselves to be so; and yet have not Courage to assert their Liberty."[49] This call to courage is a drastic departure form Augustine's "give what you command, and command what you will."[50] For Clarke it is a matter of active, chosen courage, not passive complacency—waiting for God to act so that we can—but rather that we act so that God can grant the desired and necessary help. Clarke's concern was that individuals "by long ill habits and corrupt practice, as it were [had] *given up* themselves, [they] parted with their Liberty, and yielded themselves absolutely into the Snare of the Devil, to be taken captive by him at his Will."[51] Sinners were only subject to sin so long as they declined to assert the liberty wherewith God had made them free. Humans as moral agents were unhindered in the exercise of that gift of agency and were therefore fully accountable to the extent of the gift's neglect or abuse.

Clarke explained the nature of this unhindered freedom, with an important caveat: "The True Liberty of a Rational and Moral Agent," he said, "consists in his being able to follow right Reason only, without Hindrance or Restraint. This is the Liberty of a rational Agent; the Freedom of a Man, of a Christian, of an Angel."[52] Yet at this high point he carefully distanced himself from a totally unqualified conception of human capacity, stating: "Not that in this present frail state, we can ever actually arrive at such a perfect Freedom." However, despite this caveat, he maintained the relationship between the present and eventual capacities of humankind: "By studying and practicing the Truth, the Truth of *Nature* and the Truth of *Religion*, we may and ought continually more and more to assert and improve our Freedom, till at length we arrive at the glorious Liberty of the children of God."[53] Choice and action were the symbiotic tools for *becoming* that God had granted humanity, and that becoming was in fact humans' journey to "the glorious Liberty" for which God had created them.

From Clarke's assertions in the previous paragraph, it is apparent that, for him, ascent toward perfect freedom is paved with practical adherence to commandments:

> The *highest* improvement and perfection of this Liberty in the present Life, is, when a man not only obeys the Commands of

> God, but does it habitually with ease and pleasure; when the *Commandments* of God seem *not grievous* to him, but the *yoke* of Christ is *easy*, and his *burden* light.[54]

In order then to demonstrate the scriptural basis of his conception of humankind and its ultimate dependence on Christ, Clarke quoted the Psalmist, who stated that "*his delight is in the Law of the Lord, and in his Law doeth he exercise himself day and night*"; then, most importantly, Clark quoted "our Saviour himself," who said, "*My meat is to do the Will of him that sent me, and to finish his Work.*" Clarke declared that when a person has these same sentiments, they have reached "the highest pitch of Christian Perfection upon Earth; then may it be said of such a Person, that he *continueth in the perfect Law of Liberty*" and that "though he be a *Servant* . . . he is *the Lord's free Man* . . . that because the *Son* has *made him free*, therefore *he is free indeed.*"[55] Clarke insisted that without Christ there is no path to perfection, no capacity to achieve Liberty; there would be nowhere for moral agents to go if Christ had not gone "*to preach deliverance to the captives,—to set at Liberty them that are bruised.*"[56]

## Clarke on Original Sin

That Clarke denied, albeit carefully, an Augustinian conception of humankind cannot be doubted when we consider his writings on original sin. Clarke chose as the text for another one of his sermons a passage from Ecclesiastes: "This only have I found, that God has made Man Upright, but they have sought out many inventions."[57] In this sermon, Clarke sought to establish that God does not judge humankind by the sin of Adam, although all live with its consequences. Clarke taught that the "Transgression" of "our first Parents," even though it is not identified in Genesis "nor elsewhere in Scripture" as such, "may very properly be called the *Original Sin of Men*. . . . Before it, there was no such thing as Sin upon Earth." He went on to strongly deny an Augustinian conception of original sin: "The *Original Sin of Men* therefore, was the *Actual Sin* of our first Parent; But it could not be the *Actual Sin* of any other Person, because it was committed before any other had a Being. To affirm that the *first actual Sin of Adam*, was *Imputed* to All Mankind as well as to him; is to affirm what the Scripture does not teach."[58] Here Clarke unmistakably departed from Augustine, who held that "even if ignorance and trouble were primordial features of the nature of human being, God still ought to be praised rather than blamed."[59] Clarke's conception of God would not permit a just God to commit such an act. In his "Being and Attributes," Clarke also condemned the doctrine of damnation for the innocent, perhaps a tacit disapproval of infant damnation, because the capacity of infants was wholly incommensurate with an accountability correlated with eternal misery:

> Further; that there is a *Fitness* or *Suitableness* of certain *Circumstances* to certain *Persons*, and an *Unsuitableness* of Others, founded in the *Nature of Things* and in the *Qualifications of Persons*, antecedent to *Will* and to All *Arbitrary or Positive Appointment whatsoever*; must unavoidably be acknowledged by every one, who will not affirm that 'tis *equally Fit and Suitable*, in the *Nature and Reason of Things*, that an Innocent Being should be *extremely and eternally Miserable*, as that it should be free from such Misery. There *is* therefore such a thing as *Fitness* and *Unfitness*, eternally, necessarily, and unchangeably, in the Nature and Reason of Things.[60]

A just God would not judge one individual on the actions of another, nor would he require one to account for a capacity not given. Clarke offered a similar conception in his first published work, *Three Practical Essays upon Baptism, Confirmation and Repentance* (1699), wherein he emphasized the later role of confirmation for "those baptised in their infancy,"[61] referring to a "new-born infant [as] without spot, innocent and sinless."[62]

Clarke entered into echoes of Pelagian arguments[63] when, in a sermon, he quoted Paul: "Shall the Thing formed, say unto him that formed it, Why hast thou made me thus? Hath not the Potter power over the clay, of the same lump to make one vessel unto honour, and another unto dishonour?" Clarke explained the passage with the question "Hath not God a Right to make what Variety of Creatures, and of what different Capacities, he pleases?"[64] That God created humankind, even in a "frail and fallible" condition, is indisputable according to Clarke, but the nature of that creation, and to what end, is the question.

> That though God *has* indeed made us *frail and fallible*, yet he has not made us *necessarily Wicked*; he has made us, subject and liable to *Temptation*, but not of necessity Slaves to Sin. That we are *Capable* of Corrupting ourselves, *is* indeed the Consequence of that nature which God has given us; But all *Actual* Corruptions, are the Effects of our *Free Choice*, and the Fruit of *our Own* Inventions. *God has made Man upright, but They have sought out many Inventions.*[65]

From this perspective Clarke declared: "*1st*, A justification of *God*, from all possibility of being charged with the Sins of Men: *God has made Man upright. 2ndly*, A confession, that the Sin and Misery of *Men*, is wholly owing to themselves: *But they have sought out many Inventions*."[66]

Significantly, for Clarke the nature of humankind is not determined or defined by its capacity to sin but, rather, its capacity for virtue:

> For *Temptation* is not *Sin*, but the *Tryal* and the Occasion of *Virtue*. And God, who knows how to make just *Allowances* for every one's Case, with the most exact proportion and Equity; may prove the sincere Obedience of his Creatures, by what Tryals and Temptations he himself, in his All-wise Government, thinks fit to permit. In all which, 'tis certain that God makes no Man *Wicked* by *Nature*; but every Man then sinneth, *when he is drawn away of his own Lust and inticed.*[67]

Clarke's conception of a God both omniscient and good is richly displayed in his stated understanding of the purposes of "Tryals and Tempations," which are necessary for an individual to prove "sincere Obedience."[68]

## Conclusion

Newtonian science, according to Clarke, was intimately interwoven with God's freedom, which is the source of human freedom. Clarke asserted this perspective explicitly in his Boyle lectures, and he did so again in his sermon "Of the Liberty of Moral Agents," from which this analysis drew heavily. Clarke stated:

> Now *His* Liberty consists in this, that being infinitely *Knowing* and infinitely *Powerful*, 'tis impossible he should ever be influenced by any *Violence*, or by any *Deceit*; but his *Will* is always directed by *absolute Right and Reason only* . . . [and] the *Liberty* by which he always *chooses* what is eternally and absolutely right and good, can never possibly be infringed, no not in the least degree, by any Error or Passion, by any Violence or by any Deceit.[69]

And then he asserted that the freedom of humankind is directly connected to the attributes of God that Clarke had listed. He continued:

> The Liberty of *Man*, therefore, consists proportionably in the very same things; in his being free from all those false Biasses and corrupt Inclinations, which would cause his Will to decline from the Direction of Right Reason. And where This Liberty is preserved by good men to any considerable degree of Perfection, there the Holy Ghost is pleased to express itself in such manner even concerning *Them* also, as to affirm that they *cannot sin*; I Joh. iii. 9. Which expression is therefore so far from implying their having *no Liberty* of Will at all, as some have vainly imagined; that on the contrary, it signifies their having their *Liberty so perfect* in Imitation of God, as (abating the unavoidable infirmities of human Nature) to be in *no danger* of being biassed or seduced.[70]

Clarke is consistent in maintaining the association between God and the endowment given to human creation. Clarke articulated this association for both his ecclesiastical and scientific audiences. From Clarke's Boyle lectures and sermons, we see what John Gascoigne also noted—namely, Clarke's efforts to "demonstrate that the Newtonian system was compatible with a belief in human liberty and hence moral choice."[71] Such can be observed in Clarke's correspondence with Leibniz as well.[72]

This chapter has helped establish that Clarke presented a middle path between the extremes that had been the outcome and further outgrowth of the "Antient" debate between Augustine and the Pelagians. Clarke held that human beings, through the gift of rationality, share in God's capacity to choose, to be persuaded, and to then act according to their creation by God and thereby increase further in that capacity. Consequently, individuals could justly be held accountable and eventually—or "till at length," in Clarke's words—"arrive at the glorious Liberty of the children of God."[73] As was aptly noted of Clarke by his friend and associate Benjamin Hoadly, "this Liberty, or Moral Agency, was a Darling Point to Him."[74]

## Notes

1. Margaret C. Jacob, *The Newtonians and the English Revolution, 1689–1720* (Hassocks, UK: The Harvester Press, 1976); David Nicholls, *God and Government in an "Age of Reason"* (New York: Routledge, 1995).

2. For example, Jacob wrote: "Clarke believed that the decay of moral values and consequently of social stability prefigured the physical decay of nature. If the destruction of nature is to be prevented, then the decay of moral values must cease. The principles of order and reason demand assertion, and to do this, the order inherent in nature must be affirmed and applied to the moral and social order. Thus churchmen turned to the Newtonian system as the model inherent in nature and applied its principles to the society within which they lived" (*Newtonians*, 191).

3. Some of Clarke's sermons not discussed in this anlaysis partially demonstrate the consistency of Clarke's thoughts regarding moral agency. Each sermon (listed below) can be found in the second volume of *The Works of Samuel Clarke, D. D.*, edited by John Clarke (London: Knapton, 1738): "Sermon CXLIV. Christians Ought to Endeavour to Attain Perfection," "Sermon CLVII. Different Degrees of Sinners Differently to Be Treated," "Sermon CXXXII. Of the Nature of Temptations," "Sermon CLVI. Perseverance in Religion the Only Title to the Reward of It," "Sermon CXXXI. Reason the Judge of Religious Actions," "Sermon CLV. That Godliness Generally Makes Men Happy in This Life,"; "Sermon CLIII. That True Christians Are Free from All Habits of Sin," and "Sermon CXLV. The Reward of Justice".

4. See Thomas C. Pfizenmaier, *The Trinitarian Theology of Dr. Samuel Clarke (1675–1729): Context, Sources, and Controversy* (Leiden: Brill, 1997); Ezio Vailati, ed., introduction to *"A Demonstration of the Being and Attributes of God": And Other Writings* (Cambridge:

Cambridge University Press, 1998); Eric Schliesser, "Newton and Newtonianism in Eighteenth-Century British Thought," in *The Oxford Handbook of British Philosophy in the Eighteenth Century*, ed. James A. Harris (Oxford: Oxford University Press, 2013); Sean Greeberg, "Liberty and Necessity," in *The Oxford Handbook of British Philosophy in the Eighteenth Century*; John Gascoigne, "Samuel Clarke (1675–1729), Theologian and Philosopher," in Oxford Dictionary of National Biography (Oxford: Oxford University Press, 2004); John H. Gay, "Matter and Freedom in the Thought of Samuel Clarke," *Journal of the History of Ideas* 24, no. 1 (1963): 85–105; Peter Harrison, "Newtonian Science, Miracles, and the Laws of Nature," *Journal of the History of Ideas* 56 (Oct. 1995): 531–553; and, Peter Harrison, "Was Newton a Voluntarist?" in *Newton and Newtonianism: New Studies*, ed. James E. Force and Sarah Hutton (Dordrecht, The Netherlands: Kluwer Academic, 2004).

5. James Dybikowski, "Editorial" in "Samuel Clarke," ed. James Dybikowski, special issue, *Enlightenment and Dissent* 16 (1997): 1–2.

6. Gascoigne, "Samuel Clarke."

7. Nicholls, *God and Government*, 169.

8. See Jeffrey R. Wigelsworth, "Samuel Clarke's Newtonian Soul," *Journal of the History of Ideas* 70, no. 1 (2009): 46–47; Thomas C. Pfizenmaier, *The Trinitarian Theology of Dr. Samuel Clarke (1675–1729): Context, Sources, and Controversy* (Leiden: Brill, 1997); and Maurice Wiles, *Archetypal Heresy: Arianism through the Centuries* (Oxford: Oxford University Press, 1996); see also Samuel Clarke, "Scripture Doctrine of the Trinity," in *The Works of Samuel Clarke, D. D.*, vol. 4., ed. John Clarke (London: Knapton, 1738); and Voltaire, *Letters on England* (1733), trans. Leonard Tancock (Harmondsworth: Penguin, 1980), 42–43.

9. See Voltaire, *Letters on England*, 43: "He [Clarke] . . . has confined himself to publishing a book containing all the arguments in early times for and against the Unitarians, leaving to the reader the responsibility of counting the votes and deciding. This book of the Doctor's has gained him many supporters, but prevented him from becoming Archbishop of Canterbury. I think the Doctor has miscalculated and that it would have been better to be Primate of England than an Arian parish priest." See also Gascoigne, "Samuel Clarke."

10. Pfizenmaier, *Trinitarian Theology*, 2–3.

11. Gascoigne, "Samuel Clarke."

12. See references to Clarke and Newtonianism in J. C. D. Clark, *The Language of Liberty 1660–1832: Political Discourse and Social Dynamics in the Anglo-American World* (Cambridge: Cambridge University Press, 1994); I. Bernard Cohen, *Science and the Founding Fathers: Science in the Political Thought of Thomas Jefferson, Benjamin Franklin, John Adams, and James Madison* (New York: Norton, 1995); I. Bernard Cohen, "The Newtonian Scientific Revolution and Its Intellectual Significance," *Bulletin of the American Academy of Arts and Sciences* 41, no. 3 (1987): 16–42; and Robert J. Wilson III, *The Benevolent Deity: Ebenezer Gay and the Rise of Rational Religion in New England, 1696–1787* (Philadelphia: University of Pennsylvania Press, 1984).

13. Samuel Clarke, "A Demonstration of the Being and Attributes of God" (1704) and "A Discourse concerning the Unalterable Obligations of Natural Religion and the Truth and Certainty of the Christian Revelation" (1705), in *The Works of Samuel Clarke, D. D.*, vol. 2, ed. John Clarke (London: Knapton, 1738).

14. Jacob, *Newtonians*, 33.

15. Ibid. 178. William Whiston, who was Newton's chosen successor for the Lucasian chair of Mathematics at Cambridge and was forced out for his outspoken heterodoxy, wrote that Clarke was "Master of the Chief parts of *Newtonian* Philosophy." As quoted in Jeffrey R. Wigelsworth, "Samuel Clarke's Newtonian Soul," *Journal of the History of Ideas* 70, no. 1 (2009): 45–68.

16. Samuel Clarke, "A Demonstration of the Being and Attributes of God," in *The Works of Samuel Clarke, D. D.*, vol. 2, ed. John Clarke (London: Knapton, 1738), 540.

17. Ibid., 554–555.

18. Ibid., 559.

19. Ibid., 559.

20. Ibid., 575.

21. Ibid.

22. Ibid. Throughout this chapter, I have retained the original spellings in quoted material.

23. Ibid., 574.

24. Ibid., 575.

25. Ibid.

26. Ibid., 575–576.

27. Isaac Newton, *The Principia: Mathematical Principles of Natural Philosophy*, trans. I. Bernard Cohen and Anne Whitman (Berkeley: University of California Press, 1990), 943–944. For an excellent study regarding theology and *The Principia*, see Stephen D. Snobelen, "The Theology of Isaac Newton's Principia Mathematica: A Preliminary Survey," *Neue Zeitschrift für Systematische Theologie und Religionsphilosophie* 52, no. 4 (2010): 377–412.

28. Clarke's emphasis on reason is an excellent example of what Roy Porter described as a intellectual countercurrent prevalent in the eighteenth century: "Enlightened divines instated a more optimistic (pelagian) theology, proclaiming the benevolence of the Supreme Being and man's capacity to fulfil his duties through his God-given faculties, the chief of these being reason, that candle of the Lord." (Porter, *Enlightenment: Britain and the Creation of the Modern World* [London: Penguin Books, 2000], 100).

29. See footnote 3.

30. See Gay, "Matter and Freedom in the Thought of Samuel Clarke," *Journal of the History of Ideas* 24, no. 1 (Jan.–Mar. 1963): 85–105, http://www.jstor.org/stable/2707860.

31. Gascoigne implied that Clarke's more immediate opposition was to Calvinism; however, my focus on Augustine is based on the fact that (as I demonstrate more fully hereafter) Clarke is writing in reference to participants in an "Antient" debate—hardly a description of Calvinism. See Gascoigne, "Samuel Clarke."

32. Alister McGrath, *Heresy: A History of Defending the Truth* (London: HarperOne, 2009), 165.

33. See also Tatha Wiley, *Original Sin: Origins, Developments, Contemporary Meanings* (Mahway, NJ: Paulist Press, 2002). Wiley's *Original Sin* offers an excellent summary of the debate between Augustine and Pelagius. Another important synoptic source is Mathijs Lamberigts's "Pelagius and Pelagians," in *The Oxford Handbook of Early Christian Studies*, ed. Susan Ashbrook Harvey and David G. Hunter (Oxford: Oxford University Press, 2008). And, as noted previously, Alister McGrath's *Heresy* offers excellent detail and insight into the debate's context and outcome. For further information on

Pelagius, see B. R. Rees's introduction to *Pelagius: Life and Letters*, vol. 2 (Woodbridge, UK: The Boydell Press, 1998).

34. Samuel Clarke, "Sermon XXX. Of the Grace of God," in *The Works of Samuel Clarke, D. D.*, vol. 1, ed. Benjamin Hoadly (London: Knapton, 1738), 185.

35. Clarke, "Of the Grace of God," 185.

36. Ibid.

37. Ibid.

38. McGrath, *Heresy*, 166.

39. Clarke, "Of the Grace of God," 185.

40. Ibid., 187.

41. Ibid.

42. See Clarke, "Being and Attributes," 559n18.

43. Clarke, "Of the Grace of God," 187.

44. Samuel Clarke, "Sermon XXXV. Of the Liberty of Moral Agents," in *The Works of Samuel Clarke, D. D.*, vol. 1, ed. Benjamin Hoadly (London: Knapton, 1738), 215.

45. Clarke, "Liberty of Moral Agents," 218.

46. Ibid.

47. Ibid.

48. Ibid. My emphasis.

49. Ibid. The quote continues, indicative of Clarke's keen capacity to navigate nuance: "Their *Reason* is over-ruled; and their *Passions* govern them, even *against* their Judgment." He later referenced Romans 7:22–23 (KJV).

50. McGrath, *Heresy*, 162.

51. Clarke, "Liberty of Moral Agents," 219.

52. Ibid. See also Clarke, "Being and Attributes," 575.

53. Clarke, "Liberty of Moral Agents," 219.

54. Ibid., 222.

55. Ibid.

56. Ibid.

57. Ecclesiastes 7:29 (KJV). See Samuel Clarke, "Sermons XIII, XIV. Of the Original of Sin and Misery (1723)," in *The Works of Samuel Clarke, D. D.*, vol. 2, ed. John Clarke (London: Knapton, 1738), 471, 478.

58. Clarke, "Original of Sin and Misery," 482.

59. Augustine, Reconsiderations, in *On the Free Choice of the Will, On Grace and Free Choice, and Other Writings*, ed. Peter King (New York: Cambridge University Press, 2010), 132–133.

60. Clarke, "Being and Attributes," 571.

61. J. P. Ferguson, *Samuel Clarke: An Eighteenth Century Heretic* (Kineton: The Roundwood Press, 1976), 11.

62. Samuel Clarke, *Three Practical Essays upon Baptism, Confirmation and Repentance* (1699), as quoted in Ferguson, *Samuel Clarke: An Eighteenth-Century Heretic*, 11.

63. "But most of those who, from lack of faith as much as of knowledge, deplore the status of man, are—I am ashamed to admit it—criticising the Lord's work and asserting that man ought to have been so made that he could do no evil at all, and we are then in a position where what is moulded says to its moulder: Why have you made me thus (Rom.9.20)?" [Pelagius], "[Letter] To Demetrias," in *Pelagius: Life and Letters* 2, ed. B. R. Rees (Woodbridge, UK: The Boydell Press, 1998), 38–39.

64. Clarke, "Original of Sin and Misery," 479.
65. Ibid.
66. Ibid., 480. My emphasis.
67. Ibid., 483.
68. Ibid.
69. Clarke, "Liberty of Moral Agents," 220.
70. Ibid.
71. Gascoigne, "Samuel Clarke."
72. See, for example, Samuel Clarke, "A Collection of Papers, which Passed between the Late Learned Mr. Leibnitz and Dr. Clarke, in the Years 1715 and 1716. Relating to the Principles of Natural Philosophy and Religion," in *The Works of Samuel Clarke, D. D.*, vol. 4., ed. John Clarke (London: Knapton, 1738), 671: [From Dr. Clarke's Fifth Reply] "There is no Similitude between a *Balance* being *moved* by *Weights* or *Impulse*, and a *Mind moving itself*, or *acting* upon the View of certain Motives. The Difference is, that the one is *entirely passive*; which is being subject to *absolute Necessity*: The other not only is *acted upon*, but *acts* also; which is the Essence of *Liberty*. . . . The *Motive*, or thing *considered* as in *View*, is something *extrinsick* to the Mind: The *Impression* made upon the Mind by that Motive, is the *perceptive Quality*, in which the Mind is *passive*: The *doing* of any thing, *upon* and *after*, or in consequence of, that Perception; this is the *Power of Self-Motion*, or *Action*: Which, i*n all animate Agents, is Spontaneity*; and, in *moral Agents*, is what we properly call *Liberty*." See also Steven Shapin, "Of Gods and Kings: Natural Philosophy and Politics in the Leibniz-Clarke Disputes," *Isis* 72, no. 2 (1981): 191–197.
73. Clarke, "Liberty of Moral Agents," 219.
74. As quoted in Gascoigne, "Samuel Clarke."

# Facing Forward, Looking Backward: Milton, Dryden, and the Politics of Biblical Interpretation (1660–1685)

*John J. Burke Jr.*

We all face forward. We never know for sure what lies ahead. Yet we are ever preparing for the future, consciously or not, by looking to the past. To what extent we can or should turn to the past for guidance is, of course, a contentious issue, and rightly so. Although we know that there is wisdom in the oft-repeated words of George Santayana that "those who cannot remember the past are condemned to repeat it," we have just as many or even more experiences that prove how easy and how damaging it can be to get trapped in the past. Circumstances are constantly changing, and the past may no longer have much relevance to what we will face tomorrow or even today. This is what we might call "the agony of modernization." Milton's *Samson Agonistes* (1671) and Dryden's *Absalom and Achitophel* (1681) provide particularly illuminating instances of how we turn to the past in order to face the future, revealing the tension at the heart of the modernizing endeavor. For these two poets, the past was in the Bible, or more specifically the part that we call the Hebrew Bible or the Old Testament. Both poets take advantage of a method of biblical interpretation called *typology* to help them make sense out of the swirl of contemporary events. Their poems, though, reveal the underlying slipperiness of their endeavor—the two poems in effect endorse solutions at opposite ends of the political spectrum, neither of which was ever fully realized. In so many words, both poets proved to be poor prophets of the political order that would actually come to be.

To understand the operations, poetic and otherwise, in the seventeenth century, one must first confront the central role the Bible had in the hearts and minds of the English at that time. Believed to be God's word revealed to humankind, the Bible stood as the anchor in the storm. People read the Bible in order to discover the truths that matter. Yet it is fairly obvious that there have always been many different ways of interpreting what the Bible has to say. One way that became particularly prominent in the seventeenth century is customarily described as typology, a word with a very long history.[1] What the word seems to imply, especially as typology has relevance to seventeenth-century politics, is that the Bible was believed to contain the types of anything and everything that can or will ever happen to humankind. Since the mid and late seventeenth century in England was a time of one tumultuous political upheaval after another, the Bible came to matter even more than it customarily did—and it already had mattered considerably, especially in England. The Bible is what provides us with the link between Milton and Dryden, a link that might otherwise be slighted, since the two poets, at least on the surface, are about as different as two poets can be, something that is especially visible when taking into account their opposing political views: Puritan and Royalist.

Milton's dismissive comment of Dryden's abilities ("a good rhymist, but no poet")[2] seems to play a large role in our cultural memory. Yet there is considerable evidence, even if mostly indirect, that Dryden's poetry had more of a presence in Milton's poetic psyche—even if it was a grating one—than is usually acknowledged. It is well known that with the collapse of the Puritan Commonwealth—and worse, with the restoration of the monarchy, and adding insult to injury, with the reestablishment of Anglicanism and the episcopal model of church government—that Milton's dream for the future of England had crumbled. Everything that Milton as a true believer had worked for and prayed for so tirelessly had turned into dust and ashes. He was blind. He had been imprisoned, if only briefly. He was surely embarrassed—still proud, yes, but almost completely dependent on the kindness of others.[3] What is worse, he had to endure the rise of Dryden, his poetic rival, to public acclaim. As is well known, Dryden published strikingly successful poems, first *Astraea Redux* in 1660, celebrating the

Restoration of young Charles Stuart as king, then *Annus Mirabilis* (1667), celebrating the miraculous recovery of London from both the Great Fire of 1665 and the devastations of the Plague in 1666. Both of Dryden's poems, with their Latin titles alluding, as they do, to the achievements of classical times, were in effect arguing that history was on the side of the monarchists and the Anglicans, with the further implication that God himself had approved of—even endorsed—the defeat of England's Puritans, including, most notably, the humiliation of Milton himself.

The public battle between the two began, or at least becomes visible to us, with the publication of Milton's dramatic poem known to us as *Samson Agonistes* in 1671. There is evidence that Milton had been drawn to the story of Samson as far back as the 1640s, likely when he first realized he was going blind,[4] but the origins of this dramatic poem matter less than the occasion arising for it in the decade that followed the Restoration of the monarchy in 1660. What we can be certain about is that Milton published his version of the biblical story when he was about to turn sixty-three, thus nearing the end of his life—a life that was, at least in political terms, in ruins. The question cannot help but be raised as to how a good man, maybe even a saintly man—one who had fought for what he believed was a righteous cause—could be plunged into such misery? The temptation to despair or worse had to have been nearly overwhelming. It is not surprising that under such circumstances Milton would do what he always did in such moments of severe spiritual stress: he turned to the Bible to make sense, as best he could, of why everything had gone so wrong.

The parallels between the life of John Milton and that of the biblical Samson are virtually inescapable. They may not always be exact, but it seems clear enough, given the practices of biblical typology in the seventeenth century, that they never really had to be exact, just suggestive.[5] (1) There are signs of divine election in the early lives of both men—Samson's talents being physical and/or martial, Milton's being intellectual and/or poetic. (2) Both men are struck blind—Samson by the Philistines, the enemies of God's people; Milton's blindness, so far as we know, had no such external cause. (His blindness may have been simply genetic, or it may have been, as he claimed, the result of too much reading in poor light. Whatever the reason, it was not something done to him by God's enemies.) (3) Both figures wear their hair shoulder-length or longer: Samson by the command of the God he serves, Milton perhaps for reasons having to do with the biblical Samson, but in any case stubbornly contrary to the prevailing Puritan fashion of "roundheads" or closely shorn hair.[6] (4) Both figures have considerable difficulty with women. The marital troubles of these two alpha males are believed by their men to stem from a lack of loyalty in their spouses. (5) Both of God's chosen ones experience defeat so crushing that there seems little room for hope, never mind final victory. The indication that they have indeed hit rock bottom comes when (6) they find themselves imprisoned by their foes. Yes, the literal truth is that Milton's imprisonment in 1660 as an enemy of the state was no longer than three months and may actually have been as short as three or four weeks.[7] Still, it was the emotional experience that mattered, not its factual length. (7) The enemies of the two were more than eager to exult over them in their defeat and humiliation. Milton's Samson must endure the taunts of the unbiblical Harapha, while Milton had to suffer the indignity of having his books publicly burned in August of 1660.

The sixth and seventh parallels, imprisonment and public humiliation, though the least explicit, seem to have been the ones that mattered most to Milton, for it is in these parallels that the idea of Divine Providence comes most clearly to the fore. Milton's reconstruction of the biblical story of Samson, as it is told in Judges 13–16, focuses on the Jewish hero's last moments. In the course of the dramatic poem we are reminded of the signs of God's favor that surrounded him from the time of his conception and birth, and particularly of the promise that he would be the means of Israel's victory over its enemies. Yet everything that has happened would seem to have made this impossible. This, in part, is surely why he chose to recast the story in the form of a Greek drama. Milton wanted to draw attention to the contrast between the worldview manifest in classical drama (that is, a world governed by the iron decrees of Fate) and the biblical worldview where all is governed by a very different supernatural reality, namely, the Divine Providence of the biblical God, the Almighty.

What seems to be recounted is the utter defeat of this champion of the Jews. Yet that defeat is precisely what makes his ultimate victory possible. Tragedy will be turned into a triumph for Yahweh, the God of the Hebrews. At the end of Milton's account, Samson experiences a moment of illuminating grace that at best is only implicit in the biblical account—such a moment of grace can be inferred from the biblical text, but it is still not in any way directly stated. That means that this moment is Milton's version of what must have happened and is therefore a type of what will continue to happen for God's champions:

> I begin to feel
> Some rousing motions in me which dispose
> To something extraordinary my thoughts.
> I with this Messenger will go along,
> . . . . . . . . . . . . . . . . . . . . . . . . . . . . . .
> If there be aught of presage in the mind,
> This day will be remarkable in my life
> By some great act, or of my days the last.
>
> (lls. 1381–1384; 1387–1389)[8]

It should be noted that this experience of grace is not in any sense based on reason, much less on the observable world about him. It is instead based on a stirring within, rooted in feeling. Something is going to happen that matters. At this point, though, Samson does not know what, just that he will have some part to play in it.

The divine grace that comes as a moment of inner illumination is assuring Milton's Samson that he will indeed be doing God's will by agreeing to do something that seems to be against his will, something sinful, because he is allowing himself to be brought to the Philistine theater in token homage to the pagan god Dagon. The hair on Samson's head that had been shaved as a result of Delilah's treachery has grown back, and with that his great strength has miraculously returned. Samson is still handicapped by his blindness, but when he has himself placed between the two pillars that hold up the Philistine structure he comes to understand that he can use his returning strength to push those pillars apart, thereby punishing his persecutors without any thought of mercy. His action will indeed destroy a huge number of upper-class Philistines.[9] By this action then, even though it comes about at the price of his own life,[10] Samson paves the way for Israel's later victory over its enemies.

It is not hard to see why Milton would be drawn to the story of Samson. He believed that he, too, had been elected as the instrument for bringing about God's kingdom on earth. The Puritans were drawn to the belief that they had replaced the Jews as God's chosen people. Then there was the intoxicating experience of success that had come with the establishment of the Puritan Commonwealth in England during the 1650s. Yet, all that had been achieved had come undone just a few years later. Moreover, Milton had also gone completely blind by this time. Not unlike Samson, he had been afflicted at key moments by woman troubles that left him feeling betrayed by those whom he should have been able to trust the most. He, too, had been brought low—even imprisoned, however briefly. Could it not be possible that God the Almighty would through his providential actions provide him with the occasion for some last "great act," something that would bring down the temple of the triumphant and vengeful Anglicans?

There cannot be much doubt that Milton at the end was convinced in at least one part of his psyche that he was right. We know that Milton simply did not mind standing alone against popular opinion, however intimidating—certainly not the intellectual who idolized Galileo for standing up to powerful church authorities in the name of truth and certainly not the poet who created the figure of Abdiel in *Paradise Lost*, the lone angel willing to stand up against the specious arguments of Satan and his hordes in the name of what was right. It's not likely that Milton thought he would be pulling down any great buildings, but it does seem he was hoping that by means of the strength God had given him (that is, the power of his poetry) he would somehow pull down the temple of the idolatrous Anglicans, most likely in a way that he did not fully anticipate or understand. Thus, all that he had suffered and was suffering was in fact suffused with biblical meaning.[11]

Of course, none of this ever happened. Milton would die of natural causes in 1674, three years after he had published *Samson Agonistes*, presumably still believing, or wanting to believe, that one way or another Divine Providence would bring about a result that would justify the Puritan cause, even if the poet John Milton might not live to see it happen. Up to the last, though, nothing had changed. The Anglican idolaters may have been no better than the Philistines who had persecuted the biblical

Samson, but they were still in control. Even worse, their bishops were once again in the House of Lords. True, the power of his poetry would grow in reputation and esteem, but, curiously enough, not in any way that would ever confirm, much less affirm, his brand of Puritanism.

After Milton's death in 1674, however, there was to be a dramatic change in the political climate in England. First, there would be the turmoil triggered by the revelations first made public in late 1678 by Titus Oates and then others concerning the so-called Popish Plot. In 1679, agitation over the Popish Plot would morph into the far more serious matter called the Exclusion Crisis, which centered on preventing the king's younger brother James, then the Duke of York (1633–1701), from succeeding to the throne, thereby blocking a much-feared restoration of Roman Catholicism in England. The two most prominent figures in the efforts to exclude James from the throne, though they were hardly alone, were Anthony Ashley Cooper—by this time Earl of Shaftesbury (1621–1683)—and King Charles's illegitimate son, James Walter—later James Croft or Crofts, later still James Scott, but by this time primarily known as the Duke of Monmouth (1649–1685), his highest title in the English peerage.

King Charles II, who had proved himself so adept and effective at the art of compromise, was, for any number of reasons, unwilling to bend on the issue of the rules for succession. They specified that upon the death of the monarch, if there was no legal offspring from the monarch's body, then the crown would pass to the royal male next in line. At the time this happened to be King Charles's younger brother James, younger by about three years. Depending upon one's point of view, King Charles was either proving to be stubbornly unbending in defying the will of his people or truly politically courageous by standing up for principle rather than yielding to the popular tumult of the moment. Into this situation, which had now taken the familiar shape of political gridlock, appeared anonymously Dryden's *Absalom and Achitophel* (1681), a poem among the most enduring of his poetic pieces. The title of the poem summons up a comparison of the political events then swirling about with parts of what was supposed to be a familiar story in the Bible. The reason for doing that is quite clear: it is a vigorous defense of the royalist cause. It is also intended, in my view, as a forceful rebuttal to John Milton, specifically to his *Samson Agonistes* and the case Milton was not-so-covertly making for a divine approval that would lead to a restoration of the Puritan Commonwealth, or possibly something even better. To do this, Dryden turned to another part of the Hebrew Bible, to the story of King David and his rocky relationship with his favorite son, Absalom, as this story is recounted in the books of Samuel and Kings. It seems no small accident that Dryden would be turning to the same parts of the Bible that Milton had used to compose his *Samson Agonistes.*

There are other reasons, too. They begin with the overall attractiveness of the biblical figure of David himself. Harold Bloom has described the biblical David as "the most novelistic" of the figures in the Hebrew Bible, a literary character who rivals Homer's Odysseus and Shakespeare's Hamlet in complexity and roundedness.[12] That is one way of saying that the Bible's King David is an extraordinarily engaging character. To be compared with him would naturally be flattering. Nevertheless, the full story of David, the future ruler of the united kingdom of Judea and Israel, has to be pieced together because it is told in the Bible in bits and pieces stretching from 1 and 2 Samuel, then 1 and 2 Kings, and finally spilling over into 1 Chronicles. Despite the fact that David belongs to the early history of the Jews in the Holy Land, he also has strong connections with Christianity since he is believed to be an ancestor of Jesus of Nazareth, who the Gospels tell us first came into this world, not in Nazareth where he grew up, but in Bethlehem, the city of David. David's political importance is beyond dispute since it was he who first established Jerusalem as the political and religious capital of the Jewish nation. He also designated Jerusalem as the place where a great temple was to be built to house the Ark of the Covenant. Such details tell us why David lives on in our collective memory, yet none of them figures prominently in the version employed by Dryden in his poem.

Samuel Johnson, generally speaking a hearty admirer of Dryden and his poetry, is nevertheless an insightful critic. He tells us that Dryden's *Absalom and Achitophel* is "an excellent poem of its kind," but it was not without its faults: "The original structure of the poem," he observes, "was defective; allegories drawn to great length will always break; Charles could not run continually parallel with David."[13] Johnson's point is, if anything, understated. Anyone with more than passing acquaintance with the story of David in the Hebrew Bible is going to realize quickly that there are not many parallels to be found. Though much has been made of the skillful way that Dryden mounts a creative defense of King Charles's philandering ways and the many illegitimate offspring his numerous liaisons produced—including Monmouth, the Absalom of the poet's title—the parallels quickly break down. David is reported in the Bible to have had many children indeed. In 1 Chronicles 3, his legitimate offspring are said to be numbered at nineteen by any one of the ten women who are listed. The most obvious difference between the offspring of the biblical David and those of Charles II is that David's nineteen male offspring were legitimate sons. Polygamy, as Dryden so deftly reminds us, was not only tolerated, it was the accepted, even honored, practice in biblical times. That means that each of David's sons could aspire to succeed to his father's throne, and some of them certainly did.

Much the same could be said of the father-son relationship that Dryden's title invokes. Yes, by all accounts there seems to have been a conspicuous fondness on the part of Charles toward the eldest of his illegitimate offspring, the customary number being placed at fourteen. As an infant and royal bastard, this son was given the name James. This was the royal name of his father's younger brother, who was also his uncle. Later, this uncle, as the Duke of York, would be his bitter political rival and, later still, as King James II, his executioner. The young James's last name would shift with time and circumstances, suggesting a fluid identity: James Walter or James Croft or James Scott. His titles, marriage, and early career as a young adult suggest strong paternal favor as well as some degree of talent, but he was still illegitimate, and that illegitimacy was at this time a legal barrier to any thought of his succeeding to his father's throne. The Absalom of the Bible is the third of David's sons, not the first, and he is most definitely legitimate. Both Absaloms, it is true, fall into open rebellion against their father's rule.[14] The one event that seems to matter most about the biblical Absalom is the crime of fratricide—his orchestration of the murder of his half-brother, Amnon, David's first-born by another woman—in revenge for Amnon's rape of his sister Tamar, who was also Amnon's own half-sister. There is no parallel at all for this ugly biblical event in Monmouth's rebellion. James Scott, Duke of Monmouth, did have half-sisters, but they were never the victims of such a horrific crime, at least so far as we know.[15] Nor is much made of Monmouth's having an especially gorgeous head of hair, though it is true that both Absaloms were supposed to be notable for their good looks, which are said to have contributed significantly to their ability to win over eager followers.

And then there is the matter of the parallels, or lack thereof, between the biblical Achitophel and Dryden's Achitophel—Anthony Ashley Cooper, the first earl of Shaftesbury (1621–1683). The biblical Ahitophel or Achitophel is not a particularly prominent figure. He is, it is true, represented as a wise counselor to King David who later turns on his anointed leader. We learn that he is an uncle of Bathsheba; but David's adultery with Bathsheba occurs after Achitophel's death, so that connection does not seem to matter. Instead, Achitophel is presented as a figure who counsels a military strategy that might have brought Absalom victory in his rebellion against his father and that would have allowed Absalom to take over his father's throne. However, at a crucial moment the biblical Absalom rejects his counselor's advice in favor of that of Husai, King David's secret plant and double agent, and so loses his chance for victory. The biblical Achitophel, when his advice is rejected, becomes disconsolate, returns to his home, and shortly after commits suicide (2 Samuel 17:23–24).

Absalom's rebellion does end ingloriously. We are told he was riding on a mule when unaccountably his glorious hair somehow becomes entangled in the branches of a tree (2 Samuel 18:9–11). This renders him an easy target for David's followers, who then finish him off despite his father's explicit instructions to the contrary (2 Samuel 18:15). This leads to King David's extraordinary grief over the loss of his favorite but rebellious son (2 Samuel 19:1–5).

If the parallels between the biblical account and Dryden's version of David's rule so quickly break down, as Johnson maintained that they would, how did Dryden's poem manage to become the great success, as we are told it was, when it was first published? It was, at least at first, a poem in the public domain, speaking to an issue that was presumably of concern to all the citizens of England and Scotland. (We are told it was the talk of the town.)[16] Dryden's poem did not, it is true, win a criminal conviction from a jury deliberately packed with Whigs on the charge of treason against Shaftesbury. But his poem does seem to have swung public opinion in the king's favor—it certainly quieted things down. The Exclusion Bill did not pass, and Charles's younger brother James would ultimately, for better or for worse, succeed to the throne in 1685, after the death of his older brother at the age of fifty-five.

It seems to me that we have to reconsider what mattered, and perhaps what continues to matter, about this poem. What I believe we can say, and can say fairly safely, is that the parallels don't really matter that much. It is too easy to show that they don't match very well. Something else about the poem's biblical typology must be at work to have made this poem the success it has become. The answer, I think, lies in its more general connections between the two stories and not in the exact or inexact biblical parallels. Those issues, I believe, are (1) the idea of exile, (2) its celebration of mercy over vengeance, (3) its endorsement of orderly succession to the throne, and finally (4) its firm but gentle treatment of the importance of legitimacy.

The issue of exile, while hardly unnoticed, is rarely given much prominence. I am not ready to dispute the rightness or wrongness of this, but I do think the issue may have been more important in the seventeenth century than inattention to the issue nowadays would imply. The biblical David, even though he had been anointed as king of the Jews by Samuel, spent a good many of his early years as an outlaw, dodging the various attempts to do him in by the allies of a bitterly hostile King Saul. It was during those years that David honed the political skills that would serve him so well after Saul had passed from the scene. It also helps to account for how he became such a sympathetic figure. The fact that he was treated so unfairly and that he handled his hardship with so much ingenuity contributed to a legend that won him a permanent place in the hearts of his people. It is not much of a stretch to see that those same factors were at play when young Charles Stuart was finally restored to his father's throne after having spent more than a decade on the Continent as an exile and an outlaw. It certainly seems to have been a factor in what allowed Charles to get away with some outrageous adulterous behaviors[17] while still holding on to his place in the hearts and minds of his subjects, who remembered those poignant years of exile and wandering and what they said about his character.

Perhaps one of the most remarkable features of King Charles's reign as the newly restored monarch of England was his willingness to forgive and then forget the many wrongs done to him and his family. But this is just another feature that links him firmly to the biblical King David. David's willingness to forgive and forget the wrongs that King Saul committed against him are perhaps among the most memorable in the Bible before Jesus' own words as he lay dying on the cross: "Father, forgive them for they know not what they do" (Luke 23:34). On two occasions David could easily have cut Saul's throat from ear to ear, but instead he left only physical reminders that testified to his respect for, even devotion to, his anointed king. Dryden's poem would also revive memories of David's sorrow at the death of his son Absalom, even as Joab reminds him that Absalom was ready to murder his own father in order to take possession of the throne. Joab was also, and understandably so, exasperated with his king's lack of appreciation for his loyal followers who risked their lives in order to defend him. This willingness to forgive and forget may be the most admired of Christian virtues and, as Dryden's poem reminds its audience of the link between David and Charles, might well have helped to soften the hearts of his wavering subjects.

The idea that is most visible and that holds the poem together is that of succession. As long as we believe that the people who form society need someone to rule or govern over them, orderly succession, that is, how we go from one generation to another, is going to matter. Charles's idea of how this had to happen is a mixture of two older doctrines, that of primogeniture and that of the divine right of kings.[18] From everything we can tell, Charles II felt so strongly about this issue that he was willing to risk just about everything that had been accomplished by his restoration to his father's throne in order to ensure the preservation of this principle. His secret Roman Catholic sympathies may have played a role in the king's willingness to risk it all to ensure his brother's succession, but they did not require a risk of such high daring, at least not on the surface.

Dryden is clearly most interested in the issues that surround succession in patriarchal political entities.[19] This is hardly surprising, given that the issue of succession was at the heart of the Exclusion Crisis that threatened to divide England once again into warring camps. But it is important to notice that the story of David in the Bible hardly supports the notion of succession that prevailed in Restoration England. Saul, we may remember, was the first king of the Jews, and David, with no blood relation to Saul, was to be his successor. What is more, when Samuel had decided that the new king of the Jews would be one of Jesse's sons, the choice does not go to the first or to the second or even to the third of Jesse's sons, as might be expected according to the rules of primogeniture. It goes instead to David, Jesse's last and youngest son. It is also true that David became a great favorite of the people largely because of his battlefield heroics, most spectacularly in the case of his victory over Goliath. King Charles may have on occasion conducted himself creditably on the battlefield, but there are no battlefield accomplishments that would even begin to compare favorably with those of King David.

The David of the Bible is able to overcome the murderous hostility of Saul and his years as an outlaw and exile. He is then anointed by Samuel as Saul's successor without the benefit of any connection of blood or kin, in stark contrast to the royalist assertion that succession to the throne be preserved for the next of kin. It is rather that David is the choice of Yahweh. That choice is then made known to the Jews through his servant Samuel. The newly crowned David will go on to free his people from subservience to their Philistine enemies and to establish Jerusalem as the new capital for what would then become the united kingdoms of Judah and Israel.

It is when David moves from Hebron to Jerusalem that a new issue becomes fully visible. David, like King Charles II, has had many women and sired many sons by them. In fact, there are so many that it is easy to lose count, and there may well be more than the official number. King Charles, whose legal wife proved to be barren, is said to have sired at least fourteen illegitimate offspring by various mistresses and consorts, James Scott, known as Monmouth, being but the eldest of these children. David is reported in the Bible to have had that many offspring, and more besides. There are at least nineteen sons by any one of ten women reported. Yet these are the ones who are named, and most of them, suspiciously, are sons, so it is quite possible there were many more if and when they were willing to count daughters. The most obvious difference is that David's children were considered legitimate because polygamy, as Dryden reminds us, was an accepted practice. That means that each of David's sons could and did aspire to succeed to his father's throne because birth order, from what we understand, ended up playing little or no part in deciding who would succeed the throne. Solomon, like David himself, came from the end of his family line. What mattered was divine approval, not birth order. This is a point that, if anything, would seem to favor the Puritan view of who should be the ruler of the realm. That more questions were not raised about what Dryden was blocking or ignoring in his use of the biblical materials concerning David may be a tribute to his poetic and rhetorical skills.

Dryden yet faced a trickier issue when he confronted the issue of illegitimacy.[20] James Scott, then the Duke of Monmouth, was the eldest of King Charles's many illegitimate children, and from all reports his favorite. This seems abundantly evident from the number of gifts, offices, and titles that were showered upon him by his doting father. But his father's dotage on his eldest son came to a screeching halt when it came to succession to the throne. All recognized the difficulties raised by the unlawful status of Monmouth's birth. This undoubtedly is what led to the stories that circulated among the Whigs to solve the problem: the youthful Charles, so the whispers went, had secretly married Lucy Walter when he learned she was pregnant, or perhaps before. Another possibility, that favored by Shaftesbury, would have been for Parliament to pass legislation legitimizing Monmouth, as had been done when questions were raised about the ambiguities surrounding Elizabeth Tudor's conception and birth. Either way would have smoothed his path to the throne. That of course would have been intolerable to King Charles.

That is what will allow Dryden to turn the tables on Milton at the end of his poem. He does this when Charles, in his guise as the biblical David, invokes the example of Samson, but with a purpose very different from that of Milton in his 1671 poem:

> Kings are the publick Pillars of the State,
> Born to sustain and prop the Nations weight:
> If my Young *Samson* will pretend a Call
> To shake the Column, let him share the Fall:
>
> (lls. 953–956)[21]

In other words, the biblical story of Samson's destruction of the temple of the Philistines can have a meaning quite different from the one to which Milton was pointing. This Samson is not the blind Puritan poet in his early sixties with "a Call" that would lead him to hope he can stir up the fires that would lead to a restoration of the Commonwealth of the Saints. Dryden's Samson is instead the king's overly indulged illegitimate son, the youthful, impulsive, and naïve James Scott. If Monmouth's head is full of the crazy notion that he is somehow the Samson that Milton had called for in his poem to set the people of England free from the monarchical yoke, then Dryden is demonstrating just how dangerous Milton's brand of biblical typology can be. The rebellion that Monmouth is threatening to lead would be, metaphorically, an attack on the architectural structure of his own country. If you bring down the king, then you bring down the pillar that holds up the state. The result can only be mass destruction, followed by anarchy.

Monmouth, if he continues to follow the path he has been on, will succeed not only in destroying the nation but also himself, just like the biblical Samson (like Milton's Samson).[22] Of course, Dryden had no way of knowing just how deadly accurate his King David's prophecy would prove to be. For in 1685, after the failed Rye House Plot and then the battle of Sedgemoor, Monmouth would be arrested, put on trial, and executed for high treason at the early age of thirty-six. His acts of high treason, however, were not against his father but against his uncle and namesake, the newly crowned and anointed King James II.

So what does a close look at the biblical underpinnings of these two key Restoration poems reveal? First of all, we can be sure that both poets cared deeply about their true topics: the Puritan cause in the case of Milton, the royalist cause in the case of Dryden. Second, both writers were committed Christians, though inhabiting opposite ends of the spectrum of Christianity, or at least of English Christianity. That meant that the Bible could be used to support and sustain their respective and fundamentally contradictory political positions. That in turns reminds us, if any kind of reminder is needed, of the treacheries of biblical interpretation. The most revealing moments in both cases are those in which vivid elements of the biblical accounts of both Samson and King David and his son Absalom are either marginalized or left out altogether. It is easy enough for those who look over their shoulders to pick apart or deconstruct the way that the two poets constructed their accounts and thus show how easy it might be, based on the actual biblical accounts, to come to very different conclusions.

If their poetic success is to be measured by prophetic accuracy, then curiously enough Dryden comes off the better. Milton's dream or hope that somehow Divine Providence would make it possible for the Puritans to find victory over their royalist oppressors was never to come true. Dryden, on the other hand, came much closer to predicting what would actually happen by suggesting that Monmouth, Samson-like, was engaged in actions that would bring about his own destruction and, perhaps more importantly, noting that his headstrong actions were effectively making the case for an orderly succession based on primogeniture and legitimacy. But Dryden's prophetic success was itself only temporary. He didn't even come close to anticipating what would actually happen after the Duke of York came to the throne in 1685 as King James II. James's reign was to be a brief one, and he would be overthrown by the events that are described and summed up in the phrase "the Glorious Revolution of 1688." There is nothing in the Bible that could have anticipated the stunning turn of events that would establish England as a constitutional monarchy and thus bring William and Mary as joint monarchs to the thrones of both England and Scotland. Biblical typology, it would seem, can only take us so far.

## Notes

1. Johnson's *Dictionary* (1755) provides some illumination here. Johnson offers three meanings of the word *type*, but the second is clearly the most relevant: "that by which something future is prefigured." This is followed by two illustrative quotations: the first from Book XII of Milton's *Paradise Lost* where Michael tells of "*type* / And shadows of that destin'd seed to bruise / The serpent, by what means he shall achieve / Mankind's deliverance." The

second is from a sermon by the seventeenth-century Anglican divine John Tillotson: "The Apostle shews the Christian religion to be in truth and substance what the Jewish was only in type and shadow." We should note that word *shadow* appears alongside the word *type* in both quotations. Since the word *shadow* here means what is difficult or hard to know, it's not likely that placing the two quotes together was accidental. To the contrary, it seems quite deliberate.

2. Samuel Johnson, "Life of Milton," in *The Works of Samuel Johnson*, 23 vols. (New Haven: Yale University Press, 1970–2010), 21:169.

3. Barbara Lewalski, for one, is particularly eloquent on this topic, and trenchantly so. See *The Life of John Milton: A Critical Biography* (Malden, MA: Blackwell, 2000), especially 399, 400–404, 492, 523, but also et passim.

4. As Lewalski also reminds us (*Life of John Milton*, 526), there is an admiring reference to the biblical Samson as a figure of successful resistance to political oppression in Milton's *Areopagitica* (1644), his famous, and much earlier, essay in defense of intellectual liberty. It seems clear enough that Samson had loomed large in Milton's evolving poetic consciousness.

5. The timing of the composition of *Samson Agonistes* is one of the most deeply divisive issues in Milton studies. Barbara Lewalski admits at the very beginning of her lengthy critical biography that it is one of four issues she was unable to resolve despite the years of study and research that are so abundantly evident in her book. A briefer but very well informed summary of the problem can also be found in Joseph Wittreich, *Why Milton Matters* (New York: Palgrave Macmillan, 2006), 40–48. Wittreich also treats this topic in two earlier and still valuable books: *Interpreting "Samson Agonistes"* (Princeton: Princeton University Press, 1986) and *Shifting Contexts: Reinterpreting "Samson Agonistes"* (Pittsburgh: Duquesne University Press, 2002). Mary Ann Radzinowicz, *Toward "Samson Agonistes": The Growth of Milton's Mind* (Princeton: Princeton University Press, 1978) also merits mention if for no other reason than the importance she assigns to *Samson* in Milton's intellectual and poetic development.

6. The length of Milton's hair is a much-discussed subject for obvious reasons. William Riley Parker comments as follows upon the portrait painted of Milton when he turned twenty-one: "For this solemn event John wore a black doublet and a white, falling ruff. He was doubtless self-conscious, but the painter managed to catch a pleasant, boyish expression, with alert brown eyes and just the faintest hint of a smile. At twenty-one Milton looked still seventeen. He no longer cut his hair short in Puritan fashion, but let it fall loosely to his collar, covering his ears, like a Cavalier. It was now dark brown. With his high colour and fair complexion, he was a strikingly handsome youth—a personable and intelligent-looking Bachelor of Arts." *Milton: A Biography*, 2 vols. (Oxford: Clarendon Press, 1968), I, 70. For a very different view of the meaning of Milton's hair, especially its length, see Will Fisher, *Materializing Gender in Early Modern English Literature and Culture* (Cambridge: Cambridge University Press, 2006), 147–158.

7. As William Riley Parker, perhaps the most authoritative of Milton's biographers, readily admits, we do not know the exact date when Milton was imprisoned, though we do know that he was ordered released from his imprisonment on December 15, 1660. See *Milton: A Biography*, II, 1087.

8. Citations to Milton's texts are taken from *Complete Poems and Major Prose*, ed. Merritt Y. Hughes (New York: Odyssey Press, 1957), 584–585.

9. We are not given an exact number, but the biblical account does say this regarding his (Samson's) action: "Those he killed at his death outnumbered those he had killed in his life," Judges 16:30–31. We are specifically told that Samson had earlier killed thirty of the wedding guests at Ashkelon for wheedling the answer to his riddle from his bride-to-be. We are told, too, that in his ongoing feud with the Philistines Samson had killed at least a thousand of their soldiers with the jawbone of an ass. The biblical account also estimates that in addition to the Philistines, who were the men and women of the ruling class who were in attendance at the final event, there were three thousand more watching from the roof. By these measures Samson would indeed in our day almost certainly be characterized as a mass murderer, with the number of the Philistine people killed being a fairly large multiple of a thousand. I rely, first, on the Geneva Bible (1599), but also, when appropriate on the King James Version (1611).

10. It is worth noting that some commentators have seen Samson's final heroic act as a sinful act of suicide. Nevertheless, it seems clear that Milton has accepted the mainstream tradition where Samson's final heroic act is not treated as suicide, that is, not as a sin against the Holy Spirit. This tradition of a saintly as well as a heroic Samson is said to have its origin in a New Testament verse in the Epistle to the Hebrews (11:23) where we are told Samson, along with other Old Testament heroes, is to be venerated as a model of faith in the righteousness of the Hebrew God. For an informative discussion of these issues, see F. Michael Krouse, *Milton's Samson and the Christian Tradition* (Princeton: Princeton University Press, 1949).

11. A modern and/or humanist perspective may give us to pause at this moment. We may, and possibly should, wonder what Samson's victory over his Philistine enemies may be telling us about Divine Providence, at least as that concept is conceived of in the Bible and then subsequently channeled to us through Milton's *Samson Agonistes*. The destruction of the temple of Dagon and the thousands of Philistine lives that were lost is unmistakably a bloodthirsty act of revenge. Moreover, it would appear to most of us to be an outsized and unjustified act of revenge that makes the biblical Samson indistinguishable from what we know as a suicide-bomber or, maybe more simply, a mass murderer, with nothing truly heroic about it. It is not easy to see how such savagery can be presented as "divinely sanctioned," much less easily excused and/or overlooked. For a different and possibly more sympathetic perspective on this issue, see David Ainsworth, *Milton and the Spiritual Reader: Reading and Religion in Seventeenth-Century England* (New York: Routledge, 2008). Yet, Ainsworth, curiously enough, does not deal directly with *Samson Agonistes* in this otherwise admirable study. He provides instead a detailed treatment of its 1671 companion piece, Milton's *Paradise Regained*.

12. Harold Bloom, *The Shadow of a Great Rock: A Literary Appreciation of the King James Bible* (New Haven: Yale University Press, 2011), 97–110.

13. Samuel Johnson, "Life of Dryden," in *Works*, 21:462–463.

14. I am in fact puzzled by James Winn's claim that the biblical Absalom's rebellion against King David's rule was attributed to his father's adultery with Bathsheba. *John Dryden and His World* (New Haven: Yale University Press, 1987), 350. My own reading of 2 Samuel finds no justification for this claim of cause-and-effect. Among other things, such a claim would strongly imply that King David deserved his favorite son's rebellion. It seems to me quite the contrary—that in the biblical account we are deliberately made to feel Absalom's rebellion against his father was undeserved.

15. Curiously enough, some readers, even scholars and editors, have suggested that Monmouth's part in the brutal beating of Sir John Coventry was supposed to parallel Absalom's revenge on his half-brother Amnon. Coventry was severely beaten purportedly for a slur he had made on Monmouth's father's sexuality. Coventry had suggested that King Charles loved the theater so much because he was secretly gay, despite abundant evidence to the contrary. Most readers, in any case, rightly find this proposed parallel preposterous. See, for example, the discussion of "Amnon's Murther" in *The Works of John Dryden*, 2:240–241.

16. Samuel Johnson gives vivid testimony to the popularity of Dryden's poem, which was provided to him by his own father, Michael Johnson, a bookseller in distant Staffordshire: "Of this poem, in which personal satire was applied to support of publick principles, and in which therefore every mind was interested, the reception was eager, and the sale so large, that my father, an old bookseller, told me, he had not known it equalled but by *Sacheverel's Trial*." "Life of Dryden," in *Works*: 21:404–405.

17. Many commentators seem to believe that the political troubles that Charles experienced can be directly traced to his public defiance of decent behaviors, certainly so if judged by puritanical norms. But few seem ready to note that the sexual behavior of his son ("the Protestant Duke") was not much different than that of his father. Though Monmouth sired some eight legitimate children by his wife Anna Scott, he also left behind his own batch of illegitimate children, at least four by his acknowledged mistress Eleanour Needham. It is hard to believe that such obviously scandalous behavior had completely escaped public notice by the time of the Exclusion Crisis. Perhaps less well known, but maybe not, was that in or around 1679 Monmouth became involved in a truly public adulterous relationship with Lady Henrietta Wentworth. He would go on to repudiate his wife, Anna, mother of his legitimate children, in favor of a relationship that he would claim at the end of his life to be "a true marriage." See Bryan Bevan, *James Duke of Monmouth* (London: Robert Hale, 1973), 120–126, 173–174, 231–233.

18. Macaulay in his *History of England* takes up this very point during his discussion of the theory of the divine right of kings, particularly as it had been articulated in Sir Robert Filmer's defense of this doctrine, published in 1680, a year or so before the publication of Dryden's poem: "It was gravely maintained that the Supreme Being regarded hereditary monarchy, as opposed to other forms of government, with peculiar favour; that the rule of succession in order of primogeniture was a divine institution, anterior to the Christian and even the Mosaic dispensation; . . . These absurd doctrines received no countenance from the Old Testament; for in the Old Testament we read that the chosen people were blamed and punished for desiring a king, and that they were afterwards commanded to withdraw their allegiance from him. The whole history, far from favouring the notion that primogeniture is of divine institution, would rather seem to indicate that younger brothers are under the especial protection of heaven. Isaac was not the eldest son of Abraham, nor Jacob of Isaac, nor Judah of Jacob, nor David of Jesse, nor Solomon of David" (*Everyman Edition*, 4 vols. [New York: Dutton, 1953], 1:53–54).

19. James Winn, for one, reminds us that Dryden was himself a firstborn son and that he had benefited demonstrably from his firstborn status. He was therefore especially well disposed toward the idea of primogeniture. *John Dryden and His World*, 346.

20. It seems worth noting that evidence for just how firmly the issues of primogeniture and legitimacy had taken their place at the forefront of public consciousness comes from an unexpected source. Nahum Tate was, to be sure, Dryden's associate for *The Second Part* of

*Absalom and Achitophel* (1682), but he is best known today for his revision of Shakespeare's *King Lear* (1681) for the Restoration stage. Tate's *King Lear* is remembered today primarily for "the happy ending" he "imposed" on Shakespeare's "nihilistic" tragedy (1605). What is almost certainly less well known is that Tate not only ends Shakespeare's play differently, but he also begins it differently. Moreover, he does so in a way that is directly relevant to Dryden's *Absalom and Achitophel.* Instead of beginning with the proposed division of the kingdom, as Shakespeare does, Tate begins with the earl of Gloucester's bastard son Edmund's soliloquy that begins the second act of Shakespeare's play, thereby highlighting what happens when a society's decisions to abide by primogeniture and legitimacy become subject to serious challenge.

21. John Dryden, *The Works of John Dryden*, 20 vols., H. T. Swedenborg et al. (Berkeley: University of California Press, 1968–2000), 2:33–34.

22. For another, quite different take on the meaning of Dryden's references to Samson in this poem, see Steven N. Zwicker, *Dryden's Political Poetry: The Typology of King and Nation* (Providence: Brown University Press, 1972), 94.

# *David Simple, Volume the Last*, and Rational Christian Faith

*Robin Runia*

Sarah Fielding's *The Adventures of David Simple* (1744) ends extolling the pleasures to be gained from "Tenderness and Benevolence," while its sequel, *Volume the Last* (1753), ends celebrating death as the only escape from the pain that the world will inevitably inflict on a feeling heart.[1] Accordingly, Richard Terry, in his essay "David Simple and the Fallacy of Friendship," argues that *Volume the Last* "qualifie[s] and even rescind[s] some of the ideas introduced in the earlier."[2] He uses biographical details of Fielding's financial, family, and health challenges, as well as the contrast of the novels' comic and tragic endings, to compellingly conclude that "Love, patience, and faith are the only palliative that Fielding ultimately feels able to endorse; it is through these alone that a wisely foolish man such as David Simple (in the words of Johnson's 'Vanity') 'makes the Happiness [he] does not find.'"[3] Terry's argument emphasizes *Volume the Last*'s indictment of sentiment.[4] However, closer examination of both *David Simple*'s and *Volume the Last*'s engagement with issues of faith suggests that the sequel may be considered, instead, a logical extension of its predecessor.[5] Specifically, both novels warn[6] that Christian faith must be grounded in rational principle[7] even while they also claim the potential for women's intellect to justify their moral exemplarity.[8]

Thus far, the role of religion in Sarah Fielding's work has been oft noted but insufficiently examined.[9] Linda Bree, for example, commenting on the epitaph arranged for Fielding by Dr. John Hoadly, concludes that its "reference to her piety is . . . valid: moral teaching in her fiction is consistently backed by an unobtrusive, but firmly held, set of religious principles.[10] Similarly, K. G. Hall claims that Fielding's *David Simple* "does not constitute an integrated Christian critique of society," and that the author "offers little in the way of direct comment on religion in her novel; whilst Christianity is held to be desirable and true, specific beliefs are not considered in any detail."[11]

In contrast, however, is the recent and groundbreaking work of Tera Pettella. In her essay "Devotional Reading and the Novel Form: The Case of David Simple," Pettella demonstrates how existing religious reading practices shaped the development of the sentimental novel. Petella offers a rewriting of the rise of the novel that accounts for its didacticism, episodic nature, and the proliferation of inset narratives. While this perspective offers an exciting new direction for studies of the novel by acknowledging the largely neglected role of religion, its focus on generic semblances rather than specific textual detail leaves room for further analysis of Fielding's engagement with specific Christian beliefs.[12] Mary Rooks also provides general commentary on the role of religion in Sarah Fielding's work, exploring the contrast between secular and Christian morality throughout Fielding's published works. She notes, "Despite the heavy use of heathen and secular texts in her prefatory writing, in the body of her novels Fielding's moral exemplars and directives are strikingly critical of atheism, frequently dismissive of the doctrines of ancient poets and early-modern philosophers, and often staunchly Christian in their definition of 'correct' beliefs and virtuous actions."[13] Rooks concludes that this equivocation may have resulted from Fielding's desire to avoid the religious controversy with which she grew up, and she goes on to claim that the lack of creedal affiliation in her work suggests a sort of nominal "'Christian' behavior" that includes the "importance of benevolence, good works, duty, and humility . . . the use of reason to subdue the passions and recognize virtue; and demonstrating God's mercy as essential to salvation."[14]

Significantly, these recent and important contributions have paved the way for a more detailed examination of Fielding's representations of religion. Despite what Rooks sees as Fielding's refusal to "clearly articulate an affiliation with one particular sect of Christianity" and her simultaneous espousal, as an Anglican, of "some of the core tenets of latitudinarianism (espoused by her brother) and Puritanism (espoused by Richardson),"[15] we may also see that Fielding's repeated and consistent return to specific Christian behaviors and scriptural precedent render religion the essential touchstone of everyday life.

Throughout both novels, nearly all of the various episodes make consistent mention of the role religious belief plays in everyday decision making. In *David Simple*, David's early stay with his uncle's jeweler, Mr. Johnson, is punctuated by the narrator's relation of Johnson's daughters' distinctly un-Christian choices of husbands. While David finds himself immediately attracted to the younger of Mr. Johnson's two daughters, the older daughter, we are told, catches the eye of a "rich Jew."[16] Nevertheless, "the Jew did not presently declare himself, on the consideration that she was a Christian," but he allows she may make a better mistress than a wife.[17] When Mr. Johnson promises his daughter's conversion, the couple is married, for her underdeveloped Christian beliefs turn out to be no significant obstacle:

> She was at first startled at the thoughts of changing her Religion; but as she had no more Understanding, than was just necessary to set off her own Charms, by knowing which Dress, and which Posture became her best; and had never been taught any thing more than to go to Church of a *Sunday*, when she was not wanted to stay at home to overlook the Dinner, without knowing any other Reason for it than Custom: The rich Presents the Jew made her, and his Promises of keeping her great, soon overcame all her Scruples, and she consented to have him.[18]

In this case, she lacks "Understanding" beyond coquetry, and her religion is reduced to a weekly release from domestic duties that is quickly overcome by her desires for the luxuries wealth offers her physical body.

We are next told that when a Mr. Nokes uses his wealth to convince Mr. Johnson of his own superiority to David as a match for Johnson's younger daughter, the misery that the younger daughter demonstrates at the news of her father's interest in Nokes further meditates on the role of religion in everyday decision making. When the older daughter tells the younger, "if it was my Case, I should think it no manner of Sin to disobey a Father, who imposed such unreasonable Commands on me," the younger responds, "Oh! My Dear, you quite mistake my Case; I am not troubling my head, either about the *Sin*, or my *Father*; but the height of my Distress lies in not knowing my own Mind: if I could once find that out, I should be easy."[19] Here, while the older daughter seems to have at least acquired a religious vocabulary from her church attendance, the glibness with which she justifies her sister's disregard of the commandment to honor her father and mother provides further proof of her lack of religious belief. Deepening this satire on the failures of religious education, the younger daughter's intellectual deficiency manufactures this crisis. When the younger daughter's subsequent explanation that her distress arises from the fact that she simply can't decide between Nokes's wealth and David's comely appearance, she exposes her own lack of Christian principle. Further, when she finally decides in favor of Nokes, the narrator is quick to blame her behavior on the "Temptation" his wealth offers, insisting that there is no woman "who is a perfect *Angel*" nor all "perfect *Devils*."[20] This blame insists on the moral culpability and mortality of woman according to a Christian worldview of sin, repentance, and forgiveness. It is also important to note that when David confronts his mistress's betrayal, "It cost him very little to be a Christian in that Point," and he forgives her because "Tenderness was always predominant in his Mind."[21] In each case thus far, intellectual deficiency undermines Christian behavior. Reason must undergird faith.

The next episode in which the reader is presented with the importance of Christian principle in the regulation of behavior is presented in the household of a father with three daughters. During his stay with this family, David is pleased to observe the care that the children give their patriarch on his deathbed. After the burial, however, we are told David was startled by

> a sudden Noise he knew not what to make of. At first he fancied it was the chattering of Magpyes; then he recollected, that some young female Neighbors of his, fearing lest there should be *too*

> *much Silence in their House*, kept two or three Parrots to entertain themselves with. At last he thought he heard something like the Sound of human Voices, but so confused and intermixed, three or four together, that nothing could be distinguished.[22]

The "chattering of Magypes" and "Parrots" breaks the silence necessary for reflection and rationally motivated Christian action. But David overcomes this distraction to find the three daughters in a rage, warring over a rug of their father's. At this point, David refuses to play the part of King Solomon with the babe and offer to divide the rug. This inset narrative supplements the previous critique of David's irrationality and emphasizes the important role human intellect must play in moral decision making. Nevertheless, in David's decision to flee the chaotic household rather than engage in the logical argument modeled by Solomon, David again fails to fully utilize the very intellect he finds deficient in these women.

Fielding's novel even more explicitly engages the issue of reason's relationship to Christian principle with the character of Mr. Orgueil. When David takes new lodgings and first meets Mr. Orgueil, he is struck by his new acquaintance's unusual intellectual refinement. But when Orgueil offers his perspectives on their mutual acquaintance in lodgings and around town, David is disappointed with what he hears. When David questions Mr. Orgueil's cynicism, Orgueil's reply privileges a secular moral contract over a religion he describes as "Superstition to fright me into my Duty."[23] At this point, David is unable to construct an argument to refute Orgueil's claim. We read that David is shocked, but unable to "condemn what he could not refute."[24] And when the next morning offers Mr. Spatter's assessment of Mr. Orgueil's self-idolatry, David's lament over his inability to find a "real friend" emphasizes the significance of "Obedience to *Divine Will*," by defining a real friend as one "whose every Action proceeded either from Obedience to *Divine Will*, or from the Delight he took in doing good."[25]

These characters, however, are not the only ones in the novel to highlight the essential role reason plays within the Christian faith. During the relation of her history to David, Camilla describes the moment in which she explains the machinations of her stepmother to her brother Valentine. She details his decision to expose his step-mother accordingly: "Valentine, who is very far from being passionate, (but the Passions of Men who are not subject to be ruffled, are much more to be dreaded, torn to pieces, about every Grain of Mustard-Seed or every Blast of Wind) when he had heard me out, grew outrageous."[26] Valentine's sensations motivate his unchristian lust for revenge. However, Camilla then emphasizes Valentine's eventual ability to find a level head and cool his passions (in contrast to the "Madness" and "Blindness" of their father's passion for his second wife), leading to their decision to quit their father's house.[27] This reference to Mathew 13:31–32 underscores the importance of rational intellect to Christian belief and behavior.[28]

Similarly, the inset narrative of Isabelle de Stainville insists, according to the dramatic form of the Romance histories it echoes, the necessity of reason in directing Christian conduct. While Isabelle's French and Catholic heritage may in some ways account for her and her family's excesses and failures, the opposition between sensation and religious principle is clear. Isabelle's brother's decision to become a monk, after mistakenly and jealously killing his sister's fiancé and contributing to his wife's death by shame, pits rational Christian reflection against sensuality. Specifically, the Marquis survives his wound with the help of "an Ecclesiastick of uncommon Piety," who "so pathetically enforced to him the Duty of composing his Thoughts, in order to turn them to Heaven . . . that he might live to atone, by Repentance and Virtue, for the rash Action he had committed."[29] Nevertheless, the impassioned murderer's conversion to Christian-composed thought proves only a temporary reaction to the pathetic appeals of the ecclesiastic, and the murderer yearns for suicide. Next, we read, "But, at last, the religious Impressions his Mind had received, got the better of all other Sentiments: He took a sudden Resolution to quit the World, and turn *Carthusian*, having first made over all his Estate, in equal Proportions, to me and the Mother of poor Dumont."[30] His decision to join an order of hermit monks based on a sudden impression proves yet another irrational response, so while he does avoid further sin, the absence of reason seems to preclude genuine principled Christian behavior. Similarly, Isabelle resolves, "As soon as I have settled some Affairs . . . I shall return into *France*, and execute my former Intention of taking the Veil; a religious Life being the only Relief to such Sorrows as mine."[31] She needs the opportunity for reflection offered by cloister life to live according to Christian principle. Significantly, the narrator concludes, "This whole Company were so sensible that Isabelle was in the right, in her Resolutions of retiring from a World, in which it was impossible for her to meet with anything worth her Regard, after what she had lost, that they did not attempt to dissuade her from it."[32] Her mind is currently so overwhelmed that she can only retreat from it in search of a Christian life.[33]

Finally, the most extended and most important episode in *David Simple*'s commentary on the essential role that reason plays in principled Christian behavior concerns the Atheist. Cynthia first encounters the Atheist in the company of a clergyman and a "Butterfly" on her return to London after seeking refuge from economic dependency with her generous cousin.[34] At this point, the narrator takes pains to detail the contrast between these characters, as well as Cynthia's perceptions of them. First, the reader is told that the drunken Atheist immediately attacks the clergyman, denying the existence of God and pointing to his own ill-health as proof:

> But if a good Being, who really loved his Creatures, had been the Cause of our coming into this World, undoubtedly we should have been made in such a manner, that we should neither have had Temptations, nor Power to injure ourselves . . . in my opinion *we are such low groveling Creatures*, that I can easily conceive we were made by Chance.[35]

In this satire of secular logic, the Atheist's faulty reasoning illustrates the free will bestowed on him by a benevolent Christian God even while he tries to deny it. His nonbelief also stems from a

> natural Propensity to Vice, and a Resolution to suffer all the Consequences of it, rather than deny himself any thing he liked, [which] drove all serious Thoughts as much as possible from his Mind, and [by which he] endeavoured to make use of all the Fallacies he could think on, to impose on his own Understanding.[36]

The Atheist revels in sensation at the expense of rationality, and the resulting illogic leads him further away from Christian behavior.

While the Butterfly's atheism has a different "Cause," it, too, emphasizes the importance of reason to Christian belief. We read that he

> who was naturally disposed to lead a regular Life, and whose Inclinations prompted him to nothing, which he might not have been allowed in any Religion whatever, put on all the Appearance of Viciousness he could, because he was silly enough to imagine it proved his Sense. And, as he could not think deep enough to consult on which side Truth lay, he never considered farther than what would give him the best Opportunity of displaying his Wit. He openly professed himself a great Lover of Ridicule, and thought no Subject so fit to exercise it on, as Religion and the Clergy: he therefore, as soon as the other had done speaking, ran through all the trite things that ever were said on that head . . . which at once proved his Folly, and the strong Opinion he had of his own Wisdom.[37]

The Butterfly's complete lack of direction is more than un-Christian; it proves universally "silly" in its distortion of the human ability to reason. He "can't think deep enough." He is unable to recognize truth. He is, instead, simply a pawn of fashion and its fools, and he suffers from the inability to arrive rationally at the Christian principle that should direct his behavior.

In contrast, we are told that the Clergyman responds according to his conscience and "the Duty of his Profession in this case called upon him to endeavor, at least, to convince them of their Error."[38] With "good Sense" he tries to lead them back to the path of religion.[39] And Cynthia's response further proves the essential connection made in the novel between intellect and Christian virtue: "Every Word this Gentleman spoke, and his Manner of speaking, convinced Cynthia he was not endeavouring to shew his own Parts, but acting from the true Christian Principle of desiring to do good."[40] His diction, delivery, and message illustrate a necessary link between Christian piety and rationality.

Significantly, this episode is reprised and extended at the end of the novel. As Camilla and Valentine look forward to the possibility of reconciliation with their father, David proposes going to church, "for he said he had great reason to thank his *Creator*, for giving him so much Happiness as he had found in that Company."[41] When the assent of the company is joined by a unanimous recognition of Providence's hand, the reader is told that Cynthia's thoughts return to these experiences. We read, "She had mentioned it slightly before, but now she told them all the ridiculous Arguments the Atheist made use of to prove there was no *Deity*. . . . They all admired the Clergyman's Behaviour, and David said, he heartily wished he was acquainted with him."[42] Finally, the novel conveniently ends with the Clergyman preaching at the church they determined to attend and with a rainstorm that allows David and his party to converse with him. Here, the Clergyman adds that his subsequent contact with the Atheist ended with a copy of the Atheist's deathbed repentance. He relates how the Atheist's story very carefully spells out his descent into irreligion, beginning with a description of reading bad books that proved "that the *wisest thing* a Man could do, was to give a Loose to all his *Passions*, and take hold of the present Moment for Pleasure, without depending on *uncertain Futurity*."[43] This failure of rational Christian principle then led to gambling, womanizing, confidence games, and drink. When this failure also turns out to be the cause of the Atheist cheating his "*fond-good* Brother of his Share of his Father's Patrimony," the novel comes full circle, and the Atheist is revealed to be David's brother and the cause of David's quest to find a real friend.[44]

Throughout *David Simple*, both main and peripheral characters repeatedly struggle with their rational deficiencies; eventually, the novel's repeated espousal of principled piety justifies its comedic ending. Even though David marries Camilla, he nevertheless fails to demonstrate an intellectual development or rational maturation. This imperfect resolution is exactly where *Volume the Last* picks up the narrative to offer an even more definitive argument on behalf of reason's essential role in Christian belief and behavior.

As *Volume the Last* follows David and company through one trial after another, the narrator emphasizes the fortitude of Christians. In particular, despite David and Camilla's increasing poverty, "They knew not Guilt, they know not gloomy Anguish of Mind: and as they had suffered, as yet, no material Separation, so they had not tasted of that temporary Sorrow, which, though enough to embitter our Cup, is not sufficient to subdue a Christian Mind, whose Reliance on a future State is its only Foundation for Happiness."[45] A "Christian Mind" is one buoyed by the logical conclusion that earthly life comes with no guarantee of happiness. What follows from this premise, as proven by David's misfortunes, is that comfort must be looked for only in the hereafter. Further, this comfort must not be understood as mere resignation: "For, like *Job*, David Simple submitted to the temporary Sufferings allotted him: and, from a Dependence on his Maker, acquired that Chearfulness and Calmness of Mind, which is not in the Power of the highest worldly Prosperity, without such a Dependence, to bestow."[46] David's experience has proven that money alone doesn't buy happiness. Instead, surrendering to the will of a greater power empowers him to celebrate whatever pleasures he is able to secure and maintain. Reflection leads to Christian principle, and Christian principle allows reflection. This feedback loop is key to rational piety.

In contrast, David's repeated encounters with Mr. Orgueil, who in the sequel has married and resides nearby, compare the logic of Christian principle with the irrationality of secular "Human Reason."[47] When David is forced to hire conveyance to bring his niece, Cynthia, back home from a residence with the Orgueils in which her health began to suffer dangerously, Mr. Orgueil refuses responsibility or aid:

> He was sure it was reasonable . . . that his Friend ought to be driven to suffer great Distress, in order to cure him of his Imprudence; for it was one of Mr. Orgueil's most settled Maxims, that Man, by the Use of his own Reason alone, has a Power to prevent or heal any Misfortune. He so implicitly worshiped Human Reason, that it appeared to him no less than Idolatry to dispute its Omnipotence.[48]

The narrator's linking of "Maxim" and "Human Reason" satirizes Orgueil's selfish and irrational blame and his refusal to see that "Reason alone" simply does not have the "Power to prevent or heal any Misfortune."[49] While he sees idolatry in anyone who would claim otherwise, the reader must recognize that Orgueil is the one worshiping a false idol. His worship of his own flawed and circular logic concludes with the false premise with which it begins, and he proves culpable for the very absurdity for which he blames David.

Orgueil's culpability deepens when he manipulates 1 Timothy 5:8 to further justify his selfish conclusions:[50]

> Orgueil allowed St. Paul to be a very fine Writer; for he, indeed, had human Learning before he became Teacher of the Christian Doctrines: and beside, when any Text suited Mr. Orgueil's Purpose or Inclinations, no one was more ready to quote the sacred Writings, provided he might be admitted to judge them by his own Rule of Rectitude. That Paul at such a Time became a Teacher of the Christian Doctrine, was a favourite Phrase with Mr. Orgueil; nor could he endure the Expression of St. Paul's being called to the Apostleship. And, as he believed not the Miracle of his Conversion (or, indeed, any Miracle at all) he made such Conversion the common subject of his Ridicule.[51]

Denying the religious convictions behind Paul's contributions to Christian scripture, Orgueil proves to be the worst of literary critics, manipulating passages and their contexts to prove his own point. Further, his skepticism is depicted by the narrator in distinctly irrational terms. The narrator says that Orgueil's inability to "endure" discussion of Paul's conversion and his lack of "belief" in the Resurrection function as premises upon which he bases his ridicule; the narrator's use of the parenthetical and its emphatic "indeed, any" betray Orgueil's lack of critical thinking and real inability to use careful examination and categorization to reach logical conclusions.

Mrs. Orgueil, too, suffers from irrationality, and Fielding's narrator takes pains to blame her for a lack of distinctly Christian principle. Also misreading 1 Timothy 5:8 as a celebration of her own solipsism and greed, Mrs. Orgueil "always fanc[ies] herself with-child, to keep up the Idea in Orgueil's Mind, of a growing Family."[52] This delusion backfires, however, for it was "almost incredible to what a Perplexity of Mind Mrs.

Orgueil was continually throwing herself, to prevent her Husband's ruining himself by Generosity to David and his Family. She had, indeed, the Curse of the Psalmist, of being afraid where no Fear was."[53] With this allusion to Psalms 53:4–5 (KJV), "Have the workers of iniquity no knowledge? Who eat up my people as they eat bread," Fielding exposes the fear and anxiety attendant upon Mrs. Orgueil's ignorance in contrast to the security provided by Christian principle.

Unfortunately, however, after David's financial troubles continue to escalate and his father-in-law and Valentine die, David seems to lose his grasp on the Christian principles which he formerly espoused, if not fully enacted. His mind is described as "distressed"[54] and possessing a "timidity"[55] which had "taken from him the Power of acting what, in his own Judgment, he thought best."[56] This trend only worsens when, after the death of their son David, Camilla takes ill. For two months, David hovers over her bedside, experiencing "superior Torments of his own Mind in seeing Camilla's Sufferings."[57] The narrator expounds,

> The Time she had lain in her Sickness had raised such Images in his Breast, that it was impossible any Change could be for the worse. For Time after Time did he quit her Room, when, like Job, he could almost have contended with the Almighty. And one might say with no great Impropriety, that a temporary Madness had seized his Mind. But, like his royal Example in the Scripture, though he fasted and prayed whilst his Petition could be granted, yet as soon as it was rejected, he humbly acquiesced, satisfied in the Wisdom as well as the Goodness of the great Disposer of Events."[58]

David's love of Camilla and his sensitivity to her pain drive him briefly insane. Unmoored from the Christian principle that had previously guided his behavior, he comes near to questioning the only Providential order according to which, the novel argues, one may find happiness on earth.

Eventually, however, David's reason returns and leads him back to God and away from Orgueil's example:

> Human Philosophy had little Chance of bringing him Comfort. . . . Had David been an Infidel, not all the Books composed by the

> wisest Philosophers, would have taken one Arrow from a Heart so sensible as his of every tender Connection. He would have raved to Madness, or wept himself to Death: but when the Christian Hope came over his Mind, that his Camilla was really happy,—that the Loss was all his own—and that a short Time longer struggling through Life would put an End to all his Sorrows also, and render him happy, his Grief would subside, and patient Resignation take its Place.[59]

"Human Philosophy" is ineffectual. Secular reasoning provides no comfort; only the Christian principle justifying the hope of salvation offers "patient Resignation" to the living and real "happiness" beyond the grave.

With this, the narrator again contrasts the irrational "Human Reason" of Mr. Orgueil. While suffering from kidney stones, he searches for secular philosophy to allay his fears of impending death. The narrator mocks this idolatry, explaining that "in the Intermission of his Pains, when his Body would give his Mind leave to exert his Reason (for this God whilst cloathed in Flesh, must ask that Leave), he called for all his Books of Philosophy, and supported himself by the Sayings of the Ancients."[60] This false "God" of Reason proves subject to the whims of the body. In addition, the vanity that led him to worship his own reason functions as a mere diversion from the fact of death:

> For although he fancied himself constant of Mind, and admired his own Firmness, yet the Truth was, that instead of thinking on Death, he was diverting himself with being the Admiration of the Gods; and in the Warmth of his Enthusiasm, he could fix his Mind on no other Image but that of his Self-adoration: it was amazing with what dexterous Art Orgueil mixed the Bible with the Sentiments of the ancient Heathens, till he proved that this World was made for Man; then dropped the Idea, that it was the Gift of God, and his Imagination strutted, as it were, in his own World.[61]

His irrational fancy and presumption allow him to lose touch with reality. The warmth of his blood, his sensational excesses, rival the presumption of the very religious zealots presuming to know God's will that Orgueil would mock.

Orgueil's presumption extends so far as to demand David acknowledge his secular reason as God. However, David "could not comply with [Orgueil's] Desire of admiring all those Fallacies he imposed on his own Understanding."[62] David even attempts to refute Orgueil's false reasoning, pointing to examples of philosophy's failure. He tells Orgueil "that if he had no other Comfort in his Heart, but what could arise from the admiring the Beauties of human Reason, exulting in the Dignity of his Nature, and worshipping the Strength of his own Wisdom, he would weep at the Grave of his Camilla, till like Niobe, he was dissolved into Tears."[63] Despite his own previous struggles with intellectual deficiency, David continues to uphold the rationality of Christian principle and "prove that human Wisdom can soar no higher than the Knowledge of our Dependence on God, and acting in Conformity to that Knowledge, but not even the return of David's self-possession after Camilla's death convinces him."[64] Finally, the narrator informs the reader that

> when Mr. Orgueil expected to see him most distressed and dejected, he was astonished to find with what Steadiness and Constancy he behaved. But when he perceived he could not convert him, and make him a Proselyte to the Sect of Self-worshippers, he grew angry, and at different Times introduced the Words, an Enthusiast, a Methodist, a mad Man; and at last, as an unconquerable Argument, told him, that he held Principles which were fit for nothing but old Women.[65]

The narrator's ironic labeling of Orgueil's efforts as "proselytizing" and "sectarian" resonate with Orgueil's erroneous use of "enthusiast" and "Methodist" to describe David's principled piety. David's rational approach to Christian salvation precludes the madness to which his own extreme trials might have otherwise driven him, and Orgueil's desperate attempt to undermine David's belief with reference to "old Women" merely reveals his failure to discredit David's principles.

In addition, Mrs. Orgueil provides another contrast to David's eventual calm resignation following the death of his wife; Mrs. Orgueil vividly proves the rationality of Christian principle and its necessity. Contemplating her husband's death, she writes a friend to describe "The real Distraction of [her] Soul."[66] She insists,

> As soon as I hear the dreadful Sound, *Your Husband is no more!* I know I shall be incapable of any Thought or Reflection. No Tongue can express my Distractions. I am as mad as Alicia in *Jane Shore*; could rave like Oedipus, and wish all the Stars would lose their Light; for so great are my present Torments, the universal Nature seems in one Confusion hurled.[67]

The excesses of punctuation and italics betray the hurry of her mind and prove the veracity of her failure to reflect. Her references to Nicholas Rowe's *The Tragedy of Jane Shore* (1714) and Sophocles's *Oedipus Rex* instead of the Bible link irrationality to secular literary precedent, and the link is cemented when she later erroneously assumes her husband's death and "fell a raving like an Inhabitant of Bedlam."[68]

Ultimately, however, David's return to Christian principle after the lapse caused by Camilla's illness and death proves too late, and his neglect of his body leads to his own illness and death. His deathbed repentance, once more, takes up the issue of the intellectual failures with which *David Simple* ends. David explains:

> When I revolve in my Thoughts all my past Life, the Errors of my Mind strike me strongly. . . . Friendship and Love were the only Images that struck my Imagination with Pleasure; there therefore I fixed my Pursuit, and in these I felt the Sharpness of every Disappointment.[69]

His indulgence of feeling at the expense of reason led him away from Christian piety. He acknowledges, "I exulted in the perfecting my own Scheme, and saw not what awaited me behind . . . I thought myself at home in this World, and attached my Heart to the Enjoyment of it, as strongly, though in a different Way, as does the Miser or Ambitious."[70] And he explains,

> Then, indeed, my Mind began to be seized with Fear—I was no longer my former Self—Pictures of Distress of my Family began to succeed each other in my Mind, and Terror and Timidity conquered my better Judgment . . . and my staggering Mind catched hold of every rotten Plank in hopes of Support. . . . I found my Mind in such Chains as are much worse than any Slavery of the Body . . . my Eyes were forced wide open, to discover the Fallacy of fancying any real or lasting Happiness can arise from an Attachment to Objects subject to Infirmities, Diseases, and certain Death.[71]

His emotional excesses took control; his feeling enslaved his reason and prevented him from perceiving, let alone taking, the Christian path to virtue. Ultimately, only the complete failure of secular philosophy to provide consolation in the face of death saves him, and he contrasts his own "Constancy of Mind," "weakened to [that of] a Child," with the "strong and lively Hope in the Revelation God has been pleased to send us . . . I can now sit in my Bed with a calm Resignation, to which my conquered Mind has been long a Stranger."[72] Thus, his intellect leads him back to God.

At novel's end, David dies having finally developed his Christian faith according to rational principle. Significantly, he is survived by Cynthia and his daughter Camilla. While David's peaceful death corresponds with his return to reason, Cynthia and little Camilla's survival corresponds to their consistent and superior intellect. Despite bearing witness to the impending death of her last remaining friend, Cynthia preserves her presence of mind. She preserves the Christian principle that allows her to accept the limits of earthly happiness and the promise of salvation. She does not fall prey to the irrationality of David or the Orgueils; neither does she crumple under the weight of her grief at Valentine's passing. Privileging Christian principle over emotion, she writes to David and Camilla: "your Brother, my dearest Husband died last Saturday, of a raging Fever, frequent in this Country, and has left me—but I will say nothing of myself. God comfort and preserve you to each other."[73] She glosses over her own state to argue for the value of Christian consolation in the face of earthly suffering.[74]

Further, the intellectual foundation she builds by reading "History and the Bible to the Children" nurtures their "Capacity" to create an "Understanding capable of Improvement."[75] And her model proves a strong enough influence to help little Camilla see the "Fallacies" resulting from "the Indulgence of violent Passions [that] blinds and perverts the Judgment" of Mrs. Orgueil.[76]

Finally, it is important to consider that Cynthia's and little Camilla's survival depends upon their intellectual superiority, a superiority that both *David Simple* and *Volume the Last* depict as dependent upon the logic of Christian principle. But even more important is the radical potential Fielding allows their exemplary intellect.[77] Specifically, by situating her narrative of women's superior reasoning and survival among allusions to John Milton's *Paradise Lost*, Fielding offers a radical revision of women's relationship to virtue.[78] First, in *David Simple*'s depiction of Cynthia's encounter with the Atheist, Fielding's uncanny rewriting of Milton's epic poem places Cynthia back in Eden's bower, "into a little Garden belonging to the House, in which was an Arbour."[79] However, unlike Milton's "hapless Eve,"[80] Cynthia finds repose in the Garden by "giving way to the Bent of her Mind"[81] and indulging her "Imagination."[82] Her mental activity in the garden proves healthy because her responsible management of her thoughts "exhausts . . . all unpleasing Thoughts" and provides "more agreeable Ideas."[83] Meanwhile, the Atheist, like Milton's serpent, approaches "softly, and unperceived by her."[84] But Cynthia meets him prepared. She is not "amazed."[85] Rather than allowing her "eager appetite" and "longing" to precipitate "rashness,"[86] Cynthia responds with "Courage and Resolution" to repulse her seducer according to the dictates of "reason," with "civility."[87] Meanwhile, the Atheist's physical intemperance is no match for Cynthia's practiced intellect.[88]

Further, Cynthia's ultimate survival, when viewed alongside this radical rewriting of Genesis, offers women a new and positive exemplarity reinforced by Camilla's Miltonic emotional excesses. When, upon news of her brother's death, Camilla is capable of neither speech nor tears, she is struck dumb with fear at the thought of her own husband's demise and the narrator again alludes to *Paradise*

*Lost*. When Camilla's hysteria leads her to begin questioning the justice of her father's recent passing. The narrator relates,

> It is impossible for any Words so strongly to represent the Picture of *David* and his *Camilla* at that Time, as these of *Milton*:
>
> "She silently a gentle Tear let fall<br>
> From either Eye——<br>
> Two other precious Drops that ready stood<br>
> Each in their chrystal Sluice, he, e'er they fell,<br>
> Kiss'd——"<br>
> (Fielding, *Volume the Last*, 298)[89]

In this image of the pitifully weeping Eve, Fielding sinks Camilla into an aestheticized sentimentality that indicates Camilla's pathetic passivity, her tendency for self-blame and helpless resignation. As moving as this portrait might be to some readers, the allusive dissonance it and Camilla's death offer Cynthia's bower scene and survival reinforce the novels' celebration of rational Christian principle and critique of secular reason. As such, Cynthia and little Camilla allow for exemplary women's intellect to escape sentimental stereotypes and modify women's relationship to virtue. In *David Simple* and *Volume the Last*, Sarah Fielding does much more than outline a generic "Christian" virtue of good works and humility. Instead, she details a distinctly rational Christian faith that also offers Cynthia as a new Eve, capable of using the knowledge she gained in the garden to live a life of principled piety and enjoy its consolations.[90]

## Notes

1. Sarah Fielding, *The Adventures of David Simple and Volume the Last*, ed. Peter Sabor (Lexington: University Press of Kentucky, 1998).

2. Richard Terry, "*David Simple* and the Fallacy of Friendship," *SEL Studies in English Literature 1500–1900* 44, no. 3 (2004): 525.

3. Ibid., 541.

4. Rebecca Hussey also sees *Volume the Last* as a reversal of its predecessor; however, she argues for Cynthia's status as hero according to her superior "attitude toward travel." Specifically, she concludes that the novel recommends Cynthia's ability to use her emotional susceptibility to others as a source of social critique. Rebecca Hussey, "The Sentimental

Traveler: Emotion, Movement, and Economy in Sarah Fielding's *Adventures of David Simple and Volume the Last*," *The Age of Johnson* 19 (2009): 213.

5. Janine Barchas's essay "Sarah Fielding's Dashing Style and Eighteenth-Century Print Culture" provides a wonderful example of the rewards of close-reading Fielding's work. In addition to Barchas's attention to Fielding's dashes, details of Christian belief and biblical allusion may prove in new ways the "depth of her control over the details of her writing." Janine Barchas, "Sarah Fielding's Dashing Style and Eighteenth-Century Print Culture," *ELH* 63, no. 3 (1996): 633. Betty Schellenberg argued that Fielding's own intellectual prowess can be observed through both the range of her published works as well as their marketable success. See Betty Schellenberg, *The Professionalization of Women Writers in Eighteenth-Century Britain* (Cambridge: Cambridge University Press, 2009).

6. Scott Paul Gordon also sees *Volume the Last* as an extension of *David Simple*; however, he suggests that the trope of quixotism be used to explain the novels as a critique of naïveté. According to Gordon, in the novels, "knowledge or understanding is possible only if we can shed our prejudices or hypotheses in order to see others as they really are." Scott Paul Gordon, "Suspicion and Experience in Sarah Fielding's *David Simple*," *The Practice of Quixotism: Postmodern Theory and Eighteenth-Century Women's Writing* (New York: Palgrave, 2006), 67.

7. Emily Friedman has also observed Fielding's tendency to privilege reason over emotion. Specifically, she argues that Fielding employs a variety of specific formal techniques "to provide readers spaces for their own reflection and reason-based improvement." Emily Friedman, "Remarks on Richardson: Sarah Fielding and the Rational Reader," *Eighteenth-Century Fiction* 22, no. 2 (Winter 2009–2010): 309.

8. Emma Major has explored women's religious exemplarity within a distinctly public political context. In contrast, the exemplarity offered by Fielding's work considers individual and familial contexts and consequences. See Emma Major, *Madame Britannia: Women, Church, and Nation, 1712–1812* (Oxford: Oxford University Press, 2012).

9. James Kim gets close to considering religion with his examination of sentimental irony and the way the novel is engaged in "enunciating psychological principles, and tracking the way characters deliberate in morally complex situations." However, his assessment of morality and principled action remains distinctly secular. James Kim, "Mourning, Melancholia, and Modernity: Sentimental Irony and Downward Mobility in *David Simple*," *Eighteenth-Century Fiction* 22, no. 3 (Spring 2010): 477–491.

10. Linda Bree, *Sarah Fielding* (New York: Twayne Publishers, 1996), 28.

11. K. G. Hall, *The Exalted Heroine and the Triumph of Order: Class, Women, and Religion in the English Novel, 1740–1800* (New York: Barnes & Noble Books, 1993), 55.

12. Tera Pettella, "Devotional Reading and Novel Form: The Case of *David Simple*," *Eighteenth-Century Fiction* 24, no. 2 (Winter 2011–2012): 279.

13. Mary Ann Rooks, "Wherein Lies Virtue? Secular Matters and Godly Matters in the Works of Sarah Fielding," in *Religion in the Age of Enlightenment* 3 (2012): 248–275.

14. Ibid., 261.

15. Ibid.

16. Fielding, *David Simple*, 25.

17. Ibid.

18. Ibid., 26.

19. Ibid., 27.

20. Ibid., 29.
21. Ibid., 30.
22. Ibid., 37.
23. Ibid., 55.
24. Ibid.
25. Ibid., 59.
26. Ibid., 124.
27. Ibid.
28. Matt. 13:31–32 (KJV).
29. Fielding, *David Simple*, 193.
30. Ibid., 194.
31. Ibid.
32. Ibid., 195.
33. Carol Stewart comments on the importance this inset narrative, along with that of the three daughters, to the novel's representation of female agency in relationship to filial obedience, but does not acknowledge the religious conclusion and allusions of each. See Carol Stewart, *The Eighteenth-Century Novel and the Secularization of Ethics* (New York: Ashgate, 2010), 101.
34. Fielding, *David Simple*, 138.
35. Ibid.
36. Ibid, 139.
37. Ibid.
38. Ibid.
39. Ibid.
40. Ibid., 140. Cynthia's astute and understated response to the contrast between these characters reinforces Janet Todd's reading of *David Simple* as a "sentimental novel [that] directs a blow at the passionate female and her bombastic expression." Janet Todd, *The Sign of Angellica: Women, Writing and Fiction, 1660–1800* (New York: Columbia University Press, 1989), 169.
41. Fielding, *David Simple*, 223.
42. Ibid.
43. Ibid.
44. Ibid., 228.
45. Ibid., 261.
46. Ibid.
47. Ibid., 281.
48. Ibid.
49. Ibid.
50. 1 Tim. 5:8 (KJV).
51. Fielding, *David Simple*, 282.
52. Ibid.
53. Ibid.
54. Ibid., 301.
55. Ibid., 302.
56. Ibid., 303.
57. Ibid., 327.

58. Ibid., 328.
59. Ibid., 329.
60. Ibid., 331.
61. Ibid.
62. Ibid., 332.
63. Ibid.
64. Ibid.
65. Ibid., 333.
66. Ibid., 334.
67. Ibid.
68. Ibid.
69. Ibid., 349.
70. Ibid., 341.
71. Ibid.
72. Ibid., 342.
73. Ibid., 298.
74. This pairing of women's superior intellect with Christian principle could also be seen as a softening or feminizing of masculine reason by feminized religion. Sara Gadeken has observed this kind of qualification with respect to satire in Fielding's writing. "The female satirist, if she is to be heard, must reconcile her wit with cultural demands for modesty and self-effacement." Sarah Gadeken, "Sarah Fielding and the Salic Law of Wit," *SEL* 42, no. 3 (Summer 2002): 542. David's inferior intellect and deficiency of Christian principle could also correspond to the "internal effeminacy" that Felicity Nussbaum argues motivates Fielding's creation of a "gendered hybridity that differs substantially from the distressing mixture that would complicate a national identity." Felicity Nussbaum, *The Limits of the Human: Fictions of Anomaly: Race, and Gender in the Long Eighteenth Century* (Cambridge: Cambridge University Press, 2003), 63.
75. Fielding, *David Simple*, 257, 256.
76. Ibid., 324–325.
77. Alexander Petit has also recognized the radical feminism of these novels. He argues that "by refusing to regard plot as a series of enactments of, or responses to, masculine erotic desire, Fielding argues against the rote phallocentrism intrinsic to comedy and the novel generally, and to comic closure in the novel specifically," but he also sees her position as "not in the least optimistic." Alexander Pettit, "*David Simple* and the Attenuation of 'Phallic Power,'" *Eighteenth-Century Fiction* 11, no. 2 (January 1999): 169.
78. This rewriting of Milton's text extends Mika Suzuki's argument that Fielding's work highlights her awareness of "female victimization by male language." Mika Suzuki, "Sarah Fielding and Reading," *The Eighteenth-Century Novel* 2 (2002): 92.
79. Fielding, *David Simple*, 140.
80. John Milton, "Paradise Lost," in *The Norton Anthology of English Literature*, vol. B, ed. Stephen Greenblatt et al., 1831–2055 (New York: W. W. Norton & Co., 2006), 9.404.
81. Fielding, *David Simple*, 140.
82. Ibid., 141.
83. Ibid.
84. Ibid.
85. Milton, "Paradise Lost," 9.552, 614.

86. Ibid., 9.740, 743, 780.

87. Fielding, *David Simple*, 141.

88. G. A. Starr's work with Sarah Fielding further supports the significance of Cynthia's modeling of conversation with the clergyman and with the atheist. He writes, "But she presents as normal what a modern reader is apt to find odd: David's way of regarding stories not as the mere equivalent of personal experience, but as the very substance of experience." As readers, we participate in the conversation, and our sensibility leads us toward the moral practice Cynthia models. G. A. Starr, "From Socrates to Sarah Fielding: Benevolence, Irony, and Conversation," in *Passionate Encounters in a Time of Sensibility*, ed. Maximillian Novak and Anne Mellor (Newark: University of Delaware Press), 109.

89. Milton, *Paradise Lost*, 5.130–34.

90. In this respect, Cynthia's survival shifts the focus of Lori Walk's reading of *David Simple* as primarily David's ultimate failure "to choose and create positive familial relationships as the [his] quest" to the women's potential familial agency. Lori Walk, "Questing for Family in Joseph Andrews and *David Simple*," *The Eighteenth-Century Novel* 1 (2001): 237.

# Repentance or Regret: Isabella's Religion in *The History of the Nun*

*Lisa Sikkink*

Isabella, the heroine in Aphra Behn's 1689 novella, *The History of the Nun, or, The Fair Vow-Breaker*, is a beautiful, intelligent, accomplished nun, who, through the course of the novel, breaks all her vows, loses two fortunes, suffers a miscarriage, and murders both her husbands before being executed for her various crimes. Despite Isabella's many failures, misdeeds, and false starts, at her execution she is praised by the entire city and remembered fondly. The entire ending would be highly irregular if it had occurred outside of the Behn canon. Many of Behn's heroines are involved in terrible situations that should result in equally terrible reputations for the heroines, yet often these characters are praised after their deaths.[1] Usually in a novel in which the heroine finds herself in trouble, she either redeems herself by marrying well or she dies—usually of illness or suicide—ashamed, destitute, and alone; rarely does the punished woman live on in the hearts of the people like Behn's Isabella.[2] Even when Behn's tale was adapted for the stage by Thomas Southerne in 1694 as *The Fatal Marriage, or The Innocent Adultery* and, again, in 1757 by David Garrick as *Isabella, or The Fatal Marriage*, Isabella is not mourned the way she is in Behn's original telling; instead, she is merely pitied.[3] Simply put, Behn's Isabella is to be admired for her strength, while her later incarnations are merely to be pitied—eliciting an emotional response from those around her.

I agree with the major critics that Isabella's agency in Behn's novel is most apparent when put in contrast with Southerne's and Garrick's plays, in which her agency has been systematically stripped away. The factors that highlight the differences in the character of Isabella are the amount of depth to her backstory, her second marriage, and her response when she discovers that her first husband is still alive. This chapter extends the conversation by arguing that the key to Isabella's agency is her faith: despite her many missteps, she always returns to prayer and regains her spiritual equilibrium. It is the agency of Behn's Isabella that enables her to remain in good standing with her community and the local church despite her broken vows and double homicide. She chooses to take responsibility for her crimes and is punished accordingly. She allows the government and God to judge her instead of committing suicide. Her later incarnations do not have any agency and follow an opposite trajectory; they become increasingly distraught, are unable to cope with their situations, and ultimately kill themselves. The other Isabellas do not receive secular or ecclesiastical judgment, and by committing suicide they abandon the church. These divergent paths are significant because they represent counterintuitive understandings of morality and personal responsibility.

The novel exhibits Isabella's agency through her detailed backstory (which is largely cut from the plays; the novel covers over a decade of Isabella's life), an explanation of how she decides to marry her second husband (which, in the plays, is out of need rather than desire), her reaction when she discovers her first husband is still alive, and her decision to murder both husbands—whereas her dramatic counterparts swoon away and let both their husbands and fate sort things out. These episodes in the novel highlight Isabella's determination to survive even though fate is working against her, whereas the Isabellas in the plays succumb to their circumstances and become victims who do not fight against fate but merely bewail their situations. Isabella's agency (or lack thereof) produces very different endings for the version of this character: the former continues on in the hearts of the people, while the latter commit suicide to avoid the shame of their situation. The differences represent varying conceptions of how female characters should behave in the face of overwhelming and consistent failure, while also limiting one of the few avenues of relative independence for women: the convent. Despite everything that happens in the novel, Isabella consistently returns to her faith and her tale ends on a relatively optimistic note, unlike the play versions, whose authors strip her of her faith and allow her to die miserably.

Other critics have explored the differences between these three texts and what those differences signify, but given the relative obscurity of the plays, a brief summary of the tale, highlighting the differences between the texts important to this argument, might be helpful. All three texts generally have the following plot: Isabella is a young woman who becomes a nun at age thirteen but after much suffering and deliberation breaks her vows and marries. Her husband (Henault in Behn's text, or Biron in the plays) goes to war and is presumed dead after seven years, so she marries another man (Villenoys or Villeroy, respectively). Suddenly, while her second husband is out of town, her first husband reappears and professes his eternal love for her. She panics, and this is where the texts dramatically diverge. In Behn's version, she kills both husbands and is eventually tried and executed for her crimes. In Southerne's and Garrick's versions, her first husband is killed when he is attacked on the street and her second husband survives the play, but Isabella commits suicide—even though her problems have solved themselves with the confirmed death of her first husband. The plays' endings are very subdued in the wake of Isabella's suicide. Everyone is surprised by her suicide, even though she had previously tried to stab herself, saying, "Thus I strike for him, and liberty."[4] When she finally succeeds, Villeroy only mourns the loss of his own happiness: "She's gone, and all my joys of life with her. . . . But I must live, grow gray with ling'ring grief, to die at last in telling this sad tale."[5] Villeroy is primarily concerned with his own loss and is not interested in how Isabella's despair could have been prevented, or even what will happen to her orphaned son.

The last lines of the play are delivered by Count Baldwin, who offers a trite moral about forgiving one's children. The speech has nothing to do with Isabella (despite him just having witnessed her spectacular suicide), nor the novel's original theme about the importance of keeping one's vows:

> To erring youth there's some compassion due;
> But while with rigour you their crimes pursue,
> What's their misfortune, is a crime for you.
> Hence learn, offending children to forgive:
> Leave punishment to Heav'n—'tis Heav'n's prerogative.[6]

These lines reflect what Baldwin has learned through the course of the play: Biron, his son, might have lived if only Baldwin had forgiven Biron for marrying poorly. Unlike Southerne's and Garrick's interpretations of Isabella, Behn's version remains the most moral because she attempts to follow her faith and do what is right, even though she is not terribly successful (committing murder to prevent a bigamy charge is excessive). On the other hand, Southerne and Garrick construct Isabella as a stereotype of a woman who is passive, long-suffering, highly emotional, and not terribly clear-headed, but they do not portray her as a moral woman. These later Isabellas do not have strong religious centers, like Behn's Isabella, to guide their actions. The main reason for these differences is the relationship between each of the authors and their respective version of the text. For Southerne, the tale is not about Isabella, or women at all. Instead, his version highlights the difficulties that birth order presents when determining male inheritance, as well as the importance of money for social status (as opposed to survival, the way it is for Behn). In the article "The History of *The History of the Nun*," Jacqueline Pearson thoroughly and deftly explores the differences between and significance of the various adaptations of Behn's novel. Pearson notes that the theme of keeping and breaking vows has been completely forgotten by the end of the play, whose moral emphasizes male tyranny rather than female guilt. Unlike Behn, who allows women the dignity of free will and of full moral parity with men, Southerne presents his play's heroine simply as a passive victim. . . . Both [Southerne and Garrick] at every point concentrate on her passive suffering and minimize, deny, or excuse her guilt. A complex and believable human being is transformed into an icon of virtue. . . . Abandoned or oppressed by the representatives of patriarchal power, Isabella is transformed from an active sinner into a passive sufferer."[7]

Other critics have already detailed the textual similarities and differences among these three texts, as well as how Southerne's and Garrick's changes flatten Isabella's character and make her nothing more than a victim. Pearson offers a fine summary of that conversation, particularly focusing on these two plays. In Southerne, Isabella is split into two female characters, herself and the cross-dressing Victoria, so at least there is some form of rebellious woman, but later Garrick cuts Victoria from the plot and only a passive, victimized Isabella remains. Pearson argues, "Both [Southerne and Garrick] at every point concentrate on her passive suffering and minimize, deny, or excuse [Isabella's] guilt. . . . Neither Southerne nor Garrick is willing to allow this full subjectivity to a woman."[8] Southerne's text does not allow any of the protagonists to be tainted by criminal actions, whereas Behn does not have this qualm. She thrives on unusual characters—especially women. Several of her other novels have murderous main characters—including in *The Fair Jilt*, which also demonstrates Behn's penchant for devious female characters. In *The Fair Jilt*, Miranda commits a number of heinous crimes, including sexually assaulting a monk and plotting to murder her own sister (although she largely escapes punishment for her crimes). Allowing a character full culpability for her crimes—much less allowing protagonists to commit crimes at all—is crucial if one wants to portray issues of morality or guilt. If characters are not allowed to commit and own their mistakes, they are not characters so much as stock pieces or props.

Southerne's and Garrick's plays are closely related to each other, despite Garrick's aggressive and specific agenda for adapting texts to eighteenth-century and his own personal tastes (the latter clearly shaping the former).[9] During the end of the seventeenth century, novels and plays were usually interested in ribaldry, salacious dialogue, and bed tricks. Garrick worked to make the theater a respectable venue for entertainment by improving the morality of the plays presented. He disapproved of coarse comedy and cut most of Southerne's additions to Behn's tale. The advertisement for Garrick's play explains that "the tragic part of the play has been always esteemed extremely natural and interesting," while the comic part is "not only indelicate, but immoral."[10] Garrick justified cutting huge portions of Southerne's text because it no longer fit popular tastes and morals. Interestingly, Garrick's cuts make the play much closer to Behn's original text than Southerne's play, which brings the tale, at least superficially, full circle. *Superficially* is used deliberately because he does not alter Southerne's characterization of Isabella—she is still passive, weepy, and suicidal—nor does his text allow Isabella any significant agency. Overall, changes were made to preserve the "purity" of the tragic genre while also sanitizing the play of the immoral comic plot. This is unsurprising because, as the introduction to Garrick's alterations argues, Garrick "worked mightily to mold [public] taste. . . . He became a kind of guardian of public morals, ridding the old plays of coarseness and indecency, dropping offending plays from the repertoire, and admonishing contemporary playwrights when they overstepped the bounds of good taste."[11] While Garrick was trying to sanitize Southerne's work of its salacious nature, Garrick does not appear to have read Behn's novel. Behn's writing was very popular during her lifetime and immediately after because of its salacious nature. Despite Garrick's desire to make the theater experience more virtuous, he inadvertently aligned himself with one of the most scandalous writers of the Restoration.

Southerne, however, was familiar with Behn's novel, even though his version of events is wildly different. Southerne's play was produced approximately five years after Behn's novel was published. He only acknowledges his indebtedness to Behn in the dedicatory letter to the printed version of the play, writing, "I took the hint of the tragical part of this play from a novel of Mrs. Behn's, called *The Fair Vow-Breaker*; you will forgive me for calling it a hint when you find I have little more than borrowed the question, how far such a distress was to be carried, up on the misfortune of a woman's having innocently two husbands at the same time?"[12] Here, Southerne admits that he takes great liberties with Behn's text. Many of the plot points and character names are the same, but the tone, themes, and other important components of the text are very different. From a critical perspective, Southerne's play has little in common with Behn's novel beyond a superficial summary. Given the temporal proximity of Southerne's play to Behn's novel, it seems that audiences would have been familiar with—or at least aware of—Behn's novel. Several articles, including Leah Orr's "Attribution Problems in the Fiction of Aphra Behn" and Montague Summers's "The Source of Southerne's *The Fatal Marriage*," indicate the rarity of *The History of the Nun*; these articles demonstrate that for years *The History of the Nun* was assumed to simply be a titular variant of *The Nun, or The Perjured Beauty*. It was not until the twentieth century that these misconceptions were dispelled and the novel rediscovered.[13] Also, Pearson notes that "the final scenes of Southerne's play reflect a detailed knowledge of Behn's original and an expectation that his audience will also know it and that this knowledge will color their expectations of the play. He is therefore more willing than Garrick to recall some elements of Behn's plot, while wholly altering their significance."[14]

By returning to Southerne's "hint" and what he presumes is the "question" of the tale, it becomes clear that he might be correct: once we account for all of his changes to Behn's novel regarding themes, money, and agency, he has only taken a "hint" from Behn. He disregards much of her critical exploration about gender, financial hardship, and criminality. Instead, he makes his play about a scorned younger brother, male friendship and rivalry, and the passivity of women. Given Southerne's generally privileged position, it is not surprising that he was not interested in the troubles of women. It is worth noting that he died at the advanced age of eighty-five years and was very rich. Behn died quite young, at only forty-eight, and was very poor, having been in debt for most of her life.[15] Naturally, then, the problems her female characters faced were the same problems she faced herself.[16] For Behn, the tale explores the nature of keeping and breaking vows as well as the importance of money for survival—a difficult situation for a former nun who had everything provided for her in the convent. As a woman who was often in desperate need of money, Behn writes Isabella plausibly and pragmatically. Behn is familiar with the hardships of being a woman who is in financial straits. The problems Isabella faces are ones that Behn faced—admittedly Behn did not have the benefit of Isabella's inherited fortune and aristocratic connections.

As one might expect, the titular changes reflect the thematic changes in the texts. In Behn's novel, the reader is constantly aware of both Isabella's history and her years spent as a nun, as well as her many broken vows—all things suggested in the title: *The History of the Nun*, *or the Fair Vow-Breaker*. Neither Southerne nor Garrick keep any part of Behn's title, instead opting for *The Fatal Marriage, or The Innocent Adultery* and *Isabella, or The Fatal Marriage*, respectively. "The Fatal Marriage" in Southerne's and Garrick's titles could very well suggest Isabella or either of her husbands, since each is presumed dead or dies because of the marriage. Even using Isabella's name in the title does not necessarily mean she is the subject of the play, as is often the case; it suggests that she is merely the catalyst for the action surrounding the male characters.[17] In the novel, however, Isabella is the primary actor and she is mourned because she owns her mistakes. Her later counterparts cannot cope with their problems because they have not made any choices—everything happens *to* them, not *because of* them. They are merely the victims of circumstances.

Instead of being mourned and celebrated by the community at large, Southerne's and Garrick's Isabellas are pitied because they cannot cope with their misfortunes and blame themselves instead of faulting fate or other characters. One of the key differences between the plays and the original novella is Isabella's mental toughness and resiliency, demonstrated in the text: "She was most exemplary devout in the cloister, doing more penance and imposing a more rigid severity and task on herself than was required, giving such rare examples to all the nuns that were less devout that her life was a proverb and a precedent, and when they would express a very holy woman indeed, they would say she was a very Isabella."[18] In the novel, she turns to her faith for guidance and solace. Despite her many troubles, Isabella is able to keep going and she ultimately makes peace with herself—at ease both before and during her execution.

Because in the plays Isabella is, as Pearson eloquently writes, "abandoned or oppressed by the representatives of patriarchal power, Isabella is transformed from an active sinner into a passive sufferer."[19] In the plays, Isabella cannot seem to cope with anything. She spends most of her lines in frantic distress. For much of the play she is desperate and begging, even though Behn's Isabella never stoops so low. In the beginning of the plays, Isabella begs her father-in-law for charity; she knocks on his door and cries out: "Lock'd! and fast! Where is the charity that us'd to stand in our forefathers' hospitable days at great men's doors, ready for our wants, like the good angel of the family, with open arms taking the needy in, to feed and cloath, to comfort and relieve 'em? Now even their gates are shut against their poor."[20] The novel's Isabella has enough strength of character and faith in her religion that she can persevere, whereas the Isabella in the plays lacks these traits and does not handle hardship very well. Isabella tells herself, "Let my fate determine for me; I shall be prepar'd, the worst that can befall me, is to die."[21] Without her faith and belief in heaven and divine justice, she ends up killing herself.

Southerne and Garrick dramatically alter Isabella's character so that she is virtually unrecognizable as Behn's pious nun who constantly dwells on her broken vows and their significance to her faith. Instead, she is relegated to being a secondary character at best. The plot is also changed so much that the plays are no longer about Isabella—they are about her husbands. The plays begin in media res, skipping her life as a nun, the wooing and marriage to her first husband, Biron, as well as his departure for war and subsequent supposed death. Cutting these sections of the plot for dramatic performance de-emphasizes the importance of Isabella's struggles with her faith and vows to the church—which is the titular struggle in the original text. Southerne also greatly expands the background of Biron and Villeroy and the involvement of their families, while cutting Isabella's lengthy backstory down to a short speech given by a secondary character. The nurse explains why Count Baldwin hates Isabella strictly in relation to male characters:

> this Biron, without asking the advice of his friends, . . . not having the fear of his father before his eyes, as I may say, wilfully marries this Isabella . . . after she had settled all her fortune upon a nunnery, which she broke out of to run away with him. They say they had the church's forgiveness, but I had rather it had been his father's. . . . [Count Baldwin] disinherited him; . . . and at last forc'd Biron to go to the siege of Candy, where he was killed.[22]

This abbreviated version of the complicated relationship between Biron (a.k.a. Henault) and Isabella not only relegates her to a secondary character and limits her agency but also emphasizes the actions of the male characters and removes the complexity of the novel's themes.

Behn's focus is on Isabella: her troubles, her history, her desires, her secrets, her spirituality, her passions. In Southerne's and Garrick's plays, we know relatively little about her, and she has relatively few lines and little stage time. This can be partially attributed to generic differences between novels and plays, but Isabella has fewer lines than Villeroy and (for the scenes he is present) Biron. Her lines have very little content or action; they are predominantly emotional exclamations. For example, when Villeroy attempts to persuade Isabella to marry him again, she cries out, "Oh, I have heard all this!—But must no more—the charmer is no more: My bury'd husband rises in the face of my dear boy, and chides me for my stay: Canst thou forgive me, child?" Her son responds, "Why, have you done a fault? You cry as if you had: Indeed now, I've done nothing to offend you: but if you kiss me, and look so very sad upon me, I shall cry too."[23] Even a young child of seven can see that she is unreasonably upset by the request.

Both Southerne and Garrick are more interested in Biron's family than in Isabella's, whereas we hear about Isabella's mother, father, aunt, friends, and religious sisters from Behn. One example of her support system is her close relationship with her abbess (who is also her aunt). When she and Henault are in dire straits, she pleads with her aunt and is ultimately forgiven instead of punished: "At last, one good fortune arrived to them by the solicitations of the lady abbess, and the bishop, who was her near kinsman. They got a pardon for Isabella's quitting the monastery and marrying, so that she might now return to her own country again."[24] Initially, the stated punishment for abandoning her vows was eternal banishment, but Isabella is allowed to return home to her city—and in full favor of her remaining family. The lack of punishment for her behavior does not sit well with her: "Isabella assayed to pray, but, alas, it was in vain. She was distracted with a thousand thoughts what to do, which the more she thought, the more it distracted her. She was a thousand times about to end her life and, at one stroke, rid herself of the infamy that she saw must inevitably fall upon her."[25]

In Behn's novel, Isabella's sense of loneliness is heightened by gradual losses: her parents, her aunt, her miscarried baby, and, upon leaving the convent, her friends. The contrast to the plays is important. In the male-authored texts, she is the stereotypical woman, incapable of coping emotionally, but also a slightly idealized one in that she successfully births a son for her first husband (unlike her flawed predecessor, who miscarries and does not attempt to conceive again). Her isolation is only significant once she is responsible for the isolation of a male child as well. Furthermore, in the plays, Isabella is shown as the reason for Biron's death, even though she had little to do with it. Isabella is not a character so much as a catalyst: She causes things to happen, but the play is not *about* her. Things cannot happen without her, but she is not otherwise important, or even particularly interesting.

In Southerne's and Garrick's plays, Isabella does not even start the play with a servant, just her young son. Ignoring Isabella's family contributes to her role as a victim, since she does not have a strong support system or anyone to whom she can turn for help. Garrick and Southerne even strip away her faith, which, although fraught, is a key component of her character. She has no support, not even God or her fellow nuns. Isabella's faith is central to her character, and without it the character loses its integrity and becomes flat—which is precisely what happens when Southerne and Garrick adapt Behn's novel for the stage. They shift the focus away from Isabella and her complicated history and onto her husbands' respective plights. This process results in marked thematic changes in the tale, as well as an "updating" of the story for the eighteenth century that comes from replacing Isabella's religious dilemma with the social and material dilemmas of her two husbands. Early on, Villeroy paints himself as enslaved to Isabella, even though she has consistently rejected him for years: "I'm only born to be what you would have me, the entire creature of your power, and must obey; in every thing obey you. I am going: but all good fortune go along with you."[26] By shifting the focus away from Isabella and onto Biron and Villeroy, the religious contemplation that is so frequently and centrally depicted in Behn's original work is lost. Her broken religious vows are second to her broken marriage vows; indeed, the only character who cares about her religious vows is her father-in-law. She pleads to heaven for assistance and he responds, "How dare you mention heav'n! Call to mind your purjur'd vows; your plighted, broken faith to heav'n, and all things holy: were you not devoted, wedded to a life recluse, the sacred habit on, profess'd and sworn a votary for ever? Can you think the sacrilegious wretch, that robs the shrine, is thunder-proof?"[27] That is the only instance of distress regarding her leaving the convent, although there are pages and pages of agonizing about it in Behn's novel.

Instead, in Garrick's and Southerne's versions of Isabella, it is her sexual crimes—adultery and bigamy—that take center stage, displacing Isabella's religious struggle. In the novel, Isabella's internal struggle is a prominent feature and is central to her character, but extended and constant emotional and religious struggles are difficult to portray on stage. Instead of long-winded emotional displays, Southerne opts to cut Isabella's personal moral struggles in favor of her husbands' dilemmas—which he resolves with an assassination attempt and a dramatic death scene. Susan Goulding argues in "'Stories of Nuns': Narrative Diversion and 'Sister Books,'" that "The 'stories of nuns' are not stories of young women dedicating themselves to the true service of God on earth; rather, they are subversive stories, agitating from the bottom of the power structure, that demonstrate women's power, and offer models from where women are active, and where patriarchally-defined restrictions lead only to failure."[28] Goulding's essay certainly explains why Southerne and Garrick work so diligently to remove all traces of Isabella's original personality and devotion: it would not do to have women with independent desires or minds. Goulding argues that the religious houses in Behn's novels are part of the patriarchy and are thus inherently confining for women; it is important to stipulate that, at least for Isabella, her faith is not inextricably linked to the convent. While she does struggle with her faith in the convent upon realizing her feelings for Henault, her response is to renew her pious efforts: "'Twas generally believed she was too devout, for now she redoubled her austerity, and in cold winter nights of frost and snow would be up at all hours and lying upon the cold stones before the altar prostrate at prayers, so that she received orders from the lady abbess not to harass herself so very much, but to have a care for her health as well as her soul."[29] She is tempted and tries to resist; this is significant because vows and faith are meaningless without temptation and struggle.

Even after she leaves the religious order, it is Isabella's faith that helps her cope with life. Her life with Henault is described as "the most just and pious in the world; they were examples of goodness and eminent for holy living, and for perfect loving, and yet nothing thrived they undertook. They had no children and all their joy was in each other." Even widowed and married again, "she lived more like a nun still than a lady of the world."[30] Clearly, Isabella's cloistered life shaped her personality and character in such a way that, even years later, she retains her habits of devotion, charity, and pious behavior.

The most significant differences between the novel and the plays are Isabella's responses upon discovering her first husband is still alive. Both the book and the play versions of Isabella initially welcome the reappearance of her first husband but becomes understandably distraught once he is asleep. Both versions entertain and then reject the idea of stabbing him; the difference is in the reason for the rejection: Behn's Isabella is eminently practical and says that she cannot stab him because there will be blood everywhere and it will be impossible to clean up. She ends up smothering Henault with a pillow and, using her second husband to dispose of the body, sets Villenoys up to drown. When faced with the same situation, Garrick's Isabella draws a dagger and immediately has a mental break, running around the room and shrieking until she leaves. Isabella does not return to her senses for the rest of the play and ultimately ends up killing herself. As Pearson aptly describes it, "Behn's Isabella directs a capacity for violence outwards, as murder: Southerne's (and Garrick's) more passive Isabella can only direct it inwards, as suicide, an act that, as an extreme version of approved womanly self-denial, clearly seemed to them the only authentic female heroism."[31] Also, Isabella does not kill anyone else, only herself. In Behn's novella, Isabella kills Henault and Villenoys and then is tried and executed. Instead of following Behn on this point, Southerne and Garrick invent Carlos, brother to Biron, who kills his brother out of jealousy. Southerne and Garrick also allow Villeroy to survive the play. By changing the play so that Isabella is no longer a murderer, Behn's tale loses much of its power and complexity. Behn's novel focuses on Isabella's internal struggle between her desire to be righteous, her physical needs, and her social need to be respected and honorable. Often, her physical and spiritual needs align, and that is how she understands killing her husbands as a moral act. She cannot possibly have two husbands and still be a good person, so she elects to rid herself of Henault. She subsequently kills Villenoys as a punishment for herself: she should not have the happiness and pleasure of marriage to Villenoys after killing such a good man as Henualt, who remained devoted to her his entire life.

Behn's exploration of Isabella's various and escalating struggles with her faith presents a depth of character that is not often given to clergy. Isabella cannot even pray for solace because she is so distraught by her sins. When her husband comes upon her, she cries, "'O, you can never pardon me if I should tell you, and yet, I am innocent of ill, by all that's good I am.' But her conscience accusing her at that word, she was silent. 'If thou art innocent,' said Villenoys, taking her up in his arms and kissing her wet face, 'by all that's good I pardon thee, whatever thou hast done. . . . I know thou art too good to commit a sin I may not with honour pardon.'"[32] She begs him to forgive her for her actions because her heart was in the right place, but her conscience will not let her be at ease. This unease continues throughout the rest of the novel. It is not until she is found guilty of double homicide that she can be at peace, and Isabella goes to her execution bravely. Indeed, "in Prison, she was always at Prayers, and very cheerful and easy."[33] The ending of the novel is optimistic—not for Isabella, but for Isabella's soul. She finally is treated fairly, without any special accommodations, and perhaps this will also lead to other women receiving fair treatment.

In the plays, Isabella's guilt, her lack of respite, and her lack of opportunity for redemption or punishment drive her insane and she commits suicide. In the novel, her character has been developed and strengthened through her many hardships and constant reliance on her faith, so by the end of the novel, when her crimes are discovered, she conducts herself with grace and nobility. At her execution,

> she made a speech for half an hour long, so eloquent, so admirable a warning to vow-breakers, that it was as amazing to hear her, as it was to behold her. After she had done . . . she put off her mourning veil and, without anything over her face, she kneeled down and the executioner, at one blow, severed her beautiful head from her delicate body, being then in her seven and twentieth year. She was generally lamented and honourably buried.[34]

By speaking her mind and removing her veil, Isabella demonstrates her strength of character and her ultimate goodness. While murdering her husbands was not the best way to deal with accidentally becoming a bigamist, it is only while she tries to conceal her crime that Isabella is ill at ease. Once she is discovered, she owns her mistake and, for the first time since leaving the convent, she feels comfortable during her prayers. In contrast, the Isabella of the plays spends her last moments "distracted, held by her women, her hair dishevel'd, her little son running in before, being afraid of her."[35] Her last words, instead of indicating that she has learned from her sins, are instead a plea to her son: "May thy father's virtues live in thee: And all his wrongs be buried in my grave."[36] She says that all she has to leave her son is a "kiss" and her "blessing," although the text gives the distinct impression that neither gift is worth much.[37]

Everything that Behn's Isabella attempts to do is an abortive failure, except the murder of her husbands. For example, she cannot keep her religious vows, besides her intense mourning rituals; she attempts to remain a widow after her first husband is killed, but she remarries; she is successful in her vows to her second husband, but she must kill her first to keep those vows. Isabella then realizes how the murder of the first will compromise her second husband's perception of her, so she kills him too. Throughout the story her attempts at prayer fail, and her attempts at motherhood fail when she miscarries. Isabella's only successes come when she attempts convent-like behaviors: living as a recluse in mourning, keeping a vow of silence about the murder of her husbands, living away from men and society (except her maid). If Henault's friend had not identified him at the coroner's, Isabella might have lived forever without confessing. However, it is not until she owns her many mistakes and has her secrets revealed that she can be at peace. The moment she becomes close to men, her troubles begin. Any choices she makes that lead her away from the church have terrible results, but her choice to come clean, confess, and do penance for her sins gives her freedom—both spiritually (suddenly, she can pray easily), emotionally (she has no more marital angst), financially (she is provided for in prison), and physically (it was her biological and her moral issues that got her in trouble all along; in death, these will no longer plague her). The combination of confession and penance gives her freedom and ease of mind. This is significant because it makes Isabella relatable—the reader can understand the weight of a guilty conscience and enjoy the relief when the truth is revealed. Isabella would be an easy character to idealize, especially given her description in the first portion of the novel, but Behn resists this urge, and Isabella retains her humanity, her flaws, and her shortcomings. Isabella has no experience in the world and has never had to live with the consequences of her actions, so it makes sense that she makes many mistakes. Even in doing so, however, she remains respectable. Isabella struggles with the loss of her child, her husband, and her faith. In the text, Isabella's losses are burdens without the physical representation other characters would readily see and understand. Thus there is no proof, no evidence of her suffering, only unseen emotional turmoil. Isabella's faith, while sometimes a burden, is also a balm for her wounds and a guide out of her troubles.

All three versions of Isabella might come from extraordinary circumstances, but they each have very ordinary foibles. In the case of Behn's Isabella, it is her religious struggle that makes her so relatable: the audience understands what it is like to have doubts, misgivings, and the uncertainties that Isabella expresses in her prayers and to her confidante. On the other hand, it is easy to dismiss later versions of Isabella as pathetic victims. They are pitied, but their deaths are not especially mourned—largely because they are neither relatable nor admirable. The play versions of Isabella lack initiative and guiding principles, which is a sharp contrast to Behn's Isabella, who is intelligent, devoted to her family and faith and, even in the worst circumstances, is a creative problem solver, neatly discarding both husbands and very nearly getting away with it. It is only because of a chance encounter that she does not. Because Behn's Isabella is distressed at killing her husbands, she is not an unhinged, violent sociopath. Some might even love her when she is relieved by confessing her guilt, even though we sympathize with the desire to cover up the double homicide. By removing a core component of her personality (her deeply embedded faith), all of Isabella's actions and motivations change or lose their meaning, leaving only a shell of her former self and stripping away her very soul.

## Notes

1. There are many examples of heroines and secondary characters that should suffer from terrible reputations (deserved or otherwise) but seem to escape any repercussions, even if they survive their respective ordeals. A few examples of these heroines include: Isabella from *The History of the Nun, or The Fair Vow-Breaker*, whom this paper studies; Miranda from *The Fair Jilt, or the Amours of Prince Tarquin and Miranda*, who attempts to rape a monk and tries twice to kill her sister but fails. Even though Miranda is caught, she is not executed, merely exiled. Once she repents of her sins, however, she is honored. Belvira and Moorea both escape a poor reputation despite the complicated circumstances surrounding them in *The Unfortunate Bride, or The Blind Lady a Beauty*. All three texts may be found in Paul Salzman, ed., *Oroonoko and Other Writings* (Oxford: Oxford University Press, 1994, 2009).

2. Behn, 138–190. *Fantomina* and *Moll Flanders* both provide examples of the isolated and lonely end that typically befalls most female characters with terrible reputations. Eliza Heywood's 1725 novel, *Fantomina*, has a heroine who goes to great lengths to seduce the man she loves, but she fails miserably and is ultimately sent to a convent when he refuses to marry her. In Daniel Defoe's 1722 novel, *Moll Flanders*, the heroine has many misadventures; she spends time in prison and is eventually sent to the colonies. In the end, she and her husband return to England "to spend the remainder of [their] years in sincere penitence, for the wicked lives [they had] lived." Neither of these novels has a happy ending: both heroines move away and live in relative obscurity to think on their sins. They are not praised by their communities, nor even thought of by anyone. For Behn this would have been the cruelest punishment, especially in the context of her famous passage in the preface to *The Lucky Chance*, where she writes, "I value fame almost as much as if I had been born a hero." For Behn, obscurity is its own punishment. The endings of *Fantomina* and *Moll Flanders* are fairly typical for novels about fallen women. When compared to other female characters in the genre, Isabella's ending is all the more unusual. Janet Todd explains Behn's desire for fame in the last several chapters of her 1996 biography, *The Secret Life of Aphra Behn* (New

Brunswick, NJ: Rutgers University Press). Broadview offers editions of both *Fantomina* and *Moll Flanders*: Eliza Haywood, *Fantomina*, in *Fantomina and Other Works*, ed. Alexander Pettit, Margaret Case Croskery, and Anna C. Patchias (Peterborough, Ontario: Broadview Press, 2004); Daniel Defoe, *Moll Flanders*, ed. Paul A. Scanlon (Peterborough, Ontario: Broadview Press, 2005).

3. Thomas Southerne, *The Fatal Marriage, or The Innocent Adultery*, in *Plays written by Thomas Southerne, Esq. Now First Collected with An Account of the Life and Writings of the Author*, vol. 2 (London, 1774), facsimile available via Google Books; David Garrick, *Isabella, or The Fatal Marriage*, in *The Plays of David Garrick*, ed. Harry William Pedicord and Frederick Louis Bergmann, vols. 5, 7 (Carbondale: Southern Illinois University Press, 1982). While the plays have line breaks, there are no line numbers given, so page numbers are used throughout. Since Garrick's text is almost an exact copy of Southerne's, I cite both for passages that are identical. The original spelling and punctuation is preserved throughout for Behn, Southerne, and Garrick.

4. Garrick, *Isabella*, 44; Southerne, *The Fatal Marriage*, 255.

5. Garrick, *Isabella*, 52; Southerne, *The Fatal Marriage*, 262.

6. Garrick, *Isabella*, 53; Southerne, *The Fatal Marriage*, 265.

7. Jacqueline Pearson, "The History of *The History of the Nun*," in *Rereading Aphra Behn: History, Theory, and Criticism*, ed. Heidi Hutner (Charlottesville: University Press of Virginia, 1993), 236–237.

8. Ibid., 237.

9. George Winchester Stone, Jr., and George M. Kahrl, *David Garrick: A Critical Biography* (Carbondale: Southern Illinois University Press, 1979). Stone and Karhl explore Garrick's adaptations, motivations, and techniques quite thoroughly as well as their impact on the social milieu.

10. Garrick, *Isabella*, 3.

11. Garrick, "Introduction," *Isabella*, xxi.

12. Southerne, *The Fatal Marriage*, 182.

13. Leah Orr, "Attribution Problems in the Fiction of Aphra Behn," *Modern Language Review* 108, no. 1 (2013): 30–51, http://www.jstor.org/stable/10.5699/modelangrevi.108.1.0030; Montague Summers, "The Source of Southerne's *The Fatal Marriage*," *Modern Language Review* 11, no. 2 (1916).

14. Pearson, "The History of *The History of the Nun*," 238.

15. Behn's three major biographers detail at length Behn's many struggles. See Maureen Duffy, *The Passionate Shepherdess* (London: Phoenix Press, 1977, 2000); Angeline Goreau, *Reconstructing Aphra* (Oxford: Oxford University Press, 1980); and Todd, *The Secret Life of Aphra Behn*. Again, all of Behn's biographers explore her recurring financial troubles.

16. See Duffy, *The Passionate Shepherdess*; Goreau, *Reconstructing Aphra*; and Todd, *The Secret Life of Aphra Behn*.

17. Another example that comes to mind is Shakespeare's *Othello*, in which Othello's promotion and marriage are the catalysts for Iago's manipulations and revenge.

18. Behn, *The History of the Nun*, 148.

19. Pearson, "The History of *The History of the Nun*," 237.

20. Garrick, *Isabella*, 8; Southerne, *The Fatal Marriage*, 198. It is worth noting that in Behn's novel, Isabella is a great benefactor of the poor and of women throughout her life.

21. Garrick, *Isabella*, 17; Southerne, *The Fatal Marriage*, 210.

22. Garrick, *Isabella*, 10; Southerne, *The Fatal Marriage*, 200. Italics are mine to show the emphasis on the male characters.

23. Garrick, *Isabella*, 7; Southerne, *The Fatal Marriage*, 197.

24. Behn, *The History of the Nun*, 171.

25. Ibid., 183.

26. Garrick, *Isabella*, 8; Southerne, *The Fatal Marriage*, 198.

27. Garrick, *Isabella*, 12; Southerne, *The Fatal Marriage*, 202.

28. Susan Goulding, "'Stories of Nuns': Narrative Diversion and 'Sister Books,'" *Interdisciplinary Literary Studies* 10, no. 1 (Fall 2008), 49.

29. Behn, *The History of the Nun*, 150.

30. Ibid., 171, 178.

31. Pearson, "The History of *The History of the Nun*," 238.

32. Behn, *The History of the Nun*, 185.

33. Ibid., 190.

34. Ibid.

35. Garrick, *Isabella*, stage direction, 51; Southerne, *The Fatal Marriage*, stage direction, 263.

36. Garrick, *Isabella*, 52; Southerne, *The Fatal Marriage*, 264.

37. Garrick, *Isabella*, 52; Southerne, *The Fatal Marriage*, 264.

# The *Mémoires* of Jean Marteilhe, a Huguenot Galley Slave, in the Age of Enlightenment

*Séverine Collignon-Ward*

In 1757, *les Mémoires d'un Protestant Condamné aux Galères de France pour Cause de Religion* (Memoirs of a Protestant condemned to the galleys of France because of religion)[1] were anonymously published in Rotterdam, Holland. The author, who has since been identified as Jean Marteilhe, offers with these *Mémoires* a truly unique work. They not only contribute to the Protestant Memoir—with Marteilhe offering an historical testimony as a Huguenot in the Catholic kingdom of France—but they also contribute to the Enlightenment, thanks to the author's advocating for tolerance and the Voltaire-like literary skills he employs to accomplish that goal. Therefore, these *Mémoires* deserve a place in the Age of Enlightenment, perhaps not as philosophy, per se, but as an example of skillful and persuasive writing to fight intolerance and arbitrary oppression. However, history has kept these two aspects separated, and these *Mémoires* have remained unjustly associated solely with the Protestant Memoir. With this essay, I hope to show that Marteilhe's *Mémoires* belong in the Age of Enlightenment and that they are still relevant today as an example of the power of persuasive writing.

The full title of the *Mémoires* states that *outre le récit des souffrances de l'auteur depuis 1700 jusqu'en 1713, on trouvera diverses particularités curieuses relatives à l'histoire de ce temps-là* (besides the account of the author's sufferings from 1700 until 1713, one will find several curious particularities relative to the history of that time). Since Marteilhe's account takes place in the first thirteen years of the eighteenth century, why were his *Mémoires* only published in 1757? Following the Revocation of the Edict of Nantes by Louis XIV in 1685,[2] many testimonies of the Protestants' sufferings were published, but were immediately dismissed by non-Protestants as untrue pamphlets against the Catholic Church and the king. The history of the end of the reign of Louis XIV was therefore being depicted in two very distinctive manners: the official history—a Catholic and monarchic version—on one side, and the Protestant Memoir—the version of the victims of the official history—on the other. As Jean Carbonnier explains, "Il fallait les Philosophes, il fallait l'alliance—naturelle ou contre nature on en disputera sans trêve—de la Réforme et des Lumières pour que l'on en arrivât à la tolérance" (One needed the philosophes, one needed the alliance—whether this alliance was natural or not is still subject to debate—of the Reformation and the Enlightenment in order to obtain tolerance).[3] Even though the philosophes denounced the scourge that intolerance represented, they themselves were not always tolerant toward the Protestants. When Voltaire denounced the persecutions toward Protestants and went on defending Calas and Sirven, he did it in the name of injustice, not in the name of persecuted Protestantism, per se. Nonetheless, the philosophes' writings helped establish an atmosphere of tolerance that would eventually lead to the end of the persecutions. What brings Marteilhe's work and the work of the philosophes together is, therefore, not the defense of the Protestant faith, but the belief that only an enlightened public could put an end to the reign of intolerance, and the fact that they used similar literary tools to guide readers toward the Enlightenment. This is where Marteilhe departs from his fellow Protestant writers and what renders his *Mémoires* truly unique. French historian Jules Michelet explained how:

> Ce n'est qu'à son extrème fin, quand [Louis XIV] est aux abois (1712) et va mourir, qu'on ose publier en Europe quelques détails; les légendes d'abord des saints forçats (Marolles, Lefèbvre), mais cela pour les âmes pieuses et comme livres de dévotion. . . . L'Europe y fait peu attention; le roi s'en va et

> ses victimes avec; on s'y intéresse moins; un siècle nouveau est lancé.
>
> Only at the very end, when [Louis XIV] is at bay (1712) and is going to die, does one dare publish some details in Europe; first the legends of saintly slaves (Marolles, Lefèbvre), but this is for pious souls and as worship books. . . . Europe does not pay much attention to it; the king is going and his victims with him; people are less concerned with it; this is the start of a new century.[4]

If he had published his *Mémoires* in 1713, Marteilhe would have run the risk of sinking into oblivion. By choosing to center his account on the sole praise of the Protestants, Marteilhe would have restricted his account to a Protestant readership. Voltaire strongly criticized Manichean approaches. In a letter he wrote to the Minister Moultou in January 1763, he comments on a newly published book written by a Protestant (*L'Accord parfait* by Beaumont):

> Il me semble qu'il y a un grand défaut dans ce livre, et qui peut nuire à votre cause, c'est qu'il dit continuellement que les catholiques ont toujours tort et les protestants toujours raison, que tous les chefs des catholiques étaient des monstres, et les chefs des protestants des saints. . . . Quand on attaque une secte en demandant grâce, on obtient la haine, et point de grâce.
>
> It seems to me that this book has a big flaw and that it could be prejudicial to your cause, since it continuously reiterates that Catholics are always wrong and Protestants always right, that Catholics were monsters and Protestants saints. . . . When you are asking a sect for mercy by attacking it, then you only obtain hatred, not mercy.

In 1757, the philosophes were right in the middle of their fight against intolerance. Marteilhe had understood that, at that time, the public was ready for the Memoirs of a Protestant, provided they consist of an entertaining account tinged with humor and irony, in the style of Voltaire's tales and other philosophic writings.

By adding his voice to those of the philosophes in 1757, with his own account dating back to the beginning of the century, Marteilhe's contribution shows how little had changed between 1700 to 1713 and 1757. Persecutions were still raging and it was crucial to enlighten the reader on the state of a France, whose numerous troubles still resulted from a heightened fanaticism. All these *particularités curieuses* (curious particularities) announced by Marteilhe in the title of his *Mémoires* depict the harmful effects of fanaticism emphasized by the philosophes: France had been taken over by individual passions; the search for personal gain and arbitrary power were pervasive. Fanatic clerics still reigned over the king and country. The brutal campaigns of forced conversions had failed since they either turned Protestants into hypocrites or into even more fervent proselytes. There was still a sharp imbalance between crimes and punishments. The human and economic losses were innumerable. Despite this sad depiction of the realm of France, neither the philosophes nor Marteilhe viewed the country as doomed. Tolerance was deemed possible, and in order to prove their point, they presented many examples of tolerance from numerous individuals—sometimes even from unlikely sources, such as the Turks, as well as from many countries, like England, Holland, and Russia.

However, simply lecturing readers with countless examples would most likely only bore them and keep them from joining the cause. Hence, Marteilhe and the philosophes understood that only an entertained reader could become enlightened. So, how to entertain? How to energize the reader? The following are examples of the different literary tools used by both Marteilhe and the philosophes to these ends.

## Choosing the Narrative Form

The author first needs to choose the right form for the narrative. The *Dictionnaire de l'Académie Française* (Dictionary of the French Academy) defines memoirs in these terms: "Mémoires, au pluriel, se dit Des relations de faits ou d'événements particuliers, écrites pour servir à l'Histoire"[5] (Memoirs, in its plural form, refer to the accounts of particular facts or events, written to serve history). The dilemma with this form of narrative is the question of the authenticity of the accounts related. For instance, John Leigh recalls how Voltaire's *Ingénu* was a good illustration of this "ambiguous status of 'histoire' for in pushing further its claim to veracity, the subtitle [Histoire véritable de l'Ingénu] actually serves to remind us that in the 18th century truth is not an integral component of history in all its forms."[6] The question of authenticity is crucial for Marteilhe's *Mémoires* insofar as, despite all the stylistic and factual similarities he shares with the philosophes, he aspires with his account to constitute a part of the Protestant collective Memoir. The edifice of the Protestant collective Memoir, which dated back to the Reformation, had been removed from France's official history in 1685, and needed to be rebuilt, stone by stone, through written testimonies. In his edition of the *Mémoires*, Zysberg explains how "en confrontant le texte imprimé avec, d'une part, les nombreuses lettres de forçats protestants conservées dans les 'Papier Court' et d'autre part, avec les archives des Galères de France, l'on ne doute pas de l'authenticité de ces mémoires" (by comparing the printed account with the numerous letters from Protestant galley slaves kept in the "Court Paper," and with the archives from the galleys of France, there remains no doubt regarding the authenticity of these memoirs).[7]

This form of narrative overflows with anecdotes and juicy details, making it popular with the public. French historian Pierre Nora mentions two hundred thousand publications in this form between 1700 and 1750.[8] Marteilhe states clearly in his title that the reader will find "several curious particularities relative to the history of that time." The critics have emphasized the "intérêt palpitant" (thrilling interest),[9] the "détails pittoresques" (colorful details).[10] As Michelet points out, "nul roman comparable par l'intérêt des aventures et le pathétique des situations à ces histoires trop vraies" (the interest of the adventures and the very moving situations found in these true accounts surpass all novels).[11] To the entertaining nature of the *Mémoires* is added what historian Pierre Nora calls "un incontestable cachet de vérité" (an unquestionable truth stamp).[12]

## Choosing What Information to Include

Marteilhe had indeed been carefully sorting out every piece of information and only the ones deemed "curieuses" (curious), "surprenantes" (surprising), "particulières" (particular), and "singulières" (singular) were reported in his *Mémoires*.[13] While relating his account, he remains keenly aware of his readership. The philosophes often used the same tactic and worked hard to keep the reader engaged. In his preface to *De l'Esprit des lois (The Spirits of the Laws),* Montesquieu mentions, "Ces détails même, je ne les ai pas tous donnés; car qui pourrait dire tout sans un mortel ennui?"[14] (I have not given all these particulars, for who could mention them all without a most deadly boredom?). In a letter to Minister Moultou on January 5, 1763, Voltaire explains, "Il faut être court et un peu salé sans quoi les ministres et Mme de Pompadour, les commis et les femmes de chambre font des papillottes du livre" (One needs to be short and a bit spicy otherwise the ministers, Madame de Pompadour, the clerks, and the chambermaids turn the book into curlpapers). Marteilhe deliberately protects his reader from boredom. He mentions, for instance, "Je n'ennuyerai pas mon lecteur en . . . " (I will not weary my reader by . . . ) (44). When forced to digress, Marteilhe always justifies himself to his reader. For instance, "J'ai cru que je devais cette digression au lecteur pour lui donner une idée de . . . " (I thought that I owed this digression to the reader to give him an idea of . . . ) (201) or "J'ai abrégé autant qu'il m'a été possible cette narration, pour ne pas ennuyer mon lecteur" (I have abridged this as much as possible so as not to bore my reader) (348).

## Choosing Several Plots

Another way in which to keep the reader engaged is to alternate between narrations and descriptions, and alternating between genres. For instance, Marteilhe dedicates twenty-two pages of his *Mémoires* to recount the story of the Catholic galley slave Goujon, a story that he qualifies as a "tragi-comédie" (tragicomedy) (189). Whatever the genre, Marteilhe turns out to be quite the storyteller, even getting himself caught up in the narrative momentum. Relating a battle against an English vessel, for instance, Marteilhe explains, "Nous commencions déjà à nous préparer pour l'abordage, la hache d'armes et le sabre à la main" (We were getting ready to climb on board, axes and sabers in hand) (130).

Yet galley slaves were simply unable to take part of the boarding as they were chained down, a fact that he himself describes later on: "le banc, je n'en pouvais sortir, j'y étais enchaîné" (I could not leave the bench as I was chained to it) (157), adding that "le coup de canon m'avait jeté aussi loin que ma chaîne pouvait s'étendre" (I had been thrown by the blow as far as my chain could stretch) (158). However, the reader will not hold this slight inexactitude against the narrator who, by including himself in the action with the subtle shift from the *je* (I) to the *nous* (we), has brought the level of engagement and entertainment to an even higher level. Once highly entertained, the reader is easier to persuade.

## Choosing the Persuasion Tools

### *Feigned Naivety*

The philosophes often use the perspective of a foreigner in an unknown territory to voice sharp criticism under cover of feigned naivety. Voltaire uses, for instance, the Huron of *L'Ingénu (The Ingénu),* and Montesquieu uses Usbek of the *Lettres persanes (Persian Letters).* Marteilhe uses that same feigned naivety by frequently choosing to emphasize his young age. Born in 1684, he explains how the persecution occurred in his region in 1700 and how it affected him: "la persécution m'arracha du sein de ma famille, me força de fuir hors de ma patrie, et de m'exposer, malgré la faiblesse de mon âge, aux périls d'une route de deux cent lieues" (44) (the persecution tore me away from my family, forced me to flee outside my country, and to expose myself, despite my young age, to the dangers of a journey of two hundred leagues). Other characters contribute to perpetrating this image of a young and fragile narrator by referring to Marteilhe as "my child." When meeting people of distinction, Marteilhe seems surprised, amazed, and touchingly naive, as a child would be. Upon being introduced to Queen Anne of England, he explains, "Messieurs . . . nous présentèrent à la reine, qui nous admit à l'honneur de lui baiser la main" (Misters . . . introduced us to the Queen, who let us have the honor of kissing her hand). These words allow the reader to trust the innocent and lovable child, and this helps build sympathy for his cause.

## *Appropriation of the Reader*

In *Jacques the Fatalist and His Master,* Diderot makes no secret of his appropriation of the reader: "Lecteur, qui m'empêcherait de jeter ici le cocher, les chevaux, la voiture, les maîtres et les valets dans une fondrière?" (Reader, what's to prevent me tipping driver, horses, carriage, masters, and servants into the nearest ditch?).[15] Marteilhe also has a strong presence within the discourse with expressions such as "comme j'ai dit" (like I said) (55), and "je reprends le fil de mon histoire" (I am now resuming the thread of my story) (47). However, his control and manipulation of the reader are more subtle than Diderot's. The use of the possessive adjectives found in the singular and/or plural form *mon/ mes* (my) is very common for Marteilhe and Voltaire: "mon lecteur/mes lecteurs" (my reader/my readers), "mon cher lecteur" (my dear reader), "mes amis" (my friends). This shows the consideration that the narrator has for his readership, but above all it allows the appropriation of the reader, who the narrator includes in his circle of friends. Thus, the relationship becomes more intimate when Marteilhe addresses his reader directly with turns of phrase such as, "Voyez, je vous prie . . . Considérez aussi . . . " (Please see how . . . Consider also . . . )" (259), or "Que vous dirai-je?" (What can I tell you?) (273). He also makes sure that the reader understands things the way he wants them to understand: "On comprendra peut-être que . . . Je dis que non car . . . " (One might understand that . . . I say don't because . . . ) (307), or "Je m'assure qu'on entend bien que . . . " (I want to make sure that you understand that . . . ) (316). Similarly, when the descriptions become a bit technical, especially regarding daily life aboard the galleys, Marteilhe defines every technical term, often using short parentheses[16] to prevent the reader's interest and engagement from flagging.

Should a reader be tempted to question or doubt Marteilhe's views, he does not ask them, "Qu'est-ce que cela vous fait?" (What is it to you?) (11), as Diderot would in *Jacques the Fatalist.* On the contrary, Marteilhe, who seems to anticipate these questions, uses frequent prolepses: "Il me semble entendre le lecteur demander comment . . . " (I think I hear the reader ask how . . . ) (232), or "L'on me dira peut-être ici . . . " (One might say that . . . ) (237), before concluding, "A cela je réponds . . . " (To this, I reply . . . ) (238). And Marteilhe always keeps his promises to the reader: "j'ai promis l'histoire de Goujon, je m'en acquitte" (I had promised the story of Goujon, I am carrying it out now) (172).

In his *Mémoires*, Marteilhe also relies heavily on the French *on*—in English the equivalent would be the word *one*—but it is often replaced by a passive structure that diminishes the power that this word has in French, since it can be a substitute for the collective *nous* (we). Often followed by the verb "to judge," "on juge que . . . " (one judges that . . . ), Marteilhe's personal opinion is turned into that of a larger number of people—including the reader.

This judgment is also attributed to a specific category of people: "les gens raisonnables" (the reasonable people) (166) and "les honnêtes gens" (the honest people) (358). In his *Avis au Public sur les parricides imputés aux Calas et aux Sirven (Address to the Public upon the parricides imputed to the families of Calas and Sirven),* Voltaire asks his "lecteurs sages" (wise readers) which is better between "être justes et bienfaisants" (being fair and kind) or giving into "un enthousiasme destructeur et aux plus détestables atrocités" (a destructive enthusiasm and the most detestable atrocities).[17] The skillful handling of an antithetic vocabulary is frequent in both the philosophes' works and Marteilhe's *Mémoires,* with or without mention of the reader. For instance, when Marteilhe details the arrival of the duke and his dragoons in his city to force its Protestants to renounce their faith, the persecutions are accentuated by the crescendo of the victimization. On one side, we have the victims first described as "Les bourgeois" (the townspeople), who then become "Ces pauvres bourgeois" (these poor townspeople), and finally end up as "Ces pauvres bourgeois martyrisés" (these poor tortured townspeople) (47). The use of the demonstrative adjective *ces* (these) increases empathy, since the reader feels as if he is actually attending the persecutions. On the other side, we have the dragoons with their "mission cruelle" (cruel mission) and their "cruautés inouïes" (incredible cruelties) (47).

### *Playing with the Senses and the Emotions*

Playing with readers' senses and emotions is crucial to creating a lasting impression. With his lively descriptions, Marteilhe takes the readers on a journey where they get to see and hear along with the narrator. In order to bring the reader to the scene, Marteilhe alternates between the use of indirect and direct discourse, and between the use of past and present tense, often emphasizing the value of permanence that the present tense carries. When relating his arrival in Paris with the other galley slaves, Marteilhe explains,

> Nous descendîmes devant le château de la Tournelle qui était autrefois une maison de plaisance de nos rois et qui sert présentement de lieu d'entrepôt aux malheureux condamnés aux galères pour toute sorte de crimes. On nous fit entrer dans le vaste mais lugubre cachot de la grande chaîne. Le spectacle affreux qui s'y présenta à nos yeux nous fit frémir, d'autant plus qu'on nous allait joindre aux acteurs qui le représentaient. (236)
>
> We arrived in front of the castle of the Tournelle, which was formerly a royal country cottage and which currently serves as a warehouse for all the wretches condemned to the galleys for all sort of crimes. They made us enter the vast but gloomy dungeon reserved for the great chain of galley slaves. The dreadful spectacle that presented itself in front of our eyes made us shudder, all the more since they were about to make us join the actors who were already playing it.

In this passage, the present appears twice, with the verb *sert* (serves) and with the adverb *présentement* (currently). As opposed to the previously mentioned adverb *autrefois* (formerly), *présentement* gives the impression of a spectacle that one can still see. The visual effect is reinforced by the use of expressions such as "à nos yeux" (in front of ours eyes), and the readers' senses are heightened by adjectives such as *lugubre* (gloomy) and the physical reaction that this spectacle causes ("nous fit frémir" [made us shudder]). Throughout the *Mémoires,* shudders are recurrent. Often coupled with interjections such as "Ô horreur!" (O horror!), they trigger a strong reaction from the reader who has been brought into the scene, next to Marteilhe, thanks to the lively narrative.

In the original French, the horrific scenes are also described using assonances, which provide punctuating sound to complement the visual descriptions. In the following example, Marteilhe details the cleaning of the galley, explaining how, once the *comite* (person in charge of overseeing the galley slaves) blows his whistle, the two *sous-comites* then grab their bludgeons and run from one bench to the other, using them on the lazy slaves to get them moving. The assonance in *co/cou/gou* (indicated in bold in the French original) renders each movement, each blow audible: "quand on veut le faire, le premier **co**mite donne un **coup** de sifflet qui le désigne, les deux sous-**co**mites s'arment de leur **gou**rdin sur le **cou**rsier, **cou**rant de banc en banc pour dé**gou**rdir les paresseux" (355). These stylistic effects recur too often throughout the *Mémoires* to be mere coincidences, but they unfortunately get lost in the English translations.[18]

Marteilhe constantly alternates between the accounts of the good treatment and the bad treatment that he received, therefore amplifying the different emotions felt by the reader: relief, joy, fear, and horror. After his arrest with his friend Legras, Marteilhe first explains how they were down to only "une livre et demie de pain par jour" (a pound and a half of bread daily), before adding that "le gouverneur et le major nous envoyaient tous les jours, tour à tour, suffisamment à boire et à manger. Le curé qui espérait de nous faire prosélytes, et les religieuses d'un couvent qui était dans la ville, nous envoyaient aussi très souvent à manger" (every day the governor and the major, by turns, were sending us enough to drink and to eat. The priest, who was hoping to turn us into proselytes, and the nuns from a convent in the city, were sending us things to eat very often as well), finally concluding, "si bien qu'à notre tour nous nourrissions le geôlier et sa famille" (so that we, in turn, were feeding the gaoler and his whole family) (62). Two pages later, there remains nothing of that abundance. Marteilhe and Legras are thrown in "les plus affreux cachots qu'on pouvait trouver, au pain et à l'eau, sans lit ni paille pour nous reposer" (the most frightful dungeons that could be found, receiving only bread and water, neither bed nor straw to rest upon) (64). Bad treatment seems even more atrocious when it follows good treatment. The readers' emotions are heightened by the use of hyperbole, with accounts qualified as impossible to describe and numerous superlatives such as "la persécution la plus inhumaine" (the most inhumane persecution) (44), and "le plus cruel homme" (the cruelest man) (123). "Un barbare brutal" (a brutal barbarian) (117), is one example of the pleonasms found within the *Mémoires* as well.

Not knowing what to expect next, the reader grows increasingly worried for the narrator's well-being. In his introduction to *Galley Slave,* an abridged English version of the *Mémoires,* McInerney notes, "Marteilhe's narrative keeps the reader in suspense right until the last pages, and his escape from the clutches of his captors seems by no means assured until the very end of his account."[19] What is more, Marteilhe keeps feeding that suspense by relying on numerous interrogations such as "Comment échapper à . . . ?" (How could we escape . . . ?) (44), and "Que pouvions-nous faire?" (What could we do?) (68), allowing him to invite the reader to share in his dilemma. At times, Marteilhe chooses to delay the disclosure of key information. After announcing the upcoming account of "la scène, la plus cruelle qu'on puisse s'imaginer" (the cruelest scene ever imaginable) (246), he then details for over a page the torturous search that the galley slaves had to endure before eventually disclosing that the Protestant galley slaves did not have to go through this search with the other slaves. Shaken by this violent account, the reader breathes a sigh of relief once he learns that Marteilhe and his companions were spared. However, the horror of the search stays with the readers, coopting them into Marteilhe's denunciation of such barbaric practices.

Through the description of all this suffering and ill-treatment, Marteilhe aims to push his reader toward compassion, the phenomenon that Adam Smith describes in his *Theory of Moral Sentiments* as "the emotion we feel for the misery of others, when we either see it, or are made to conceive it in a very lively manner."[20] In *Mémoires,* compassion can be found between Protestants, between Catholics, between Protestants and Catholics, and between Turks and Protestants. Compassionate people are moved and tears flow in the *Mémoires* as they do in Voltaire's *Candide.*[21] However, as in Voltaire's work, laughter is never far behind.

### *Using Irony and Humor*

As too much violence can kill the violence, Marteilhe intersperses his account of the persecutions with entertaining facts. In the beginning of his *Mémoires,* he explains, "Avant d'en venir au détail de ce que les Réformés de cette province eurent à souffrir, le lecteur ne sera pas fâché que je le régale d'un fait assez divertissant, arrivé au château de La Force tandis que le duc s'y reposait de ses fatigues, et pour fruit de son heureuse expédition . . . "(46) (Before relating what the reformed in this province had to suffer, I must amuse my reader with a rather diverting scene which took place at the castle of La Force, while the duke was resting after the fatigues of his successful expedition). Marteilhe then proceeds to tell the reader about the ironic harangue made by a lawyer from the reformed religion to the duke:

> Le duc, assis sur son siège de cérémonie, ayant à ses côtés ses quatre jésuites, admit à son audience Grenier qui commença sa harangue en ces termes: "Monseigneur, votre grand-père était un grand guerrier; votre père un grand dévot, et vous, Monseigneur, vous êtes un grand chasseur." Le duc l'interrompit pour lui demander comment il savait qu'il était un grand chasseur, puisqu'en effet ce n'était pas là sa passion dominante. "J'en juge, repartit Grenier, par vos quatre limiers qui ne vous quittent pas", en lui montrant les quatre jésuites. (46–47)
>
> The duke, seated in his ceremony chair, with his four Jesuits by his side, admitted Grenier to an audience who began his speech in these words: "Monseigneur, your grandfather was a great warrior; your father a great saint, and you, Monseigneur, you are a great hunter." The duke interrupted him, to ask him how he knew that he was a great hunter, as in reality hunting was not his main passion. "I judge of it, replied Grenier, by your four bloodhounds who never leave your side," as he pointed to the four Jesuits.

This funny anecdote renders the funny Protestant Grenier more appealing than the cruel Duke of La Force.

In *Voltaire: A Sense of History,* John Leigh notes, "History may well be an overwhelming joyless catalogue of crimes and wars, but, since 'l'édification des Français consiste à rire' this material will have to lend itself to comic treatment . . . Voltaire seems to come close to regarding laughter as a necessary release valve."[22] So does Marteilhe, and his

*Mémoires* are full of comic puns, expressions, anecdotes, and ironies. With the exception of two compassionate members of the Catholic Church, every other Catholic cleric present in the *Mémoires* is given an ironic treatment by Marteilhe. Everyone accepts a priori the precepts such as "un bon chrétien" (a good Christian). In Marteilhe's *Mémoires,* this precept, strategically placed by the author, loses all its Christianity, as in the following example about the four Jesuit fathers who are counseling the duke regarding the forced conversions of Protestants: "Ces Pères, en bons chrétiens, commençaient à demander qu'on punit Grenier de son insolence" (These fathers, as good Christians, began to demand that Grenier should be punished for his insolence) (47). Thus, any expression made of the adjective *bon* (good) followed by a religious term such as *chrétien* (Christian) is turned into an example of antiphrasis. Marteilhe had previously said of the duke that "il commença, pour donner une idée de la douceur de sa mission et de l'esprit de ses conseillers, à exercer des cruautés inouïes contre ses vassaux de la Religion Réformée" (he began, in order to give an idea of the gentleness of his mission, and the spirit of his counsellors, to exercise unheard-of cruelties against those of his vassals who belonged to the reformed faith) (45). When Marteilhe takes up his pen, whoever ends up giving a hypocritical renunciation of his faith, to avoid being sent to the galley, becomes "un bon catholique romain" (a good Roman Catholic).

Criticism is also channeled through rewording. In his *Traité sur la Tolérance (Treatise on Tolerance),* Voltaire mentions a "Chrétien compatissant" (Christian and charitable man), who prescribes that "l'extinction totale des Protestants en France n'affaiblirait pas plus la France qu'une saignée n'affaiblit un malade bien constitué" (the entire extirpation of the Protestants in France would not weaken that kingdom more than a plentiful bleeding would a patient of sound constitution). After having mentioned how this writer had published "un petit code de persécution, intitulé *l'Accord de la religion et de l'humanité* (c'est une faute de l'imprimeur: lisez de l'inhumanité)" (a small code of persecution titled *The Harmony of Religion and Humanity* [but this last word seems to be an error of the press, and should be read Inhumanity])," Voltaire then proceeds to refer to the work each time as *"l'Accord de la religion et de l'inhumanité"* (The Harmony of Religion and Inhumanity).[23] Marteilhe also uses epanorthosis, a literary device that consists of rewording what has just been said, either to qualify it, to weaken it, to retract it, or to expose it with more energy.[24] When arriving at the Tour Saint Pierre, Marteilhe mentions the presence of Jesuit fathers in these terms: "comme il se trouva là, soit par hasard ou de dessein prémédité, deux pères jésuites, ils nous prirent nos livres de dévotion et notre sentence; sans nous avoir jamais voulu rendre ni l'un ni l'autre" (there happened to be two Jesuit fathers there, either by chance or by prearranged design. They took our books of devotion and the copy of our sentence and never returned either one) (107). The use of the *ou* (or) allows for a subtle criticism, since it appears to offer an alternative. Replaced in Marteilhe's skillfully written narrative, the reader always ends up favoring the latter qualifier. Marteilhe often adds *métaboles,* the process that consists of accumulating synonyms in order to express an idea or describe an object with an accrued precision:[25] "L'évêque de Tournai ayant appris la froideur ou plutôt la négligence ou l'ignorance de ce curé à nous convertir, nous envoya son chapelain" (the Bishop of Tournay, having heard of the indifference, or rather the negligence or the ignorance of this priest in converting us, sent one of his chaplains) (87). In the end, the reader will view this priest as indifferent *and* negligent *and* ignorant.

In Marteilhe's *Mémoires,* as well as in the philosophes' works, criticism is often made through a third party, especially through representatives of another religion. It allows for a subtle criticism of the Catholic rites and superstitions. Criticism goes through what Jean Starobinski calls *désacralisation* (desecration), a process that consists in reclaiming objects in secular language or in the language of another religion. Coupled with the air of naivety we have previously mentioned, this process becomes funny and ironic insofar as the narrator seems to take seriously what he is enunciating. In *La Promenade du Sceptique (The Promenade of the Skeptic),* Diderot places religion in a military context where God becomes "le gouverneur en chef" (the commanding officer), the clergy "l'état major" (the joint staff), the Jesuits "les enrôleurs" (the enlisters), and baptism "l'enrôlement" (the enlistment).[26] In Montesquieu's *Lettres persanes (Persian Letters),* the priest becomes "le dervis" (the dervish), the king and the pope become "deux magiciens" (two magicians), and the rosary "des petits grains de bois" (little balls of wood).[27] In Voltaire's "Pot-Pourri," the pope becomes "un petit homme qui fait des marionnettes" (a little puppeteer) and the Roman Church "Mme Gigogne, une danseuse" (Mrs. Gigogne, a dancer).[28] In Marteilhe's *Mémoires,* the rosary turns into a rasp used for shredding tobacco (56). With the help of the Turk Galafas, Marteilhe first desecrates the Catholic rites and, to add to the irony, he then has some Catholic clerics make them sacred once again. Here is the story: Two thieves have stolen a silver vase used to hold the holy oil for conducting last rites, and they sell it to a Turk named Galafas. Once purchased, Galafas uses the oil to grease his shoes and then uses a hammer to change the form of the vase, which he finally buries in the ground. Unfortunately for him, one of the thieves is caught soon after and, convicted of the theft, he informs against Galafas, who ingenuously confesses and explains, "J'en ai graissé mes souliers. Si j'avais eu de la salade, je l'en aurais garnie, car j'ai goûté cette huile qui était très bonne" (I used this oil to grease my shoes. If I had had some salad, I would have tossed some on it as I tasted this oil and it was very good) (346). The anecdote continues with the priest removing Galafas's shoes,

> Quel autre que lui aurait osé porter ses mains profanes sur ces souliers sanctifiés par ces saintes huiles? Ce fut enfin avec de grandes cérémonies et des battements de poitrine qu'on mit les souliers de Galafas, la boîte aplatie et toute la terre qu'on jugea qui avait touché cette boîte, dans une nappe de l'autel, que quatre prêtres portaient, tenant chacun un coin de la nappe, et chantant les hymnes d'affliction jusques à la grande église, où tout fut enterré sous l'autel (345–46)
>
> Who but a priest could have ever dared touching with his layman's hands what had been sacred by the holy oil? Finally, it was with great ceremonies that the shoes, the vase, and all the earth, which was thought to have touched the vase, were put into a cloth, each corner of which was held by a priest and

> carried in the most mournful procession and with penitential hymns to the great church where all was buried under the altar.

This anecdote becomes even more ironic since, according to Lavisse, at the time, any Turk converting to the Catholic faith would receive a pair of . . . shoes![29]

## Subtly Praising the Protestants

Marteilhe also uses the Turks to indirectly praise the Protestants that they consider their "frères en Dieu" (brothers in God) (199). However, throughout his *Mémoires,* Marteilhe uses extreme caution in his praise for the Protestants, and he never gives in to a Manichean temptation, where every Protestant would be good and every Catholic would be evil. He talks about bad Protestants as well as good Catholics. As explained previously, Manichean approaches were strongly criticized by the philosophes, especially Voltaire, who denounced all forms of intolerance. In another letter to Moultou,[30] Voltaire mentions the need for a book about the horrors of the Protestant persecutions, but "qui pût se faire lire avec quelque plaisir, par les gens mêmes qui n'aiment point lire, et qui portât les cœurs à la compassion" (that could be read with pleasure, by those who do not like to read and that would make hearts become compassionate).

Marteilhe's *Mémoires* met these expectations that Voltaire had for a work that would not be tinged with an exaggerated bias but whose style would rather bring as wide a readership as possible toward tolerance. My research has not yet allowed me to establish whether or not the philosophes had read Marteilhe's *Mémoires.* It is likely that Voltaire heard about the translation that was published in 1758 by Oliver Goldsmith, since they knew each other. Unfortunately, Goldsmith's translation did not do justice to the *Mémoires,* as he made numerous emphatic additions, present in the English title itself where he added the following: "comprehending an account of the various distresses he suffered in slavery, and his constancy in supporting almost every cruelty that bigoted zeal could inflict or human nature sustain," turning the *Mémoires* into the kind of account Voltaire would criticize.

Fortunately, Marteilhe is being rediscovered by modern readers thanks to the new French edition of the *Mémoires* published by Zysberg first in 1982, then in 1989. In 2003, a French story about his ordeal, titled "Prisonnier du Roi-Soleil" (Prisoner of the Sun King), was published for children ages eight through twelve in the collection *Je lis des Histoires Vraies* (I am reading true stories).[31] With his growing public, Marteilhe's *Mémoires* are far from being obsolete. Let's hope that his *Mémoires* will continue to enlighten readers to come and encourage new generations of writers to pursue the work of Marteilhe and the philosophes: skillful and persuasive writing to fight intolerance and arbitrary oppression.

## Notes

1. This and all translations are mine. The French quotes originate from Jean Marteilhe, *Mémoires d'un galérien du Roi-Soleil*, ed. André Zysberg (Paris: Mercure de France, 1989).

2. The Revocation of the Edict of Nantes is the name often given to Louis XIV's Edict of Fontainebleau, dated 1685, since this edict revoked Henri IV's Edict of Nantes, promulgated in 1598, which put an end to the liberties that had been granted to the Protestants in the kingdom of France.

3. Jean Carbonier, "La Révocation permanente," *Réforme 2084* (1985).

4. Jules Michelet, *Histoire de France. Louis XIV jusqu'en 1700*, vol. 9 (Lausanne: Editions Rencontre, 1966), 406.

5. *Dictionnaire de l'Académie Française*, 4th ed. (1762), http://artfl-project.uchicago.edu/content/dictionnaires-dautrefois.

6. John Leigh, *Voltaire: A Sense of History* (Oxford: Voltaire Foundation, 2004), 181.

7. Jean Marteilhe, *Mémoires d'un galérien du Roi-Soleil*, ed. André Zysberg (Paris: Mercure de France, 1989), 11.

8. Pierre Nora, *Les Lieux de Mémoire*, vol. 1, *La République* (Paris: Gallimard, 1984), 375.

9. Michel Bonnefoy, *Jean Artigues: Cévénol (1630–1701): Galérien pour la foi* (Charly: Edité à compte d'auteur, 1996), 49. Gaston Tournier, *Les Galères de France et les galériens protestants des XVIIe et XVIIIe siècles*, vol. 1 (Montpellier: Les Presses du Languedoc, 1984), 25.

10. Samuel Mours, "Note sur les galériens protestants (1683–1775)," *Bulletin de la Société de l'Histoire du Protestantisme Français* 116 (1970): 181.

11. Michelet, *Histoire de France*, 425.

12. Nora, *Les Lieux de Mémoires*, 359.

13. All these adjectives are recurrent throughout the *Mémoires*.

14. Montesquieu, *De l'Esprit des lois*, 2 vols. ed. Victor Goldsmith (Paris: Garnier-Flammarion, 1979), 116.

15. Diderot, *Jacques le Fataliste et son maître,* ed. J. Assézat (Paris: Garnier Frères, 1885), 254.

16. For instance: "Mais la hardiesse du capitaine anglais est admirable; car comme il avait prévu cet événement, il s'était tenu tout prêt avec ses grappins (qui sont des crocs de fer attachés à des chaînes) . . . " (But the courage of the English captain was admirable; he had foreseen what would happen and was therefore ready with his grapnels [which are iron hooks attached to chains] . . . ) (151).

17. Voltaire, "Avis au Public sur les parricides imputés aux Calas et aux Sirven," in *L'Affaire Calas et autres affaires,* ed. Jacques Van den Heuvel (Paris: Gallimard, 1975), 222–223.

18. In the first English translation of Marteilhe's *Mémoires,* dated 1758 and titled *The Memoirs of a Protestant Condemned to the Galleys of France for his Religion, written by Himself,* the translator, James Willington (a pseudonym for Oliver Goldsmith), took liberties with the original French and added many personal touches to the narrative. The aforementioned passage was translated in these terms: "the Comite gives Orders for doing it by the Whiftle. The Sub-Comites with their Whips, go from Seat to Seat, and have not Mercy on thofe they fee lazy" (233). Other translations, highly abridged versions of the *Mémoires,* fail to render the stylistic effects or simply omit this passage altogether.

19. Vincent McInerney, introduction to *Galley Slave,* by Jean Marteilhe (Great Britain: Seaforth Publishing, 2010), 23.

20. Adam Smith, *The Theory of Moral Sentiments or, An Essay towards the analysis of the principles by which men naturally judge concerning the conduct and character, first of their neighbours, and then afterwards of themselves* (Philadelphia: Anthony Finley, 1817), 1.

21. The word *larmes* (tears) and the verb *pleurer* (to cry) in its various forms are recurrent in both works.

22. Leigh, *Voltaire,* 198.

23. Voltaire, *Traité sur la Tolérance,* ed. Jacques Van den Heuvel (Paris: Editions Gallimard, 1975), 117, 121–122.

24. "Épanorthose, figure de pensée qui consiste à revenir sur ce que l'on vient d'affirmer, soit pour le nuancer, l'affaiblir et même le rétracter, soit au contraire pour le réexposer avec plus d'énergie." CNRTL, Centre National des Ressources Textuelles et Lexicales, http://www.cnrtl.fr/definition/épanorthose.

25. "Métabole, Procédé qui consiste à accumuler des expressions synonymes pour exprimer une idée ou décrire un objet avec une précision accrue." CNRTL, Centre National des Ressources Textuelles et Lexicales, http://www.cnrtl.fr/definition/métabole.

26. Diderot, *"La Promenade du Sceptique ou les allées,"* in *Œuvres complètes de Diderot,* vol. 1 (Paris: Garnier-Frères Libraires-Editeurs, 1875), 191–192, 195–196.

27. Montesquieu, *Lettres persanes,* ed. Jean Starobinski (Paris: Gallimard, 1973), 92.

28. Voltaire, *"Pot-Pourri,"* in *Romans et contes,* ed. René Pomeau (Paris: Garnier Flammarion, 1966), 300–301.

29. Ernest Lavisse, "Sur les galères du Roi," *Revue de Paris,* November 1897, 250—"Un Turc qui se convertissait recevait une paire de souliers."

30. Dated October 1766.

31. Jean-Benoît Durand, *Prisonnier du Roi Soleil,* Je lis des Histoires Vraies (Paris: Fleurus Presse, Février 2003), 4–32.

# "The Agreeable Contrast": British Caricatures of the 1745 Jacobite Rebellion

*Monika Renate Barget*

"The agreeable contrast" is the telling headline of several eighteenth-century satirical prints published between 1746 and 1749 that address issues concerning good leadership and just government. These prints are generally classified as political caricatures of the failed 1745 Jacobite rebellion led by Charles Edward Stuart in Scotland, and they encapsulate the contested and many-voiced political and religious identity of mid-eighteenth-century Britain.

On the one hand, such caricatures uncover the enduring vigor of anti-Catholic sentiment and the incessant reference to English laws and liberty as powerful patterns of argumentation. This suggests that Britain was quickly developing into a modern nation-state with distinctly insular traditions in church and state. On the other hand, such caricatures disclose that the European age of Enlightenment was also shaped by self-confident aristocratic cosmopolitanism and religious irenicism. The fact that these variations of British identity were especially embraced by adherents of the perishing Stuart dynasty does not make them any less valid. Allegations of backwardness and bigotry voiced by the Hanoverian faction must therefore be scrutinized, and the inventive caricatures of the 1745 rebellion testify that the diverse protest movements that made up Jacobitism may have been reformist in their own right.

Political caricatures are a highly controversial and revealing genre of early modern art. Both the Reformation and the mid-seventeenth-century crisis were heydays of acrimonious printed satire, and the Jacobite rebellions of the eighteenth century equally inspired derisive graphical representations.[1] The campaign of 1745 tragically proved to be the last decisive attempt made by the exiled Stuart dynasty to recapture the throne of Great Britain, which they had lost in the Glorious Revolution of 1688.

Twenty-four-year-old Stuart prince Charles Edward, grandson to King James II of England, hoped to land with a French army in Scotland and march on London, but for various reasons the campaign failed. After the Battle of Culloden in April 1746, the Jacobite army dispersed, and Charles Edward fled to France. On his way through the Highlands, he was assisted by young Scotswoman Flora McDonald, who had at some point disguised the prince as an Irish servant.

Media all across Europe were eager to report on the prince's adventurous escape—especially since royal soldiers had previously declared him dead and the royal government, fearing he was still alive, had issued urgent warrants to track him down and kill him on the spot. From a military point of view, the sudden breakup of Charles Edward's troops was a severe setback for the Jacobite cause, but this did not yet sound the death knell for Jacobitism as a political and cultural movement.

The very end of the actual campaign in Britain even stimulated a media debate on the assets and weaknesses of both Charles Edward and his major opponent, the Duke of Cumberland. William Augustus, Duke of Cumberland, was four months younger than Charles Edward and was the third son born to King George II and his wife, Caroline. Trained as an army officer early on, William was entrusted with the command of the royal troops fighting Charles Edward in Scotland. After the crucial Battle of Culloden, the duke became known as "the butcher"[2] because eyewitnesses accused him of disproportionate cruelty against both his enemies and his own soldiers. Supporters of King George, however, widely praised him as one of the bravest officers in history and had Roman-style silver medals coined in his honor. From 1746 to around 1750, these irreconcilable perceptions of the recent past finally evolved into a multimedia-based battle of words and pictures, in which continental observers from France, the Dutch Republic, and Italy also played an important part. The up-and-coming genre of political caricatures especially proves how complex and creative this debate really was.

The exchange of witty headlines and visual vulgarities referring to the opposing party augmented the caricatures of the 1745 Jacobite rebellion from an artist's monologue to a many-voiced quarrel. The makers of the prints were also attentive recipients. Specifically, the recurrent motif of the "agreeable" or "true" contrast between Charles Edward and William Augustus illustrates this dialogue and gives a pointed account of eighteenth-century expectations of a worthy ruler.

In order to grasp and appreciate these caricatures to the fullest, one must always consider their "hybrid"[3] production and perception. The majority of satirical graphics, for their part, did not consist of pictures alone but, rather, combined visual and verbal elements to form "iconotextual constructs."[4] Therefore, the relation of visual satires to the written word as well as performance and sound still offer a lot to explore in present-day historiography and will prove a most exciting and valuable outlook for the sociopolitical interpretation of rebellion prints.[5] An impressive stock of Jacobite eighteenth-century prints is held by the National Library of Scotland. Most of these prints form part of the so-called Walter Biggar Blaikie Collection, which dates back to the nineteenth century.

This chapter will interpret three caricatures from this collection that were published after the Battle of Culloden and the subsequent failure of the 1745 Jacobite rising. Like several other contemporaneous prints, they draw on a direct and extremely personal comparison of the two antagonists in imagery, inscriptions, subtitles, and, above all, speech bubbles. These broadsides not only exemplify the central arguments of pro- and anti-Jacobite propaganda in Britain but also attest to widespread interrelations between satire and serious political and religious iconography.

Interestingly enough, two of these prints—*The Agreeable Contrast* and *A Jacobite Satire*—have been described as overtly pro-Jacobite in the comprehensive British Museum catalog published in 1877, whereas *The Agreeable Contrast between the Formidable John of Gant and Don*

*Carlos of Southern Extraction* was not judged to be politically biased.[6] All the prints deserve a careful cross-media analysis as proposed by M. Dorothy George in her study *English Political Caricature to 1792: A Study of Opinion and Propaganda*.[7] The fact that most of the prints kept in the Walter Biggar Blaikie Collection cast a truly damning light on the Duke of Cumberland does not imply that these prints express undivided support for the Stuart cause, nor were they necessarily lighthearted; their humor ranges from insinuating burlesque to melancholic sarcasm that almost restrains the laughter.

Before the eighteenth century, the term *caricature*, in its present-day spelling and meaning, did not exist in the English language. It is a word borrowed from the Italian term *caricatura*, which was already frequently used in the seventeenth century and denoted exaggerated and thus fundamentally fictional representations.[8] In English, however, this Italian term contrasted and eventually mingled with *character* or *characterisme*,[9] which gave the idea of visual satire a more realistic notion.[10] Early modern dictionaries help us understand the linguistic and art historical implications of this English usage, which initially saw a "character" in drawing, painting, or print as a revealing yet true-to-life imitation.[11] In contrast to highly formalized and flattering portraiture, a "character" was aimed at a simple, reduced, but increasingly truthful depiction of its object. Especially under the influence of famous engraver William Hogarth, this notion of a minimalistic, hand-drawn sketch remained an important aim of eighteenth-century satirical representation, which was increasingly referred to as "caricature."[12]

Regarding style and mode of production, British caricatures were strongly influenced by Dutch satire prints from around 1696 to 1750, and art historians agree that it was only in 1750 to 1780 that an independent caricatural symbolism emerged within the British Isles.[13] English artists' greatest endeavor was to establish a clear aesthetic distinction between themselves and French and Italian models of the time. This struggle was by no means limited to satires, however, and equally included the field of history painting. In the first half of the century, William Hogarth contributed most to the search for a distinctly British style of art, and his contemporary Henry Fielding described Hogarth's eye-catching satirical works as "comic history painting."[14] Caricature as we find it in Enlightenment England is a daring blend of "imago" (a timeless icon) and "historia" (a pictorial narrative). With undoubted success, British caricatures were then destined to be commented on, collected, and appreciated abroad.

Consequently, the period from 1780 to 1820 has frequently been described as the peak of classical political caricatures throughout all of Europe, even more so as they began to form a lasting link with journalism and newspaper publishing.[15] The fact that many caricatures were published anonymously hinders a proper analysis of their production and their producers' motivations. Especially oppositional prints were hardly ever signed by their engravers, and they lack reference to printers and booksellers. Not even overtly Jacobite artists such as Sir Robert Strange are known to have produced any caricatures at all. Among Strange's most celebrated works are portraits of the Stuart family, glass engravings, and, last but not least, plates for new banknotes, intended to be printed after a successful Stuart restoration.

The most renowned anti-Jacobite caricaturist might have been George Bickham the Younger, born in London in 1704. We also know that Anthony Walker produced anti-Jacobite material after the Battle of Culloden. The majority of the engravers who made the prints of the Blaikie Collection, however, have never been identified. This is why we must rely on the rare recipients' comments and on comparisons with related media to understand the intentions behind graphic satires. Literary sources such as street ballads, odes, epics, and drama help enlighten the allegories, puns, and nicknames frequently used in the eighteenth century.

Following the general tastes and cultural controversies of their time, the more elaborate caricatures display rococo finesse as well as moral concerns and enlightened thoughtfulness. At first sight, they are often rude and seem to appeal only to man's worst instincts; but the attentive spectator can also discover serious political reasoning and even social awareness. Print 19.8 from the Blaikie Collection was published in 1746 and deals with the "agreeable contrast" between handsome, energetic Bonnie Prince Charlie, and overweight, ill-tempered William Augustus, Duke of Cumberland.

Anon. *The Agreeable Contrast*. Engraving, 10 1/4 x 6 1/8, 1746. Walter Biggar Blaikie Collection. National Galleries of Scotland. Shows overweight, ill-tempered William Augustus, Duke of Cumberland.

The comic effect of this picture is produced by a fable-like combination of the two men with an animal describing their virtues and vices. While the wind hound is attributed to Bonnie Prince Charlie on the left, the Duke of Cumberland is—obviously less flatteringly—compared to an elephant. In contemporary perception, both animals were connected with a fighting spirit. However, the elephant was seen as an exotic, rude animal of the wilderness, and the greyhound was considered to be a well-behaved, domesticated pet that was indispensable for aristocratic hunting expeditions. The caption beneath the picture frame reads "Shews [*sic.*] that a Greyhound is more agreeable than an Elephant, and a genteel personage more agreeably Pleasing than a Clumsey one, a Country lass is better than a town trollop and that Flora was better pleas'd than Fanny to be had of the author in Bromley Street."[16]

Furthermore, the picture features four speech bubbles in order to express the purported sentiments of the four persons more fully. Bonnie Prince Charlie proclaims "Mercy & Love, Peace etc."[17]

and does not fail to attract Flora McDonald, who replies, "O'h the agreeable creature wt. a Long tail he has."[18] The Duke of Cumberland is apparently calling Charles Edward names, but only the first and last letters of the two swear words are given. And Fanny, the duke's mistress, seems to address both William Augustus and Charles Edward when she says, "Let no body Like Me be Deceived w.th such a pittifull tail."[19] The British Museum catalog lists this print among the few surviving examples of pro-Jacobite graphics,[20] but this print might just as well have been produced by a mildly oppositional engraver who wished to keep aloof from either party. Both men, after all, seem to get their share of mockery, especially since the visual conflation of violence and obscenity gives the print disturbing ambiguity.

In regard to form, the print encompasses several levels of communication that must be carefully distinguished. While the headline and the bottom lines directly address the reader, the speech bubbles create fictional communication between the depicted human beings.[21] Set in front of a simple, two-dimensional landscape, the figures' interaction evokes a performance on stage. In turn, this theatrical or cinematic effect gives the readers spatial and emotional distance from what they see, as well as connects the amusement to a sense of superiority and wisdom. The formal arrangement reflects the inbuilt idea of careful observation and decision-making, even though the range to choose from might not be entirely satisfactory.

Both in image and text, the engraver played with hidden meanings and colloquialisms of the time. The female name Fanny,[22] for example, is a common slang expression for vulva, and the animal tails denote the male sexual organ. "To be had"[23] is another highly ambivalent expression in the context of the engraving, and the mention of "Bromley Street"[24] may also have had an immodest connotation to eighteenth-century readers.[25] Bonnie Prince Charlie's promise of love, peace, and mercy might seem airy and too good to be true, but it is nevertheless presented as preferable to the Duke of Cumberland's ugliness and cruelty, which is stereotypically expressed in his butcher's apron and raised knife.

The central conflict is, after all, between bad taste and the congruency of noble character and beauty. The decisions that the men and the two women have to make bear a strong sexual connotation. It is striking, indeed, that eroticism and lewdness almost surpassed warfare and royalty as the most frequent element in both verbal and visual satires of the 1745 Jacobite rebellion. And in this respect, the caricatures of the Forty-Five Rebellion are very different from earlier satire prints against Charles Edward's father, James Francis Stuart.[26]

From the mid-eighteenth-century onward, eroticism was frequently displayed in the many *before and after* pictures of the time and in popular *fête galante* (French: "festival of gallantry") paintings, which soon developed into more realistic and more detailed *tableaux de mode* (French: "paintings depicting the current [upper-class] lifestyle").[27] The predominant aesthetics of Protestant morality had gradually mingled with an undercurrent of aristocratic hedonism in post-Restoration England, and the satire prints of the day also allowed for a more positive representation of earthly pleasures.[28] But as David Taylor has recently shown in his analysis of dancing in political caricatures, eroticism in eighteenth-century prints frequently served as a witty symbol of social hierarchies and coalitions. Against this background of "sexual politics,"[29] naïve Flora McDonald and lavish Lady Fanny provided perspicuous allegories that questioned whether the British nation was still healthy. Court politics, corruption, city dwelling, and urban luxury were heavily criticized not only in this very print but also in many writings of the time. In more general terms, the juxtaposition of Flora, the judicious country girl, and Fanny, the disappointed court lady, also illustrate a growing conflict between aristocratic self-esteem and bourgeois values.

In contrasting the physical and sexual qualities of Charles, William, and their beloved ladies, the body politic is redefined: king and people are no longer a single body, united by blood and heritage, but a freely formed cohabitation, bound by love or divided by mistrust and disappointment.[30] In many other prints of the time, the political bodies of kings and leading politicians appeared to be secularized in the course of scientific progress because they were sometimes laid open to scrupulous medical and psychological analysis.[31] The constitution of the state, which was (according to early modern English belief) constantly threatened by foreign war and popish plots, was seen as the

[Ebersley, W.]. *The Agreeable Contrast between the Formidable John of Gant and Don Carlos of Southern Extraction.* Engraving. Size not indicated, 1749. Walter Biggar Blaikie Collection. National Galleries of Scotland.

very model wherein a legitimate ruler was expected to fit. Royal prerogative was clearly subordinate to common law, and a worthy king ought to reflect true Britishness in his own person.[32] Accordingly, the female figures portrayed in these prints were not only supposed mistresses but also personifications of the entire British people, whose welfare depended on a responsible monarch.[33] A politician's individual being became a measurement of his ability to rule, and the accusation of administrative "corruption" was often combined with allegations of "seduction"—in a very literal sense.[34]

To a certain degree, such erotica may also be viewed as a revision of violence and law enforcement, which had dominated the depiction of earlier revolts and repression. All throughout Europe, exorbitant punishments now tended to be seen as a moral weakness of the executing governments, and being in control also meant that state officials should withhold their own lust for revenge.[35] In accordance with philosophical considerations of universal justice, humanity, and sportsmanship, many eighteenth-century caricatures, too, presented political struggles for power as nonviolent tournaments and competitions of talents.

*The Agreeable Contrast between the Formidable John of Gant and Don Carlos of Southern Extraction,*[36] from 1749, also centers on the idea of a potential ruler's courteousness, but it is impossible to understand this print, held at Edinburgh, if one does not know the corresponding London print *The Agreable* [*sic*] *Contrast between the British Hero, and the Italian Fugitive.*[37]

The London print seems to have been published immediately after the Battle of Culloden, and several copies of this anti-Jacobite mockery are kept by the British Museum and the Queen's private collections today. *The British Hero, and the Italian Fugitive*[38] blames Charles Edward Stuart's upbringing in continental Europe and his Catholic religion for his military failure. Sitting at his writing desk, Bonnie Prince Charlie is absorbed in "Romish Legends,"[39] his elbow leaning on "The Popes Bull."[40]

Anon. *The Agreable Contrast between the British Hero, and the Italian Fugitive.* Engraving and etching on laid paper, 230 mm x 296 mm, 1746. Lewis Walpole Library, lwlpr01230. Yale University Library.

The Duke of Cumberland's bravery and his military skills are, in contrast, depicted in the engraving placed on the floor. His image is also full size, and he is shown as a proud leader. Together with Britannia, he points his finger at the Stuart prince to laugh at his fainthearted flight. Thus the text below the framed image expresses praise of Cumberland's military achievements: "Here Happy Britain tells her Joyfull Tales, / And may again Since Williams Arms prevails."[41]

The engraver who imitated and obverted this anti-Jacobite print[42] kept Charles Edward in the same position, but showed the Duke of Cumberland only as another picture in picture in the foreground. In this imaginary print within the print, the Duke of Cumberland is on his knees and is inappropriately courting two women. Britannia, for her part, complains to the young Stuart prince about the moral decline of William Augustus. Again, this print has been classified as pro-Jacobite by the authors of the nineteenth-century British Museum catalog of printed satires,[43] but its overall message is even more ambiguous than that of the elephant-greyhound satire.

The nicknames "John of Gant" for the Duke of Cumberland and "Don Carlos" for Prince Charles were commonly used in satires of the day, but neither had a positive connotation. The headline itself even suggests a bias in favor of the duke, but Bonnie Prince Charlie is the most prominent figure. Reading at his writing desk, he is relaxed and calm, although it is not clear what book he is holding. Even though the bookshelf in the background is filled with sophisticated philosophical and political literature on "the original laws"[44] and "the original contract,"[45] Charles Edward rests his arm thoughtlessly on the Magna Carta, and the prince's dreamy look suggests that he is occupied with a fanciful novel instead of serious studies. On the one hand, this print certainly is a statement in favor of Charles Edward's overall education, which clearly exceeded the learning achieved by the Duke of Cumberland; but on the other hand, the print discloses playfulness and maybe even self-irony, which may have come from either Hanoverian or Jacobite adherents. Britannia, after all, is presented as helpless and upset, and while she expects due support from Charles Edward, he does not even lend her an ear. Taking similar prints into consideration, this complex, independent approach to conflict and opposing parties seems to have been a popular feature of political caricature in general.[46] How far pro-Hanoverian artists could go in scorn for their own party is, after all, reflected in William Hogarth's much-debated painting *March of the Guards to Finchley*,[47] which was publicly exhibited in 1750 and was ill received by King George II.[48]

This is why one-sided attributions of political caricatures to a single party do not always do justice to these multilayer works of art. Once more, the print on "Don Carlos" and "John of Gant" strongly personalizes politics and religion, as well as questions whether a leader is fit to rule in both fundamental and symbolic ways. The facts that neither the Duke of Cumberland nor Charles Edward Stuart are explicitly named and that traditional outward signs of royalty, such as crowns, ermine coats, andmilitary decorations are omitted draw our attention to the personal traits and physical features meant to speak for themselves.[49] Toward the end of the century, this interest in psychology and the physical manifestations of the human character developed into academic typology and physiognomy, and the first English edition of Lavater's *Essays on Physiognomy*,[50] in 1797, was illustrated with earlier eighteenth-century caricatures by Hogarth and his contemporaries.[51] In his own writings, Hogarth had in fact paid great attention to the face as both the physical and moral center of the human body: "How soon does a face that wants expression, grow insipid, tho' it be ever so pretty?—The rest of the body, not having these advantages in common with the face, would soon satiate the eye, were it to be constantly exposed, nor would it have more effect than a marble statue."[52]

Last but not least, "the invention of the first person"[53] in eighteenth-century art was closely related to the idea of collective characterizations.[54] Individuality not only became detached from office and rank but also formed new bonds with national identity. This marked another significant shift with regard to content. In 1715, when James Francis tried to reclaim the British crown, the anti-Stuart propaganda had wholeheartedly focused on French support for the Jacobites and tried to denounce the exiled Pretender as a foreign invader. In the opinion of his opponents, Francis's Catholic faith implied that he was fatally attached to continental

Anon. *Britannia Sitting between Prince Charles and Cumberland Weighing Mercy and Butchery.* Etching, 157 mm x 256 mm, 1746. Walter Biggar Blaikie Collection, SNPG 1.16, National Galleries of Scotland.

manners and ignorant of British laws and customs. By 1745, however, both French subsidies for the Stuarts and the Catholic self-representation of James II's offspring had abated or transformed, and neither the multi cultural and religiously tolerant Stuart court in Italy nor the personal character of Charles Edward Stuart substantiated enemy stereotypes of backward, heteronomous fanatics.[55] Subsequently, pro- and anti-Stuart propaganda in Britain sought new communicational strategies, although long established patterns of argumentation were by no means given up. Due to the strong Highland support for Bonnie Prince Charlie, the Stuart cause was increasingly identified with a patriotic striving for Scottish hereditary rights, which fostered a hitherto unsurpassed dispute about the nature and destiny of Great Britain. This is most strongly emphasized in the untitled print No. 2834 from the British Museum in London (Blaikie Collection No. SNPG.1.16).[56] This print reiterates the contrast between mercy and cruelty and has a clear pro-Jacobite message, but it also shows that transitions from and to serious political iconography in heraldry or history painting remained in flux. Britannia is seated on a throne between the Duke and the Pretender, holding a balance, in which "mercy"[57] outweighs "butchery."[58] The additional imagery used to describe the pre-eminence of mercy is the biblical motif of the wolf and the lamb, taken from Isaiah 11:6. This Bible verse is in fact a description of the virtuous king, the Messiah, coming to restore the people of Israel and bringing harmony to all creation.

Although the print carefully avoids any hint of confessional divisions—in sharp contrast to anti-Jacobite propaganda of the time—familiar Old Testament symbolism is introduced to express the qualities of a good king and the moral concepts of Christian humanism. Right behind the Duke of Cumberland with his bloody axe, the engraver depicted several bodies suspended from a gallows beside a decapitated head and an arm lying on a blazing altar. These were signs of pagan human sacrifice and idolatry, which pointed to religion as a matter of conduct and integrity. References to the Bible as the written foundation of all Christian communities indicate that Jacobitism was denominationally diverse, and by then less High Church oriented than it had been immediately after the Glorious Revolution. One may even suggest that Jacobitism had transformed from a political faction rooted in Britain's Anglican establishment to a sociocultural network far beyond the British Isles.[59] Both before and after Culloden, Jacobites may have identified with the ancient Jews in exile, painfully anticipating the advent of their savior. In the course of time, many Jacobites even came to terms with being a minority loyal to a "king over the waters,"[60] who was not likely ever to return. In their letters to James Francis and his court, Irish Catholic priests frequently praised the advocating influence that the Stuarts in Italy could exert on continental rulers and, above all, the Pope. Fr. James MacKenna, a member of the Augustinian Order, called James Francis "our great patron"[61] and "our gr. Prone [Padrone] Benjesu."[62] Frs. Francis d'Evereux, Ioannes Plunket, J. Brady, and John O'Neill wrote to James Francis in 1748: "As your Majesty is of all the Princes in the world the most conspicuous for your attachment to the true religion and zealous practice of it, all remonstrances relating to the good of religion may be made to your Majesty without the least fear of giving offence and all possible succour expected from your Majesty in that and every other way be, Sir, your Majesty's most loyal, most faithful subjects and ever humble servants."[63] This aesthetic of virtue and confidence, rather than a desire for political change, is also reflected in post-1745 Jacobite prints. In this context, the verses inscribed at the bottom of the engraving are especially revealing:

> Look here upon this picture, and on this, The counterfeit Presentment of two Persons, See what a Grace is seated on this Brow, like Mars to threaten & Command, God hath seem'd to set his Seal, To give the World Asurance [*sic*] of a Man, Look you now on the other, Blasting his wholsom [*sic*] Country. Have you Eyes, Could you on this fair Mountain leave to feed and batten on this Moor. Ha! Have you Eyes? You cannot call it Love, for at your Age, The heyday of the blood is tame, it's humble, And waits upon ye Judgment, and what Judgment would step from this to this?[64]

This text is a reference to Shakespeare's *Hamlet,* act 3, scene 4, and is based loosely on Hamlet's conversation with Gertrude, his mother.[65] In the play, Hamlet shows Gertrude a picture of the dead king, his murdered father, and a picture of the current king, his uncle and Gertrude's second husband. Hamlet furiously asks his mother what has driven her to marry such a rotten man. In this case, it is the British nation that must answer for their own blinded choice, and both the necessity of careful inspection and the responsibility of selection are taken into consideration. A further profound feature of the print is the divisive, but not altogether unusual, combination of Scottish patriotism with an open claim to see Bonnie Prince Charlie rule over a united Great Britain. Still today, the tension of a common British interest and an independent cultural and political heritage fuels debate over Scottish autonomy, and the idea of a general British identity was probably even more heavily contested in the mid-eighteenth century.[66]

In this example, the Young Pretender is depicted in Scottish military dress and is framed by crowned Scottish thistles, but the presence of Britannia as a personification of a united kingdom counters this tendency. Prior to 1745, Scottish Jacobites had refused King George I and King George II mainly because they came from the continent, not because they weren't Scottish. Critics of the Act of Union saw their aims unite only gradually with the wider appeal of Jacobitism. French propaganda before 1746 had been far more anti-English than any pro-Stuart literature from Scotland, but the peculiar conditions of the 1745 rebellion, which involuntarily drew its basic support from the north of Britain, gave the Stuart cause a new separatist turn. While the Stuarts themselves generally commissioned courtly portraits depicting members of the family as leading European noblemen in fashionable dress or armor, many of the small-scale portraits of Bonnie Prince Charlie (circulated in Scotland from 1745 onward) tended to emphasize the prince's alleged Scottishness. Edward Corp has already mentioned the stylistic differences between courtly Stuart portraits from Italy and France and the copies spread in Scotland in his exhibition catalog *The King Over the Water: Portraits of the Stuarts in Exile after 1689*.[67] However, he discusses these differences predominantly in terms of inferior British artistic qualification. On the contrary, there might also have been a forceful political motivation for the fact that British Jacobite artists did not focus on ribbons and laces as much as continental court painters did. A deliberate simplification of royal dress and symbols of power could serve the purpose of expressing the populism of the Stuart family.

This idea was embraced by both anti- and pro-Stuart caricaturists, and it was also reflected elsewhere in popular culture of the day. After Charles Edward had fled from Britain back to France in summer 1746, his supporters in Edinburgh planned to stage his twenty-sixth birthday, in December, as a public feast that was deliberately rooted in Scottish folklore and local traditions. On Christmas Eve 1746, George Keppel, Third Earl of Albemarle and Lord of the Bedchamber to the Duke of Cumberland, sent an urgent letter to London, reporting that "a surprising, audacious and impudent attempt was made [last Saturday] by several People of this Town to celebrate the Birth day of the Pretender's Son, the Women distinguishing themselves by Wearing Tartan Gowns with Shoes & Stockings of the same kind, & white Ribbands on their heads and breasts."[68]

In the long run, selective commemoration of the 1745 Jacobite rebellion on both sides molded the English stereotype of the stubborn, backward, and rakish Scotsmen for many decades to come. One man severely affected by these powerful trends in British satire was John Stuart, Earl of Bute, who served as privy councilor, secretary of state, and prime minister to George III from 1760 to 1763. Accused of being obstinate and arrogant and ofhaving a passionate liaison with Augusta, the Dowager Princess of Wales, Lord Bute was often depicted as a covetous Scotsman in Highland dress.[69] Many of these caricatures strongly resembled those of Bonnie Prince Charlie and Flora McDonald. "Omnia vincit amor"[70]—"love overcomes all things"—was the motto ascribed to John Stuart, and the big black jackboot in the satire prints ridiculed his Christian name as well as the Scottish pronunciation of "Bute."[71] Being of a more delicate nature, John Stuart did not take the attacks in text and pictures lightly. In a letter to his son Charles, he admitted, "I never put my foot in Town without someone to worry me—people who are never abused wonder I mind anonymous writers, but few feel for others what they would do in their own case—besides, some are by nature shielded with callosity. I was cast in a different mould."[72]

Although the Jacobite rebellion of 1745 had been a military failure, it nevertheless continued to have strong effects on Britain's political, religious, and communicational culture. In regard to media history, British caricatures of the eighteenth century marked an important connecting link between informational long distance communication, in a Luhmannian sense, and the sensuous immediacy of representative art.[73] Caricatures were not only collected but increasingly reflected upon—both in regard to their content and their aesthetic nature.[74] Jean André Rouquet's *Description du tableau de M. Hogarth, qui represente La marche des gardes à leur rendez-vous de-Finchley*[75] on Hogarth's famous satirical painting, for instance, discussed both the artistic quality and the political implications at great length. Rouquet's famous question, "D'où vient que les oreilles sont plus chaste que les yeux?"[76] ("Why is it that the ears are chaster than the eyes?") summarizes the attraction that people of all social classes had to visualized debate and criticism of both politics and individual politicians. As Diana Donald has stated in her comprehensive study on visual satires in Georgian England, "Caricature was not 'a style of art, in which a father of any pretensions to good taste would desire to see his daughter excel.'"[77] However, as popular access to what had formerly been considered high art increased and as artists aimed to represent the simple truths of everyday life, the elitist definition of art and its purpose was challenged and transformed. Although government officials seem to have collected satirical prints primarily to produce evidence for potential seditious libel charges, their letters exchanged on the subject contributed to the gradual appreciation of such prints as artistic expressions.[78]

How extensively caricatures were reprinted, collected, and discussed across social boundaries is, after all, reflected in cheap and popular magazines like the *British Antidote* of the 1760s, which served as yearly anthologies of all the satires printed during the past months.[79] In this respect, caricatures did not necessarily attempt to represent a true event promptly and realistically; on the contrary, caricaturists often wished to form a collective identity beyond the daily mutations of history. The greatest strength of eighteenth-century caricatures was that their condensed messages allowed for long-dated responses "in easy connivance"[80] with contemporary verbal expression. Visual quotations from other printed satires were frequent in eighteenth-century rebellion caricatures even years later, and they created extensive dialogues and catchy political narratives that were gladly received by contemporary collectors. None of the iconographical and stylistic features mentioned above were invented in the eighteenth century, but the way in which they were refined and distributed during this period constituted a new artistic and political awareness.

All in all, caricatures of the 1745 rebellion defined a lasting framework for later British caricatures, both in content and style, and they mark the first half of the century as an age of cultural and social transition from pre-Enlightenment concepts of bravery and honor to the Age of Sensibility and republican reasoning.[81] While private and public character appeared to intertwine, church and state as organizational systems of society were more clearly separated. But as individual ability and personal responsibility were stressed, religion as a source of dignity and morality became important for other reasons. Even the unashamed erotic symbolism of political communication was anything but incompatible with these redefined values, but helped to distil sophisticated discourse down to forceful catchwords.

Printed caricatures transmitted such ideas to wider audiences, and their cross-border circulation linked national controversies to related issues abroad. In this sense, the formation of eighteenth-century nations was peculiarly embedded in pan-European discourse, and Christian humanism often served to counterbalance patriotism and isolation.

## Notes

1. "Over the past fifteen years, scholars of eighteenth-century Britain have come to place increasing importance on the caricature, as both a counter-aesthetic and a rich repository of cultural information." David Francis Taylor, "Coalition Dances: Georgian Caricature's Choreographies of Power," *Music in Art* 36, no. 1–2 (2011): 117.

2. Cf. two contemporary poems "On William, Duke of Cumberland" and "Up and rin awa', Willie," collected by Gilbert Samuel Macquoid, *Jacobite Songs and Ballads*, edited, with notes, *Historical Collection from the British Library* (London: The British Library, 2013), 277–279.

3. "This linear model has been reinforced by the illustrative practices of secondary literature. Typically, for example, pendant texts are cropped. This may be in the interest of reprography but it is arguably symptomatic also of a dualism which continues to inform the unwillingness to address the hybrid nature of the genre." Eirwen E. C. Nicholson, "Soggy Prose and Verbiage: English Graphic Political Satire as a Visual/Verbal Construct," *Word & Image* 20 (2004): 35.

4. In her essay "Soggy Prose and Verbiage," Eirwen Nicholson names four major categories thereof. Apart from caricatures, which consisted of a single, isolated picture, there were satire sheets wherein words appeared "within the 'frame' of the pictorial image" (*inscription-picture relationship*), satire sheets containing words only "within the physical boundaries of the 'carrying medium'" (*subscriptio*), and satires whose accompanying words appeared on separate sheets (especially when the graphic satire was part of a longer pamphlet). Cf. ibid., 28. Also Hans-Peter Wagner, *William Hogarth. Das graphische Werk. Ein kommentierter Auswahlkatalog* (Trier: Wissenschaftlicher Verlag Trier, 2013), back cover.

5. Julius Ralph Ruff, *Violence in Early Modern Europe: 1500–1800*, New Approaches to European History (Cambridge: Cambridge University Press, 2001), 21.

6. Frederic George Stephens and Edward Hawkins, *Catalogue of Prints and Drawings in the British Museum. Division I: Political and Personal Satires*, ed. British Museum, Department of Prints and Drawings, vol. III.1 (March 28, 1734, to ca. 1750) (London, 1877), 599, 622, 627, and 753.

7. Mary Dorothy George, *English Political Caricature to 1792: A Study of Opinion and Propaganda* (Oxford: Clarendon Press, 1959).

8. " —adversary of connoisseurs. (. . .) And in 1743, Hogarth published his *Characters & Caricaturas* [2591], 'Being perpetually plagued from the mistakes made among the il-

literate by the similarities in the sound of the words...' . . . But caricature and the burlesque were destined to transform the emblematical print, and here the amateur made his contribution with drawing that was incorrect and expressive, and art superbly practiced by Max Beerbohm. . . . The print-sellers (in 1756) used the words 'Character' and 'Caricatura' indiscriminately for collections of prints by Townshand and others, and in 1758 Hogarth returned to the distinction with *The Bench* [3662]." Ibid., 111–1112.

9. "Characterisme, a lively description, and as it were painting forth any person by any Orator or Poet, as that of Catiline by Cicero and such like." Edward Phillips, *The Nevv Vvorld of Vvords. Or a General English Dictionary Containing the Proper Significations, and Etymologies of All Words Derived from Other Languages* (London: printed by W.R. for Robert Harford at the Angel in Cornhill, 1678), 47. "Characterisme, a lively description of a person" / "characterize, to describe; also to take in characters or short-hand." Elisha Coles, *An English Dictionary Explaining the Difficult Terms That Are Used in Divinity, Husbandry, Physick, Philosophy, Law, Navigation, Mathematicks, and Other Arts and Sciences Containing Many Thousands of Hard Words, and Proper Names of Places, More than Are in Any Other English Dictionary or Expositor* (London: Printed for Peter Parker, 1692), 25.

10. "Hogarth particularly disliked caricature because it was an Italian fashion that was being introduced to England by the same people who dealt in foreign 'old master' paintings and drawings. These dealers and drawing masters encouraged their pupils and patrons to think more highly of what was old or continental than of modern English art. At the base of his design Hogarth contrasts 'characters' taken from Raphael's cartoons (in the Royal Collection, now in the Victoria and Albert Museum, London) with caricatures by Leonardo, Carracci, and the fashionable contemporary Italian, Pier Leone Ghezzi. Above, a crowd of expressive, but not caricatured, faces demonstrate the variety and subtlety of character." "William Hogarth, *Characters and Caricaturas*, a Print," The British Museum, accessed January 5, 2014, http://www.britishmuseum.org/explore/highlights/highlight_objects/pd/w/william_hogarth,_caricaturas.aspx.

11. "CARICATURA, n.s. [Ital. Caricatura] A ridiculous representation of a person or circumstance, without loss of the resemblance. Brown. To CARICATURE. v.a. To ridicule. Lord Lyttleton. CARICATURIST. n.s. He who caricatures persons or things." Samuel Johnson and Alexander Chalmers, *Samuel Johnson's Dictionary of the English Language* (London: Studio Editions, 1994), 98. "CHARACTER. n.s. [character, Lat.] A mark; a stamp. Wicliffe. A letter used in writing or printing. Shakspeare. The hand or manner of writing. Spenser. A representation of personal qualities. Denham. An account of any thing. Addison. The person with his assemblage of qualities; a personage. Dryden. Personal qualities; a particular constitution of the mind. Pope. Adventitious qualities impressed by a post or office. Atterbury." Ibid., 108.

12. Direct anticipations of modern caricatures are rather found in the Italian fourteenth-century tradition of "pitture ridicule," described by Klaus Krüger, "Das Sprechen und das Schweigen der Bilder," in *Der stumme Diskurs der Bilder: Reflexionsformen des Ästhetischen in der Kunst der frühen Neuzeit*, ed. Valeska von Rosen, Klaus Krüger, and Rudolf Preimesberger (Munich: Dt. Kunstverlag, 2003), 32.

13. Helen Pierce, *Unseemly Pictures: Graphic Satire and Politics in Early Modern England* (New Haven: Yale University Press, 2008), 27.

14. "Published in London, England, AD 1743 Hogarth's subscription ticket announces that he is a comic artist, not a caricaturist. This etching was designed as a subscrip-

tion ticket—a receipt presented to all those who had placed an advance order for Hogarth's series, *Marriage à la Mode*. It refers to Henry Fielding's preface to Joseph Andrews (1742), where Fielding had praised Hogarth as a comic history painter and drawn a parallel distinction between the comic and the burlesque in writing and between comedy and caricature in painting. The comic painter imitates nature, while the caricaturist distorts and exaggerates nature." "William Hogarth, *Characters and Caricaturas*." Also Ronald Paulson, *Popular and Polite Art in the Age of Hogarth and Fielding* (Notre Dame, IN: University of Notre Dame Press, 1979); Peter Jan de Voogd, *Henry Fielding and William Hogarth: The Correspondences of the Arts* (Amsterdam: Rodopi, 1981).

15. Nicholson, "Soggy Prose," 37.

16. Anon., *The Agreeable Contrast*, engraving, 1746, Walter Biggar Blaikie Collection, National Galleries of Scotland.

17. Ibid.

18. Ibid.

19. Ibid.

20. "Amidst a shower of anti-Jacobite prints, but three pro-Jacobite examples are described in this volume, and due to the period in question, these are 'The Agreeable Contrast,' No. 2833, the nameless engraving here styled 'A Jacobite Satire', No. 2834, and 'The Butcher,' No. 2843." Stephens and George, *Catalogue*, III.1 (March 28, 1734, to ca. 1750): xxxix.

21. Examples of different levels of communication within pictures are also given in Krüger, "Das Sprechen," 25. "Es ist, so kann man sagen, der Versuch einer darstellungslogisch plausiblen und konsistenten Verknüpfung von extern gerichteter Präsentation, bei der die gemalte Schrift als Substitut für die nicht malbare Sprache fungiert, und zugleich von bildintern sich entfaltenden, mit eben dem Geschriebenen *be*fassten und ihm innerlich *er*fassten Emotionen und Empfindungen der dargestellten Protagonistin."

22. Anon., *Agreeable Contrast*.

23. Ibid.

24. Ibid.

25. All we know about Bromley Street today is that it was a busy London district traditionally connected with seafaring and home to one of the city's largest graveyards. Since the late seventeenth-century, it was also known for its Spanish Coffee House where auctions took place: Anon., *A Curious Collection of Paintings, Being Most Originals: By the Best Masters, Both Antient & Modern: ... Will Be Sold by Auction, at the Spanish-Coffee-House, at the Corner of Bromley-Street in Holbourn, on Friday the 27th of This Instant November, 1691. The Sale Begins at Four of the Clock in the Afternoon, and Will Continue on Saturday, Monday, &c. till All Are Sold off* (London: s.n, 1691). The daily influx of travelers and goods from abroad might also have given rise to certain crimes and an atmosphere of shadiness.

26. Anti-Jacobite caricatures prior to the 1745 rebellion were generally much more complex and contained many heraldic, mythological, or biblical references. Prints such as Anon., *The Traytors Coat of Arms, size not indicated*, ([London]: s.n., 1715), British Library, and *The Jacobites Hopes, Or, Perkin Rideing* [*sic*] in Triumph, engraving and etching, 144 mm x 189 mm, published by William Pennock, 1711, BM Satires 1495: Broadsides British 1709 Imp, British Museum London, were also rich in emblematic usage of animals and objects but did not highlight human individuality. For the influence of emblem books on political satires and the English genre of "hieroglyphical prints," cf. George, *English Political Caricature*, 7–9.

"But the advance in English graphic satire produced by High Church and Low Church excitements was not followed up for many years. There is almost nothing on the Peace (though there were many Dutch prints), on the accession of the Hanoverians and the Tory rout, or on the Fifteen." Ibid., 71.

27. Jörg Ebeling, "Tableaux de Mode—Studien zum Aristokratischen Genrebild in Frankreich in der Ersten Hälfte des 18. Jahrhunderts" (Philipps Universität, 2012), http://archiv.ub.uni-marburg.de/diss/z2012/0074/pdf/dje.pdf.

28. David Francis Taylor analyzed dancing in caricatures as "an erotic motif" and explained how political coalitions and hierarchies, above all "disjunction and inappropriate union," were symbolized by "sexual sublimation": "The minuet is thus not just an image of politics, but of sexual politics—of a certain kind of power (desire) that has been codified and contained through dance." Taylor, "Coalition Dances," 129.

29. Ruth Kenny, "Sexual Politics: Or John Stuart, Earl of Bute and Augusta, Dowager Princess of Wales in English Graphic Satire, 1760–1762," *Immediations* 1, no. 1 (2004): 21.

30. Marilyn Morris, *Sex, Money, and Personal Character in Eighteenth-Century British Politics* (New Haven: Yale University Press, 2014), 24–25.

31. Nicholson, "Soggy Prose," 30.

32. "Royal tastes and royal portraiture dominated the seventeenth-century artistic landscape, with the collections and commissions of the court and the elite championed by the studies of Roy Strong, Oliver Millar and their successors, primarily informing our understanding of the visual arts during this period. It is a history of art born out of Continental influences, whether via the patronage of acclaimed foreign artists such as Van Dyck and Rubens or the experiences brought back from the European sojourns of Inigo Jones. By contrast, the development of purely 'English art' over the course of the seventeenth century has been given short scholarly shrift, and it is rarely considered to emerge from the shadow of portraiture." Pierce, *Unseemly Pictures*, 3–4.

33. In her essay on the famous print series *Marriage à la Mode*, engraved by Hogarth, Christine Riding says that criticism of the "aspirant bourgeois" was just as common in popular satire as was the fierce criticism of the noblemen's idleness. Mark Hallett and Christine Riding, *Hogarth* (London: Tate, 2006), 141. Also cf. Morris, *Sex*.

34. The debates on *An Essay on Woman. A Poem*, written by J. W. (John Wilkes) Senator in 1763, reflected the importance of the female body, above all the noblewoman's, as a symbol of collective virtue and success. In several publications, Wilkes and his supporters outlined seduction and fornication not only as moral failures but employed them as political accusations: "I shall always remain persuaded, that you have been the cause of all our internal commotions; that you tempted the woman to destroy not only her own peace, but the tranquility of this once happy country; a foreigner, unacquainted with our laws, manners, constitution, the thought of subverting such a government could never have spontaneously entered into her mind: schemes of this enormous size do not belong to women; they are not the original devisers of such over-grown mischiefs; they are first misled themselves, and then indeed are wondrous capable of misleading others: you, my Lord, have been the wiley seducer, you the culprit of the public, and against you did I always wish to see the vengeance of the people, the justice of the laws directly and immediately pointed." Anon., *A Letter to the Earl of Bute* (London, 1771), 6. In Samuel Johnson's "Essay on Woman"—a response to John Wilkes's outwardly pornographic satires on the assumed relationship between John Stuart, Earl of Bute, and the Dowager Princess of

Wales—Johnson, for his part, defended "the fond affectioned female mind" and discussed the value of marriage and gender equality. Samuel Johnson, *An Essay on Woman, a Poem, And, Sensibility. A Political Epistle Addressed to Charlton Leighton, Esq.* (London, 1772).

35. "The expansion of state justice injected a measure of violence into European life through the corporal and capital punishments that the penology of the day employed, yet we will see this brutality eventually diminishing along with violent crime itself." Ruff, *Violence*, 3.

36. [Ebersley, W.], *The Agreeable Contrast between the Formidable John of Gant and Don Carlos of Southern Extraction*, engraving, 1749, Walter Biggar Blaikie Collection, National Galleries of Scotland.

37. Anon., *The Agreable Contrast between the British Hero, and the Italian Fugitive*, engraving and etching, 1746, Satires British Stephens series, BM Satires 2832, British Museum London. This print is described in Stephens and George, Catalogue, III.1 (March 28, 1734, to ca. 1750): 599.

38. Anon., *The Agreable Contrast between the British Hero, and the Italian Fugitive.*

39. Stephens and George, *Catalogue*, III.1 (March 28, 1734, to ca. 1750): 599.

40. Ibid.

41. Anon., *The Agreable Contrast between the British Hero, and the Italian Fugitive.*

42. The name of the engraver given in the imprint, W. Ebersley, is apparently a pseudonym.

43. Stephens and George, *Catalogue.*

44. [Ebersley, W.], *Agreeable Contrast.*

45. Ibid.

46. "Kunst definiert sich als Differenz zur Realität." Hans Körner, "Die enttäuschte und die getäuschte Hand: Der Tastsinn im Paragone der Künste," in van Rosen, Krüger, and Preimesberger, *Der stumme Diskurs der Bilder*, 222.

47. Cf. Douglas Fordham, "William Hogarth's The March to Finchley and the Fate of Comic History Painting," *Art History: Journal of the Association of Art Historians*, no. 24 (2004): 95–128.

48. When Hogarth attempted to dedicate the painting to his own King George II of England, the king was said to have reacted in anger: "Does he intend to mock my soldiers?" ["Will er meine Soldaten verhöhnen?," quoted in Wagner, *William Hogarth*, 157]. Consequently, Hogarth instead chose to keep the painting, and he authorized engraved copies that were executed by Luke Sullivan and dedicated to the King of Prussia.

49. Cf. essay on late seventeenth- and early eighteenth-century relations between royal courts and the public sphere: Jörg Jochen Berns, "Der nackte Monarch und die nackte Wahrheit: Auskünfte der deutschen Zeitungs- und Zeremoniellschriften des späten 17. und frühen 18. Jahrhunderts zum Verhältnis von Hof und Öffentlichkeit," *Daphnis* 11 (1982): 315–349.

50. Johann Caspar Lavater, *Lavater's Essays on Physiognomy: With Ornamental Caricatures, and Finished Portraits. Translated from the Last Paris Edition, by the Rev. C. Moore* (London, 1797).

51. Diana Donald, *The Age of Caricature: Satirical Prints in the Reign of George III* (New Haven: Yale University Press, 1996), 12.

52. William Hogarth, *Analysis of Beauty: Written with a View of Fixing the Fluctuating Ideas of Taste* (London, 1753), 36.

53. Hallett and Riding, *Hogarth*, 24.

54. Wolfgang Harms, "Feindbilder im illustrierten Flugblatt der frühen Neuzeit," in *Feindbilder: Die Darstellung des Gegners in der politischen Publizistik des Mittelalters und der Neuzeit*, ed. Franz Bosbach, *Bayreuther Historische Kolloquien* 6 (2006), 141–177 and 235–242.

55. "James wollte damit unter Beweis stellen, dass die Stuarts trotz ihres Katholizismus bereit waren, den protestantischen Glauben ihrer potentiellen Untertanen in England und Schottland zu dulden. Mitten im Zentrum des sonst wenig toleranten katholischen Europa wurde der Hof der Stuarts damit zu einer kleinen Hochburg der Toleranz. . . . Jakobiten fand man am russischen Hof genauso wie in der Armee der Habsburgermonarchie, im preußischen Herr oder in den zahlreichen Freimaurerlogen des Kontinents, von den vielen jakobitischen Adelsfamilien in Frankreich ganz abgesehen." Ronald G. Asch, *Die Stuarts: Geschichte einer Dynastie* (Munich: Verlag C. H. Beck, 2011), 124.

56. Anon., *A Jacobite Satire on the Duke of Cumberland: Britannia Sitting between Prince Charles and Cumberland Weighing Mercy and Butchery*, etching, 157 mm x 256 mm, 1746, Satires British Stephens series: BM Satires 2834, British Museum London. This print is described in Stephens and George, *Catalogue*, III.1 (March 28, 1734, to ca. 1750): 627.

57. Anon., *A Jacobite Satire.*

58. Ibid.

59. Asch, *Stuarts*, 120–124.

60. Edward Corp, *The King over the Water: Portraits of the Stuarts in Exile after 1689* (Edinburgh: The Trustees of the National Galleries of Scotland 2001). Exhibition catalog.

61. Fr. James MacKenna to James Edgar, Elixim in Brabant, February 22, 1745, *Ireland in the Stuart Papers: Correspondence and Documents of Irish Interest from the Stuart Papers in the Royal Archives, Windsor Castle*, ed. Patrick Fagan, vol. 2: *1743–1765* (1st ed.) (Dublin: Four Courts Press, 1995), 24.

62. Fr. James MacKenna to James Edgar, Dublin, July 30, 1748, ibid., 89.

63. Frs. Francis d'Evereux, Ioannes Plunket, J. Brady, and John O'Neill to James Francis Stuart, ibid., 98.

64. Anon., *Britannia.*

65. "Look here upon this picture and on this, The counterfeit presentment of two brothers. See, what a grace was seated on this brow? Hyperion's curls, the front of Jove himself, An eye like Mars to threaten and command, A station like the herald Mercury, New-lighted on a heaven-kissing hill—A combination and a form indeed Where every god did seem to set his seal To give the world assurance of a man. This was your husband. Look you now, what follows. Here is your husband, like a mildewed ear Blasting his wholesome brother. Have you eyes? Could you on this fair mountain leave to feed And batten on this moor? Ha, have you eyes? You cannot call it love, for at your age, The heyday in the blood is tame, it's humble, And waits upon the judgment. And what judgment Would step from this to this? Sense sure you have, Else could you not have motion. But sure that sense Is apoplexed, for madness would not err, Nor sense to ecstasy was ne'er so thralled, But it reserved some quantity of choice To serve in such a difference." Full transcription of ibid. For a more detailed analysis, cf. George, *English Political Caricature*, 97.

66. Douglas Fordham, "State, Nation, and Empire in the History of Georgian Art," *Perspective: La Revue de l'INHA. actualités de la recherché en histoire de l'art*, no. 1 (2012): 115.

67. Corp, *King over the Water*.

68. The National Archives of the United Kingdom (hereafter cited as TNA), "SP 54/34/4F: Albemarle, Reporting Charles Edward's Intention to Return from France, Bringing Aid" 1746, State Papers Scotland, Secretaries of State: State Papers Scotland Series II.

69. Donald, *Age of Caricature*, 50.

70. John Pridden, *The British Antidote to Caledonian Poison: Containing Fifty-Three Anti-Ministerial, Political, Satirical, and Comic Prints, for Those Remarkable Years 1762, and 1763*, 7th ed. (London: 1764), 49.

71. Donald, *Age of Caricature*, 50.

72. John Stuart, Earl of Bute, in a letter to his son Charles, dated November 1778, *A Prime Minister and His Son, from the Correspondence of the 3rd Earl of Bute and of Lt.-General Sir Charles Stuart,* compiled by Violet Stuart Wortley and Rennell Rod (London: John Murray, 1925), 141.

73. Certain caricaturists like Gillray especially appealed to "people of high rank, good taste and intelligence," while the "enlarged public for caricature, which the success of specialist suppliers of the 1780s and 1790s indicates, was not a socially homogeneous body." Donald, *Age of Caricature*, 4–8. Cf. also Andreas Würgler, *Medien in der frühen Neuzeit*, vol. 85 of *Enzyklopädie deutscher Geschichte* (1st ed.) (Munich: Oldenbourg Wissenschaftsverlag, 2009), http://ebooks.ciando.com/book/index.cfm/bok_id/29611.

74. When George stated in 1959 that "the earliest English prints [were] scarcely caricatures, seldom intentionally comic, and only by exception works of art," her definition of art remained unclear, even more so as she seemed to contrast artistic value with the significance of a print as a "historic document." George, *English Political Caricature*, 13.

75. Jean André Rouquet, *Description du tableau de M. Hogarth, qui represente La marche des gardes à leur rendez-vous de-Finchley : ... Cette lettre de Mr. Rouquet, ... a été écrite a un de ses amis à Paris* (London, 1746).

76. Ibid., 6.

77. Donald, *Age of Caricature*, 16.

78. The National Archives of the United Kingdom hold several collections of engraved seventeenth- and eighteenth-century caricatures in their State Papers series. These prints were sent to government officials in their own time and informed the royal administration not only of satires concerning their own monarchs, but also recorded political developments abroad. A set of six engraved caricatures of the late seventeenth century (TNA, "SP 9/202/1/35" [engraved caricatures, Dutch Republic, seventeenth century]), for example, contains caricatures of both Charles II and Louis XIV that seem to have been imported from abroad. Jacobite satires directed against the Hanoverian succession or the Whigs were observed with special care (TNA, "SP 46/170/102-106" [Printed satirical broadsheets, London, early eighteenth century], State Papers Domestic: Supplementary), and "disrespectful caricatures of the Royal Family" (cf. TNA, "HO 42/28/108," February 13, 1794, Home Office: Domestic Correspondence, George III) still concerned the administration in the late eighteenth century. But at the same time, caricatures favorable to England or to the Protestant succession were much appreciated, and the ambassadors' decent collecting efforts have helped to preserve individuals prints that were either deliberately banned

and destroyed or accidentally lost in their countries of origin (cf. TNA, "SP 9/144: Le Consulte degli Animali Parlanti, a political satire. Sent to Williamson in 1666 by Giles Jones, English consul in Venice" [Italy, 1666], State Paper Office: Williamson Collection, Pamphlets, Miscellaneous).

79. For example, Pridden, *British Antidote*; John Pridden, *The Scots Scourge: Being a Compleat Supplement to the British Antidote to Caledonian Poison: Containing Fifty-Four Anti-Ministerial, Political, Satiric, and Comic Prints, during Lord Bute's Administration, down to the Present Time*, 6th ed. (London: 1765); Anon., *The Comick Magazine; Or, Compleat Library: Of Mirth, Humour, Wit, Gaiety, and Entertainment. By the Greatest Wits of All Ages & Nations. Enriched with Hogarth's Celebrated (...) Prints.* (London: 1797).

80. Donald, *Age of Caricature*, 50.

81. Fordham, "State," 116.

# Religion and the Late German Enlightenment: Four New Translations of Schiller and Goethe

*Paul E. Kerry*

The four translations presented here of little-known pieces by Friedrich Schiller and Johann Wolfgang von Goethe provide bright glimmers of late German Enlightenment thinking and its engagement with religion.[1] The two pieces by Schiller spring from anecdotal historical episodes, one involving far-flung transatlantic Jesuit settlements and the other an incident that took place much nearer to home in Thuringia; the latter piece is a report of female boldness and courage against the backdrop of a full-fledged Reformation war. The two pieces by Goethe are concerned with pressing topics of his time. He takes the occasion, in response to a question from university students, to offer his visionary view of how religious harmony and coexistence could replace religious rancor and division. He also sets forth his suggestions for how to commemorate the Reformation without causing religious strife in Germanic lands exhausted by the Napoleonic wars.

The two Schiller prose pieces were published in 1788 under the titles "Jesuitenregierung in Paraguai" ("Jesuit Rule in Paraguay") and "Herzog von Alba bei einem Frühstück auf dem Schlosse zu Rudolstadt im Jahre 1547" ("The Duke of Alba at a Breakfast in the Rudolstadt Castle in the Year 1547").[2] The two Goethe prose pieces are an article from the periodical *Morgenblatt* (referred to simply as the *Morgenblatt* essay) published in 1816 and another article presumably written in the same year but published posthumously in 1895, given the title "Zum Reformationsfest" ("On the Reformation Festival"). These writings provide snapshots of German Enlightenment thinking both before and after the French Revolution, the ensuing Napoleonic wars, and the French military occupation. Of course, these themes are not exhausted by these writings by two of Germany's most acclaimed authors, but they are productive lenses through which to understand the late German Enlightenment's engagement with religion.

Schiller's "Jesuit Rule in Paraguay" (see appendix A) has a rich Enlightenment context and specifically fits into Schiller's interest in Jesuits, intrigue, and conspiracy theories.[3] Ritchie Robertson shows how Schiller deployed the figure of the Jesuit in some of Schiller's most well-known works, including *Wallenstein*, *Maria Stuart*, *Fiesco*, and "Der Geisterseher" ("The Ghost-Seer").[4] Schiller's Jesuit characters are entangled in machinations and schemes, topics that drew on headlines and rumors and catered to the tastes of the late eighteenth-century public. They also reflect the trends of anti-Jesuitism and anti-Catholicism that swept through Europe. The suppression of Jesuits gained momentum in the latter half of the eighteenth century in Catholic kingdoms such as Portugal and Spain (and their colonies), France, and Austria. This suppression was also advanced by the Pope in 1773.[5]

The specific historical context for Schiller's "Jesuit Rule in Paraguay" was that of the Jesuit reductions in the seventeenth and much of the eighteenth centuries.[6] The Jesuit order had established a series of settlements in Latin America that crossed the frontiers of present-day Paraguay, Argentina, and Brazil. The Jesuits used these settlements to exploit the labor of natives and proselytize them, but the settlements also protected natives to some degree from slave traders. Montesquieu's *Spirit of the Laws* (1748), Voltaire's *Candide* (1759), and other Enlightenment writings reflect an awareness of the Jesuit reductions in Paraguay and show that the distant native settlements entered the European imagination as a foil to European civilization.[7] Spain and Portugal disputed the geographical boundaries in their New World colonies during the tumultuous period of the War of the Austrian Succession and the Seven Years' War.[8] The Spanish-Portuguese treaty of 1750, known as the Treaty of Madrid, attempted to settle the border dispute between the two kingdoms. This endeavor required the relocation of nearly thirty thousand native inhabitants, often called "Indians," who lived in several Jesuit settlements within the disputed area. The natives refused to migrate voluntarily and fought to defend their homes, their way of life, and their relative economic prosperity. The Spanish and Portuguese sent a combined military force that crushed all resistance.[9] As Robertson describes: "Many strange stories about these events reached Europe. It was widely believed that the Jesuits held a vast and wealthy empire with an Indian as its nominal ruler, and that the Jesuits had commanded an Indian army."[10] These so-called reports from the field were often fanciful and, as with Voltaire's or Franklin's use of such field reports, could be employed as vehicles for Enlightenment criticism of superstition, rural narrowness, and religion.

Schiller's "Jesuit Rule in Paraguay" begins with the capture of two richly adorned and well-armed Europeans who were fighting with questionable courage alongside the native inhabitants against the military forces, Spanish or Portuguese, sent to oust the Indians. Only under the duress of interrogation and torture do the two suspicious Europeans reveal that they are in fact Jesuit priests. They claim that they are chaplains and that their aim was to pacify the unbridled and violent passions of the Indians. This reflects a Eurocentric prejudice wherein native peoples are viewed as being more prone to impulse and recklessness and less given to reason and restraint. Upon a search of the priests' belongings, a notebook is found with a secret text written in cipher along with its key. The rest of Schiller's piece is a purported reproduction of the decoded subject matter in the notebook.

The strategy here is to present the voice of a disinterested editor who is sharing the uncovered contents of this notebook, which turn out to be Jesuit instructions for the natives. The reader is meant to be shocked and repulsed by what is revealed by the neutral editor. The notebook is a set of "commandments" written for the native fighters that highlights the blatant perversion of the Christian (Catholic) faith and the sophistry and priestcraft of the Jesuits—their deceit, scheming, and exploitation and mistreatment of the natives. The notebook teaches that Jesuits are angelic beings to whom natives owe the strictest obedience (and that any deviation on the part of the natives is punished by eternal damnation). All material fruits of Indian labor are delivered to the Jesuits. The priests' role is to teach natives to become skillful in exterminating those deemed enemies of God, identified as white Europeans, particularly the Spanish and Portuguese. The notebook inculcates hatred of Europeans and commands murder and daily acts of violence against them, with the promise of eternal life and maidens in paradise. Sexual violence against women is also condoned.

Schiller's anecdote magnifies and amplifies the Enlightenment attack on the abuse of religion by profligate, reprobate, and depraved clerics. Religion is shown to be merely a pretext for the most vile and debased behavior of hypocritical priests, whose distorted teachings corrupt the indigenous inhabitants. The natives are clearly manipulated pawns in thrall to renegade and devious Jesuit cabals for their expansionist political and military aims. The special bond that ought to exist between a teacher and learner, missionary and convert, has here been grossly perverted. The spiritual bankruptcy of the priests and their flagrant abuse of the natives are completely exposed in "Jesuit Rule in Paraguay."

In Schiller's "The Duke of Alba at a Breakfast in the Rudolstadt Castle in the Year 1547" (see appendix B), a far different ethos prevails. When powerful men who are meant to be honorable have reneged on a promise, it is a less powerful but truly honorable female who courageously intervenes to protect her townspeople. This piece has been classified by scholars as a work of literary prose with a "tension and terseness"[11] that anticipates Heinrich von Kleist's masterful short stories. It blends the characteristics of a historical anecdote and an eighteenth-century morality tale, in which the "focus is on moral character and event over actual history."[12] It was not uncommon for Enlightenment histories to highlight character and leadership. Nevertheless, there is a specific historical context to the brief but compelling anecdote. It is set in the early modern period, and its background is the religious and political conflict occurring in the Germanic lands during the Reformation. In particular, the events it portrays take place in the wake of the Schmalkaldic War, directly after the Battle of Mühlberg in Saxony in 1547. During this battle, an alliance of Protestant princes was vanquished by a coalition of Catholic rulers under the command of the Holy Roman Emperor, Charles V.[13]

In the narrative, as the imperial Spanish part of the army withdraws, a Protestant countess in Thuringia, Catherine of Schwarzburg, is able to secure from the Emperor himself a guarantee of protection. He promises that her townspeople and their property will be spared from looting and other degradations from the passing troops. In return, she promises to provide the army with provisions. She carefully takes other precautions to safeguard her people and their possessions.

Catherine is also called on to provide breakfast in her Rudolstadt castle for the victorious Catholic princes, including the Duke of Alba. Alba, known as the Iron Duke, is one of the leading generals of his day, widely respected and feared. During breakfast, Catherine learns that soldiers in several villages were driving off the villagers' cattle. She complains to the breakfasting Catholic princes, but they laugh it off as the incidental collateral damage of war. In a daring move, Catherine orders her servants to quietly arm themselves and politely surround her guests. She then declares her disappointment at how abysmally the Emperor's word has been kept. This incredibly bold and potentially fatal intervention works, and the oxen are restored to her people. The anecdote concludes on a note illustrating how she shelters a persecuted Lutheran reformer and theologian.

If Schiller's pieces offer readers the concrete specificity of historical examples, then Goethe's pieces offer a utopian vision of future possibilities. In 1784–1785, Goethe limned the beginnings of an epic poem, *Die Geheimnisse* (*The Mysteries*), that he never completed. The fragment intrigued many of his readers over the years, including a group of intrepid and intellectually curious university students from Königsberg. In late 1815, the students read and discussed *The Mysteries*, and after forming their own interpretation, decided to write to Goethe himself (by that point established as the leading author in the Germanic lands) and ask how he had intended to develop the epic.[14] Their audaciousness was rewarded in a spectacular way that must have exceeded their highest expectations. In the spring of 1816, Goethe not only responded to their query but did so publicly in one of the leading literary periodicals of the day, the *Morgenblatt für gebildete Stände* ("Morning paper for cultured classes"). Thus, three decades after he had first published the fragment, the German master revealed his ostensible purpose. Goethe did so by outlining the narrative sweep of how his planned epic would have progressed.

Why would Goethe, a storied and established figure throughout Europe, have written back to a small group of student readers? He recognized that young people were attempting to orient themselves in wake of the havoc that Napoleon's wars had wrought throughout central Europe, devastation that included the destruction of life and property, political confusion, and, not least, spiritual malaise.

Goethe explains in his *Morgenblatt* essay (see appendix C) that had he completed *The Mysteries*, his epic would have featured a monk, Brother Markus. This monk would have come upon a remote mountain province, which Goethe likens to the holy mountain Montserrat, thereby evoking in literary shorthand both the geography and spirituality of his own envisioned setting. Brother Markus would have found twelve knights who had withdrawn from the world to lead contemplative lives. These, Goethe continues, would have functioned as representatives of twelve world religions. Brother Markus "would have visited each of the knight-monks in their living quarters and learned, through observation of climatic and national differences, that the finest men from all ends of the earth assemble here, where each worships God in his own most individual way and in stillness." This reflective approach resonated with Goethe, who had felt sympathy with German Pietism in his younger years.[15]

Goethe's outline exhibits a gendered weakness in his framing: the twelve religions are all represented by men only. This evinces a common blind spot in the thinking of Enlightenment philosophers, at least many of the male thinkers.[16] Of course, Goethe's projected epic takes place in an earlier historical age, within traditional male religious and military orders.

Goethe's protagonist, Brother Markus, occupies an anthropological position as he spends time with each knight and observes individual living quarters. The Enlightenment notion that climatic and cultural differences contribute to religious ones mediates a purely theological notion of such differences. Goethe's thinking here reflects that of the theologian and philosopher Johann Gottfried Herder, who also gave credence to the influence of geography on culture.

Moreover, as these representatives of the world's faiths all dwell in close proximity, a hope is put forward that this is in fact possible, not merely theoretically but practically, as a lived reality—namely, that people with different belief systems can get along with each other. It is important to remember that before these men came to this mountain, they had been cavaliers—mounted soldiers. Perhaps Goethe is alluding metaphorically to the European religious wars, suggesting that after centuries of religious conflict, these faiths had matured and lived in concord one with another and that a new dawn of possibility might be on the horizon. Harmonious coexistence was of course a major aim of German Enlightenment writing, not least Gotthold Ephraim Lessing's *Nathan the Wise* on world religions and Immanuel Kant's *Perpetual Peace* on world affairs. In fact, a few decades after Goethe's death, before the end of the nineteenth century, the first Parliament of World's Religions assembled in the United States. In life, Goethe had already heard word of such possibilities as he read about ninety different Christian denominations coexisting peacefully in New York.[17] After the catastrophe of the First World War, an imperfect League of Nations seemed to embody Kant's vision.

The architectural imagery in the *Morgenblatt* essay offers an interesting perspective on the structure of each knight-monk's living quarters. There are walls, a floor, and a ceiling within which each religion may flourish and unfold in uniqueness; where members may worship according to the dictates of their conscience; and where each faith's rituals, traditions, and history may be preserved and celebrated. Perhaps this boundedness represents civil society, a protected social space that allows for religious freedom as well as freedom from religion among its citizens and that insists on the difficult peaceful negotiation of religious and other differences. The implication is that there are boundaries between each worldview, secular or religious. Both make up a part of the landscape, but neither inhabits all of the landscape. A quintessential tension of Enlightenment thought is this recognition of the liminality of interstitial spaces between faiths and between faith and civil society. It is in the interstices that tolerance occurs and humility arises about one's own beliefs vis-à-vis those of others. Goethe read and admired the writings of Benjamin Franklin, who put forward the necessity of religious modesty. Franklin compared a sectarian to "a Man travelling in foggy Weather: Those at some Distance before him on the Road he sees wrapt up in the Fog, as well as those behind him, and also the People in the Fields on each side; but neer him all appears clear—Tho' in truth he is as much in the Fog as any of them."[18]

There is a hint of the Enlightenment's encyclopedic thinking in Goethe's ambitious attempt to be global by insisting on the presence of twelve different faiths. Although twelve religions would certainly not encompass every denomination, and the number does have obvious Christian resonances, Goethe is using the Christian trappings and numerology symbolically to make his expanded vision of religious diversity understandable by drawing on the shared historical and religious heritage of his readers.

In *The Mysteries*, the twelve are not assembled around Jesus as their Master, but "they have gathered themselves around a man called *Humanus*," for they felt an affinity with him. Goethe is of course only providing an outline to these students who have sought to plumb the depths of meaning of his epic fragment; even so, he is uncharacteristically blunt in sending the message that the humane or humanity is at the center of this set-apart group of men who strive after holiness. Indeed, Goethe describes Humanus as the "mediator" of this hallowed band.

In Christology, the role of Jesus as mediator between humanity and the divine is well established. Yet Goethe suggests here that Humanus mediates interconfessionally. As religions become more humane, they become more peaceful and fulfill their loftiest ends. It seems that Goethe puts forward an Enlightenment Golden Rule, a Goethean Rule, for all religions. In his view, each faith flourishes and becomes the best version of itself as its members focus on their common humanity with members of other faiths and treat them humanely. In the *Morgenblatt* essay, Goethe expresses the desire to show readers that in each religious tradition mediated by Humanus, "one would have found each manifestation of God and virtue, no matter how marvelously expressed, to be worthy of all honor and love."

The phrase "no matter how marvelously expressed" reveals Goethe's vision of the diversity of religions in the broadest possible ways. This thought was reflected four years prior to Goethe's penning of *The Mysteries*, when he wrote a letter to the Swiss pastor Johann Kaspar Lavater, who had been pressing for Goethe's conversion. The letter contains this line: "In our Father's apothecary shop are many prescriptions."[19] This is clearly an allusion to John 14:2: "In my Father's house are many mansions." Goethe's hermeneutic implies a multiplicity of pathways to spiritual well-being. He presses not merely for religious toleration but for religious appreciation. His aim is to challenge readers to overcome their own prejudices about other faiths and instead rejoice that so many manifestations of God and pathways to worship are available.

Goethe's sketch continues with the news that after a long life in the community, Humanus prepares to depart. Through his writing, Goethe signals that this departure occurs when religions are able to embody a humane spirit and lay aside abuse, deceit, hatred, and hypocrisy. This idea fits the trajectory of the German Enlightenment set out by Lessing, Kant, Herder, and others—namely, that maturity is linked to a religion's development and ability to accept responsibilities concerning humanity. The European religious wars of the earlier centuries—which threatened to continue in the late eighteenth century with the infamous Revocation of the Edict of Nantes—could now be overcome if each faith embraced the dignity of humanity as one of its highest ideals.

Goethe, who as a German understood the atomizing effects of the Reformation, replaces the three major religions with twelve and uses the plural title *Die Geheimnisse* to underscore religious diversity and, by implication, heterodoxy. There are many religious mysteries, each with truth claims, that must learn to live with one another in peace. As Goethe once commented in a letter a decade after he wrote the *Morgenblatt* essay: "Fortunately, we are left with the conviction that many things that would like to exclude each other can and must co-exist: the World Spirit is more tolerant than one thinks."[20]

There is one more crucial element to Goethe's outline of *The Mysteries* that must be elucidated. He employs a strategy that Mozart used in *The Magic Flute* (1791): the reader becomes a participant. Goethe is subtle and yet linguistically explicit about this transformation. He changes the word that he wields to describe the reader from that of a passive "listener" to that of an active "participant." Just as members of the audience find themselves initiated into Enlightenment thinking in the same way that the protagonists are initiated into the Mysteries of Isis in *The Magic Flute*, Goethe holds out hope that readers would have become more tolerant, appreciative, and humane towards the wondrous diversity of beliefs in the same way that Brother Markus (who is projected to have replaced Humanus) would have done.

Goethe applied this thinking about the peaceful coexistence of religions to his own context. The year 1817 marked a great anniversary in Germany: the tercentenary of the Reformation, which, in custom, began with Martin Luther supposedly nailing his ninety-five theses to the Castle Church door in Wittenberg on 31 October 1517. One of Goethe's closest friends, the musician Carl Friedrich Zelter, wrote to Goethe to inquire whether the subject of the Reformation might be suitable for a cantata.[21] The fruitful letter exchange with Zelter in November 1816 stimulated Goethe's thoughts on the actual celebration of the Reformation itself.[22] What were the possible social and political ramifications of celebrating the Reformation in the Germanic lands as they sought to heal, regroup, and rebuild after the madness and cruelty of Napoleon's military campaigns that had ended in his ultimate defeat only a little over a year ago?

Goethe penned an essay that captured his thinking on the practical implications of celebrating the Reformation. This essay, "On the Reformation Festival" (see appendix D), reveals Goethe's deep concerns about how divisive a national celebration of the Reformation could be, given that members of other faiths lived in the German territories, including many Catholics who feared "jeering arrogance as well as new division and separation."

Goethe wondered how it would be possible for German Lutherans to joyfully celebrate this important anniversary without alienating other religious denominations. He was under no illusion that Protestantism and Catholicism could be reconciled, for he understood that their differences were not merely theological but also concerned completely different worldviews on authority. Moreover, if Protestants chose to celebrate on the traditional date of October 31, this might offend Catholics because that was the day Luther "declared an irrevocable war on the Papacy." Goethe reasoned: Why not select a different date?

Goethe also held that the meaning of the Reformation could be more broadly interpreted to encompass self-reformation and general protests against injustice. He importuned elsewhere: "We must reform ourselves and protest against others on all days, if not in the religious sense."[23] Goethe believed that a central element of the Reformation was protest, a positive right and personal responsibility that, according to him, nests in the freedom of thought.

In "On the Reformation Festival," Goethe is primarily concerned with helping Germans move toward harmonious coexistence and cooperation. Ultimately, he sets forth that by selecting a date in October associated with another celebration, the negative effects of a narrower confessional festival could be subsumed into a national celebration. He muses that by commemorating the Reformation along with the German victory at Leipzig (known as the *Völkerschlacht*, or Battle of the Nations, October 16–19, 1813), all Germans would be able to celebrate. This would frame Luther's achievement (a stand against tyrannical rule over religious thought) as the equivalent of the overthrow of Napoleon's armies (a revolt against tyrannical political rule). Both of these events were monumental acts of protest in the name of liberty—religious and political.

Goethe also had practical reasons in mind for celebrating the Reformation on a different day. Germans would feel the economic squeeze if both celebrations were held within a couple weeks of each other; moreover, celebrating the events separately would be emotionally exhausting. Another salient reason echoes his concern in his *Morgenblatt* essay. He argues that if both events were celebrated within two weeks of each other, the Reformation festival would call to remembrance "conflict and discord" and cause a celebrant to "tell himself that he must separate himself from those with whom he celebrated fourteen days previously and to whom he felt deepest and strongest alliance and now through this separation offend them."

On the other hand, merging the two celebrations into one festival might help transcend religious division and inspire unity among Germans, who existed in a patchwork quilt of various polities. Goethe sought to "edify" all in celebrating the "freedom of the nation from foreign domination and the freedom of thought from doctrinaire restraints."[24] Certainly the defense against Napoleonic invasion and

French imperialism was transregional and interdenominational.[25] Yet, Goethe envisioned an even greater possibility, one that might transcend nationalism; he thought that this celebration was an opportunity to create "a festival of purest humanity."

Goethe wanted to go beyond a specifically Christian festival and imbue a spirit that would uplift all, "not only the Christians, but also Jews, Muslims, and heathens." In his attempt to break out of a dominant Western religious paradigm, he introduced a new concept, that of an inclusive "Welftfest," or global festival, that would produce a joyful and loving "harmony."

Goethe and Schiller were deeply engaged in the Enlightenment effort not only to address religious hypocrisy and abuse but also to draw on the highest religious ideals and practices to foster a flourishing civil society. May these new translations of four of their overlooked texts throw fresh light for anglophone readers on these and other themes in the relationship between the German Enlightenment and religion.[26]

## Appendix A: "Jesuit Rule in Paraguay"

*Friedrich Schiller*[27]

In a military operation that preceded the Battle of Paraguay, waged between the Jesuits and the united Spanish-Portuguese army on September 12, 1759, two Europeans who had fought with doubtful bravery were captured along with other Indian prisoners. Both were dressed completely differently from the remaining prisoners. They wore red Hussar riding attire, from which two small sleeves dangled from the shoulders. Their helmet was adorned with a plume of red feathers, and both wore a large chain of diamonds around their necks. Their horses were likewise richly adorned. Their weapons consisted of a large saber and a musket. When the men were undressed, an exceedingly fine breastplate was found on their bodies, as well as a short pistol and two daggers. The Indians who were captured with them, fell to their knees reverentially as the Europeans appeared before them and the Indians smote themselves upon the breast—while they pronounced repeatedly the word *Kau*. One of the Europeans seemed to accept this homage with embarrassment; however, the Indians were no less worshipful. The European uttered not a word. He was beaten and tortured; some involuntary grunts in Portuguese were pressed out of him owing to the pain, but that was all that one obtained from him. The other one proved to be more open and freer and soon admitted that he was a Jesuit. He had, he claimed, led his Indians into battle as their chaplain and spiritual support, to check, as he stipulated, their excessive rage and to inculcate in them a milder attitude towards the enemy. Finally, he revealed that he was Father Rennez and the other prisoner, prompted by his colleague's example, grew more talkative and confessed that he was a Jesuit and chaplain to the Indians, and that his name was Father Lenaumez. As their pockets were searched, a small book was found, the discovery of which made them extremely uneasy. It was written in unknown ciphers; however, a key in Latin was contained in the margin. This script at first appeared to be an Indian war law, but turned out to be the main principles of the religion, which the Jesuit order had wanted to instill in their Indian subjects. I share them here because they should interest inquisitive people and perhaps impart some information about Jesuit rule in Paraguay.

Hearken, o man! The commandments of God and of holy St. Michael:

1. God is the aim of all human actions.
2. God is the source of all courage and strength.
3. Courage is a virtue of the body as well as of the soul.
4. God does not do anything without reason.
5. Courage is given to people so they can defend themselves.
6. People must defend themselves against their enemies.
7. The white men are the enemies, who come from far-off regions to wage war, and are accursed of God.
8. The Europeans, for example the Spanish and Portuguese, are some of these people cursed by God.
9. God's enemies cannot be our friends.
10. God commands that we wipe out his enemies and advance into their lands, in order to exterminate them.
11. To destroy one cursed by God, such as a Spaniard, one must also be willing to lose one's worldly life, so that one gains an eternal one.
12. Whosoever speaks with a European or understands their language will be condemned to hell fire.
13. Whosoever kills a European will be blessed.
14. Whosoever spends a day without having carried out an act of hatred and execration against a European will be damned to eternal fire.

15. God allows him who despises worldly possessions and is constantly ready to contend with the devil's minions to do as he pleases with a woman.
16. Whosoever falls in battle against the Europeans will be sanctified.
17. Whosoever fires a cannon against the enemies of God will find divine favor, and all of his sins will be forgiven him.
18. Whosoever, despite great danger to himself, recaptures a castle and a fortress that white men unlawfully occupy, shall amongst all the damsels of heaven take for himself a beautiful wife.
19. Whosoever causes the enlargement of the borders of our kingdom shall take four beautiful wives from amongst all the daughters of God.
20. Whosoever is the means of extending our weapons to Europe will have many beautiful maidens in paradise.
21. Whosoever is devoted to the fruits of the earth shall not enjoy the fruits of heaven.
22. Whosoever fathers more children will have more glory in heaven.
23. Whosoever drinks wine shall not enter into the kingdom of God.
24. Whosoever does not hearken to his Kau and is not humble, will go to hell.
25. The Kau are sons of God who came from heaven through Europe that they might help the peoples of the earth oppose the enemies of God.
26. The Kau are angels of God who have descended to the nations to teach them how one enters God's kingdom and the skill of exterminating God's enemies.
27. All fruits of the field and products of labor are to be offered to the Kau so that they can be used to eradicate the nations that are friends of the devil.
28. Whosoever falls from the grace of his Kau and dies will not be sanctified in the hereafter.
29. Whosoever pleases the highest Kau will be sanctified.
30. Every man is subject to his Kau and is to go whithersoever bidden, give whatsoever is demanded, and do whatsoever is commanded.

31. People are on the earth to fight against the devil and his friends so that they may enter the kingdom of God, where there is eternal joy and the incomprehensible satisfaction of every desire.

# Appendix B: "The Duke of Alba at a Breakfast in the Rudolstadt Castle in the Year 1547"

*Friedrich Schiller*[28]

While leafing through an old chronicle of the sixteenth century (*Res in Ecclesia et Politica Christiana gestae ab anno 1500 ad an. 1600* by J. Soeffing, Doctor of Theology, Rudolstadt, 1676), I find the following anecdote, which for more than one reason deserves to be rescued from oblivion. I find the story confirmed in a text with the title, *Mausolea manibus Metzelii posita* by Fr. Melch. Dedekindo [1638]. One can also look it up in Spangenberg's *Adelspiegel*, part I, volume 13, page 445.

A lady of German nobility, descended from a family distinguished already in former times through heroism, and that had given the German Empire an Emperor, nearly made the dreaded Duke of Alba tremble through her resolute conduct. In 1547 when Emperor Charles V and his army, after the Battle of Mühlberg, were passing through Thuringia to Franconia and Swabia, the widowed Countess Catherine of Schwarzburg, by birth Princess of Henneberg, obtained from him, through a confidential correspondence, a letter of protection that would guarantee her subjects would not suffer at the hands of the (Imperial) Spanish army. In exchange, she promised to deliver bread, beer, and other provisions from Rudolstadt at a reasonable rate to the Spanish troops who would cross at the bridge of the Saale River. She was prudent and quickly dismantled the bridge that lay very near the town and had it rebuilt further away, so that the close proximity of the town would not lead her rapacious military guests into temptation. At the same time, she granted permission to the inhabitants of every village that lay on the army's path to safeguard their most valued possessions in the Rudolstadt castle.

Meanwhile, the Spanish general approached the town, accompanied by Duke Henry of Brunswick with his sons, and sent a messenger ahead to request breakfast in the castle of the Countess of Schwarzburg for him and his party. Such a modest request, made by one who stood at the head of a wartime army, could not really be refused. His Excellency would be welcome to partake, was the answer, if he could be satisfied with what the house could offer. At the same time, her reply did not fail to mention the conditions of the letter of protection and a reminder that its promise ought to be conscientiously observed.

A friendly reception and a well-furnished table awaited the Duke at the castle. He had to admit that the ladies of Thuringia kept an excellent kitchen and understood the obligations of hospitality. They had hardly sat down when a messenger called the Countess out of the dining hall and informed her that in a few villages the passing Spanish soldiers had used force to drive off the peasants' cattle. Catherine was the mother of her people; she held that an injustice against the poorest of her subjects was also an offence against herself. Incensed over his broken promise, yet not abandoning her presence of mind, she ordered her servants to arm themselves with all speed and silence, and to bolt the castle gates; she then made her way to the dining hall, where the princes were still at the breakfast table. Here she complained to them in the most moving language of the plight of her subjects, and how poorly kept had been the word of the Emperor. They answered her with laughter and said that such little accidents were merely a convention of war and unavoidable. "We shall see about that!" she exclaimed indignantly. "My poor subjects must have returned them that which is theirs, or by God!"—She raised her voice in a threatening manner, "*the blood of princes for the blood of oxen!*" With this terse declaration she left the room, which was filled a few moments later with armed men, who, with sword in hand, yet with much deference, positioned themselves behind the chairs of the princes, ready to serve breakfast. At the entrance of this battle-ready company, the Duke of Alba turned pale; astonished, the other guests looked at one another mutely. Cut off from the army, surrounded by a superior force of sturdy men, what remained for him to do except, no matter the conditions, be patient and reconcile with the offended lady? Henry of Brunswick collected himself first then burst into loud laughter. He seized the reasonable way out by turning the entire scene into something jovial, and extolled the Countess for her maternal concern for the welfare of her people and the resolute courage she had demonstrated. He bade her be at peace and took it upon himself to obtain from the Duke of Alba that which fairness required. Moreover, he actually brought the latter to the point where the Duke, on the spot, wrote up an order to his army to return straightway the stolen livestock to their owners. As soon as the Countess of Schwarzburg learned that the restoration had taken place, she thanked her guests most cordially, and they, in turn, with much courtesy took their leave.

It was undoubtedly this event that earned the Countess Catherine of Schwarzburg the sobriquet the Heroic. She is renowned for her steadfast efforts to advance the cause of the Reformation in her lands, already introduced there by her husband, Count Henry [XXXII], to abolish the monasteries and improve instruction in schools. She gave protection and support to many Protestant preachers who suffered persecution for the sake of religion. Among these was Caspar Aquila, pastor of Saalfeld, who, in his younger years had accompanied the army of the Emperor to the Netherlands as a military chaplain. Because he refused to christen a cannon ball, he was stuffed into a mortar by unruly soldiers to be shot into the air, a fate he, fortunately, escaped because the powder would not ignite. A second time his life was in danger and a price of 5,000 florins placed on his head because the Emperor was enraged against him for attacking his *Interim*[29] measures against Protestant territories from the pulpit. Catherine allowed him, at the request of the townspeople of Saalfeld, to be conveyed secretly to her castle, where she hid him for several months and cared for him with the noblest human kindness, until he could be seen in public again without fear. She died universally honored and mourned in the fifty-eighth year of her life and in the twenty-ninth year of her rule. The church in Rudolstadt safeguards her remains.

## Appendix C: "*The Mysteries*: A Fragment from Goethe"

### *Johann Wolfgang von Goethe*[30]

My worthy countrymen, especially the younger ones, have for a long while shown me much trust, which seems to be increasing at present. Each and every sincere striving for the good and beautiful is encouraged anew, especially after liberation from external pressures and restoration of inner peace, each sincere struggle for the good and beautiful may again be found favorable. However, it is seldom that I can express the gratitude and empathy with which I recognize this new state of affairs, for time is too short to do justice to such worthy obligations. Consequently, to my own regret, many letters remain unanswered, many questions unexplained, many problems unsolved.

I can report, however, that among this multitude of wishes and requests, several are to be found which reflect a common interest, as they are repeatedly sent to me; I have therefore undertaken to make explanations on these points by and by in the *Morgenblatt*, and thereby hope as far as is possible to satisfy my distant, often unknown friends and others who perhaps hold similar wishes. May the following contribute to this desired end.

----------------------------------------

A group of young students in one of the most prominent cities of Northern Germany has determined in its meetings to read works of poetry and then discuss them, thereby making profitable use of their hours together. This same society has read my poem,

*The Mysteries*

and given it considerable attention. As the students could not agree upon the meaning of the work, they decided to request of me that I, if possible, clear up the matter, although I must acknowledge that they have shared with me a rather insightful interpretation, which the majority of them apparently agree upon. As I found their endeavor so full of good will, sense, and propriety, I shall eagerly strive to give an explanation; for this enigmatic work has busied the interpretive faculties of many a reader, and I in my literary pursuits will probably never arrive at the point where I can complete it; and so it shall remain as it is now, as it was when its composition was first interrupted in the middle of the eighties.

While I presume that the reader is acquainted with the poem of which we speak, I shall nevertheless provide the following as a synopsis: You will recall that a young monk loses his way in a mountainous region, and at last comes upon a magnificent building lying in a pleasant valley, the outer appearance of which indicates that it is the abode of pious, but enigmatic men. He finds twelve knights who, after surviving stormy lives filled with difficulty, suffering, and danger, have committed themselves to live here and serve God in stillness. A thirteenth, whom they recognize as their captain, is preparing to leave them; by what means, they do not know; but he had recently begun to tell them his life's story, and the monk, whom the company graciously receives, becomes aware of a good part of it. A mysterious night-vision of solemn boys, whose torches light the garden in their hurried procession, concludes the fragment.

With regard to the broader intent, to the general plan, and thereby the purpose of the poem, I shall divulge that the reader is led through a sort of ideal Montserrat, and after he has made his way through various stretches of lofty mountains, rocks, and cliffs, he shall in turn come upon broad and pleasant plains. One would have visited each of the knight-monks in their living quarters and learned, through observation of climatic and national differences, that the finest men from all ends of the earth assemble here, where each worships God in his own most individual way and in stillness.

The reader or hearer would have become aware of the most varied ways of experiencing the world that develop in or are impressed upon humanity through atmosphere, geography, ethnicity, necessity, and habit. This would be represented here, in this place, through outstanding individuals who desire the highest training and education and, although singly imperfect, through community life are worthy and called to express this diversity.

So that this community life may be possible, they have gathered themselves around a man called *Humanus*, which they would not have decided to do had they not all felt a similarity and affinity with him and thereby been drawn to him in some manner. This intercessor has now unexpectedly chosen to depart from them and they give ear to the story of his former exploits. He is not the sole teller of the story, however, for each of the twelve can relate a portion of the great course of his life, they having all come in contact with him at some point along the way.

Here it would have been revealed, that each specific religion had flowered to the pinnacle of its virtue and beneficence at the point when it drew close to—yes, even fully unified itself with—this supreme leader and mediator. These epochs were to be embodied and personified in the twelve representatives, so that each acknowledgement of God and virtue, be it ever so remarkable, would be worthy of all honor and devotion. And now Humanus could in fact part ways with the assemblage, for his spirit had become manifest in every one of the followers, and he now belonged to all, no longer needing any form of earthly raiment himself.

When, according to this outline, the listener, the participant was led in spirit through all lands and times and experienced the most joyous of what the love of God among men in so many forms brings forth, the most pleasant feeling and perception would arise, and neither deviation, misuse, nor distortion, for which every religion has been hated at some point in its history, would have surfaced.

As the entire plot unfolds during Holy Week and the emblem of the order is the cross encircled by roses, it is easy to conclude that the eternal continuance of an exalted humanistic state, sealed by the festival of Easter—the date on which Humanus departs—would have revealed itself pleasingly in this story.

So that such a beautiful society is not left without a head and intermediary, the poor pilgrim, Brother Markus, will be ordained in the high office through miraculous fate and revelation; for he, without studious circumspection, without struggling for the unachievable, and with humility, devotion, and faithful, pious diligence, has proven himself more than worthy to preside over such a company while he yet sojourns upon the earth.

Had this poem been completed and published thirty years ago, as it was envisioned and begun, it would have preceded its time. And although mankind's ideas have broadened in the intervening years, our feelings become purer, our views clearer, it may gratify some to see these generally recognized sentiments clothed in poetic robes, that their convictions might grow firmer, for it is alone through his convictions—on his own Montserrat—that man can find peace and contentment.

Weimar, the 9th of April [1816]. *Goethe.*

## Appendix D: "On the Reformation Festival"

*Johann Wolfgang von Goethe*[31]

The Reformation Festival, to be celebrated on the 30th of November in 1817 [correct date: 31 October] is already causing a considerable commotion in the minds of Germans. The Protestants anticipate this epoch with joy; the Catholics fear jeering arrogance as well as new division and separation that such a day would produce. Many suggestions have been put forward as to how this festival should be celebrated. The thought occurred to me that we should reschedule it for the 18th of October. When this date was chosen for the observance of the Annual Festival it was done so, in a certain sense, by chance. On this day, Luther declared an irrevocable war on the Papacy; nevertheless, there are important days both before and—especially—after this date, which might just as easily have been selected. The Battle at Leipzig, on the other hand, is a definitive festival day, while the entire year of 1817, and the year following, might well be seen as celebratory for the Protestants. As I have thus claimed that the Reformation Festival is a moveable holiday, having only been incidentally set for the 30th [correct date: 31st] of October, I shall endeavor to set forth the justifications, which have persuaded me to offer the suggestion to reschedule.

A celebration of two festivals so close to one another—not even 14 days apart—must detract from the festivity of both, and the second of the two is likely to suffer from a lack of splendor. For the festival on the 18th of October exhausts the economic reserves of many Germans, whose talents or efforts are required for the event; and these, though they willingly give of themselves, desire afterward an interval of repose.

2. A still higher consideration factors in, for not only are the funds reserved for these indulgent donations of talent and the outward décor of the festival depleted; but the spirit of festivity is also exhausted; whoever heartily shares in the celebration, cheer, and feasting, will on the 30th [correct date: 31st] feel a certain emptiness and find himself unable to muster a similar measure of enthusiasm.

3. And in the end, no greater festival can be found in any sense of the term than that of all the German people. It will be celebrated by all believers and is in this sense even more than a national festival; a festival of purest humanity. Nobody asks what is the confession of the man in the territorial reserve, all go unified to church and are edified by the same religious service; all stand together in one great circle about the bonfire, and are illuminated by the same flame. The Spirit lifts all in the remembrance of that day whose glory lies indebted not only to the Christians, but also the Jews, Muslims, and heathens. Imagine the spirit of this great world festival (*Weltfest*) turned back upon a specific church festival in which a person of pure disposition often cannot have a fullness of joy because he is reminded of conflict and discord, a monstrous disaster of some few centuries. And what is worse, that he must tell himself that he must separate himself from those with whom he celebrated fourteen days previously and to whom he felt deepest and strongest alliance and now through this separation offend them. And exactly the delight of a loving harmony one will miss as they stand before their torches and lights of all sorts, which clearly cannot reconstruct the feelings of the previous festival.

In any Protestant region where only few Catholics live, these Catholics will never fail to shut themselves up in their homes during such a festival; and conversely, in Catholic regions, where Protestants are a small minority, these Protestants shall only be granted a celebration of the uttermost stillness.

# Notes

1. See Paul E. Kerry, "'Diesen Kuss der ganzen Welt!' Locating German Enlightenment through the Tolerance Discourse," *Religion in the Age of Enlightenment* 3 (2012): 301–328.

2. See the Appendices for all translations.

3. Schiller found this anecdotal report in a work by Johann Christoph Harenberg, *Pragmatische Geschicte des Ordens der Jesuiten* (1766), and published it with very slight alterations. See NA 19/1, 391. I will reference major Goethe and Schiller editions by volume and page numbers and refer to each as FA (Frankfurt edition), MA (Munich edition), WA (Weimar edition), NA (National Edition): Johann Wolfgang von Goethe, *Sämtliche Werke. Briefe, Tagebücher und Gespräche*, eds. Dieter Borchmeyer et al., 40 vols., Frankfurter Ausgabe (Frankfurt am Main: Deutscher Klassiker Verlag, 1985–2013); J. W. v. Goethe, *Sämtliche Werke nach Epochen seines Schaffens*, Münchner Ausgabe, eds. Karl Richter et al., 20 vols (Munich: C. Hanser, 1985–1998); J. W. v. Goethe, *Goethes Werke*, ed. im Auftrage der Grossherzogin Sophie von Sachsen, 143 vols, Weimarer Ausgabe (Sophienausgabe) (Weimar: Hermann Böhlaus Nachfolger, 1887–1919); Friedrich Schiller, *Schillers Werke*, Nationalausgabe, eds. Julius Petersen et al., 43 vols. (Weimar: Hermann Böhlaus Nachfolger, 1943–).

4. Ritchie Robertson, "Schiller and the Jesuits," *Schiller: National Poet—Poet of Nations. A Birmingham Symposium*, ed. Nicholas Martin, Amsterdamer Beiträge zur neueren Germanistik 61 (Amsterdam: Rodopi, 2006), 179–200.

5. "Christine Vogel: The Suppression of the Society of Jesus, 1758–1773," European History Online, published by the Institute of European History, last modified December 3, 2010, http://www.ieg-ego.eu/vogelc-2010-en.

6. Ibid.

7. Girolamo Imbruglia, *The Jesuit Missions of Paraguay and a Cultural History of Utopia (1568–1789)* (Leiden: Brill, 2017).

8. See *The Jesuit Suppression in Global Context: Causes, Events, and Consequences*, ed. Jeffrey D. Burson and Jonathan Wright (New York: Cambridge University Press, 2015), passim.

9. NA 19/1, 391–392.

10. Robertson, "Schiller and the Jesuits," 192.

11. Nicholas Martin, "Playing with the Rules: Schiller's Experiments in Short Prose Fiction, 1782–1789," in Jeffrey L. High, *Schiller's Literary Prose Works New Translations and Critical Essays*, ed. Jeffrey L. High (Rochester: Boydell and Brewer, 2008), 188–201, 194.

12. Jeffrey L. High, preface to *Schiller's Literary Prose Works New Translations and Critical Essays*, ed. Jeffrey L. High (Rochester: Boydell and Brewer, 2008), xvii–xx, xvii. See also in the same volume Ian Codding's translation, "The Duke of Alba's Breakfast at Rudolstadt Castle in the Year 1547 (1788)."

13. NA 19/1, 395.

14. The letter from the students is found in FA 20, 1473–1475. For a more comprehensive treatment of Goethe's *Morgenblatt* essay and "On the Reformation Festival," see Paul E. Kerry, *Enlightenment Thought in the Writings of Goethe. A Contribution to the History of Ideas* (Rochester: Camden House, 2009), 90–108.

15. Hans-Georg Kemper and Hans Schneider, eds., *Goethe und der Pietismus* (Tübingen: Verlag der Franckeschen Stiftung Halle im Max Niemeyer Verlag, 2001).

16. See Carla Hesse, *The Other Enlightenment: How French Women Became Modern* (Princeton: Princeton University Press, 2010); Karen O'Brien, *Women and Enlightenment in Eighteenth-Century Britain* (Cambridge: Cambridge University Press, 2009); Patricia Fara, *Pandora's Breeches: Women, Science & Power in the Enlightenment* (London: Pimlico, 2004).

17. FA 13, 72.

18. Benjamin Franklin, *Autobiography and Other Writings*, ed. Ormond Seavey (Oxford: Oxford University Press, 1993), 120. See Paul E. Kerry, "From Weimar, with Love: Benjamin Franklin's Influence on Johann Wolfgang von Goethe's Self-Fashioning," *Benjamin Franklin's Intellectual World*, eds. Paul E. Kerry and Matthew S. Holland (Madison, NJ: Fairleigh Dickinson University Press, 2012), 153–166.

19. Letter to Lavater, 4 October 1782; WA IV/6, 66.

20. Letter to Carl Friedrich Reinhard, 12 May 1826; WA IV/41, 30.

21. 4–5 November 1816; MA 20.1, 466. At the same time, a local society in Weimar formulated plans for the construction of a Luther monument. See 14 November 1816; MA 20.1, 474–478.

22. MA 20.1, 477.

23. FA 13, 161.

24. James J. Sheehan, *German History 1770–1866* (Oxford: Clarendon Press, 1993), 406.

25. There were initial pockets of sympathy for the highest ideals in the earliest phase of the French Revolution that had disappeared in the course of the descent into terror, invasion, and occupation. Ulrich Raulff argues that Schiller did not follow this pattern and that no evidence of his sympathy for the French Revolution is found, only his horror at the execution of the French monarch. "Schiller, der Enthusiasmus, die Historie," in *Friedrich Schiller und der Weg in die Moderne*, ed. Walter Hinderer (Würzburg: Königshausen & Neumann, 2006), 325–338.

26. Interest in Enlightenment strands in the Germanic lands seems to be dwindling in the Anglosphere with the decline of German as a secondary school language option and the closure of German departments and majors at some universities. I presented a paper on the late German Enlightenment at the 47th Annual Conference of the British Society for Eighteenth-Century Studies in January 2018 and could not find in the titles of the papers (over ninety panels were offered) any with the word German in it, nor any on an overtly eighteenth-century German topic save one.

27. Translated by Paul E. Kerry and Alan S. Ostler.

28. Ibid.

29. The *Interim* is a 1548 decree of Charles V that attempted to regulate religious affairs after the defeat of the Protestant Schmalkaldic League.

30. Translated by Paul E. Kerry and Brigham Cheney.

31. Ibid.

# Managing Overseas Missions: The SPCK in the Scilly Islands, 1796–1819

*Bob Tennant*

While historians have studied modern Christian missions to the remoter parts of northern Britain, studies on corresponding parts of southern Britain do not seem to exist. The present chapter helps correct this, with the additional consideration that the mission to the Scillies, an archipelago in the Atlantic off the southwestern tip of Cornwall, was to an anglophone population[1] that was culturally underresourced and geographically remote. Whereas the bishop of Nova Scotia could visit the Bermudas by a regular, direct route, the traveler from London, from where the Scillies mission was directed, had to travel via coastwise shipping to Penzance and then by fishing boat. When the secretary of the Society for Promoting Christian Knowledge (SPCK) visited the Scillies in 1798, he completed his voyage from Penzance by the Royal Navy warship HM gun brig *Assault*.[2] The comparison is apt because the Society for the Propagation of the Gospel in Foreign Parts (SPG) and SPCK missions to the Scillies and Canada served as test-beds for future missions to the colonist populations of India, Australia, New Zealand, and South Africa.

I have suggested elsewhere[3] that a synoptic view of the modern Protestant missions (and, beyond them, a general theory that could also include the Catholic and Orthodox missions) might be approached through systems analysis. The present chapter prepares the way for such work by offering a study of the administrative mechanisms of specific missionary transactions. The problems experienced were those typically found in contemporary colonies—the challenge of "New Light" Methodism, conflicts with civil government; tests of mutual loyalty; speed of communications; accuracy in making and implementing decisions; and the balance between corporate policy and local initiative, between management techniques at the center and staff morale on the ground, and between the provision of resources and their acceptability in the local situation.

We will first consider certain aspects of the SPCK's committee structure and then its handling of two episodes: first, the restaffing of the mission in 1796 and, second, the economic crisis of 1818.

## The SPCK Scilly Islands Mission Committee

The SPCK mission to the Scilly Islands was the result of a bequest to the Society in 1752. It was intended as an "off-islands" supplement to the parish on the main island of St. Mary, whose living was in the gift of the lord proprietor, the Duke of Leeds. The mission was launched in 1765 by establishing schools—not churches—on each island. In 1796 the missionary was Revd. Mr. Davies, who had served since 1781. The St. Mary's minister was Revd. Mr. Troutbeck, his predecessor.[4] The islands' schools were dame schools,[5] not charity schools (which were usually conducted by men) and hence did not figure into the statistics published in the SPCK's annual accounts.[6] In 1796 their total roll was 202 children.[7] The missionary on Tresco was described as an "assistant minister,"[8] and the mission's financial affairs, including the disbursement of salaries, were conducted by the St. Mary's minister, who was charged with the religious and educational affairs of St. Mary's and with superintending the schools on the other islands.

The chief surviving record of the SPCK's activity in the Scilly Islands is the minute book of the meetings of its Scilly Islands Mission Committee from 1796 to 1825.[9] The volume dates to December 1796; an entry in the minutes for December 12, 1796, reads: "Resolved to get a minute book and enter past minutes." The secretary, George Gaskin,[10] thus copied into it the previous six months' transactions, beginning with the Extraordinary General Meeting of June 3, 1796, which had been reestablished after a period of inactivity. He made a few obvious mistakes in doing so—most notably, the meeting of November 21, 1796, being recorded as November 28, the date of the following meeting—but there is no evidence that the record was edited. The minutes can be regarded as accurate, and after about December 1796 they are the original fair copy. The book also contains records of some (but not all) Scillies-related decisions by the main SPCK general committee (colloquially, "the board") that do not appear in its own minutes. That the board judged it acceptable to insert its own decisions into the proceedings of the committee indicates the constitutional balance between them. The committee was appointed by the board from among its own membership. It may thus be described strictly as an executive subcommittee. It was not a policy-making body or an instrument of governance, which was the prerogative of the board, and did not have an existence apart from the board's. Its membership was both clerical and lay, but the attendance of a bishop (bishops could attend any meetings) was exceptional.[11] It met on an as-needed basis rather than as part of a cycle of monthly meetings that has become the standard operating procedure in modern administration. Sometimes years passed without the board convening; it had not yet been appreciated that there was a need to routinely integrate board policy discussions with committee executive actions. Thus, there was a high threshold to be overcome for an operational matter to be considered in the strategic context (by the board), and, consequently, there was an institutional lack of grip. When the committee finally approached the board for guidance in 1796, the mission in the islands had become almost nonfunctional.

The board's response to the approach on March 15, 1796, was to ask the committee "to consider the State of the Society's Mission to the Islands of Scilly" and "to form a plan, to be reported to the Society, for the proper establishment of the Scilly Mission."[12] This report was put to an Extraordinary General Meeting at the Bartlett Buildings headquarters on Friday, June 3, 1796, attended by twenty-five members and chaired by Samuel Horsley, the bishop of Rochester.[13] Three of the seven clergy present eventually gave the society's anniversary sermon at St. Paul's,[14] while all were not only dedicated attendees of its board but also served the SPG. Some were to serve the national society, too.

The report began with a geographical description of the six inhabited islands: St. Mary's (800 inhabitants), Tresco (600), St. Martin's (150), St. Agnes (200), "Bryer or Brehar" (80), and Sampson (30). The missionary lived on Tresco, and each island had a church, except Sampson. Because of the war with Revolutionary France, there was also a military garrison, although the prominence of military invalids indicates that it was a recuperative staging post to service in active units. A dynamic Methodist presence on the islands was regarded as hostile to the SPCK's objectives:

> Considerable, and indeed, almost insuperable, difficulties have attended the perfect discharge of [pastoral] duties. . . . [Because of these] the Holy Sacrament of the Lord's Supper hath not been administer'd in St: Agnes for a considerable number of Years. . . . the Liturgy of the Church, and a Sermon, have been, in his absence from [the off-islands] . . . read by Lay Readers. – It is apprehended that some occasional duties have been also perform'd by these Persons. It is also apprehended that Sectaries have intruded themselves among the People in all the Islands, even St: Mary's itself, and that their influence has produced no good effects, respecting both the state of Religion, and civil Government. . . . The imperfect manner in which ecclesiastical duties have hitherto been discharg'd in the Island of St. Agnes, so deeply affected the Committee, that they were almost induc'd to recommend it to the Society, to incur the expence of sending a second Missionary, and therefore they have very great satisfaction in informing the General Meeting, that the lord proprietor of the Islands has offer'd to direct his Minister at St: Mary's, to take upon himself the whole charge of the duty at St: Agnes, if the Society will please to allow him a proper compensation for that additional duty. The annual Sum, which the Committee beg leave to propose, is 25£. . . .

> The Proprietor has indicated he will grant land for a house and donate building stone, through his agent.[15]

The Duke of Leeds, as the lord proprietor, could direct the activities of the minister at St. Mary's and remove him "at his pleasure,"[16] which was not legally possible on the mainland. Meanwhile, clerical appointments in the English parochial system were based on a system of patronage that often put the gift of a ministry in the hands of a lay individual. Once in place, the minister was regulated by the diocesan bishop and the church courts.[17] Directing that the St. Mary's minister also take on St. Agnes might not provide additional resources of personnel or finances to resist the Methodist "sectaries," but it did—at least notionally—provide an ordained minister in the place of improvised lay administration that could easily morph into, or stimulate, Methodist arrangements.

## The First Episode: Staffing the Mission, 1796

The first of the two episodes we shall examine is the restaffing of the mission after being unchanged for almost twenty years. The Extraordinary General Meeting had reconstituted the committee as "a standing Committee to effect the great purposes intrusted to their Care."[18] It was thus expected to remain actively in being, to assume greater executive powers, and to make all decisions not directly affecting ministerial prerogatives, such as confirmation of the proposed deployment of ordained missionaries[19] and arrangements for an official inspection.[20] Otherwise, the committee now acted in its own name for the society, for example, writing directly to the vice chancellors of Oxford and Cambridge Universities for possible missionaries.[21]

During the remainder of 1796, the committee met and worked sixteen times, which culminated in a second report. Unusually, a bishop (in fact, Samuel Horsley) attended to lend the weight of his office to any negotiations with third parties, such as the proprietor, who had attended as many as five of its earlier meetings. In the following three years the committee was to meet sixteen, seventeen, and ten times, respectively, before subsiding to between four meetings a year and none. Throughout, it comprised mainly William Jackson (later the bishop of Oxford; nine attendances of the sixteen between June 10, 1796, and December 19, 1796), Charles Layard (fifteen attendances),[22] Richard Shackleford (sixteen),[23] Gaskin (twelve), Adrian Crawford (fifteen), and a Mr. Ackland (thirteen).[24]

The existing ministers, Troutbeck and Davies, were probably too old for the climate and conditions. The new report wrote off both men, and the proprietor consented: "Mr. Tremayne is appointed [by the Duke] to St. Mary's, in the Room of Mr. Troutbeck."[25] Both names suggest a local origin, and neither appears to have possessed a university degree. Following the trawl of the universities, there were three applicants to replace Davies, of whom Reverend David Evans of Wadham College was preferred because he was supported by Dr. Wills, the Oxford vice chancellor[26] (the SPCK was always predominantly led by Oxford men).[27] Evans had been ordained a deacon in 1792 by John Butler, the bishop of Oxford, and ordained a priest in 1794 by John Douglas of Salisbury. Both bishops had preached for the SPG (1784 and 1793, respectively), and Butler had preached for the SPCK as well (1780). Evans had been a grammar school master and was serving as curate of Cholsey in Douglas's diocese.[28] Secretary Gaskin immediately wrote to Davies, ending his employment retrospectively (from July 5) and advising him that no more "Bills" (drafts on an imprest) would be accepted and that his pension and gratuities would not be paid until he had left the islands. The committee intervened to soften this brutality (July 28) but pressed Tremayne to meet Evans (July 21).

Evans was to be paid one hundred pounds per annum (double Davies's salary, as befitted a university graduate), with a twenty-five-pound grant for expenses "on entering upon his Mission." His duties were to "take as much as possible out of the hands of the Lay Readers the performance of every ecclesiastical duty, and . . . he will on week days frequently visit the Islands, for the purpose of baptizing, visiting the sick, and burying the dead." He was not to work a one-day week. The new house, garden (for growing vegetables),[29] and boat were included in the terms of employment.[30] He was thus to have better resources, a smaller population to administer to, fewer islands, and better accommodation. A new, sound boat was essential; local sea conditions on the extreme eastern Atlantic seaboard are notoriously stormy.

The committee was minded to link the improved resources to more detailed management. As early as its meeting on July 21, the committee had decided that "the best move would be to allow the Missionary for the Expences of each Voyage, provided that his Account of them shall not exceed Ten, or Fifteen Pounds a Year." Expenses, that is, would henceforward be paid for individual journeys from an annualized imprest that required frequent reports and strengthened the financial incentive to do parochial work.

Only four days after the confirmation of Evans's employment, the committee learned on August 1 that he had submitted a testimonial from a suspected Methodist. Wills was approached for clarification, but the same meeting pressed on with the proprietor's half of the new arrangement, writing to Tremayne with the offer of twenty-five pounds for the additional duties. By August 8, Wills had arranged a replacement testimonial from Bishop Douglas—a response both reassuringly authoritative and very prompt, especially given that Douglas was probably in Salisbury, not London.[31] Assurance that Evans was not sympathetic to Methodism was necessary because one of his first tasks was to reclaim his church from Methodist use.[32]

The arrangements then broke down. Extended negotiations had been held with Tremayne (committee meetings on October 24, 27, and 31 and November 7) and were then settled on the mainland. With his mother to care for, Tremayne wished to receive the additional twenty-five pounds but proposed to subcontract to an unnamed third party—a widespread contemporary practice wherein bishops would often license such curates retrospectively, if they heard of them at all. The society, however, vetoed the proposal and appointed one Daniel Taylor to the St. Agnes role (November 21).[33] Tremayne finally withdrew altogether from the Scillies and was eventually replaced by the proprietor.[34]

Tremayne had misread the committee. Horsley was so firmly against the practice that in his primary visitation charge at his next diocese, St. Asaph, he felt it necessary to explain his policy at length.[35] An incumbent had the right to appoint a curate if he brought the proposed appointee "before the bishop to make the proper enquiry into the regularity of his orders, the godliness of his life and conduct, and his ability to instruct the people."[36] However, while a diocesan might not have the right to veto the arrangement in principle, any question of an incumbent's nonresidence was a legitimate matter of interest. Tremayne was, moreover, not even an incumbent but subject to dismissal at the proprietor's pleasure. The society in effect made two assertions. The first was that the islands, and the proprietor's parish on them, were not as certainly included in the mainland parochial system as their nominal inclusion in the Exeter diocese might suggest. In this the islands resembled the overseas colonies, where the political and legal underpinnings of ecclesiastical authority to a great extent flowed from the realities of local power. The second assertion was that the society's policy actually determined the scope and methods of missionary clergy's exercise of their ministry. The main distinction between a conventional cleric and a missionary was not that the latter evangelized the heathen but that his ministry was task based and subject to administrative direction.[37]

Before passing to the second episode, it may be noted that the society was at pains to resource the reestablished mission with practical and theological books, and this gives some insight into how its relationship to the population was understood. On December 12, 1796, the society

> resolved to send 200 copies of Mrs Trimmer's Charity School Spelling Book (2 parts); 100 psalters; 100 Testaments Brev.; 100 Bishop Wilson's bound Treatise on the Holy Sacraments; 500 Stonhouse's Admonitions (on sheets); 1 large Bible with Apocrypha and marginal references, two do. Prayer Books; one Nelson's Fasts & Festivals; one Whole Duty of Man; one Osterwald's Arguments; 1 set of the Society's tracts; 1 copy of Duke's Lectures; 1 compleat set of Bp Wilson's Works; 6 of the Selection of Bp Wilson's Sermons; 100 of a pastoral letter from a Minister to his Parishioners; 500 Catechism broke in short questions; 100 Psalters to be presented by the Missionary to the commanding Officer, Major Bowen, to be distributed to the Invalids under his Command; 100 Xian Soldier for the same purpose; 400 Brev. Prayer Books; 12 Cambridge

> Minion and 12 Oxford do.; a folio prayer book for the inscription of Marriages, Baptisms, and Burials, from whence they may be transmitted to the Register at St. Mary's.

This package appears to have served four functions. One was to provide the missionary with a library of basic theology and apologetics; the second, to resource acts of worship in the islands' churches; the third, to minister to the garrison; and the fourth (the folio prayer book), to provide rudimentary civil administration. Providing six sets of Wilson's selected sermons suggests that one might be lodged with a key lay member on each island—potentially a resource for the private study of orthodox texts for those who might otherwise explore the unorthodox. The missionary was a minister and teacher, a church- and school-builder, not an evangelist in the narrower sense familiar to the Methodist circuits.

One omission in this catalog was to be taken up with great vigor by the Evangelicals through the British and Foreign Bible Society (founded in 1804): the mass distribution of the Bible. The prominence of the works of Thomas Wilson, bishop of Sodor and Man from 1698 to 1755, is explained by his having administered to an island population and been deeply interested in the colonial missions. His *Essay towards an Instruction for the Indians*[38] was standard issue to SPG missionaries. The SPCK thus exerted ecclesiastical, theological, and administrative direction over the mission. A year and a half later, the Society's "General & Anniversary" meeting of June 19, 1798,[39] chaired by the 1774 anniversary preacher, Dr. Robert Pool Finch,[40] decided in a discussion of Layard's report from the committee to send Secretary Gaskin to the oslands on a "visitation" of its mission, but not of the proprietor's parish.

## The Second Episode: Infrastructural Developments, 1818–1819

The other episode to be examined happened twenty years later. The Scilly mission had been firmly reestablished, and its oversight was a matter of low-key routine. David Evans remained the society's missionary on Tresco, with the Revd. Mr. Selby serving St. Agnes. The annual published report had shrunk from two pages to a single sentence: "The Rev. Mr. Evans, of Tresco, and the Rev. Mr. Selby, of St. Agnes, continue in the discharge of their respective duties, in the Scilly Islands."[41] Serious problems had arisen, however, that were neither ecclesiastical nor educational. Rather, they were about the economic and political relationship of the islanders to the government and the lord proprietor.

When the committee assembled in Bartlett's Buildings on Wednesday, May 29, 1817, it was for the first time since June 10, 1814, and for only the seventh time in the decade. Over the next twelve meetings (between May 29, 1817, and May 24, 1819) the committee, while less close-knit than in 1796–1797, was distinctly more heavyweight. Its nine members included Secretary Gaskin (twelve meetings), Shackleford (twelve—still an active member), Joseph Watson (nine),[42] and Josiah Pott (seven—archdeacon of London and "Treasurer for General Designs"). Additionally, those attending three meetings included William Howley (the bishop of London and a future primate) and George Pelham (the bishop of Exeter and at least nominally the islands' diocesan). Pelham was deeply interested in missionary policy; he attended the SPG board fifteen times between February 1805 and June 1807 as bishop of Bristol (out of twenty-five meetings, an exceptional commitment). His subsequent twenty-eight attendances (1808–1825) included a group of eight in 1818–1820.[43]

Perhaps by calculation, Pelham attended the May 29, 1817, meeting and consequently chaired the committee, as was his duty under Rule III. This had the fortunate effect of uniting the committee and diocese in his person. The subject was a dispute between Selby and the proprietor's steward. Selby had been active in a campaign by the islanders for exemption from the salt tax (salt was used in the curing of fish, an export to the mainland)[44] and had been removed from the islands' council by the duke because of "[your] Resistance to the Legal Authorities [i.e., the steward, acting on the Lieutenant-Governor's behalf] and your unauthorised Interference in Matters which belong to them." It had not helped that the campaign had been successful.

Matters had clearly been simmering for some years, and the duke even threatened to ask the bishop of Exeter to remove Selby from his pastoral duties, something beyond Pelham's competence.[45] It is very likely that Selby had been cooperating with the local Methodists on this campaign and even putting himself at their head. Gaskin tabled a file on the case from the duke, together with

> several Letters from Mr. Selby, in one of which, dated Apr: ult: he tenders a resignation of his station, as Missionary from this Society to the Scilly Islands. Whereupon, the Committee unanimously Agreed in opinion, that, not being satisfied with the conduct of the Rev. Mr. Selby, in his situation of Missionary to the Scilly Islands, it would be proper for the Society willingly to accept his resignation, but to pay his Salary to Midsummer next.

Thus the committee, on behalf of the society, accepted the version of events given by the proprietor and his steward instead of the version of their own employee, whose resignation was taken as an admission of fault. The committee also refused to meet a builder's claim for money owing on Selby's new house.[46] Not until January 19, 1818, did the committee soften its position, and only then because of the outcome of a case in law:

> Read Letters from the Revd. Mr. Selby, dated, at Penzance, one in December, another Decr: 11, another Dec: 17:—another Dec: 26: & another Jany: 6, 1818, detailing particulars respecting discord between him, & the Steward of Scilly, of ill treatment which he had experienced from the Steward, & other persons, of the appeal he had made to the Magistrates at Penzance, for redress, & of the success wch had attended that appeal, enclosing several papers connected with that discord, & requesting [that] the half years rent . . . for the House occupied by him, might be discharged by the Society. . . . Agreed in opinion that it will not be proper that the draft should be accepted . . . [but] as he appears to have been very ill used, he be authorized, by a Letter from the Secretary to draw upon him for a donation of 20£.

Having accepted Selby's resignation, the society moved quickly (March 2, 1818) to accept a Cornish member's offer to recommend a successor. This was Mr. James Lane, who was not yet in holy orders and who, like Troutbeck and Tremayne before him, did not hold a university degree. According to the committee minutes of May 22, 1818, Pelham ordained him as deacon. Events then moved quickly, the secretary reporting direct to the board. By the committee's October 5 meeting, Evans had been retired and Lane, still a deacon, was appointed not to St. Agnes but to Tresco. This was done by the board, not the committee, which was on vacation. It is notable that when Lane was ordained a priest by Pelham in Exeter Cathedral on November 15, 1818, he was not recorded as being assigned a cure; employment by a missionary society was distinct from incumbency in the church.[47]

Lane's activities were threefold and intertwining. He negotiated with the islands' Methodists, encouraged economic development, and administered the population as deacon and, from November 1818, as priest. This stimulated local demand for additional ministry.

The big issue for the islanders was economic, but the society approached the issue indirectly through its educational provision. On Tresco, and despite the SPCK's support for the islands' dame schools, the Methodists had built (at local expense) and fitted out (at mainland expense) "a commodious room, for the purpose of a School in the week, & a Methodist Chapel on the Sunday & [Lane] suggests that this room would be admirably adapted for a School, upon the System of Dr. Bell, wherein all the Children of the Island might be taught, if an allowance of 20£ per ann: could be made for this purpose."[48] The room had been built two years prior on a plot granted by the proprietor, but no teacher had been appointed, and the building was apparently unused. The committee urged that Lane "endeavour to get entire possession of the Room . . . by an offer to take upon himself, for the Society, the Charge of providing a Master and Books, for the education of the Children of the Island." Simultaneously, he was required to inspect the existing SPCK-funded schools in the Scillies.

The significance of this minute is complex. The National Society, established with SPCK support in 1812, was committed to the Bell "monitor" system of education, which, in contemporary assessments, was low-cost and methodologically scientific.[49] The Methodists, like other dissenting churches and movements, supported the rival "Joseph Lancaster" system, which as developed in imitation of Bell's system but excluded the Church of England's catechism. They had offered the prospect of schooling greatly superior to the old dame school system but had not delivered. The SPCK was now committed to revolutionizing its schools and activating idle infrastructure.[50] An exploratory meeting (October 30, 1818) established that "the Inhabitants . . . have no means of securing this room from the hands of the Methodists," suggesting the prevailing of an off-island Methodist influence, but the islanders would build a schoolhouse themselves if the society could meet the costs of sixty pounds. The committee authorized Lane to buy the Methodists' building at full cost for use as both a "daily" and a Sunday school, with the implication that the SPCK would build if necessary. With a population of six hundred, and assuming three years' schooling, there would have been about sixty potential scholars on Tresco[51] and thus no case economically for two schools. The dispute could not avoid the fact that, from sheer circumstance, an educational monopoly was at stake.

These negotiations exemplified the missionary task of creating infrastructure but also acted as a base for Lane's other main activity. Poverty was chronic and exceptionally severe. The islanders "daily . . . flock around him, for medicines, wine, white bread, apples, meat, & so on." He gave up drinking wine, distributing it instead. He reported that a "public subscription" had been set up "as he had been told for the sole purpose of procuring materials to open a fishery for the future employment & maintinance of the Inhabitants, but he rather thinks that their present exigances are likewise to be supplied from the same source, & that it is to be distributed by a Committee formed of the most reputable persons at St. Mary's."[52]

The phrase "the most reputable persons" implied "non-Methodists" and made an appeal to mutual loyalties. Even before the meeting, someone had suggested the idea of an SPCK-sponsored subscription fund; Howley and Lord Kenyon had each pledged ten pounds, subject to the committee's recommendation to the board. The fund, which had already received three hundred pounds via committee approval during the meeting on January 11, 1819, was put under Lane's supervision, greatly raising his status. He was immediately "added to the Sub-Committee, acting under that established at Penzance."[53] Acting beyond his competence, Gaskin had already "ventured to authorise" Lane to draw thirty pounds in addition to his usual imprest allowance. The committee gave its retrospective approval and agreed on an additional and immediate grant of fifty pounds for "relief to the distressed poor in the other Islands, under the superintendence of the committee for relief at St: Mary's, amongst whom it is presumed Mr: Lane has been enrolled." By this the committee meant the main, Penzance-based committee "for relief at St Mary's." The SPCK was demanding that Lane be invited to join the senior committee too. Lane would now be the leading figure in the project unless he mishandled things. While "presumed" is, in the last analysis, a demand,[54] the unconditional release of such large quantities of funds was a bold action, scarcely conceivable in the previous century.

During the same meeting (January 11, 1819), the committee asked Lane to prepare "plans, by which the unemployed & distressed poor of the Islands may be set to work, for their own lasting advantage, & at the same time be paid for it, from the monies intrusted to the Society's disposal, for their relief, & advantage." In mainland England (especially urban England), this would have meant some sort of workhouse system. One suspects the committee envisaged something like a smokehouse for exporting kippers or mackerel, which would be a significant employer of both men and women. The "fishery Establishment" that had been discussed on the islands turned out to be deep-water boatbuilding. Lane intervened in this project, which would have diverted charitable moneys to the better-off fisher folk. He withheld further disbursements and succeeded in diverting the project into

> small Boats . . . [T]he Boats about to be furnished to the Islanders from another quarter, are of a very different class to those [to

> be] provided by the Society's Collection; the former being much too large for any other purpose but that of deep fishing, so that without the latter, the Inhabitants would be at as great a loss as ever, for Boats to procure Kelp, manure, & for their little trafick, whch he thinks it right to confess that he is still of opinion the 100£ cannot be more advantageously laid out.[55]

The committee agreed and authorized the disbursement of one hundred pounds for small boats, as well as fifty pounds for relief work. This constituted a definite and principled application of the society's strategic policy of creating socially and economically functioning small family units.[56] Also, by concentrating on the production of fertilizer (a scarce necessity, given the islands' paucity of livestock and therefore of animal manure), this policy approached the long-term problem of maintaining adequate food supplies.

The mission benefited substantially from the society's quick and decisive responses to the questions of educational provision and economic self-reliance and from Lane's own accuracy of analysis and vigor of action. Already by late 1818, the presence of a new and active minister, despite being only a deacon, had stimulated a petition for a resident minister on St. Martin's, signed by 101 of its 150 inhabitants. The committee immediately agreed (November 13, 1818) to a joint arrangement with the St. Agnes vacancy. Gaskin was asked to approach Pelham and to ask the St. Martin's inhabitants about the possibility of erecting a house. Pelham concurred, although he was unable immediately to identify a missionary candidate (December 14, 1818).

## Some Concluding Observations

The history of the modern Protestant missions is strewn with examples of doctrinaire micromanagement from the home committees. In the present case, a feature of the management problems will be noticed. Both episodes began with revivals of the committee and radical changes of staffing and resourcing. Thus, previously satisfactory arrangements and the competence of existing staff to introduce solutions for new problems had degenerated parallel to the committee's own activity. Selby, in attempting to take a lead without committee backing on a vital local interest, came to constitute a source of instability unacceptable to the proprietor's steward and was viewed as subversive of the seniority of the St. Mary's minister, whose living, though in the gift of the duke, had been occupied by a former SPCK missionary since 1773. The SPCK, working in close partnership with the proprietor, could not judge independently the merits of any case involving the working relationship. The SPCK came to regret its brutal treatment of its employee, but only when he had proved his case at law, while its compensation to him was ex gratia and therefore without prejudice to its relationship with the proprietor. This was an example of the priority of mission over person that missionaries of all societies had to accept. Troutbeck, in the early stages of the war with Revolutionary France, seems to have prioritized the garrison over the civilian population—its officers would be his social equals at least—while Davies was working at low intensity. Both may be suspected of suffering from low morale and bad practice bred by managerial neglect. Tremayne's case illustrates a clash of cultures and his misunderstanding of the difference between a beneficed clergyman and a missionary employee. The only nonfinancial support accorded by the society to the missionaries was their being acknowledged in the annual published account. Never reported to the wider membership and the reading public were the issues discussed in the present chapter. These were featured only in the committee minutes, not even those of the board—and the committee met only in times of operational crisis. The mission was perhaps more isolated than if it had been in Canada, where the recently established bishops held visitations. In contrast, the first "visitations" to the islands were not by the bishop of Exeter but by Gaskin in 1798 and again in 1819; "visitation" was a courtesy term, for Gaskin was not playing an ecclesiastical role but a managerial one on behalf of an employer with the right to dismiss. The diocesan bishop's role at St. Mary's, even by 1819, was restricted to ordaining those would-be clergy who were not graduates. Informally, St. Mary's was a "peculiar."

In the second case study, the fixed points—the speed and creativity of decision-making and communications between the Penzance committee, the missionary in the islands, and the society in London—were remarkable.

Together, working by mutual trust and establishing a dominant financial weight, they secured the position of the church in the Scillies from being overwhelmed by the "New Light" Methodists (who were seen as sectarian), laid the groundwork for a modern educational system, and offered economic subsistence to the many, rather than comparative comfort to the few. The only improvisation was Gaskin's unauthorized increase of Lane's imprest. Apart from that, the Scilly Islands represented a textbook application of policy, even if, behind the record, it is easy to discern the extreme austerity of the islanders' lives. The main shortcoming of the society's remote management was its failure to require regular committee meetings and thus maintain governance as well as crisis management. This affected the missionaries' morale, inflicted injustice on Selby, and ended other missionaries' service too abruptly, especially that of Davies. Poor governance led to failures of management, but this prevented the committee from developing an excessively schematic system of control. A healthy balance was maintained between the prerogatives of the center and the missionaries' judgments about delivering spiritual, educational, and pastoral support to isolated communities.

The Cambridge University Library's permission to quote from the SPCK MS archives is gratefully acknowledged. This article is the product of research financed by a British Academy grant.

## Notes

1. There is no indication of any language barrier (the Cornish language being only a century from near extinction), whereas, in other domestic missions, the SPCK published Welsh and Manx Bibles. The Society in Scotland for Promoting Christian Knowledge published a corresponding Gaelic version.

2. 1799 Account, pp. 142–143, appended to Thomas Rennell's Anniversary Sermon.

3. Bob Tennant, *Corporate Holiness: Pulpit Preaching and the Church of England Missionary Movement, 1760–1870* (Oxford: Oxford University Press, 2013), introduction. The present essay might be read in association with the second chapter of *Corporate Holiness*. For an extended discussion of the term *missionary*, see chapter 1 of the same work.

4. SPCK Accounts for 1779, pp. 91–93, appended to Robert Markham's *Anniversary Sermon* (London: Francis and Rivington, 1779) and for 1780, pp. 11–12, appended to John Butler's 1780 *Anniversary Sermon* (London: Rivington, 1780).

5. This is confirmed in SPCK secretary Gaskin's report of his visitation and published in the 1799 Account, p. 146.

6. The SPCK's published annual reports were contained in annually updated "Accounts [of the SPCK]," and included constitutional, narrative, and financial elements.

7. SPCK Account, pp. 133–135, appended to George Isaac Huntingford's *1796 Anniversary Sermon* (London: Rivington, 1796).

8. See successive annual Accounts.

9. Cambridge University Library, SPCK.MS A11/1.

10. Gaskin, of Trinity College, Oxford, succeeded his father-in-law as secretary of the SPCK in 1783. See *Oxford Dictionary of National Biography*, W. M. Jacob, "Gaskin, George (1751–1829)."

11. This informal concession paralleled the bishops' constitutional rights in the SPG, an "incorporated" society in which a bishop, once "erected" to membership, became one of the individuals who collectively formed the legal person that was the society.

12. SPCK.MS A1/32.

13. Horsley was a leading conservative theologian and dedicated diocesan bishop whose series of charges was well-respected and referenced by his peers. He was also a consistent attendee at the SPG Board with almost twice the rate of attendance as the average: 41 Boards as a bishop in 148 months. See Tennant, *Corporate Holiness*, appendix 1.

14. Horsley in 1793, Henry Whitfeld (spelled "Whitfeild" in the minute book) in 1798, and John Buckner (as bishop of Chichester) in 1800. Technically, the anniversary was that of the Society of Patrons of the Anniversary Meeting of the Charity Schools (of the Cities of London and Westminster), but the SPCK sponsored the event financially and arranged the preachers.

15. MS A11/1: Extraordinary General Meeting, June 3, 1796, Report of the Committee. In the present article, transcriptions pay minimal attention to the originals' orthography and entirely omit paragraphing and other features of layout.

16. SPCK.MS A11/1, Report to the Extraordinary General Meeting of June 3, 1796.

17. Patronage and incumbency are discussed in W. M. Jacobs, *The Clerical Profession in the Long Eighteenth Century, 1680–1840* (Oxford: Oxford University Press, 2007), 74–80.

18. From the Committee's Second Report, appended to the minute of its meeting of November 28, 1796.

19. For example, the Board meeting of 6 December 1796 (SPCK MS A1/32, p. 119).

20. June 19, 1798 Board (SPCK MS A1/32, p. 311).

21. Committee, June 10, 1796; see also Second Report, first page.

22. Charles Layard, of St John's, Oxford, ordained a deacon December 21, 1771, ordained a priest February 27, 1774; died May 21, 1803. Source: Clergy of the Church of England Database (CCEd).

23. Richard Shackleford, of St. John's College, Oxford, a stalwart of both the SPCK and the SPG. Ordained a deacon by Thomas Newton (January 20, 1766) and ordained a priest by Robert Lowth (December 20, 1767). Source: CCEd.

24. The Acland family was subsequently famous in the SPG and colonial church, providing a twentieth-century bishop of Bombay.

25. Committee, July 21, 1796.

26. *Oxford Dictionary of National Biography*, Philip Carter, "John Wills (1741–1806)."

27. Committee, July 21, 1796. As what seems to have been a precaution against disappointment, the vice chancellor's support was mentioned in the year's published Account, p. 151, appended to Edmund Law's 1797 *Anniversary Sermon* (London: Rivington, 1797).

28. CCEd, person ID: 73540.

29. Eventually of three acres (1798 Account, p. 144, appended to Henry Whitfeld's Anniversary Sermon).

30. Initially Evans had to live in Davies's "uncomfortable" old house; see 1797 Account, p. 151, appended to John Law's 1797 sermon.

31. As his pattern of attendance at the SPG Board shows (although his last meeting had been in May 1794), Douglas, like most contemporary bishops, lived in London for the parliamentary sessions and in his diocese in the summer recess.

32. 1797 Account, p. 152. When visiting in 1798 Gaskin found no "Enmity to the Church of *England*, or any Disaffection to Government" among the Methodists (1799 Account, p. 144).

33. The date is recorded incorrectly as November 28.

34. Committee, November 28, Second Report.

35. Primary visitation charge at St. Asaph, August 1806, in *Theological Works*, volume III (London: Longman, 1830), 128–129.

36. Ibid.

37. The Church Missionary Society was to exercise central control even over the marriages of nonordained, locally recruited colonial staff. See Tennant, *Corporate Holiness*, chapter 3.

38. First edition, London: J. Osborn and W. Thorn, 1740. Subsequently published with the main title, T*he knowledge and practice of Christianity made easy to the meanest capacities.*

39. Cambridge University Library: SPCK.MS A1.

40. SPCK Rule III (printed in all published annual Accounts): "That the Chair be filled Monthly by a Choice of one of the Members present, and that at each Monthly Meeting a Chairman shall be declared, who shall preside (except when a Bishop is present) at every Meeting of the Committee, during his Month; but in his Absence, his Place may be supplied by such Member, as the Society, or Committee, shall agree upon for that Day."

41. This example from p. 60 of the Account appended to William Howley's SPCK Anniversary Sermon (London: SPCK, 1814).

42. Founder of an asylum for deaf and mute children in Bermondsey. See *Oxford Dictionary of National Biography*, M. C. Curthoys, "Watson, Joseph (1764/5–1829)."

43. Attendances at SPG meetings, 1751–1870, are given in Tennant, *Corporate Holiness*, appendix 1.

44. The minute book (SPCK.MS A11/1) has, stapled inside its cover, a letter from the Duke of Leeds to the lieutenant governor of the islands, enclosing a letter of August 1813 from the treasury agreeing to receive an annual request from the islanders for this exemption. This agreement did not constitute a binding precedent.

45. This correspondence is similarly enclosed in the minute book.

46. "Agreed in opinion that the legality of these claims cannot be admitted," Committee, December 8, 1817.

47. Committee, December 14, 1818. See also CCEd's "evidence" of Pelham episcopacy for his ordaining of Lane as a priest.

48. Committee, October 5, 1818.

49. Andrew Bell, *Extract of a Sermon on the Education of the Poor* (London: T. Cadell, 1807), e.g., p. 17. See also *An Experiment in Education, Made at the Male Asylum at Eamore, Near Madras* (London: Cadell and Davis, 1805), with its advertising of its "machine"-like and "experimental" nature (pp. 6, 13–14). The present author has discussed the Bell system in several publications, including *Corporate Holiness* (chapter 4) and "Hard Labour: Institutional Benevolence and the Development of National Education," in *Oxford Handbook of the Modern British Sermon 1689–1901*, ed. K. Francis and W. Gibson (Oxford: Oxford University Press, 2012), pp. 365–367 passim.

50. In his *Oxford Dictionary of National Biography* article on Watson, a committee member, W. M. Jacobs notes his activity on behalf of the National Society and the Bell system.

51. Tresco's share of the 202 pupils for all six islands given in the Report.

52. Committee, October 30, 1818.

53. Letter from Mr. J. E. Gordon (evidently one of St. Mary's "reputable persons"), December 23, 1818, reported to the committee of 11 January 1819.

54. During the March 6, 1819, meeting, the committee received a report of Lane's election, communication delayed by bad weather.

55. Letter from Mr. J. E. Gordon, December 23, 1818.

56. Tennant, *Corporate Holiness*, chapter 2.

# Bibliography

Adams, Brooks. *The Emancipation of Massachusetts: The Dream and the Reality*. Boston: Houghton Mifflin, 1962.

Adams, Abigail. "To Mrs. Smith, 10 March 1794." In *Letter of Mrs. Adams, The Wife of John Adams*. Edited by Charles Francis Adams. Boston: Wilkins, Carter, 1848.

Ainsworth, David. *Milton and the Spiritual Reader: Reading and Religion in Seventeenth-Century England*. New York: Routledge, 2008.

Albemarle, reporting Charles Edward's intention to return from France, bringing aid (SP 54/34/4F). State Papers Scotland, 1746. Secretaries of State: State Papers Scotland Series II. National Archives of the United Kingdom.

*Allgemeine Zeitung des Judentums* XVIII, no. 22: 258.

Anonymous. *A Jacobite Satire on the Duke of Cumberland: Britannia Sitting between Prince Charles and Cumberland Weighing Mercy and Butchery*. 1746. Etching. Satires British Stephens Series. British Museum London.

Anonymous. *The Agreable Contrast between the British Hero, and the Italian Fugitive*. 1746. Engraving. Satires British Stephens Series. British Museum London.

Anonymous. *The Agreeable Contrast*. 1746. Engraving. Walter Biggar Blaikie Collection. National Galleries of Scotland.

"Art. 30." *The Monthly Review, or Literary Journal* 20 (1759).

Artem'eva, Tatiana V. *Ot slavnogo proshlogo k svetlomu buduschemu: Filosofiia istorii i utopiia v Rossii epohi Prosveschenia*. St. Petersburg: Aleteiia, 2005.

Asch, Ronald G. *Die Stuarts: Geschichte einer Dynastie*. Munich: Verlag C. H. Beck, 2011.

Atiba, E. "The Rhetoric of Liberty: John Wesley and the Polemics of the American Revolution." Honors thesis, Duke University, 1996.

Augustine. "Reconsiderations." In *On the Free Choice of the Will, On Grace and Free Choice, and Other Writings*, translated and edited by Peter King. New York: Cambridge University Press, 2010.

*Avraam Sergeevich Norov, Puteshestvie k semi tserkvam upominaemym v apokalipsise*. St. Petersburg: Tip. III ontel'nenniia Sobstvennoi e. i. v. kantseliarii, 1847. Reprints, St. Petersburg: Tip. P. P. Soiskin, 1890; Moscow: Indrik, 2005.

Baagø, Kaj. *Vaekkelse og wirkeliv I København og omegn I første halvdel af det 19. Århundrede*. Copenhagen: Gad, 1960.

Baehr, Stephen. *The Paradise Myth in Eighteenth-Century Russia. Utopian Patterns in Early Secular Russian Literature and Culture*. Stanford: Stanford University Press, 1991.

Bailey, Francis. *Supplement to the Account of the Reverend John Flamsteed, the First Astronomer-Royal*. London: Glavard College, 1837.

Bailyn, Bernard. *The Origins of American Politics*. New York: Vintage, 1970.
Baker, Frank. "The Shaping of Wesley's 'Calm Address.'" *Methodist History* 14 (1975).
Bang, Jacob Peter. *De stora väckelserörelserna: en historisk och psykologisk framställning*. Stockholm: Svenska kristliga studentrörelsen, 1926.
Barchas, Janine. "Sarah Fielding's Dashing Style and Eighteenth-Century Print Culture." *ELH* 63, no. 3 (1996): 633.
*Bartleby.com: Great Books Online*. Accessed November 24, 2015. http://www.bartleby.com/297/154.html.
Batalden, Stephen K. "Musul'manskii i evreiskii voprosi v Rossii epokhi Aleksandra i glazami shotlandskogo bibleista i puteshestvennika." In *Voprosy Istorii*. 2004.
Bautz, Friedrich Wilhelm. "Isaac da Costa." In *Biographisch-Bibliographisches Kirchenlexicon*. Edited by Friedrich Wilhelm Bautz. Berlin: Verlag Traugott Bautz, 1993.
Bell, Andrew. *An Experiment in Education, Made at the Male Asylum at Eamore, Near Madras*. London: Cadell and Davis, 1805.
———. Extract of a Sermon on the Education of the Poor. London: T. Cadell, 1807.
———. "Hard Labour: Institutional Benevolence and the Development of National Education." In *Oxford Handbook of the Modern British Sermon 1689–1901*. Edited by K. Francis and W. Gibson. Oxford: Oxford University Press, 2012.
Bell, Daniel. "The Return of the Sacred: The Argument about the Future of Religion." In *Bulletin of the American Academy of Arts and Sciences* 31 (1978).
Berlin, Isaiah. "The Counter-Enlightenment." In *The Dictionary of the History of Ideas*. Edited by Philip P. Wiener. New York: Charles Scribner's Sons, 1968.
Berns, Jörg Jochen. "Der nackte Monarch und die nackte Wahrheit: Auskünfte der deutschen Zeitungs- und Zeremoniellschriften des späten 17. und frühen 18. Jahrhunderts zum Verhältnis von Hof und Öffentlichkeit." *Daphnis* 11 (1982).
Bevan, Bryan. *James Duke of Monmouth*. London: Robert Hale, 1973.
Beyreuther, Erich. *Die Erweckungsbewegung*. Göttingen, Germany: Vandenhoeck and Ruprecht, 1977.
Birnbaum, Pierre, and Ira Katznelson, eds. *Paths of Emancipation: Jews, States, and Citizenship*. Princeton: Princeton University Press, 1995.
Bloom, Harold. *The Shadow of a Great Rock: A Literary Appreciation of the King James Bible*. New Haven: Yale University Press, 2011.
Bogatzky, Carl Heinrich. *God's Thoughts of Peace in War, Published in These Turbulent and Trying Times, for the Consolation of the Afflicted and the Awakening of the Careless and Profligate*. Translated and edited by James Sayre. London: 1779.
Bonnefoy, Michel. *Jean Artigues: Cévénol (1630–1701): Galérien pour la foi*. Charly: Edité à compte d'auteur, 1996.
Bradford, William. *History of Plimouth Plantation*. 2008. http://www.gutenberg.org/files/24950/24950-h/24950-h.htm.

Brattle, Thomas. "A Copy of a ms. Letter." In *Collections of the Massachusetts Historical Society, for the year 1798*. Boston: Johnson Reprint Co.

———. "An Account of Some Eclipses of the Sun and Moon, Observed at Cambridge, in New-England."

———. *An Almanack of Coelestial Motions of the Sun and Planets, with Their Principal Aspects, for the Year of the Christian Aera 1678; Being in Our Account the Third After Leap-Year and from the Creation, 5627, the Vulgar Notes of Which Are . . . Calculated for the Longitude of 315.gr and 42.gr.30. min of North Latitude*. Cambridge, Massachusetts: S. Green and S. Green, 1678. Photocopy of the original in the Watkinson Library, Hartford, CT, 1954.

———. *Eclipse of the Moon 5 April 1707, Observed at Boston*. Boston: 1707.

Bree, Linda. *Sarah Fielding*. New York: Twayne Publishers, 1996.

Burr, George Lincoln, ed. *Narratives of the Witchcraft Cases, 1648–1706*. New York: Charles Scribner's Sons, 1914.

Burson, Jeffrey D., and Jonathan Wright, eds. *The Jesuit Suppression in Global Context: Causes, Events, and Consequences*. New York: Cambridge University Press, 2015.

Butler, John. *Appendage to Anniversary Sermon*, pp. 11-12. London: Rivington, 1780.

Butler, Jon. *Awash in a Sea of Faith: Christianizing the American People*. Cambridge, MA: Harvard University Press, 1990.

Calef, Robert. *More Wonders of the Invisible World*, in *Narratives of the Witchcraft Cases, 1648–1706*. Edited by George Lincoln Burr. New York: Charles Scribner's Sons, 1914.

Carbonier, Jean. "La Révocation permanente." In *Réforme 2084*. 1985.

Carter, Philip. "John Wills (1741–1806)." In *Oxford Dictionary of National Biography*.

Cash, Arthur H. *John Wilkes: The Scandalous Father of Civil Liberty*. New Haven,: Yale University Press, 2007.

Cassirer, Ernst. *Die Philosophie der Aufklärung*. Tübingen: J. C. B. Mohr-Siebeck, 1932.

Cherikover. "Prosveshchenie." In *Evreiskaia Entsiklopediia*, 16 vols. St. Petersburg: Brokgaus-Efron, 1906–1913.

Clark, J. C. D. *The Language of Liberty 1660–1832: Political Discourse and Social Dynamics in the Anglo-American World*. Cambridge: Cambridge University Press, 1994.

Clarke, Samuel. "A Collection of Papers, which Passed between the Late Learned Mr. Leibnitz and Dr. Clarke, in the Years 1715 and 1716. Relating to the Principles of Natural Philosophy and Religion." In *The Works of Samuel Clarke, D. D.*, vol. 4. Edited by John Clarke. London: John and Paul Knapton, 1738.

———. "A Demonstration of the Being and Attributes of God" (1704). In *The Works of Samuel Clarke, D. D.*, vol. 2. Edited by John Clarke. London Knapton, 1738.

———. "A Discourse concerning the Unalterable Obligations of Natural Religion and the Truth and Certainty of the Christian Revelation" (1705). In *The Works of Samuel Clarke, D. D.*, vol. 2. Edited by John Clarke. London: Knapton, 1738.

———. "Scripture Doctrine of the Trinity." In *The Works of Samuel Clarke, D. D.*, vol. 4. Edited by John Clarke. London: Knapton, 1738.

———. "Sermon XXX. Of the Grace of God." In *The Works of Samuel Clarke, D. D.*, vol. 1. Edited by Benjamin Hoadly. London: Knapton, 1738.

———. "Sermon XXXV. Of the Liberty of Moral Agents." In *The Works of Samuel Clarke, D. D.*, vol. 1. Edited by Benjamin Hoadly. London: Knapton, 1738.

———. "Sermons XIII, XIV. Of the Original of Sin and Misery (1723)." In *The Works of Samuel Clarke, D. D.*, vol. 2. Edited by John Clarke. London: Knapton, 1738.

———. *The Works of Samuel Clarke, D. D.* Edited by Benjamin Hoadly. 4 vols. London: John and Paul Knapton, 1738.

———. *The Works of Samuel Clarke, D. D.* Edited by John Clark. 4 vols. London: John and Paul Knapton, 1738.

———. *Three Practical Essays upon Baptism, Confirmation and Repentance* (1699).

Cohen, I. Bernard. "The Newtonian Scientific Revolution and Its Intellectual Significance." *Bulletin of the American Academy of Arts and Sciences* 41, no. 3 (1987).

———. *Science and the Founding Fathers: Science in the Political Thought of Thomas Jefferson, Benjamin Franklin, John Adams, and James Madison*. New York: Norton, 1995.

———. *Vilna*. Philadelphia: Jewish Publication Society of America, 1992.

Coles, Elisha. *An English Dictionary Explaining the Difficult Terms That Are Used in Divinity, Husbandry, Physick, Philosophy, Law, Navigation, Mathematicks, and Other Arts and Sciences Containing Many Thousands of Hard Words, and Proper Names of Places, More than Are in Any Other English Dictionary or Expositor*. London: Printed for Peter Parker, 1692.

Cope, Kevin L. "Tea at a Hexagonal Table? Gregarious Insects and the Outer Limits of Eighteenth-Century Sociability." In *La sociabililté en France et en Grande-Bretagne au Siècle des Lumières: L'èmergence d'un nouveau modèle de société,*. Edited by Norbert Col and Allan Ingram. Paris: Éditions Le Manuscrit, 2015.

Corp, Edward. *The King over the Water: Portraits of the Stuarts in Exile after 1689*. Edinburgh: The Trustees of the National Galleries of Scotland, 2001. Exhibition catalog.

Costa, Isaac da. *Bezwaren tegen den Geest der Eeuw*. Leiden: L. Herdingh and Son, 1823.

Cowley, Abraham. *To the Royal Society*. From the editor's copy of *Works*. The Abraham Cowley Text and Image Archive. Accessed September 15, 2014. http://cowley.lib.virginia.edu/works/RoyalSociety.htm.

Cracraft, James ed. "Feofan Prokopovich." In *The Eighteenth Century in Russia*. Oxford: Clarendon Press, 1973.

Crews, Robert. "Empire and the Confessional State: Islam and Religious Politics in Nineteenth-Century Russia." *The American Historical Review* 108, no. 1 (2003): 50–83.

Curthoys, M. C. "Watson, Joseph (1764/5–1829)." In *Oxford Dictionary of National Biography.*

Dampier, William Cecil. *A History of Science and Its Relations with Philosophy and Religion*. Cambridge: Cambridge University Press, 1944.

Dawidowicz, Lucy S. *The Golden Tradition: Jewish Life and Thought in Eastern Europe*. New York: Holt, Reinhart, and Winston, 1967. Reprint, Syracuse, NY: Syracuse University Press, 1996.

de Madariaga, Isabel. *Russia in the Age of Catherine the Great*. London: Phoenix, 2003.

———. *Politics and Culture in Eighteenth-century Russia*. London: Routledge, 1998.

Defoe, Daniel. *Moll Flanders*. Edited by Paul A. Scanlon. Peterborough, Ontario: Broadview Press, 2005.

Descartes, Rene. *Discourse on the Method of Rightly Conducting the Reason, and Seeking Truth in the Sciences*. Translated by John Veitch. Chicago: Open Court, 1913.

———. *The Meditations and Selections from the Principles of Rene Descartes*. Translated by John Veitch. Chicago: Open Court, 1927.

*Dictionnaire de l'Académie Française*. 4th ed. Paris: Académie Française, 1762. http://artfl-project.uchicago.edu/content/dictionnaires-dautrefois.

Diderot. "La Promenade du Sceptique ou les allées." In Œuvres complètes de Diderot, vol. 1. Paris: Garnier-Frères Libraires-Editeurs, 1875.

———. *Jacques le Fataliste et son maître*. Edited by J. Assézat. Paris: Garnier Frères, 1885.

Ditchfield, G. M. *The Evangelical Revival*. London: University College London Press, 1998.

Dixon, Simon. "'Prosveshchenie': Enlightenment in Eighteenth-century Russia." In *Peripheries of the Enlightenment*. Edited by Richard Butterwick, Simon Davies, and Gabriel Sánchez Espinosa, vol. 2008:01 of *Studies on Voltaire and the Eighteenth Century*. Voltaire Foundation, 2008.

———. *Catherine the Great*. New York: HarperCollins, 2009.

Donald, Diana. *The Age of Caricature: Satirical Prints in the Reign of George III*. New Haven: Yale University Press, 1996.

Dryden, John. *The Works of John Dryden*. Edited by H. T. Swedenborg et al. 20 vols. Berkeley: University of California Press, 1968–2000.

Duffy, Maureen. *The Passionate Shepherdess*. London: Phoenix Press, 1977, 2000.

Dukes, Paul. "The Russian Enlightenment." In *The Enlightenment in National Context*. Edited by Roy Porter and Mikuláš Teich. Cambridge: Cambridge University Press, 1981.

Durand, Jean-Benoît. "Je lis des Histoires Vraies." In *Prisonnier du Roi Soleil*. Paris: Fleurus Presse, Février 2003.

Dwight, Timothy. *A Discourse of Some Events of the Last Century, Delivered in the Brick Church in New Haven, On Wednesday, January 7, 1801*. New Haven, 1801.

———. "A Sermon Preached at Northampton on the Twenty-Eighth of November 1781: Occasioned by the Capture of the British Army Under the Command of Earl Cornwallis." Hartford: Nathaniel Patten, 1781.

———. "Letters on the Religion of New England." In *Travels in New-England and New-York*. New Haven, 1822.

Dwight, Timothy. *The Triumph of Infidelity: A Poem*. Printed in the World: 1788.

Dybikowski, James. "Samuel Clarke." Special issue, *Enlightenment and Dissent* 16 (1997).

Ebeling, Jörg. "Tableaux de Mode—Studien zum Aristokratischen Genrebild in Frankreich in der Ersten Hälfte des 18. Jahrhunderts." PhD diss., Philipps Universität, 2012. http://archiv.ub.uni-marburg.de/diss/z2012/0074/pdf/dje.pdf.

[Ebersley, W.] *The Agreeable Contrast between the Formidable John of Gant and Don Carlos of Southern Extraction*. 1749. Engraving. Walter Biggar Blaikie Collection. National Galleries of Scotland.

Edwards, Jonathan. *The History of Redemption*. New York: T. J. Swords, 1793.

Efron, John. "Orientalism and the Jewish Historical Gaze." In *Orientalism and the Jews*. Edited by Ivan Davidson Kalmar and Derek J. Penslar. Lebanon, NH: Brandeis University Press, 2005.

Elliott, Clark A., and Margaret W Rossiter. *Science at Harvard University: Historical Perspectives*. Bethlehem, PA: Lehigh University Press, 1992.

Elukin, Jonathan. "Maimonides and the Rise and Fall of the Sabians: Explaining Mosaic Law and the Limits of Scholarship." *Journal of the History of Ideas* 63, no. 4 (October 2002).

"Épanorthose." CNRTL (Centre National des Ressources Textuelles et Lexicales), 2012. http://www.cnrtl.fr/definition/épanorthose.

Ezio Vailati, ed. Introduction to *"A Demonstration of the Being and Attributes of God": And Other Writings*. Cambridge: Cambridge University Press, 1998.

Faggionato, Rafaella. *A Rosicrucian Utopia in Eighteenth-Century Russia: The Masonic Circle of N.I. Novikov*. Dordrecht: Springer, 2005.

Fara, Patricia. *Pandora's Breeches: Women, Science & Power in the Enlightenment*. London: Pimlico, 2004.

Feiner, Shmuel. "Towards a Historical Definition of the Haskalah." In *New Perspectives on the Haskalah*. Edited by Shmuel Feiner and David Sorkin. London: Littman Library of Jewish Civilization, 2001.

———. *Haskalah and History: The Emergence of a Modern Jewish Historical Consciousness*. Translated by Chaya Naor and Sondra Silverston. Oxford: Littman Library of Jewish Civilization, 2004.

———. *The Jewish Enlightenment*. Philadelphia: University of Pennsylvania Press, 2003.

Ferguson, J. P. *Samuel Clarke: An Eighteenth Century Heretic*. Kineton: The Roundwood Press, 1976.

Feuchtwanger, Edgar. "The Jewishness of Conservative Politicians: Disraeli and Stahl." In *Two Nations: British and German Jews in Comparative Perspective*. Edited by Michael Brenner et al. Tübingen: Mohr Siebeck, 1999.

Fielding, Sarah. *The Adventures of David Simple and Volume the Last*. Edited by Peter Sabor. Lexington: University Press of Kentucky, 1998.

Fisher, Will. *Materializing Gender in Early Modern English Literature and Culture*. Cambridge: Cambridge University Press, 2006.

Fishman, David. *Russia's First Modern Jews: The Jews of Shklov*. New York: New York University Press, 1995.

Fordham, Douglas. "State, Nation, and Empire in the History of Georgian Art." *Perspective: La Revue de l'INHA. actualités de la recherché en histoire de l'art*, no. 1 (2012).

———. "William Hogarth's The March to Finchley and the Fate of Comic History Painting." *Art History: Journal of the Association of Art Historians*, no. 24 (2004).

Franklin, Benjamin. *Autobiography and Other Writings*. Edited by Ormond Seavey. Oxford: Oxford University Press, 1993.

Freeze, ChaeRan. "When Chava Left Home: Gender, Conversion, and the Jewish Family in Tsarist Russia." In *Jewish Women in Eastern Europe, Studies in Polish Jewry* 18 (2005).

Friedman, Emily. "Remarks on Richardson: Sarah Fielding and the Rational Reader." *Eighteenth-Century Fiction* 22, no. 2 (Winter 2009–10): 309.

"Friedrich Christian Lesser (1692-1754): Prediger und Historiker." City of Nordhausen website. http://www.nordhausen.de/allgemein/cblock_lang.php?CBlNr=11512.

Frisch, Johann Leonard. *Beschreibung von Allerley Insecten in DeutschLand: Nebst Nützlichen Anmerckungen und Nöthigen Abbildungen von diesem kriechenden und fliegenden inländischen Gewürme, zur Bestätigung und Fortsetzung der grüdlichen Entdeckung, so einige von der Natur dieser Creaturen heraus gegeben, und zur Ergäntzung und Verbesserung der Andern*. Berlin: 1720–1738.

Füßl, Wilhelm. "Friedrich Julius Stahl." In *Biographisch-Bibliographisches Kirchenlexicon*. Edited by Friedrich Wilhelm Bautz. Berlin: Verlag Traugott Bautz, 1995.

Gadeken, Sarah. "Sarah Fielding and the Salic Law of Wit." *SEL* 42, no. 3 (Summer 2002): 542.

Garrick, David. *Isabella, or The Fatal Marriage*. In *The Plays of David Garrick*. Edited by Harry William Pedicord and Frederick Louis Bergmann, vols. 5, 7. Carbondale: Southern Illinois University Press, 1982.

Gascoigne, John. "Samuel Clarke (1675–1729), Theologian and Philosopher." In *Oxford Dictionary of National Biography*. Oxford: Oxford University Press, 2004.

Gay, John H. "Matter and Freedom in the Thought of Samuel Clarke." *Journal of the History of Ideas* 24, no. 1 (Jan.–Mar. 1963): 85–105. http://www.jstor.org/stable/2707860.

Geiger, Abraham, and Wiener, Max, ed. *Abraham Geiger and Liberal Judaism: The Challenge of the Nineteenth Century*. Cincinnati: Hebrew Union College Press, 1981.

———. *Abraham Geiger and Liberal Judaism: The Challenge of the Nineteenth Century*. Compiled with a biographical introduction by Max Weiner and translated by Ernst J. Schlochauer. Philadelphia: Jewish Publication Society of America, 1962.

———. *Was hat Mohammed aus dem Judenthume aufgenommen?* Baden, 1833. Republished in F. M. Young, *Judaism and Islam*. Madrasa: M.D.C.S.P.C.K. Press, 1898. Reprinted with new introduction by Moshe Pearlman. 1902.

George, Mary Dorothy. *English Political Caricature to 1792: A Study of Opinion and Propaganda*. Oxford: Clarendon Press, 1959.

Gessen, Iulii. "Ravinskie uchilishcha v Rossii." In *Evreiskaia entsiklopediia*, vol. 13. St. Petersburg: Brokgaus-Efron, 1906–1913.

———. "Khvol'son, Daniil Avraamovich." In *Evreiskaia Entsiklopediia*, vol. 15. St. Petersburg: Brokgaus-Efron, 1906–1913.

Gingrich, Owen. *God's Universe*. Cambridge, MA: The Belknap Press of Harvard University Press, 2006.

Gintsburg, David. "80-letie D. A. Khvol'son." In *Novosti*. November 21, 1899.

Goethe, Johann Wolfgang von. *Goethes Werke*. Weimarer Ausgabe (Sophienausgabe). Edited by im Auftrage der Grossherzogin Sophie von Sachsen. 143 vols. Weimar: Hermann Böhlaus Nachfolger, 1887–1919.

———. *Sämtliche Werke nach Epochen seines Schaffens*. Münchner Ausgabe. Edited by Karl Richter et al. 20 vols. Munich: C. Hanser, 1985–1998.

———. *Sämtliche Werke. Briefe, Tagebücher und Gespräche*. Frankfurter Ausgabe. Edited by Dieter Borchmeyer et al. 40 vols. Frankfurt am Main: Deutscher Klassiker Verlag, 1985–2013.

Goncharova, Ol'ga M. *Vlast' traditsii i novaia Rossia v literaturnom soznanii vtoroi poloviny XVIII veka*. St. Petersburg: Izd-vo RHGI, 2004.

Gordon, Scott Paul. "Suspicion and Experience in Sarah Fielding's David Simple." In *The Practice of Quixotism: Postmodern Theory and Eighteenth-Century Women's Writing*. New York: Palgrave, 2006.

Gordon, William. *The History of the Rise, Progress and Establishment of the United States*. 2nd ed. 3 vols. New York: Samuel Campbell, 1794.

Goreau, Angeline. *Reconstructing Aphra*. Oxford: Oxford University Press, 1980.

Gottesman, Ronald, ed. *The Norton Anthology of American Literature*. New York: Norton, 1979.

Goulding, Susan. "'Stories of Nuns': Narrative Diversion and 'Sister Books.'" *Interdisciplinary Literary Studies* 10, no. 1 (Fall 2008).

Graetz, Michael. "The Jewish Enlightenment." In *German-Jewish History in Modern Times*. Edited by Michael Meyer, vol. 1. New York: Columbia University Press, 1996.

Grbić, Dragana. "*Telemachus*: Dositej Obradović's Last Wish. The Serbian Reception of Fénelon." In *Fénelon in the Enlightenment: Traditions, Adaptations, and Variations*. Edited by Christoph Schmitt-Maaß, Stefanie Stockhorst, and Doohwan Ahn. Amsterdam: Rodopoi, 2014.

Greenberg, Sean. "Liberty and Necessity." In *The Oxford Handbook of British Philosophy in the Eighteenth Century*. Edited by James A. Harris. Oxford: Oxford University Press, 2013.

Greenwood, Isaac. *A Brief Account of Some of the Effects and Properties of Damps*. Boston: Royal Society, 1729.

Grundtvig, Nikolaj. *Uebersicht der Welt-Chronik vornähmlich des Lutherischen Zeitraums*. Translated by Johann Volkmann. Nuremberg: Raw'schen Buchhandlung, 1837.

Habermas, Jürgen. *The Structural Transformation of the Public Sphere: An Inquiry into a Category of Bourgeois Society*. Cambridge, MA: MIT Press, 1994.

Hall, K. G. *The Exalted Heroine and the Triumph of Order: Class, Women, and Religion in the English Novel, 1740–1800*. New York: Barnes & Noble Books, 1993.

Hall, Michael G. *The Last American Puritan: The Life of Increase Mather*, 1639–1723. Middleton, CT: Wesleyan University Press, 1988.

Hallett, Mark, and Christine Riding. Hogarth. London: Tate, 2006.

Hammond, Geordan. *John Wesley in America: Restoring Primitive Christianity*. Oxford: Oxford University Press, 2014.

Harman, P. M. *Metaphysics and Natural Philosophy: The Problem of Substance in Classical Physics*. Sussex, UK: Harvester Press, 1982.

Harms, Claus. "Thesen zum Reformationsjubiläum 1817." In *Ausgewählte Schriften und Predigten*. Edited by Gottfried Ernst Hoffman. Flensburg: Ch. Wolff, 1955.

Harms, Wolfgang. "Feindbilder im illustrierten Flugblatt der frühen Neuzeit." In *Feindbilder: Die Darstellung des Gegners in der politischen Publizistik des Mittelalters und der Neuzeit*. Edited by Franz Bosbach. *Bayreuther Historische Kolloquien* 6 (2006).

Harrison, Peter. "Newtonian Science, Miracles, and the Laws of Nature." *Journal of the History of Ideas* 56 (Oct. 1995): 531–553.

———. "Was Newton a Voluntarist?" In *Newton and Newtonianism: New Studies*. Edited by James E. Force and Sarah Hutton. Dordrecht, The Netherlands: Kluwer Academic, 2004.

Hatch, Nathan O. *The Sacred Cause of Liberty: Republican Thought and the*

*Millennium in Revolutionary New England*. New Haven: Yale University Press, 1977.

Haywood, Eliza. *Fantomina*. In *Fantomina and Other Works*. Edited by Alexander Pettit, Margaret Case Croskery, and Anna C. Patchias. Peterborough, Ontario: Broadview Press, 2004.

Heitzenrater, Richard P. *Wesley and the People Called Methodists*. Nashville, TN: Abingdon Press, 1995.

Hempton, David. *The Religion of the People: Methodism and Popular Religion, c. 1750–1900*. London: Routledge, 1996.

Hendrix, Lee. "Of Hirsutes and Insects: Joris Hoefnagel and the Art of the Wondrous." *Word and Image: A Journal of Verbal/Visual Enquiry* 11, no. 4 (1995).

Herbert, Thomas Walter. *John Wesley as Editor and Author*. Princeton: Princeton University Press, 1940.

Hertz, Deborah. *How Jews Became Germans: The History of Conversion and Assimilation in Berlin*. New Haven: Yale University Press, 2007.

Heschel, Susannah. *Abraham Geiger and the Jewish Jesus*. Chicago: University of Chicago Press, 1998.

Hesse, Carla. *The Other Enlightenment: How French Women Became Modern*. Princeton: Princeton University Press, 2010.

High, Jeffrey L. Preface to *Schiller's Literary Prose Works New Translations and Critical Essays*. Edited by Jeffrey L. High (Rochester: Boydell and Brewer, 2008).

Hogarth, William. *Analysis of Beauty: Written with a View of Fixing the Fluctuating Ideas of Taste*. London, 1753.

———. Characters and Caricaturas. 1743. Engraving. The British Museum.

Holland, Lynwood M. "John Wesley and the American Revolution." *A Journal of Church and State* 5 (1963).

Hooker, Edna M. "The Significance of Numa's Religious Reforms." *Numen* 10, no. 2 (1963): 129.

Horowitz, Brian. *Jewish Philanthropy and Enlightenment in Late-Tsarist Russia*. Seattle: University of Washington Press, 2009.

Hoyt, Sarah F. "The Etymology of Religion." *Journal of the American Oriental Society* 32, no. 2 (1912): 128.

Hughes, Merritt Y., ed. *Complete Poems and Major Prose*. New York: Odyssey Press, 1957.

Hunter, Michael. *Robert Boyle Reconsidered*. Cambridge: Cambridge University Press, 1994.

Huntingford, George Isaac. *1796* Anniversary Sermon. London: Rivington, 1796.

Hussey, Rebecca. "The Sentimental Traveler: Emotion, Movement, and Economy in Sarah Fielding, *Adventures of David Simple and Volume the Last*." *The Age of Johnson* 19 (2009): 213.

Imbruglia, Girolamo. *The Jesuit Missions of Paraguay and a Cultural History of Utopia (1568–1789)*. Leiden: Brill, 2017.

Institute of European History. "Christine Vogel: The Suppression of the Society of Jesus, 1758–1773." European History Online. Last modified December 3, 2010. http://www.ieg-ego.eu/vogelc-2010-en.

Israel, Jonathan I. *Radical Enlightenment: Philosophy and the Marking of Modernity, 1650–1750*. New York: Oxford University Press, 2001.

Jacob, Margaret C. *The Newtonians and the English Revolution, 1689–1720*. Hassocks, Sussex: The Harvester Press, 1976.

Jacob, W. M. "Gaskin, George (1751–1829). *Oxford Dictionary of National Biography*. Oxford: Oxford University Press, 2004.

Jacobite Songs and Ballads. Historical Collection. British Library.

Jacobs, W. M. *The Clerical Profession in the Long Eighteenth Century, 1680–1840*. Oxford: Oxford University Press, 2007.

Jennings, Theodore W. *Good News to the Poor: John Wesley's Evangelical Economics*. Nashville, TN: Abingdon Press, 1990.

Johnson, Samuel. *An Essay on Women, a Poem, And, Sensibility. A Political Epistle Addressed to Charlton Leighton, Esq*. London, 1772.

———. "Life of Milton." In *The Works of Samuel Johnson*. 23 vols. New Haven: Yale University Press, 1970–2010.

———. Samuel Johnson to John Wesley. In Ellis Sandoz, *Political Sermons of the Founding Era*, 2 vols. Liberty Press: 1991.

———. *Taxation No Tyranny: An Answer to the Resolutions and Address of the American Congress*. London, 1775.

Johnson, Samuel, and Alexander Chalmers. *Samuel Johnson's Dictionary of the English Language*. London: Studio Editions, 1994.

Jones, W. Gareth. *Nikolay Novikov: Enlightener of Russia*. Cambridge: Cambridge University Press, 1984. Bartlett, Roger, and Hartley, Janet, eds. *Russia in the Age of Enlightenment: Essays for Isabel de Madariaga*. New York: St. Martin's Press, 1990.

Kamenskii, Aleksandr. *Pod seniiu Ekateriny: Vtoraia polovina XVIII veka*. St. Petersburg: Lenizadat, 1992.

Katz, Jacob. *Out of the Ghetto: The Social Background of Jewish Emancipation, 1770–1870*. New York: Schocken Books, 1978.

Kelley, Brooks Mather. *Yale: A History*. London: Yale University Press, 1974.

Kemper, Hans-Georg, and Hans Schneider, eds. *Goethe und der Pietismus*. Tübingin: Verlag der Franckeschen Stiftung Halle im Max Niemeyer Verlag, 2001.

Kennedy, Rick. "The Alliance between Puritanism and Cartesian Logic at Harvard, 1687–1735." In *The American Enlightenment*. Edited by Frank Shuffleton. Rochester: University of Rochester Press, 1993.

———. "Thy Patriarchs' Desire: Thomas and William Brattle in Puritan Massachusetts." PhD diss., University of California, Santa Barbara, 1987.

———. *Aristotelian and Cartesian Logic at Harvard: Charles Morton's Logick System and William Brattle's Compendium of Logick*. Publications of the Colonial Society of Massachusetts, 1995.

Kenny, Ruth. "Sexual Politics: Or John Stuart, Earl of Bute and Augusta, Dowager Princess of Wales in English Graphic Satire, 1760–1762." Immediations 1, no. 1 (2004).

Kerry, Paul E. "'Diesen Kuss der ganzen Welt!' Locating German Enlightenment through the Tolerance Discourse." *Religion in the Age of Enlightenment* 3 (2012).

———. *Enlightenment Thought in the Writings of Goethe. A Contribution to the History of Ideas*. Rochester: Camden House, 2009.

———. *Enlightenment Thought in the Writings of Goethe: A Contribution to the History of Ideas*. New York: Camden House, 2001.

———. "From Weimar, with Love: Benjamin Franklin's Influence on Johann Wolfgang von Goethe's Self-Fashioning." *Benjamin Franklin's Intellectual World*. Edited by Paul E. Kerry and Matthew S. Holland. Madison, NJ: Fairleigh Dickinson University Press, 2012.

Kheraskov, Mikhail M. *Kadm i Garmonia*. Moscow: Universitetskaia tipografia u N. Novikova, 1789.

———. *Numa Pompilii, ili protsvetauschii Rim*. Izdanie chetvertoe. Moscow: Vol'naya Tipografiia M. Ponomareva, 1809.

———. *Plydor, syn Kadma i Garmonii*. Moscow: V Tip. I. Zelennikova, 1794.

———. "'Vladimir Vozrozhdennyi' in Kheraskov." In Kheraskov, M. M., *Tvoreniia M. Kheraskova, vnov' ispravlennyia i dopolnennyia. Chast' II*. Moscow: V Universitetskoi Tipografii, 1797.

Khvol'son, Daniil Avraamovich. *Die Ssabier und der Ssabismus*. St. Petersburg: Buchdruckerei der Kaiserlichen Akademie der Wissenshaften, 1856.

Khvol'son, E. A. "D. A. Khvol'son, (Orientalist) 1819–1911, Zhivnennii put samouchni-potchetnogo chleni Akademii nauk," Sankt-Peterburgskii filial arkiv—Rossiiskoi Akademii Nauk.

———. "Kharakteristika semiticheskikh narodov." *Russkii Vestnik* 97 (1872).

Kidd, Thomas S. *The Great Awakening: The Roots of Evangelical Christianity in Colonial America*. New Haven: Yale University Press, 2007.

Kim, James. "Mourning, Melancholia, and Modernity: Sentimental Irony and Downward Mobility in David Simple." *Eighteenth-Century Fiction* 22, no. 3 (Spring 2010): 477–91.

Klink, Abraham. "Groen van Prinsterer en Stahl." In *Groen van Prinsterer in Europese Context*. Edited by Jan de Bruijn and George Harinck. Hilversum: Verloren, 2004.

Krouse, F. Michael. *Milton's Samson and the Christian Tradition*. Princeton: Princeton University Press, 1949.

Krug, Burkard. "Erik Pontoppidan." In *Biographisch-Bibliographisches Kirchenlexicon*. Edited by Friedrich Wilhelm Bautz. Berlin: Verlag Traugott Bautz, 1994.

Lamberigts, Mathijs. "Pelagius and Pelagians." In *The Oxford Handbook of Early Christian Studies*. Edited by Susan Ashbrook Harvey and David G. Hunter. Oxford: Oxford University Press, 2008.

Lambert, Frank. *Divinity: George Whitefield and the Transatlantic Revivals*. Princeton: Princeton University Press, 1994.

———. *James Habersham: Loyalty, Commerce and Politics in Colonial Georgia*. Athens: University of Georgia Press, 2015.

Lampe, Johan Fredrik. *Bergens Stifts Biskoper Og Praester, Efter Reformationen*. Christiana: Gammer Meyers Boghandel, 1895.

Larsen, Karen. *A History of Norway*. Princeton: Princeton University Press, 1948.

Lavater, Johann Caspar. *Lavater's Essays on Physiognomy: With Ornamental Caricatures, and Finished Portraits. Translated from the Last Paris Edition, by the Rev. C. Moore*. London, 1797.

Lavisse, Ernest. "Sur les galères du Roi." *Revue de Paris*, November 1897.

Leigh, John. *Voltaire: A Sense of History*. Oxford: Voltaire Foundation, 2004.

Lesser, Friedrich Christian, and Pierre Lyonnet. *Insecto-Theology: Or, a Demonstration of the Being and Perfections of God, from a Consideration of the Structure and Economy of Insects . . . with Notes by P. Lyonnet*. Edinburgh: 1799.

Letter from Mr. J. E. Gordon, December 23, 1818, reported to the Committee of 11 January 1819.

Leverett, John. *John Leverett's Diary, 1707–1723*. In *Papers of John Leverett: An Inventory 1652–1724, 1730*, box 8. Harvard University Archives.

———. The Papers of John Leverett 1652–1724, 1730. Harvard University Archives.

Levin, David. *Cotton Mather: The Young Life of the Lord's Remembrancer, 1663–1703*. Cambridge, MA: Harvard University Press, 1978.

Lewalski, Barbara. *The Life of John Milton: A Critical Biography*. Malden, MA: Blackwell, 2000.

Liebeschuetz, W. "The Religious Position of Livy's History." *The Journal of Roman Studies* 1, no. 2 (1967): 48.

Lilienthal, Max. "My Travels in Russia." In *Max Lilienthal, American Rabbi: Life and Writings*. Edited by David Philipson. New York: Bloch, 1915.

Lilla, Mark. "Numa Pompilius and the Idea of Civil Religion in the West." *Journal of the American Academy of Religion* 72, no. 4 (2004): 888.

Lindhardt, Poul Georg. *Grundtvig: An Introduction*. London: SPCK, 1951.

Litvak, Olga. *Conscription and the Search for Modern Russian Jewry*. Bloomington: Indiana University Press, 2006.

Livy (Titus Livius Platavinus). *The Early History of Rome*. Books I–V of *The History of Rome from Its Foundation*, translated by A. De Selincourt. London: Penguin, 1971.

Löwith, Karl. *Meaning in History*. Chicago: University of Chicago Press, 1949.

Luther, Martin. "Wider das Papsttum zu Rom, vom Teufel gestiftet." In *D. Martin*

*Luthers Werke: kritische Gesammtausgabe*. Edited by Karl Drescher. Weimar: Hermann Böhlau Verlag.

Lutnick, Solomon. *The American Revolution and the British Press 1775–1783*. Columbia: University of Missouri Press, 1967.

Macaulay. *History of England*. Everyman Edition. 4 vols. New York: Dutton, 1953.

MacKenna, Fr. James. Fr. James MacKenna to James Edgar, February 22, 1745. In *Ireland in the Stuart Papers: Correspondence and Documents of Irish Interest from the Stuart Papers in the Royal Archives, Windsor Castle*, 1st ed.. Edited by Patrick Fagan, vol. 2. Dublin: Four Courts Press, 1995.

Magnus, Alv Johan. *Veirydder med gnagsår, Hans Nielsen Hauge og vekkelsen som forandret Norge*. Ottestad: Prokla-Media, 1996.

Magnus, Shulamit S. "Good Bad Jews: Converts, Conversion, and Boundary Redrawing in Modern Russian Jewry, Notes toward a New Category." In *Boundaries of Jewish Identity*. Edited by Susan A. Glenn and Naomi B. Sokoloff. Seattle: University of Washington Press, 2011.

Mahaffey, Jerome Dean. *Preaching Politics: The Religious Rhetoric of George Whitefield and the Founding of a New Nation*. Waco, TX: Baylor University Press, 2007.

———. *The Accidental Revolutionary: George Whitefield and the Creation of America*. Waco, TX: Baylor University Press, 2011.

Major, Emma. *Madame Britannia: Women, Church, and Nation, 1712–1812*. Oxford: Oxford University Press, 2012.

Marker, Gary. *Publishing, Printing, and the Origins of the Intellectual Life in Russia, 1700–1800*. Princeton: Princeton University Press, 1985.

Markham, Robert. *Anniversary Sermon*. London: Francis and Rivington, 1779.

Marsden, George. *Jonathan Edwards: A Life*. New Haven: Yale University Press, 2004.

Marteilhe, Jean. *Mémoires d'un galérien du Roi-Soleil*. Edited by André Zysberg. Paris: Mercure de France, 1989.

Martin, Nicholas. "Playing with the Rules: Schiller's Experiments in Short Prose Fiction, 1782–1789." In *Schiller's Literary Prose Works New Translations and Critical Essays*. Edited by Jeffrey L. High. Rochester: Boydell and Brewer, 2008.

Massachusetts General Court. "Provoking Evils (1675)." In F*ive Hundred Years: Exploring American Traditions*. Edited by Scott Casper. Boston: Simon and Schuster, 2000.

Mather, Cotton, and Increase Cotton. *Some Few Remarks upon a Scandalous Book against the Government and Ministry of New England, Written by One Robert Calef*. Boston, New England: T. Green, 1701.

———. *Diary of Cotton Mather*. New York: Frederick Ungar, 1911.

———. *Memorable Providences, Relating to Witchcrafts and Possessions*. NIn *Narratives of the Witchcraft Cases, 1648–1706*. Edited by George Lincoln Burr. New York: Charles Scribner's Sons, 1914.

———. *Some Few Remarks upon a Scandalous Book, against the Government and Ministry of New-England, Written, by One Robert Calef. Detecting the Unparrallel'd Malice & Falsehood, of the Said Book; and Defending the Names of Several Particular Gentlemen, by Him Therein Aspersed & Abused.* Boston: T. Green, 1701.

———. *The Christian Philosopher: A Collection of The Best Discoveries in Nature, with Religious Improvements.* Gainesville: Scholar's Facsimile and Reprints, 1721.

———. *The Wonders of the Invisible World, in Narratives of the Witchcraft Cases, 1648–1706.* Edited by George Lincoln Burr. New York: Charles Scribner's Sons, 1914.

Mather, Increase. "Heavens Alarm to the World, or, A Sermon Wherein Is Shewed, That Fearful Sights and Signs in Heaven Are the Presages of Great Calamities at Hand." Boston: John Foster, 1681. In *Sabin's Dictionary of Books Relating to America*. 1997.

Mather, Increase. *Kometographia*. Boston: S.G. for S.S., 1683. In *Sabin's Dictionary of Books relating to America*, 1997.

McGrath, Alister. *Heresy: A History of Defending the Truth.* London: HarperOne, 2009.

McInerney, Vincent. Introduction to *Galley Slave*, by Jean Marteilhe. Great Britain: Seaforth Publishing, 2010.

Menken, Gottfried. *Über Glück und Sieg der Gottlosen.* Frankfurt, 1795.

"Métabole." CNRTL (Centre National des Ressources Textuelles et Lexicales), 2012. http://www.cnrtl.fr/definition/métabole.

Meyer, Michael A. *The Origins of the Modern Jew: Jewish Identity and European Culture in Germany, 1749–1824.* Detroit: Wayne State University Press, 1967.

Michelet, Jules. Louis XIV jusqu'en 1700. In *Histoire de France*. Lausanne: Editions Rencontre, 1966.

Middlekauff, Robert. *The Glorious Cause: The American Revolution, 1763–1789.* New York: Oxford University Press, 2005.

Miller, Perry. *The New England Mind from Colony to Province.* Cambridge, MA: Harvard University Press, 1953.

Mills, Frederick V., Jr. "New Light on Methodists and the Revolutionary War." *Methodist History* 28 (1989): 60.

Milton, John. *Paradise Lost.* In *The Norton Anthology of English Literature*, 9th ed.. Edited by Stephen Greenblatt et al., vol. B. New York: W. W. Norton & Co., 2006.

Montesquieu. *De l'Esprit des lois.* Edited by Victor Goldsmith. 2 vols. Paris: Garnier-Flammarion, 1979.

———. *Lettres persanes.* Edited by Jean Starobinski. Paris: Gallimard, 1973.

Morris, Marilyn. *Sex, Money, and Personal Character in Eighteenth-Century British Politics.* New Haven: Yale University Press, 2014.

Mours, Samuel. "Note sur les galériens protestants (1683–1775)." *Bulletin de la Société de l'Histoire du Protestantisme Français* 116 (1970).

Mundt, William F. *Sinners Directed to the Saviour: The Religious Tract Society Movement in Germany, 1811–1848*. Zoetermeer: Uitgeverij Boekencentrum, 1995.

Murdock, Kenneth Ballard. *Increase Mather, the Foremost American Puritan*. New York: Russell and Russell, 1953.

Nathans, Benjamin. *Beyond the Pale: The Jewish Encounter with Later Imperial Russia*. Berkeley: University of California Press, 2002.

Newton, Isaac. "The Argument for a Deity." In *The Portable Enlightenment Reader*. Edited by Isaac Kramnick. New York: Penguin Books, 1995.

———. *Mathematical Principles of Natural Philosophy and His System of the World*. Berkeley: University of California Press, 1966.

———. *The Principia: Mathematical Principles of Natural Philosophy*. Translated by I. Bernard Cohen and Anne Whitman. Berkley: University of California Press, 1990.

Nicholls, David. *God and Government in an "Age of Reason."* New York: Routledge, 1995.

Nicholson, Eirwen E. C. "Soggy Prose and Verbiage: English Graphic Political Satire as a Visual/Verbal Construct." *Word & Image* 20 (2004).

Noll, Mark A. *America's God: From Jonathan Edwards to Abraham Lincoln*. New York: Oxford University Press, 2002.

———. *Christians in the American Revolution*. Reprint of 1977 edition, Vancouver: Regent College Publishing, 2006. Reprint of 1977 edition.

Nora, Pierre. *La République*. Vol 1 of *Les Lieux de Mémoire*. Paris: Gallimard, 1984.

Norov, Avraam Sergeevich. *Puteshestvie po Egiptu i Nubii v 1834–1835*. St. Petersburg: Tip. III ontel'nenniia Sobstvennoi e. i. v. kantseliarii, 1853.

———. *Puteshestvie po Sitsilii v 1822 g.* St. Petersburg: Tip. A. Smirdina, 1828.

———. *Puteshestvie po Sviatoi Zemle v 1835 g.* 2 vols. St. Petersburg: Tip. A. Smirdina, 1838.

———. Norov to the Minister of Finance Petr Fedorovoch Brok. The Russian State Historical Archive. 1955.

Nussbaum, Felicity. *The Limits of the Human: Fictions of Anomaly: Race, and Gender in the Long Eighteenth Century*. Cambridge: Cambridge University Press, 2003.

O'Brien, Glen. "John Wesley's Rebuke to the Rebels of British America: Revisiting the 'Calm Address.'" *Methodist Review* 4 (2012).

———. "Freedom in the Atlantic World: John Wesley and George Whitefield on Slavery." In *Wesley and Whitefield? Wesley versus Whitefield?* Edited by Ian Maddock, 161-182. Eugene, OR: Pickwick, 2018.

O'Brien, Karen. *Women and Enlightenment in Eighteenth-Century Britain*. Cambridge: Cambridge University Press, 2009.

Obshchestvo dlia rasprostraneniia prosveshchenie mezhdu evreiiami v Rossii. *Sovremennyi kheder*. St. Petersburg: 1912.

Okenfuss, Max J. *The Rise and Fall of Latin Humanism in Early-Modern Russia: Pagan Authors, Ukrainians and the Resiliency of Muscovy*. Leiden: Brill, 1995.

Omel'chenko, O. A. *Zakonnaia monarkhiia' Ekateriny II: Prosveschennyi absoliutizm v Rossii*. Moscow: Iurist, 1993.

Orlovsky, Daniel T. *The Limits of Reform: The Ministry of Internal Affairs in Imperial Russia, 1802–1881*. Cambridge, MA: Harvard University Press, 1981.

Orr, Leah. "Attribution Problems in the Fiction of Aphra Behn." *Modern Language Review* 108, no. 1 (2013).

Otdel Rukopisei—Rossiskaia natsional'niia biblioteka. St. Petersburg, f. 531, d. 416, "Khvol'son, D. A. pis'ma A. S. Norovu." 18 September 1850.

———. St. Petersburg f. 531, d. 631, "Khvol'son, D. A., orientalist, pis'ma Avraamu Sergeevichu Norovu, 1854–1859, Die Erbauer der Piramiden."

Outram, Dorinda. *The Enlightenment*. Vol. 7 of *New Approaches to European History*. Cambridge: Cambridge University Press, 1995.

Pagden, Anthony. *The Enlightenment and Why It Still Matters*. Oxford: Oxford University Press, 2015.

Parker, William Riley. *Milton: A Biography*. 2 vols. Oxford: Clarendon Press, 1968.

Paul Salzman, ed. *Oroonoko and Other Writings*. Oxford: Oxford University Press, 1994, 2009.

Paulson, Ronald. *Popular and Polite Art in the Age of Hogarth and Fielding*. Notre Dame, IN: University of Notre Dame Press, 1979.

Pearson, Jacqueline. "The History of *The History of the Nun*." In *Rereading Aphra Behn: History, Theory, and Criticism*. Edited by Heidi Hutner. Charlottesville: University Press of Virginia, 1993.

Pelagius. Pelagius to Demetrias. In *Pelagius: Life and Letters*. Edited by B. R. Rees. Woodbridge, vol. 2. Suffolk: The Boydell Press, 1998.

———. *Pelagius: Life and Letters*. Edited by B. R. Rees. 2 vols. Woodbridge, Suffolk: The Boydell Press, 1998.

Peschio, Joe. *The Poetics of Impudence and Intimacy in the Age of Pushkin*. Madison: University of Wisconsin Press, 2012.

Pettella, Tera. "Devotional Reading and Novel Form: The Case of David Simple." *Eighteenth-Century Fiction* 24, no. 2 (Winter 2011–12): 279.

Pettit, Alexander. "*David Simple* and the Attenuation of 'Phallic Power.'" *Eighteenth-Century Fiction* 11, no. 2 (January 1999): 169.

Pfizenmaier, Thomas C. *The Trinitarian Theology of Dr. Samuel Clarke (1675–1729): Context, Sources, and Controversy*. Leiden: Brill, 1997.

———. *The Trinitarian Theology of Dr. Samuel Clarke (1675–1729): Context, Sources, and Controversy*. Leiden: Brill, 1997.

Philipson, David, ed. *Max Lilienthal, American Rabbi: Life and Writings*. New York: Bloch, 1915.

Phillips, Edward. *The Nevv Vvorld of Vvords. Or a General English Dictionary*

*Containing the Proper Significations, and Etymologies of All Words Derived from Other Languages*. London: printed by W.R. for Robert Harford at the Angel in Cornhill, 1678.

Phips, William. "Letters of Governor Phips to the Home Government, 1692, 1693." In *Narratives of the Witchcraft Cases, 1648–1706*. Edited by George Lincoln Burr. New York: Charles Scribner's Sons, 1914.

Pierce, Helen. *Unseemly Pictures: Graphic Satire and Politics in Early Modern England*. New Haven: Yale University Press, 2008.

Piksanov, Nikolai K. "Masonskaia literature." In *Istoriia russkoi literatury v 10 t. T. IV: Literatura XVIII veka Ch. 2*. Moscow: Izd-vo AN CCCR, 1947.

Pinter, Walter M., and Don Karl Rowney, eds. *Russian Officialdom: The Bureaucratization of Russian Society from the Seventeenth to the Twentieth Century*. Chapel Hill: University of North Carolina Press, 1980.

Plutarch. *Lives*. Vol. 1 of *Loeb Classical Library*, translated by Bernadotte Perrin. Cambridge, MA: Harvard University Press, 1914.

Polunov, Alexander. *Russia in the Nineteenth Century: Autocracy, Reform, and Social Change, 1814–1914*. Armonk, NY: M. E. Sharpe, 2005.

Pontoppidan, Erich. *Die Kraft der Wahrheit den atheistischen und naturalistischen Unglauben zu besiegen. In verschieden historischen Beyspielen solcher Religionspötter vorgestellt, welche sich entweder bekehrt und Gott die Ehre gegeben oder auch ein Ende mit Schrecken genommen haben*. Translated by Christian Gottlob Mengel. Leipzig: Friedrich Christian Pelt, 1757.

———. *Unvorgreifliche Bedenken über die natürliche Ursache der vielen und starken Erdbeben, und des ungewöhnlichen Wetters, welches man seit einziger Zeit so wohl in als außer Europa vernommen hat*. Translated by Christian Gottlob Mengel. Leipzig: Friedrich Christian Pelt, 1757.

Pope, Alexander. *An Essay on Man* I:6. Accessed November 24, 2015, through *Representative Poetry Online*. http://rpo.library.utoronto.ca/poems/essay-man-epistle-i.

Porter, Roy. *Enlightenment: Britain and the Creation of the Modern World*. London: Penguin Books, 2000.

Price, Richard. *Observations on the Nature of Civil Liberty, the Principles of Government, and the Justice and Policy of the War with America*. London, 1776.

Pridden, John. *The British Antidote to Caledonian Poison: Containing Fifty-Three Anti-Ministerial, Political, Satirical, and Comic Prints, for Those Remarkable Years 1762, and 1763*. 7th ed. London: 1764.

Prinsterer, Guillaume Groen van. *Ongeloof en Revolutie: Eene Reeks van Historische Voorlezingen*. Leiden: S. and J. Luchtmans, 1847.

Proskurina, Vera. *Mify imperii: literature i vlast' v epokhu Ekateriny II*. Moscow: Novoe literaturnoe obozrenie, 2005.

Prowse, K. R. "Numa and the Pythagoreans: A Curious Incident." *Greece & Rome* 11, no. 1 (1964): 39.

Quincy, Josiah. *The History of Harvard University*. 2 vols. Cambridge, MA: John Owen, 1840.

Racaut, Luc. "Religious Polemic and Huguenot Identity." In *Society and Culture in the Huguenot World*. Edited by Raymond Mentzer and Andrew Spicer. New York: Cambridge University Press, 2002.

Radzinowicz, Mary Ann. *Toward* Samson Agonistes: *The Growth of Milton's Mind*. Princeton: Princeton University Press, 1978.

Raeff, Marc. "The Well-Ordered Police State and the Development of Modernity in Seventeenth and Eighteenth Century Europe: A Comparative Approach." *The American Historical Review* 80, no. 5 (1975): 1229.

Raeff, Marc. *Michael Speransky, Statesman of Imperial Russia, 1772–1839*. The Hague: M. Nijhoff, 1957.

Raisin, Jacob S. *The Haskalah Movement in Russia*. Philadelphia: Jewish Publication Society of America, 1913.

Raulff, Ulrich. "Schiller, der Enthusiasmus, die Historie." In *Friedrich Schiller und der Weg in die Moderne*. Edited by Walter Hinderer. Würzburg: Königshausen & Neumann, 2006.

Raymond, Allan. "'I Fear God and Honor the King': John Wesley and the American Revolution." *Church History* 45 (September 1976).

Rein, Siegfried. *Friedrich Christian Lesser (1692–1754): Pastor, Physicotheologe und Polyhistor*. Nordhausen: Friedrich-Christian-Lesser Stiftung, 1993.

Rennell, Thomas. Appendage to *Anniversary Sermon* (1799), pp. 142-43. Society for Promoting Christian Knowledge (SPCK) account, 1799.

Reznik, Semen. "Krovavyi navet v rossii istoriko-dokumental'nye ocherki." In *Vestnik* 24 (November 23, 1999).

Riasanovsky, Nicholas V. *Nicholas I and Official Nationality in Russia, 1825–1855*. Berkeley: University of California, 1959.

Richter, Melvin. "Appreciating a Contemporary Classic: The Geschichtliche Grundbegriffe and Future Scholarship." In *The Meaning of Historical Terms and Concepts: New Studies on Begriffsgeschichte*. Edited by Hartmut Lehmann and Melvin Richter. Washington, DC: German Historical Institute, 1996.

*Rimskaia istoria. Ot sozdania Rima do bitvy Aktiiskia toest' po okonchanie Respubliki*. St. Petersburg: Sanktpeterburgskaia Imperatorskia Akademii Nauk, 1761–67.

Robertson, Ritchie. "Schiller and the Jesuits." In *Schiller: National Poet—Poet of Nations. A Birmingham Symposium*. Edited by Nicholas Martin, *Amsterdamer Beiträge zur neueren Germanistik* 61. Amsterdam: Rodopi, 2006.

Robie, Thomas. "A Letter to a Certain Gentleman Desiring a Particular Account May Be Given of a Wonderful Meteor That Appeared in New England, on December 11, 1719."

———. "An Ephemeris of the Coelestial Motions, Aspects and Eclipses, etc. for the Year of the Christian Era, MDCCX." Boston: 1710. In *Early American Imprints* (1985), 1.

Rooks, Mary Ann. "Wherein Lies Virtue? Secular Matters and Godly Matters in the Works of Sarah Fielding." *Religion in the Age of Enlightenment* 3 (2012): 248–75.

Rosen, Valeska von, Klaus Krüger, and Rudolf Preimesberger, eds. *Der stumme Diskurs der Bilder: Reflexionsformen des Ästhetischen in der Kunst der frühen Neuzeit*. Munich: Dt. Kunstverlag, 2003.

Rouquet, Jean André. *Description du tableau de M. Hogarth, qui represente La marche des gardes à leur rendez-vous de-Finchley : ... Cette lettre de Mr. Rouquet, . . . a été écrite a un de ses amis à Paris*. London, 1746.

Ruben, Bruce L. *Max Lilienthal: The Making of the American Rabbinate*. Detroit: Wayne State University Press, 2011.

Ruff, Julius Ralph. *Violence in Early Modern Europe: 1500–1800. New Approaches to European History*. Cambridge: Cambridge University Press, 2001.

Sack, August Wilhelm Friedrich. *Vertheidigter Glaube der Christen*. Berlin, 1773.

Sainsbury, J. *John Wilkes: The Lives of a Libertine*. Aldershot: Ashgate, 2006.

Schaff, Philip. "Friedrich August Gottreu Tholuck." In *The New Schaff-Herzog Encyclopedia of Religious Knowledge*. Edited by Samuel Jackson. Grand Rapids: Baker, 1953.

———. *The Creeds of Christendom with a History and Critical Notes*. London: Harper and Brothers, 1919.

Schellenberg, Betty. *The Professionalization of Women Writers in Eighteenth-Century Britain*. Cambridge: Cambridge University Press, 2009.

Scherbatov, Mikhail M. "Puteshestvie v zemlu ofirskuiu." In *Izbrannye trudy*. Moscow: ROSSPEN, 2010.

Schlereth, Eric R. *An Age of Infidels: The Politics of Religious Controversy in the Early United States*. Philadelphia: University of Pennsylvania Press, 2013.

Schliesser, Eric. "Newton and Newtonianism in Eighteenth-Century British Thought." In *The Oxford Handbook of British Philosophy in the Eighteenth Century*. Edited by James A. Harris. Oxford: Oxford University Press, 2013.

Schorsch, Ismar. "Converging Cognates: The Intersection of Jewish and Islamic Studies in Nineteenth Century Germany." *Leo Baeck Institute Year Book* 55, no. 3 (September 2010).

Scott, John T. "Politics as the Imitation of the Divine in Rousseau's *Social Contract*." *Polity* 26, no. 3 (1994): 496.

Sewall, Samuel. *The Diary of Samuel Sewall*. New York: Farrar, Straus, and Giroux, 1973.

Shainker, Ellie. "Imperial Hybrids: Russian-Jewish Converts in the Nineteenth Century." PhD diss., University of Pennsylvania, 2010. ProQuest (3414113).

Shapin, Steven. "Of Gods and Kings: Natural Philosophy and Politics in the Leibniz-Clarke Disputes." *Isis* 72, no. 2 (1981).

Sheehan, James J. *German History 1770–1866*. Oxford: Clarendon Press, 1993.

Schiller, Friedrich. *Schillers Werke*. Nationalausgabe. Edited by Julius Petersen et al. 43 vols. Weimar: Hermann Böhlaus Nachfolger, 1943.

Sibley, John Langdon. *Biographical Sketches of Graduates of Harvard University, in Cambridge, Massachusetts*. 3 vols. Cambridge, MA: Charles William Sever, 1967.

Silverman, Kenneth. *Timothy Dwight*. New York: Twayne, 1969.

Skarsten, Tryge R. "Rise and Fall of Grundtvigianism in Norway." *The Lutheran Quarterly* 17 (1965).

Smith, Adam. *The Theory of Moral Sentiments or, An Essay towards the analysis of the principles by which men naturally judge concerning the conduct and character, first of their neighbours, and then afterwards of themselves*. Philadelphia: Anthony Finley, 1817.

Smith, Douglas. *Working the Rough Stone: Freemasonry and Society in Eighteenth-Century Russia*. DeKalb, Ill.: Northern Illinois University Press, 1999.

Snobelen, Stephen D. "The Theology of Isaac Newton's Principia Mathematica: A Preliminary Survey." *Neue Zeitschrift für Systematische Theologie und Religionsphilosophie* 52, no. 4 (2010).

Sorkin, David. *The Transformation of German Jewry, 1780–1840*. Oxford: Oxford University Press, 1990.

Southerne, Thomas. *The Fatal Marriage, or The Innocent Adultery*. In *Plays written by Thomas Southerne, Esq. Now First Collected with An Account of the Life and Writings of the Author*, vol. 2. London, 1774.

Southey, Robert. *The Life of Wesley and the Rise and Progress of Methodism*. Edited by Maurice Fitzgerald. 2 vols. London: 1925.

Stahl, Friedrich Julius. *Was ist die Revolution? Ein Vortrag auf Veranstaltung des Evangelischen Vereins für kirchliche Zwecke am 8. März gehalten*. Berlin: Wilhelm Schultze, 1852.

Stampfer, Shaul. *Families, Rabbis, and Education: Traditional Jewish Society in Nineteenth-Century Eastern Europe*. Oxford: Littman Library of Jewish Civilization, 2010.

Stanislawski, Michael. *Tsar Nicholas I and the Jews: The Transformation of Jewish Society in Russia, 1825-1855*. Philadelphia: Jewish Publication Society of America, 1983.

Stanwood, Owen. *The Empire Reformed: English America in the Age of the Glorious Revolution*. Philadelphia: University of Pennsylvania Press, 2013.

Starr, G. A. "From Socrates to Sarah Fielding: Benevolence, Irony, and Conversation." In *Passionate Encounters in a Time of Sensibility*. Edited by Maximillian Novak and Anne Mellor. Newark: University of Delaware Press.

Stearns, Raymond. *Science in the British Colonies of America*. Urbana: University of Illinois Press, 1970.

Stephens, Frederic George, and Edward Hawkins, eds. *Catalogue of Prints and Drawings in the British Museum. Division I: Political and Personal Satires*. 4

vols. British Museum, Department of Prints and Drawings (March 28, 1734, to ca. 1750). London: British Museum, 1877.

Stewart, Carol. *The Eighteenth-Century Novel and the Secularization of Ethics*. New York: Ashgate, 2010.

Stone, George Winchester, Jr., and George M. Kahrl. *David Garrick: A Critical Biography*. Carbondale: Southern Illinois University Press, 1979.

Stout, Harry S. *The Divine Dramatist: George Whitefield and the Rise of Modern Evangelicalism*. Grand Rapids, MI: William B. Eerdmans, 1991.

Stroumsa, Sarah. *Maimonides in his Portrait of a Mediterranean Thinker*. Princeton: Princeton University Press, 2009.

Stuart, John. John Stuart, Earl of Bute, to Charles Stuart, November 1778. In *A Prime Minister and His Son, from the Correspondence of the 3rd Earl of Bute and of Lt.-General Sir Charles Stuart,* compiled by Violet Stuart Wortley and Rennell Rod. London: John Murray, 1925.

Summers, Montague. "The Source of Southerne's *The Fatal Marriage*." *Modern Language Review* 11, no. 2 (1916).

Suzuki, Mika. "Sarah Fielding and Reading." *The Eighteenth-Century Novel* 2 (2002): 92.

Taylor, David Francis. "Coalition Dances: Georgian Caricature's Choreographies of Power." *Music in Art 36*, no. 1–2 (2011): 117–130.

Tennant, Bob. Corporate Holiness: Pulpit Preaching and the Church of England Missionary Movement, 1760–1870. Oxford: Oxford University Press, 2013.

Terry, Richard. "*David Simple* and the Fallacy of Friendship." *SEL Studies in English Literature 1500–1900* 44, no. 3 (2004): 525.

*The Edinburgh Magazine: Or, Literary Miscellany* 10 (1789).

*The Gentleman's Magazine*, September 1789.

The Massachusetts General Court. "Provoking Evils." 1675.

*Theological Works*, vol. 3. London: Longman, 1830.

Tholuck, August. "Abriss einer Geschichte der Umwälzung, welche seit 1750 auf dem Gebiete der Theologie in Deutschland statt gefunden." In *Vermischte Schriften grösstentheils apologetischen Inhalts*. Hamburg: Friedrich Perthes, 1839.

———. *Die Lehre von der Sünde und vom Versöhner, oder die wahre Weihe des Zweiflers*. Hamburg: Friedrich Perthes, 1830.

———. "Ueber Apologetik und ihre Litteratur." In *Vermischte Schriften grösstentheils apologetischen Inhalts*. Hamburg: Friedrich Perthes, 1839.

———. "Vorwort zur ersten Auflage." In *Die Lehre von der Sünde und vom Versöhner Die Lehre von der Sünde und vom Versöhner, oder die wahre Weihe des Zweiflers*. Hamburg: Friedrich Perthes, 1854.

Thomas, Peter D. G. *John Wilkes: A Friend to Liberty*. Oxford: Oxford University Press, 1992).

Thyssen, Anders Pontoppidan, and Thodberg, Christian. "A Brief Biography." In *N.F.S. Grundtvig: Tradition and Renewal*, translated by Edward Broadbridge.

Edited by A. P. Thyssen and C. Thodberg. Copenhagen: Det Danske Selskab, 1983.

Todd, Janet. *The Secret Life of Aphra Behn*. New Brunswick, NJ: Rutgers University Press, 1996.

———. *The Sign of Angellica: Women, Writing and Fiction, 1660–1800*. New York: Columbia University Press, 1989.

Tournier, Gaston. *Les Galères de France et les galériens protestants des XVIIe et XVIIIe siècles*. Montpellier: Les Presses du Languedoc, 1984.

Troitskii, Ilia. "Pamiati professora Daniila Abramovicha Khvol'sona 23 Marta 1911." *Tserkovnyi Vestnik*, no. 14–15 (April 7, 1911).

Ulrich, Johann Heinrich Friedrich. *Von der Reformation bis auf unsre Zeiten*. Vol. 2 of *Geschichte der Christlichen Kirche für christliche Leser aus allen Ständen*. Frankfurt: Johann Philipp Reiffenstein, 1782.

van Eijnatten, Joris, and Fred van Lieburg. *Niederländische Religionsgeschichte*. Göttingen: Vanenhoeck and Rupprecht, 2011.

van Lieburg, Fred, ed. *Opwekking van de natie: Het protestantse Réveil in Nederland*. Amsterdam: Verloren, 2012.

Vickers, Jason E. "Honouring the King: The Politics of Divine Right." In *Wesley: A Guide for the Perplexed*. London: T & T Clark, 2009.

Viswanathan, Gauri. *Outside the Fold: Conversion, Modernity, and Belief*. Princeton: Princeton University Press, 1998.

Voltaire. "Avis au Public sur les parricides imputés aux Calas et aux Sirven." In *L'Affaire Calas et autres affaires*. Edited by Jacques Van den Heuvel. Paris: Gallimard, 1975.

———. *Letters on England* (1733). Translated by Leonard Tancock. Harmondsworth: Penguin, 1980.

———. "Pot-Pourri." In Romans et contes. Edited by René Pomeau. Paris: Garnier Flammarion, 1966.

———. *Traité sur la Tolérance*. Edited by Jacques Van den Heuvel. Paris: Editions Gallimard, 1975.

Voogd, Peter Jan de. *Henry Fielding and William Hogarth: The Correspondences of the Arts*. Amsterdam: Rodopi, 1981.

Wagner, Hans-Peter. *William Hogarth. Das graphische Werk. Ein kommentierter Auswahlkatalog*. Trier: Wissenschaftlicher Verlag Trier, 2013.

Walk, Lori. "Questing for Family in *Joseph Andrews* and *David Simple*." *The Eighteenth-Century Novel* 1 (2001): 237.

Wallet, Bart. "Het Réveil als joodsche Hervorming." In *Opwekking van de natie: Het protestantse Réveil in Nederland*. Edited by Fred van Lieburg. Hilversum, The Netherlands: Verloren, 2012.

Ward, W. Reginald, and Richard P. Heitzenrater, eds. *Journal and Diaries VI (1776–1786)*. Vol. 23 of *The Works of John Wesley*. Nashville, TN: Abingdon Press, 1995.

Weisensel, Peter R. *Prelude to the Great Reforms: Avraam Sergeevich Norov and Imperial Russia in Transition.* In *Minnesota Mediterranean and East European Monographs*, A Modern Greek Studies Yearbook Supplement, no. 4. Minneapolis: University of Minnesota, 1995.

Weisensel, Peter. *Prelude to the Great Reforms: Avraam Sergeevich Norov and Imperial Russia in Transition.* Minneapolis: University of Minnesota Press, 1995.

Wemyss, Alice. *Histoire du Réveil, 1790–1849.* Paris: Les Bergers et Les Mages, 1977.

Wengeroff, Pauline. *Rememberings: The World of a Russian-Jewish Woman in the Nineteenth Century.* Translated by Henny Wenkart and with an afterword by Bernard D. Cooperman. Bethesda: University Press of Maryland, 2000.

Wesley, Charles. "Hymns on Patriotism," 23, lines 67–72. Cited in Donald S. Baker, "Charles Wesley and the American War of Independence." *Proceedings of the Wesley Historical Society* 34 (1964): 161.

Wesley, John. "Thoughts upon Slavery." In *Works.* 3rd ed.. Edited by Thomas Jackson. 14 vols. London: Wesleyan Methodist Book Room, 1872. Reprint, Grand Rapids: Baker Book House, 1979.

———. 31 March 1780. In *The Letters of John Wesley, A.M.* Edited by John Telford, 7:3–16. London: Epworth Press, 1931.

———. *An Account of the Conduct of the War in the Middle Colonies. Extracted from a late author.* 1780.

———. *An Extract from A Reply to the Observations of Lieut. Gen. Sir William Howe, on a Pamphlet, entitled,* Letters to a Nobleman. 1781.

———. *An Extract of a Letter to the Right Honourable Lord Viscount H[ow]e on his Naval Conduct in the American War.* 1781.

———. John Wesley to Brian Bury Collins, 11 March 1784. In *The Letters of John Wesley, A.M.* Edited by John Telford, 7:214. London: Epworth Press, 1931.

———. John Wesley to Charles Wesley, 2 June 1775. In *The Letters of John Wesley, A.M.* Edited by John Telford, 6:152–53. London: Epworth Press, 1931.

———. John Wesley to Charles Wesley, 4 April 1783. In *The Letters of John Wesley, A.M.* Edited by John Telford, 7:173–74. London: Epworth Press, 1931.

———. John Wesley to Charles Wesley. 17 October 1775. In *The Letters of John Wesley, A.M.* Edited by John Telford, 6:179. London: Epworth Press, 1931.

———. John Wesley to Christopher Hopper, 25 October 1780. In *The Letters of John Wesley, A.M.* Edited by John Telford, 7:36–37. London: Epworth Press, 1931.

———. John Wesley to Christopher Hopper, 26 December 1775. In *The Letters of John Wesley, A.M.* Edited by John Telford, 6:199. London: Epworth Press, 1931.

———. John Wesley to the Earl of Dartmouth. 14 June 1775. In *The Letters of John Wesley, A.M.* Edited by John Telford, 6:155–60. London: Epworth Press, 1931.

———. John Wesley to the editors of the Freeman's Journal, 23 March 1780. In *The Letters of John Wesley, A.M.* Edited by John Telford, 7:3–9. London: Epworth Press, 1931.

———. John Wesley to Lord North, 15 June 1775. In *The Letters of John Wesley,*

*A.M.* Edited by John Telford, 6:147-48. London: Epworth Press, 1931.

———. John Wesley to the Printer of the Public Advertiser, 12 January 1780. In *The Letters of John Wesley, A.M.* Edited by John Telford, 7:370–73. London: Epworth Press, 1931.

———. John Wesely to Thomas Coke, In *The Letters of John Wesley, A.M.* Edited by John Telford, 7:36. London: Epworth Press, 1931.

———. John Wesley to Thomas Rankin. 13 August 1775. In *The Letters of John Wesley, A.M.* Edited by John Telford, 6:173. London: Epworth Press, 1931.

———. John Wesley to Thomas Rankin, 20 October 1775. In *The Letters of John Wesley, A.M.* Edited by John Telford, 6:182. London: Epworth Press, 1931.

———. John Wesley to Thomas Rankin, 21 April 1775. In *The Letters of John Wesley, A.M.* Edited by John Telford, 6:147–48. London: Epworth Press, 1931.

———. *Some Observations on Liberty Occasioned by a Late Tract.* London, 1776.

———. *The Doctrine of Original Sin.* Bristol: E. Farley, 1757.

———. *The Letters of John Wesley, A.M.* Edited by John Telford. 8 vols. London: Epworth Press, 1931.

———. "Upon Our Lord's Sermon on the Mount: Discourse the Second." In *The Works of John Wesley: Sermons I.* Edited by Albert C. Outler, 1–33. Nashville, TN: Abingdon, 1984.

Weststeijn, Thijs. *The Visible World: Samuel Van Hoogstraten's Art Theory and the Legitimation of Painting in the Dutch Golden Age.* Amsterdam: Amsterdam University Press, 2008.

Wheeler, Robin. *Palmer's Pilgrimage: The Life of William Palmer of Magdalen.* Bern: Peter Lang, 2006.

Whitefield, George. "An Answer to the First Part," and "An Answer to the Second Part of an Anonymous Pamphlet." In *The Works of the Rev. George Whitefield.* London: 1771.

Whittaker, Cynthia H. *The Origins of Modern Russian Education: An Intellectual Biography of Count Sergei Uvarov.* DeKalb: Northern Illinois University Press, 1984.

———. *Russian Monarchy: Eighteenth-Century Rulers and Writers in Political Dialogue.* DeKalb, Ill.: Northern Illinois University Press, 2003.

Wigelsworth, Jeffrey R. "Samuel Clarke's Newtonian Soul." *Journal of the History of Ideas* 70, no. 1 (2009).

———. "Samuel Clarke's Newtonian Soul." *Journal of the History of Ideas* 70, no. 1 (2009).

Wiles, Maurice. *Archetypal Heresy: Arianism through the Centuries.* Oxford: Oxford University Press, 1996.

Wiley, Tatha. *Original Sin: Origins, Developments, Contemporary Meanings.* Mahway, NJ: Paulist Press, 2002.

Willhite, Fred H., Jr. "Rousseau's Political Religion." *The Review of Politics* 27, no. 4 (1965): 508.

Wilson, Robert J., III. *The Benevolent Deity: Ebenezer Gay and the Rise of Rational Religion in New England, 1696–1787*. Philadelphia: University of Pennsylvania Press, 1984.

Wilson, Thomas. *Essay towards an Instruction for the Indians*. First edition, London: J. Osborn and W. Thorn, 1740. Subsequently published with the main title, *The* knowledge and practice of Christianity made easy to the meanest capacities.

Winn, James. *John Dryden and His World*. New Haven: Yale University Press, 1987.

Wirtschafter, Elise. *The Play of Ideas in Russian Enlightenment Theater*. DeKalb, Ill.: Northern Illinois University Press, 2003.

Withers, Charles W. J. *Placing the Enlightenment: Thinking Geographically about the Age of Reason*. Chicago: University of Chicago Press, 2007.

Witte, Leopold. *Das Leben Doktor Friedrich August Gottreu Tholuck's*. Leipzig: Velhagen and Klasing, 1886.

Wittreich, Joseph. *Interpreting Samson Agonistes*. Princeton: Princeton University Press, 1986.

———. *Shifting Contexts: Reinterpreting* Samson Agonistes. Pittsburgh, PA: Duquesne University Press, 2002.

———. *Why Milton Matters*. New York: Palgrave Macmillan, 2006.

Wolff, Larry. *Imagining Eastern Europe: The Map of Civilization on the Mind of the Enlightenment*. Stanford: Stanford University Press, 1994.

Würgler, Andreas. *Medien in der frühen Neuzeit*. Vol. 85 of *Enzyklopädie deutscher Geschichte*. 1st ed. Munich: Oldenbourg Wissenschaftsverlag, 2009. http://ebooks.ciando.com/book/index.cfm/bok_id/29611.

Zaionchkovskii, P. A. *Pravitel'stvennyi apparat samoderzhavnoi Rossii v XIX v*. Moscow: 1978.

Zele, Adam Scott. "John Wesley's America." PhD diss., Duke University, 2008.

*Zhtiia slavnyh v drevnosti muzhei pisannye Plutarhom*. St. Petersburg: Tip. Suhoput. kadet. korpusa, 1765.

Zwicker, Steven N. *Dryden's Political Poetry: The Typology of King and Nation*. Providence: Brown University Press, 1972.

# Index

## A



## B

## C



## D

## H

## L



## M

## N

## O



## P

## R



## S

## T



## U



## V



## Y



## W

## Z

# Contributors

**Monika Barget** is a postdoctoral researcher and project manager in the "Letters 1916–1923" team at Maynooth University (Ireland). From 2013 to 2017, she was a PhD candidate in the interdisciplinary research group "Early Modern Revolts" at the University of Konstanz (Germany). Her research focuses on British imperial politics and the political iconography of the Enlightenment.

**Andreas Berg** has recently completed his PhD thesis on mystical discourses in late eighteenth-century Russia. His primary interest is in the interrelationship between religion and the Enlightenment. More broadly, he is interested in the enduring value of metaphysics, especially from the perspective of Russian intellectual history.

**John J. Burke Jr.** is emeritus professor of English at the University of Alabama in Tuscaloosa. His more recent publications have focused on the various uses of history in the long eighteenth century. They appear in *Religion in the Age of the Enlightenment*; *1650–1850: Ideas, Aesthetics, and Inquiries in the Early Modern Period*; and most recently *An Expanding Universe: The Project of Eighteenth-Century Studies.*

**Séverine Collignon-Ward** teaches French at Grand Valley State University. Her research interests include eighteenth-century literature, business French, and the use of technology in the foreign language classroom.

**Kevin L. Cope** is the Adams Professor of English Literature and a member of the comparative literature faculty at Louisiana State University. The author of *Criteria of Certainty*, of *John Locke Revisited*, and of *In and After the Beginning*, Cope has written scholarly essays on topics ranging from the early-modern fascination with miracles to colossalism in modern culture. He edits the annual journal *1650-1850: Ideas, Aesthetics, and Inquiries in the Early Modern Era* and has served for over a decade as the general editor of *ECCB: The Eighteenth-Century Current Bibliography*. A member of the National Governing Council of the American Society for University Professors, Cope is regularly referenced in publications such as the *Chronicle of Higher Education* and *Inside Higher Ed* and is a frequent guest on radio and television news and talk shows.

**Douglass Madison Furrh** is an assistant professor of American literature at Colorado State University–Pueblo. His most recent essays on Melville will appear in *Texas Studies in Literature and Language* and *Nineteenth-Century Prose*, respectively.

**Paul E. Kerry** is a research fellow at the Voltaire Foundation, visiting fellow in the Centre for Theology and Modern European Thought as well as the Programme for the Foundations of Law and Constitutional Government, and a supernumerary research and teaching fellow at the Rothermere American Institute at the University of Oxford. He is an associate professor of history at Brigham Young University and a visiting fellow at the Centre for Women, Peace, and Security at LSE

**Andrew Kloes** received his PhD in the history of Christianity from the University of Edinburgh in 2016. His chapter is based on research that he completed during an Advanced Theological Studies Fellowship at Kampen Theological University in the Netherlands. He currently works as a historian in Washington, D.C. His book on the German Protestant awakening movement (1815–1848) is forthcoming with Oxford University Press.

**Brett C. McInelly** is a professor of English at Brigham Young University, where he specializes in eighteenth-century British literature and culture. He has published extensively on the literary reception of Methodism in the eighteenth century and is the author of *Textual Warfare and the Making of Methodism* (Oxford University Press, 2014).

**Glen O'Brien** is a research coordinator at Eva Burrows College in the University of Divinity, Melbourne, and is a member of the university's Centre for Research in Religion and Social Policy. He has published widely in Wesleyan and Methodist studies. He coedited *Methodism in Australia: A History* (Routledge 2015) with Hilary M. Carey and is the author of *Wesleyan-Holiness Churches in Australia: Hallelujah under the Southern Cross* (Routledge, 2018).

**Jonathan D. Pike** received an MSt in theology from the University of Oxford, with an emphasis in science and religion, as well as an MA in history from Oxford Brookes University. He is pursuing a PhD at Heidelberg University in Germany and researches the nexus of theology and political thought in the long eighteenth century.

**Andrew C. Reed** is an assistant professor of comparative religion at Brigham Young University, where he specializes in nineteenth-century Russian and Jewish history. He has published in the fields of Russian, Jewish, and Mormon history.

**Robin Runia** is an associate professor of English at Xavier University of Louisiana. She has published essays on gender, genre, and race in *Restoration and Eighteenth-Century Theatre Research* and *Journal of Early Modern Cultural Studies*. She's the editor of *The Future of Eighteenth-Century Feminist Scholarship: Beyond Recovery* (Routledge, 2018).

**Lisa Sikkink** is finishing her dissertation, "Femme Fatale: Women's Violence in Early Modern English Drama," for her PhD in English literature at the University of Memphis. She received her MA from Washington State University and is currently a staff member at the University of Memphis's McWherter Library.

**Bob Tennant** (1949–2014) was an honorary research fellow at Durham and Glasgow Universities. His publications include "Conscience, Consciousness, and Ethics" in Joseph Butler's *Philosophy and Ministry* (2011) and *Corporate Holiness, Pulpit Preaching, and the Church of England Missionary Societies, 1760–1870* (2013). He was also a consultant editor and contributor to *The Oxford Handbook of the British Sermon, 1689–1901*.